A Most Opulent Iliad:
Expansion, Confrontation and Cooperation on the
Southern Moroccan Frontier (1505-1542)

A Most Opulent Iliad:

Expansion, Confrontation and Cooperation on the Southern Moroccan Frontier (1505-1542)

by

Matthew T. Racine

LAKE GEORGE PRESS
SAN DIEGO

A most opulent Iliad: Expansion, confrontation and cooperation on the southern Moroccan frontier (1505-1542) / by Matthew T. Racine – 1st ed.

ISBN-13: 978-0615600567
ISBN-10: 0615600565

© 2012 Lake George Press.
All Rights Reserved.
First edition.

Cover photos:
Large Photo: Frank Douwes, with permission used under Creative Commons 3.0 Attribution license.
Inset Photos: By Author

CONTENTS

Acknowledgements i

Abbreviations Used.. iii

Portuguese Morocco as A Frontier Society: An Introduction 1

Chapter One: Historical Background.. 10

Chapter Two: The Portuguese (and European) Population in Portuguese Cities in Southern Morocco 28

Chapter Three: Non-Christians and New Christians in Portuguese Cities in Southern Morocco.. 65

Chapter Four: Food, Construction, and Justice: Logistics and Order on the Portuguese-Moroccan Frontier 90

Chapter Five: Trade and Economy 123

Chapter Six: Political Alliances on The Frontier: Forging Trust and Loyalty Out of Chaos and Suspicion..150

Chapter Seven: Military Violence in Portuguese Southern Morocco: Preparation, Action, and Response 206

Chapter Eight: Captivity and the Captured: Slavery and Sequestration along the Portuguese-Moroccan Frontier 245

Conclusion: Lessons from the Frontier....................................282

Appendix 1: Maps 293

Appendix 2: Important Leaders in Portugal and Morocco 297

Appendix 3: List of *Capitães* in Southern Morocco from 1505-1542.299

Appendix 4: Top Portuguese Office Holders Other than *Capitães* 303

Appendix 5: Weights and Measures 319

Bibliography of Sources 322

Index...341

Quem compilasse, n'um volume de historia, as batalhas e cercos sustentados pelos portuguezes na conquista e na defeza das praças d'Africa, teria escripto uma opulentissima Illiada.

He who sets down, in a single volume of history, the battles and sieges endured by the Portuguese in the conquest and defense of the African fortresses, will have written a most opulent *Iliad.*

From the "Introduction" to Agostinho de Gavy de Mendonça, *História do Cerco de Mazagão* (Lisbon: Bibliotheca de Classicos Portuguezes, 1890), 6.

ACKNOWLEDGEMENTS

I first want to admit openly that this book would not have been possible without the work of scholars before me, especially those who have transcribed and published numerous documents from Portuguese archives. Without those published collections as a foundation on which to base my archival research, I would have been rudderless in a churning sea of information (if I am permitted to mix metaphors).

The research presented herein is the culmination of a long, arduous, and somewhat circuitous process, none of which would have been possible without financial assistance from various sources. The History Department at the University of California at Santa Barbara provided several grants throughout my time in graduate school to fund research, writing, conference presentations, and travel. The Graduate Division of UCSB provided a Humanities and Social Science research grant to fund work on several areas of the dissertation on which this book is based. The Luso-American Development Foundation funded my initial research trip to Lisbon in 1997. The J. William Fulbright Fellowship provided for a wonderful year of research in Lisbon from September 1999 through May 2000. While in Lisbon, the staffs at the Instituto dos Arquivos Nacionais/Torre do Tombo and the Biblioteca Nacional assisted me with great courtesy and professionalism.

Financial aid, of course, means nothing without the assistance of helpful and knowledgeable mentors. I would like to thank Dr. Francis A. Dutra, my dissertation director, whose vast knowledge of Portuguese history has always amazed me, and whose uncanny ability to secure large sums of money for his students to conduct research has sustained me. Dr. Sarah Cline earns my gratitude for her insight, her humanity, her patience, and her refusal to tolerate laziness. Dr. J. Sears McGee's reading and research seminars on English history taught me time and again that just because four or five books have been written

Acknowledgements

about a topic does not mean that there is nothing more to say. I thank Dr. Dwight Reynolds for introducing me to the wonders of Arabic literature and music and for his unshakeable faith in his students. I must also thank Dr. Jeffery Russell whose fabulous writing seminar allowed me to understand that, while extremely difficult, it is possible to write well. My first publication, "*A Pearle for a Prynce*: Jerónimo Osório and Early Elizabethan Catholics," resulted from editing completed in large part under Dr. Russell's direction. Finally, I would like to thank Dr. Ivana Elbl, Martin Elbl, Dr. James Powers, Dr. Kathryn Ringrose, and Dr. Mary Elizabeth Perry for their kind words at the 1999 meeting of the Society for Spanish and Portuguese Historical Studies. Keep paying it forward.

Anyone who has completed a written work of any length knows that colleagues, friends, and family are indispensable in the process. Among my colleagues, I would like to thank Dr. Brian Carniello, whose intense intellectual curiosity reminded me why I was doing all this; Dr. Jim Emmons, with whom I share many gustatory pleasures; Dr. Jason Kelly, who rarely has a bad idea; Dr. Nancy Stockdale, whose enthusiasm and energy are unmatched; and Dr. José Valente, whose friendship and insights have helped me more than he could possibly realize. Among my friends, I would like to thank Dr. Erik Conklin, who said the perfect thing more than once; Timothy Haeg, who pointed me in this direction and who, even in death, inspires me; and Ryan Welty, whose friendship so many years ago meant so much. I would also like to single out Mécia de Sena for her kindness and generosity that made my stay in Lisbon in 1999-2000 such a pleasure.

I am grateful to my parents for all their support and constant encouragement throughout all these years. Thanks to my grandparents for taking the time to read the produce of my scholarly endeavors. To my wife, Jenny, for so many years of loving encouragement and profound understanding, I owe you a debt that I can never repay. I would never have finished this book if not for you.

And, finally, to Luke and Mia: Always look to the future and know that I will be behind you no matter what you do.

ABBREVIATIONS USED

AJ	Fr. Luís de Sousa, *Anais de D. João III*, 2 vols. (Lisbon: Livraria Sá da Costa, 1954).
AA	Bernardo Rodrigues, *Anais de Arzila*, 2 vols. (Lisbon: Academia das Ciências, 1915).
ANTT	Instituto dos Arquivos Nacionais/Torre do Tombo, Lisbon
CC	Corpo Cronológico collection of ANTT. Citations are listed as Part, Maço (Bundle), Document (e.g., CC II, 23, 17).
CdGA	The Cartas dos Governadores de Africa collection of ANTT
CDM	Damião de Góis, *Crónica do Felicíssimo Rei D. Manuel* 4 vols. (Coimbra: University of Coimbra Press, 1949-55). Citations listed as Part:Pages.
CJ	Chancelaria de D. João III in ANTT. Citations listed as Book, Folio.
CM	Chancelaria de D. Manuel in ANTT. Citations listed as Book, Folio.
CSC	*Chronique de Santa-Cruz du Cap de Gué*, ed. and trans., Pierre de Cenival (Paris: Paul Geuthner, 1934).
DCC	Antonio Baião, *Documentos do Corpo Chronologico Relativos a Marrocos (1488 a 1514)* (Coimbra: University of Coimbra Press, 1925).
DIB	Ahmed Boucharb, *Dukkāla wa'l-isti`mār al-Burtughālī ila sanat ikhlā' Āsafi wa Azammūr [Dukkala and Portuguese colonization until the Year of the Evacuation of Safi and Azamor]* (Casablanca: Dār al-thaqāfa, 1404/1984).
EI(1)	*Encyclopedia of Islam* (Leiden: Brill, 1913-1936).
EI(2)	*Encyclopedia of Islam* New edition (Leiden: Brill, 1954-2001)

Abbreviations

GTT	*As Gavetas da Torre do Tombo* 12 vols. (Lisbon: Centro de Estudos Históricos Ultramarinos, 1960-1977).
HP	Damião Peres, ed., *História de Portugal* 8 vols. (Barcelos: Portucalense Editora, 1928-1954).
MFS	Robert Bartlett and Angus MacKay, eds., *Medieval Frontier Societies* (New York: Oxford University Press, 1989).
NA	Núcleo Antigo collection of ANTT. Citations are listed as Number of Document, Folio (e.g., NA 597, f. 122).
Qur'ān	English translations taken from *The Koran*, trans. N. J. Dawood (New York: Penguin, 1994) and will be cited as (Surah:Verse).
SIHMP	Pierre de Cenival, ed., *Les Sources Inédites de L'Histoire du Maroc. Première Série – Dynastie Sa`dienne, Archives et Bibliothèques de Portugal* 5 vols. (Paris: Paul Geuthner, 1934-53).

Portuguese Morocco as a Frontier Society: An Introduction

PORTUGUESE Morocco is a broad topic, both geographically and temporally, and it has not received the scholarly attention that it deserves. The basic outlines of the political and military history have been sketched by previous historians, mainly Portuguese and French. Scholarly effort has focused overwhelmingly on the capture of Ceuta in 1415 and the disaster at Tangiers in 1437.[1] The only two passable outlines of the entire history (1415-1769) of the Portuguese in Morocco were written in the 1930s by David Lopes.[2] Furthermore, of the eight fortresses where the Portuguese had an extended presence, only Ceuta and post-1542 Mazagão have received extensive study.[3] This is not without reason, as these cities have the richest archival records, with the majority of these records covering the period after the mid-sixteenth century.

---

[1] See, for example, Isabel M. R. Mendes Drumond Braga and Paulo Drumond Braga Braga, *Ceuta Portuguesa (1415-1656)* (Ceuta: Instituto de Estudios Ceutíes, 1998); Vitorino de Magalhães Godinho, "Ceuta e Marrocos," in Idem, *A Economia dos Descobrimentos Henriquinos* (Lisbon: Livraria Sá da Costa, 1962), 109-127; John Vogt, "Crusading and Commercial Elements in the Portuguese Capture of Ceuta," *Muslim World* 59 (1969): 287-299. For the most recent and best account of the events of 1415 and 1437, see Peter Russell, *Prince Henry "the Navigator": A Life* (New Haven: Yale University Press, 2001).

[2] These appeared in António Baião, Hernâni Cidade, and Manuel Múrias, eds., *História da expansão portuguesa no mundo* 3 vols. (Lisboa: Editorial Atica, 1937) and Damião Peres, ed., *História de Portugal* 8 vols. (Barcelos: Portucalense Editora, 1928-1954). The version appearing in Baião, et. al., has been reprinted as David Lopes, *A expansão em Marrocos* (Lisbon: Teorema, 1989). A modern, but much shorter outline has been published by António Dias Farinha, *Os portugueses em Marrocos* (Lisbon: Instituto Camões, 1999).

[3] Braga and Braga, *Ceuta Portuguesa* and the bibliography in the back of that volume; António Dias Farinha, *História de Mazagão durante o período filipino* (Lisboa: Centro de Estudos Históricos Ultramarinos, 1970); J. Goulven, *La Place de Mazagan sous la domination portugaise* (Paris: 1917).

Introduction

Studies of the remaining cities were conducted mainly in the first half of the twentieth century. As such, these studies focused primarily on the political and military aspects of the Portuguese presence, with some attention paid to economic aspects as well.[4] Very little was or has been said of the social and cultural aspects of the Portuguese presence or the effects of this presence on Moroccans themselves. Moreover, little study has been undertaken of the ways in which the Moroccans and the Portuguese interacted with each other, whether in conflict or in concert, both at the individual and group levels.[5]

This study moves beyond the political and military history of this period. It will focus on the southern Moroccan fortresses (Safi, Azamor, Mazagão, and Santa Cruz) from the late fifteenth century until 1542, when all but Mazagão were abandoned by the Portuguese. This study is, in effect, a survey of the various aspects of Portuguese and Moroccan life during the period of the most extensive Portuguese influence in the region. Within this survey structure, however, the notion of Portuguese Morocco as a frontier society with contested and ever-shifting boundaries and expectations is used as a way to understand more deeply various issues, from the macrocosmic problems of political relations between Portuguese and Moroccan politicians to the microcosmic realities of everyday life. As Robert Burns points out, "The movements of any actor in the frontier drama . . . must be assessed against the international pressures, limitations, and

---

[4] Joaquim Figanier, *História de Santa Cruz do Cabo de Gué (Agadir) 1505-1541* (Lisboa: Agência Geral das Colónias, 1945); J. Goulven, *Safi au vieux temps des portugais* (Lisbon: 1938); David Lopes, *Textos em aljamia portuguesa; estudo filológico e histórico*, 2nd ed. (Lisboa,: Imprensa nacional, 1940); Durval R. Pires de Lima, *História da dominação portuguêsa em Çafim (1506-1542)* (Lisbon: 1930); Robert Ricard, "Sur le chronologie des fortifications portugaises d'Azemmour, Mazagan, et Safi," in *III Congresso do Mundo Português* (Coimbra: 1940), 107-117. This bias continues even today: Pedro Dias, "As fortificações portuguesas da cidade magrebina de Safi," *Oceanos* 28 (1996): 12-14; Martin M. Elbl, "Portuguese Urban Fortifications in Morocco: Borrowing, Adaptation, and Innovation along a Military Frontier," in *City Walls: The Urban Enceinte in Global Perspective*, ed. James D. Tracy (New York: Cambridge University Press, 2000), 349-385.

[5] Some exceptions include Isabel M. R. Mendes Drumond Braga, *Entre a Cristandade e o Islão: cativos e renegados nas franjas de duas sociedades em confronto* (Ceuta: Instituto de Estudios Ceutíes, 1998); Matthew T. Racine, "Service and Honor in Sixteenth-Century Portuguese North Africa: Yahya-u-Ta`fuft and Portuguese Noble Culture," *Sixteenth Century Journal* 32 (2001): 67-90; José Alberto Rodrigues da Silva Tavim, *Os judeus na expansão portuguesa em Marrocos durante o século XVI: origens e actividades duma comunidade* (Braga: Edições APPACDM Distrital de Braga, 1997).

options affecting him."[6] In Morocco, issues were extremely complex for everyone, but especially the native Moroccans who had to deal with numerous political and cultural frontiers in a highly fragmented and decentralized situation. Therefore, we should augment Burns' assertion with two others that will guide much of the analysis in this book.

The first is that "countries in which the units of political power and governance are multiple and which lack a central, stable, unchallenged supervisory source of jurisdiction and power have their own internal complex frontiers and have to devise their own working solutions for dealing with the problems raised by such frontiers."[7] Control of southern Morocco in the first half of the sixteenth century was contested by four major competing political authorities: the Portuguese; the Wattasids, headquartered in Fez; the Hintati, rulers of Marrakech until 1524; and the Sa`adid Sharifs, rising to power in the Sus region after 1510.[8] In addition to these more powerful leaders, there were hundreds of tribal governments, several large tribal confederations, and a number of independent urban governments. Moreover, these "internal complex frontiers" were not just political, but also cultural, religious, and ethnic. For instance, animosity existed between Moroccans of Berber and Arab ethnicity. Daily reality could be complex, confusing, and overwhelming.

Secondly, "as a rule the issues motivating conflicts [on a frontier are] local and personal, with the result that there [is] a local search for stability and local arrangements [evolve] as one of the principal mechanisms which [respond] to the destabilizing effects of these conflicts."[9] For instance, we see tribal groups and cities repeatedly changing alliances, hoping to find a relationship that allowed them maximum freedom and wealth while offering protection from harm. As Moroccan historian Ahmed Boucharb describes the situation, Moroccans had no security "either for their lives, the lives of

---

[6] Robert I. Burns, "The Significance of the Frontier in the Middle Ages," in *MFS*, 320.

[7] Rees Davies, "Frontier Arrangements in Fragmented Societies: Ireland and Wales," in *MFS*, 80.

[8] See chapter one for more background information on these Moroccan leaders.

[9] José Enrique López de Coca Castañer, "Institutions on the Castilian-Granadan Frontier, 1369-1482," in *MFS*, 147.

their family members, or for their possessions."[10] These negotiated alliances typically included tribute paid to the protecting power and a promise to not fight for any of that power's adversaries and often to supply some troops for the armies of their protector.

The concept of the frontier has been useful to historians ever since Frederick Jackson Turner's employment of the term at the American Historical Association's meeting in 1893, and in his essay, "The Significance of the Frontier in American History." Since then, his theory has received various treatments by numerous historians: embellished, used as a starting point, modified to the point of being unrecognizable, and wholly refuted. The idea of the frontier, as a region where two or more peoples or ideologies meet, is nevertheless a very useful concept today. This is the case despite Turner's use of the term "frontier" to describe the boundaries of an area *lacking* civilization and which ceased to be a frontier once civilization had *settled* it. Turner was, moreover, discussing a very specific "American frontier," which differed from what he called the "European frontier," or "a fortified boundary line running through dense populations."

But Turner's idea was more than the bipolar meeting of civilization and savagery. Turner's American frontier was associated with "the changes involved in crossing a continent, in winning a wilderness, and in developing at each area of this progress out of the primitive economic and political conditions of the frontier into the complexity of city life." In other words, Turner did not see the frontier simply as a geographical boundary or a region, but rather "a complex process, always in a state of becoming."[11]

---

[10] Ahmed Boucharb, "Les conséquences socio-culturelles de la conquête ibérique du littoral marocain," *Relaciones de la península ibérica con el magreb (siglos xiii-xvi): actas del coloquio*, Mercedes García-Arenal and María J. Viguera (Madrid: Instituto Hispano-Árabe de Cultura, 1988), 488. For a similar interpretation of the mental state of Muslims who fell under Christian control in Valencia during the thirteenth century, see Robert I. Burns, "Spanish Islam in Transition: Acculturative Survival and its Price in the Christian Kingdom of Valencia, 1240-1280," in Idem, *Moors and Crusaders in Mediterranean Spain* (London: Variorum, 1978), XIII:94.

[11] Burns, "Significance of the Frontier," 308; Frederick Jackson Turner, "The Significance of the Frontier in American History," in Idem, *The Frontier in American History* (San Francisco: Holt, Rinehart and Winston, 1962), 2-3; George Wolfskill and Stanley Palmer, "Introduction," in *Essays on Frontiers in World History*, eds. Wolfskill and Palmer (College Station: Texas A&M University Press, 1983), 4.

Turner posited the belief that culture was modified by the environment in which it found itself, arguing, for example, that the frontier of North America helped explain the differences between European and American society. The frontier provided a place for immigrants and the poor to settle, and, after a time, they eventually reconnected with "civilization" on the Atlantic Coast and were incorporated into the greater society of the United States.[12] The frontier and its abundant natural resources decreased the dependence of the United States on other nations for trade goods and economic growth. Furthermore, as a consequence of the material needs of frontier settlers for goods from the coastal regions of the continent, the national government had to be strengthened over state governments in order to create ways to supply them. In short, the frontier largely explains the growth in the economic power and the governmental centralization of the United States. The frontier strongly promoted individualism and therefore democracy, in the United States initially, then spreading to Europe. Finally, the "American intellect" owes its unique traits, such as practicality, acuteness, lack of artistic sentiment, and restless, nervous energy to the frontier.[13]

From these examples, it is clear that Turner's notion of the frontier can be used to help explain political, economic, social, cultural, and intellectual change. We should note that, although Turner focuses only on a single, moving frontier line within the United States, the examples he uses throughout his essay give rise to the possibility of multiple frontiers: between Europeans ("civilization") and Indians ("savagery"), between the Anglicized coast and the more Germanic and Scottish interior, between trappers and traders and settled farmers, etc. In other words, a "frontier" is simply any border separating two cultural groups or ideologies viewed as different (in one or more ways) from each other. This perception of difference must be held both by contemporaneous participants and by temporally or culturally distant observers.

It is in this sense that the "frontier," and the contested space for which the term serves as a shorthand, is a fitting heuristic for the analysis of the Portuguese occupation of the southern portion of

---

[12] Turner, "Significance of the Frontier," 22-23.

[13] Turner, "Significance of the Frontier," 23-27, 30, 37.

Introduction

Morocco from 1505-1542. I do not, of course, mean to say that it was somehow a "meeting point between savagery and civilization" or that it demarcates the edge of "free land" open to European settlement,[14] but rather that it was a meeting point of the different: religions, political systems, social customs. The Portuguese language seems to have acknowledged that life on the frontier was different from life in, say, Lisbon, with the use of the word *fronteiro* to describe nobles and other military men who served on a frontier in general and in the Moroccan fortresses in particular.[15] It should be noted here that there were many similarities between the Portuguese and the Moroccans, meaning that in some cultural areas, there was no frontier. That is, the encounter was in no way as startling as that between the Portuguese and the Brazilian Indians.

Recent frontier historians have used the concept in a variety of ways. Walter Prescott Webb viewed the entire western hemisphere as a "Great Frontier" for England and Western Europe. Webb believed that this frontier was important for the economic boom it created for Europe. This economic success, in turn, enabled the development of capitalism, participatory democracy, and the modern concept of progress.[16] While these grand claims are questionable, the idea that an expanse of land newly exploited by an alien culture leads to economic success is extremely useful in an understanding of the Portuguese frontier in Morocco. As shown in chapter five, one of the central successes of the Portuguese was the acquisition of Moroccan textiles, horses, and gold to be used to purchase slaves in sub-Saharan Africa. At the same time, Morocco provided a market for European cloth and Indian spices. Morocco was a keystone of the Portuguese imperial economy.

---

[14] Turner, "Significance of the Frontier," 3.

[15] Paulo Drumond Braga, "A expansão no norte de África," in *A expansão quatrocentista*, ed. A. H. de Oliveira Marques (Lisbon: Editorial Estampa, 1998), 300 and António Dias Farinha, ed., *Crónica de Almançor, sultão de Marrocos (1578-1603), de António de Saldanha* (Lisbon: Instituto de Investigação Científica Tropical, 1997), 657. Castilians used their word *frontero* to describe nobles who led attacks on the kingdom of Granada in the fourteenth and fifteenth centuries. Charles J. Bishko, "The Spanish and Portuguese Reconquest, 1095-1492," in *A History of the Crusades*, ed. Harry W. Hazard (Madison: University of Wisconsin Press, 1975), 441, 450.

[16] Walter Prescott Webb, *The Great Frontier* (Boston: Houghton Mifflin, 1952).

Charles J. Bishko, in many ways a direct inheritor from Turner, saw the frontier as the "spatial transplantation of population and culture with resulting evolutionary modification." Which is to say that as a conquering group defeats another group and occupies its land, the two cultures and peoples mix, creating a new population and modified institutions. Although many Portuguese undoubtedly desired a complete conquest of Morocco and its people, we know with hindsight that this was not ever remotely close to occurring. Furthermore, even in the regions where the Portuguese dominated, they permitted the Moroccans to maintain most of their cultural, religious, and even political systems with little interference so long as they remained orderly and paid their tribute.

Historians such as Robert I. Burns and Thomas Glick represent another interpretation of the frontier notion with a more anthropological focus, studying the "interaction of cultures, both by osmotic interchange and in the wake of violent conquest."[17] Most of these historians, however, study frontiers that – while they may have lasted for decades or even centuries – eventually disappeared as the conquering group digested the conquered group, assimilating those nutrients deemed necessary and expelling the rest as waste. This is to say, the group that moved into the territory labeled as the frontier eventually made that frontier part of itself. In the case of Portuguese Morocco, the final part of the process is reversed.

Although the Portuguese expanded forcefully into Morocco, creating a frontier region resembling that of the various Iberian Christian-Islamic frontiers, they were eventually met with stiff native resistance and forced to all but abandon southern Morocco in less than forty years. Consequently, the Portuguese-Moroccan frontier region returned, to a great extent, to an identity that it previously held before the arrival of the Portuguese, though Morocco too had been changed in

---

[17] Burns, "Significance of the Frontier," 315 and T. Glick, *Islamic and Christian Spain in the Early Middle Ages: Comparative Perspectives on Social and Cultural Formation* (Princeton: 1979). See also the analysis of Lawrence J. McCrank, "Cistercians as Frontiersmen," in *Estudios en homenaje a don Claudio Sánchez Albornoz en sus 90 años* 3 vols. (Buenos Aires: Cuadernos de História de España, Anexos, 1983), 2:313-360. Charles J. Bishko, "The Castilian as Plainsman: The Medieval Ranching Frontier in La Mancha and Extremadura," in *The New World Looks at its History: Proceedings of the Second International Congress of Historians of the United States and Mexico*, ed. Archibald R. Lewis and Thomas F. McGann (Austin: University of Texas, 1963), 47-69.

certain ways by the experience.¹⁸ In fact, if one judges the success of the early European colonialists by their constant increase in landed territory under control, the Portuguese abandonment of the majority of their southern Moroccan holdings in 1542 might be seen as the first and perhaps only European colonial "failure" of the sixteenth century.¹⁹ This book, therefore, examines how a group of colonizers successfully pushes the frontier back *and* how it fails to consolidate those gains.

This book is divided into eight chapters. Chapter one provides a brief history of the Portuguese in Morocco from 1415 until 1769. Where germane, this chapter offers information about Moroccan political leaders, such as the Wattasids, the Hintati, and the Sa`adids. Readers familiar with this history should feel free to skim or entirely skip this chapter. Chapter two provides an account of the Portuguese and European populations living within Portuguese fortresses in southern Morocco. Overviews of various governmental officials and the occupations that employed the residents of the fortresses fill the bulk of this chapter. Special attention is given to the roles and status of Portuguese women. Chapter three examines the Jewish and Muslim residents of the Portuguese cities, with attention paid to their occupations as well as the general manner in which they interacted with the Portuguese. Also included in this chapter are discussions of New Christians and *mouriscos*, Jews and Muslims who had converted to Christianity.

The fourth chapter discusses various logistical concerns. The topics examined include how food was supplied to the fortresses, how housing was allocated and built, and how order was maintained within the fortresses. These issues have been generally ignored by previous histories of this period. Chapter five focuses on the economic and commercial aspects of the Portuguese presence in Morocco. It provides an overview of the well-known place that Morocco served in

---

[18] One of the most extensive modifications (not discussed in any detail in this book) was in the way Moroccans waged war. See Weston F. Cook, Jr., *The Hundred Years War for Morocco: Gunpowder and the Military Revolution in the Early Modern Muslim World* (San Francisco: Westview Press, 1994).

[19] Mary Karasch makes similar remarks about the frontier in Brazil in the eighteenth and nineteenth centuries. Mary Karasch, "Interethnic Conflict and Resistance on the Brazilian Frontier of Goiás, 1750-1890," in *Contested Ground: Comparative Frontiers on the Northern and Southern Edges of the Spanish Empire*, ed. Donna J. Guy and Thomas E. Sheridan (Tucson: University of Arizona Press, 1998), 115.

Portuguese imperial commerce, as well as examines the little-discussed forms of local trading between Moroccan Muslims, Jews, and the Portuguese.

The sixth chapter examines an issue that has been almost entirely neglected by previous historians: Portuguese alliances with Moroccan tribal and village leaders. A good deal of information is known about truces and peace agreements concluded between the Portuguese and the Wattasids, the Hintati, and the Sa'adids. It was alliance with local leaders, however, that composed the bulk of Portuguese diplomatic efforts in the region. The creation and maintenance of these alliances was perhaps the single greatest concern of Portuguese kings and Portuguese leaders in Morocco.

Chapter seven addresses the issue of military violence in the Moroccan frontier zone, examining the cost of preparing to conduct military actions as well as defending against them. It provides two case studies of sieges – of Safi (1510) and of Santa Cruz (1540-1541) – conducted by Moroccans against Portuguese fortresses, demonstrating a significant change over time in both Portuguese and Moroccan attitudes toward siege warfare. Chapter eight examines one of the most common consequences of military violence: captivity and enslavement. Captivity, while a constant worry for all people living in the frontier zone, has not been explored in any detail by studies of the Portuguese presence in southern Morocco. Chapter eight examines the lives of Portuguese and Moroccan captives, the mechanisms by which some were able to regain their freedom, and the general political implications of captive-taking and captivity. Finally, the last chapter will review the conclusions reached by this study and will also offer some possibilities as to how the Portuguese failure to hold Moroccan territory might have been mitigated or avoided altogether.

The Portuguese occupation of southern Morocco as well as other regions of North Africa was a complex undertaking that the Portuguese kings hoped would culminate in their conquest of Fez and Marrakech. They intended on staying in Morocco indefinitely. It is my hope that the information provided in this study will illuminate an ignored area of history and encourage others to turn their attention to it. Once a more complete accounting of the Portuguese experience in Morocco is made, the information may help expand inquiry into comparative studies of European colonization.

Chapter One: Historical Background

THIS chapter is strictly a chronological account of Portuguese efforts to expand into Morocco. There is little in the way of new analysis of the events, though some historiographical information is discussed, both in the main text and in the footnotes. In addition to an account of Portuguese expansion, this chapter contains brief descriptions of important Moroccan political leaders who figure in the remainder of this study.

The history of Portuguese conquest in Morocco begins in 1415. On 21 August of that year, a Portuguese force of 20-30,000 invaded Ceuta and took the city in a day.[1] As a reward for their participation in the conquest, King D. João I (1385-1433) granted the title of Duke of Coimbra to his son, D. Pedro, and the title of Duke of Viseu to his son, D. Henrique ("Henry the Navigator"). In August 1418, the first major attack against Portuguese-held Ceuta was launched by the Marinid sultan, Abu Sa`īd `Othman, known to the Portuguese as the King of Fez. Another siege, joined by troops from Granada, Tunis,

---

[1] The reasons behind this invasion have been the subject of scholarly debate for nearly a century. Marxist historians argue that a rising bourgeoisie wanted to expand and secure a source of Moroccan grain and access to Eastern goods. David Lopes and others argue that very little grain was sold at Ceuta and the true reason for the invasion was a continuation of the Reconquest ideal and the need to protect the Portuguese coast from Moroccan pirates. A. H. de Oliveira Marques agrees with both of these reasons and adds that the invasion canalized the restless energy of Portuguese nobles who wanted to fight somewhere. António Dias Farinha argues that the invasion was a way for the newly ascendant Avis dynasty of Portugal to gain legitimacy in the eyes of Europe and the Church. Finally, Bailey Diffie and George Winius suggest that the conquest of Ceuta was a preemptive move to close off North Africa to Aragonese and Castilian expansion. For summaries of these (and other, less influential) opinions, see Paulo Drumond Braga, "A expansão no norte de África," in *A expansão quatrocentista*, ed. A. H. de Oliveira Marques (Lisbon: Editorial Estampa, 1998), 250-256; António Dias Farinha, *Os portugueses em Marrocos* (Lisbon: Instituto Camões, 1999) 7-8; Bailey W. Diffie and George D. Winius, *Foundations of the Portuguese Empire, 1415-1580* (Minneapolis: University of Minnesota Press, 1977), 49.

Marrakech, and Bugis, was put in place in 1419.² Both attempts failed. Smaller efforts were made by local *mujahiddin*, who came to assault the walls and with whom individual Portuguese knights longed to fight in order to distinguish themselves.³ Portuguese-controlled Ceuta would face small-scale raids and occasional sieges for years to come.

There was no more Portuguese conquest activity in Morocco until 1437. It is possible that D. João I was thinking of launching another invasion at the end of his reign, though he died in 1433 before he could realize this.⁴ However, his son, King D. Duarte (1433-1438), was persuaded by the hawks at court, including D. Henrique, to launch an assault on Tangiers. D. Fernando, the king's youngest brother, apparently even threatened to depart Portugal and look for some kind of heroic/crusading enterprise in the service of another sovereign.

It was not simply the opportunity to conduct a crusading raid against Islam that convinced D. Duarte. His advisors argued that the conquest of Tangiers would take pressure off Ceuta and help to block Castilian ambitions in the Straits of Gibraltar. As usual, the Portuguese interest in Morocco was never exclusively dominated by simplistic motivations of religious antagonism. The king secured financing of this enterprise from the Portuguese *cortes* and a bull of crusade from the Church. The papacy had supported Portuguese and Spanish efforts in the reconquest of Iberia and continued that support wherever Christians fought Muslims.⁵ Moreover, to raise a sufficient number of men for the invasion force, D. Duarte allowed for people involved in civil and criminal legal proceedings to join the army in

---

² Weston Cook Jr., *The Hundred Years War for Morocco: Gunpowder and the Military Revolution in the Early Modern Muslim World* (San Francisco: Westview Press, 1994), 90, cites Gomes Eanes de Zurara, *Crónica de Guiné*, chapter 5, who states that the size of this army was approximately 100,000 men. Cook says that this number is improbable.

³ Paulo Drumond Braga, "A expansão," 242-5 and "Introduction," in *SIHMP*, 1:VIII.

⁴ Luís Filipe F. R. Thomaz, "Expansão portuguesa e expansão europeia – reflexões em torno da génese dos Descobrimentos," in Idem, *De Ceuta a Timor* (Lisbon: Difel, 1994), 89.

⁵ Diffie and Winius, 70-73; Cook, 86; Charles J. Bishko, "The Spanish and Portuguese Reconquest, 1095-1492," in *A History of the Crusades*, ed. Harry W. Hazard (Madison: University of Wisconsin Press, 1975), 399, 409-410.

exchange for a pardon.⁶ The final force, led by D. Henrique, was somewhere between 7-10,000 men.

Unlike in 1415, the Moroccans were prepared for this assault. 'Abd al-Haqq (Lazaraque), still a young child when he succeeded his assassinated father in 1420, was Marinid sultan in name only; true power lay in the hands of the regent, vizir Abu Zakariya al-Wattas (d. 1448). The vizir joined troops from Marrakech, Velez, and Fez to form a massive army, while the *qā'id* (leader) of Tangiers, Salah ibn Salah, brought in reinforcements of men and artillery from Granada.⁷ This army, perhaps up to 100,000 men, met the Portuguese in Tangiers and quickly forced them to surrender.

In order to save his men from captivity, D. Henrique promised to give up Ceuta, leaving his brother, D. Fernando, as a hostage to guarantee this oath.⁸ D. Fernando would later die in captivity (1443). During his captivity, King D. Duarte planned to rescue him either by force or subterfuge by having a Castilian merchant help him escape. In fact, a desperate D. Duarte had commenced the process of surrendering Ceuta when he died in 1438, permitting the queen, D. Leonor, and D. Pedro (regents while D. Afonso V remained a minor) to interrupt this process. Twice more the regent was on the verge of attempting a rescue or trading Ceuta for D. Fernando, but this never happened. D. Fernando's death transformed him into a martyr for the Christian faith, earning him the name, "Infante Santo," or Holy Prince.⁹

D. Duarte's son, D. Afonso V (1438-1481; later known as "The African" because of his crusading in Morocco), succeeded his father in 1438, reaching his majority in 1448. While still a minor, the Portuguese

---

⁶ Note that the use of criminals in the assistance of conquest and colonization continued in later years in Morocco and elsewhere in the Portuguese empire. See chapter two of this book and Timothy J. Coates, *Convicts and Orphans: Forced and State-Sponsored Colonizers in the Portuguese Empire, 1550-1755* (Stanford: Stanford University Press, 2001).

⁷ "Introduction," in *SIHMP*, 1:IX and Cook, 86, 93.

⁸ The use of hostages was common in interactions with Portuguese and Moroccans. See chapter six for details.

⁹ See the chronicle of his captivity: Fr. Joao Álvarez, *Chronica do Infante Santo D. Fernando* ed. Mendes dos Remedios (Coimbra, 1911). See also, Paulo Drummond Braga, "O Mito do 'Infante Santo'," in *Ler História* 25(1994): 3-10. For a detailed discussion of the Tangiers incident, see Peter Russell, *Prince Henry "the Navigator": A Life* (New Haven: Yale University Press, 2001), 167-194.

turned more to the exploration of the African coast, ignoring further Moroccan expansion. Nevertheless, the papacy had issued a bull of crusade in 1443, giving Portugal title to several unconquered areas, including Alcácer Ceguer (Qsar al-Saghir) and Tetuan. D. Afonso V had considered an invasion of neighboring Granada, and after the fall of Constantinople in 1453, he considered a crusade against the Turks, but no other European monarchs showed interest. He then directed his energies toward Morocco.

Morocco had many rich ports and cities that anyone with D. Afonso's crusader mentality would want to conquer and plunder. In 1458, D. Afonso settled on Alcácer Ceguer because of its proximity to Ceuta, thus making for a stronger hold on that city and because Alcácer Ceguer had become a base for corsair activity directed against the Portuguese Algarve. About 25,000 men were assembled for an invasion force. D. Henrique, despite his advanced age, was active in raising troops in the Algarve and participated in the expedition. After a difficult voyage, the Portuguese landed near Alcácer Ceguer and conquered the city after a three-day siege. Post-conquest activity followed a familiar pattern. The Portuguese quickly consecrated the central mosque as a church, while D. Afonso disbursed coats of arms and other awards for distinguished service. In 1458 and in 1459, Marinid forces besieged Alcácer for seven weeks each time, but were unable to break the Portuguese, who could re-supply from the sea.[10]

During 1463 and 1464, D. Afonso returned to Morocco in an attempt to capture more territory. For these campaigns, the king relied on the financial backing of a Bruges merchant based in Lisbon, Martim Leme. Already, Portugal's Moroccan endeavors were becoming a drain on the Portuguese treasury requiring the king to borrow money. The king remained in North Africa for nearly a year, hoping to accomplish some great feat, but he succeeded at little other than spending money and losing several hundred men. The most disastrous of these adventures was an attempt in January 1464 to capture Tangiers. During this expedition, over two hundred Portuguese were killed and one

---

[10] Cook, 88. All Portuguese fortresses in Morocco without exception could be supplied by water.

Historical Background

hundred were taken captive, a large portion of them nobles and military leaders.[11]

The 1460s gave rise to many internal changes in Morocco, changes that would eventually lead to opportunities for the Portuguese to conquer large areas of Morocco. The year 1465 brought the Idrisid revolution and its assassination of Marinid sultan `Abd al-Haqq. He was replaced by the Idrisid sharif, Mawlay Muhammad bin `Ali. Mawlay Muhammad was unable to rest easy in power, however, for in 1471, Fez was besieged and eventually conquered by Muhammad al-Seikh, *qā'id* of Arzila and the son of vizir Abu Zakariyā al-Wattas, who inaugurated a new dynasty, the Beni Wattas or Wattasids, in 1472.[12]

D. Afonso V learned of this chaos and decided to invade Morocco again. In 1467, the Portuguese bombarded Tangiers from the sea, but made no attempt to take the city. In 1468 or 1469, D. Afonso sent his son, D. Fernando, the Duke of Viseu, to attack Al-Anfa (modern Casablanca) in retribution for the city's embargo against Portuguese grain buyers. The city was conquered easily when the inhabitants fled before the Portuguese; however, because the Portuguese were short on men, they could not occupy the city. Instead, they razed its ramparts and then returned to Portugal.[13]

D. Afonso carried out a better-planned invasion in 1471, this time, against the city of Arzila. This city was a good target because it would be easier to conquer than Tangiers, and once conquered, Tangiers would cease to have a reason to be held by the Muslims, for it would be flanked by Christian fortresses. D. Afonso again received financial backing from Martim Leme and from various English merchants, who would be given the right to free trade in all Portuguese territories. This expeditionary force had about 30,000 men, a force whose size one historian calls "monstrous."[14]

With its leader, Muhammad al-Sheikh, away campaigning against Fez, Arzila was taken by the Portuguese in four days. The

---

[11] "Introduction," in *SIHMP*, 1:XI. For more on the experiences of Portuguese captives, see chapter eight.

[12] "Introduction," in *SIHMP*, 1:XI and Jamil M. Abun-Nasr, *A History of the Maghrib in the Islamic Period* (New York: Cambridge University Press, 1987), 115.

[13] "Introduction," in *SIHMP*, 1:XI and Cook, 97.

[14] Cook, 97-98.

Portuguese had killed 2,000 Moroccans and captured 5,000, including two wives and one son of the absent *qā'id*. Muhammad al-Sheikh eventually signed a peace treaty with D. Afonso, giving him Arzila and recognizing him as sovereign of all the Moroccan cities he had captured, as well as giving him the right to occupy Tangiers. In return, D. Afonso recognized al-Sheikh as the legitimate sovereign of Fez and, in exchange for the mortal remains of the Infante Santo, returned al-Sheikh's captive family members. The occupants of Tangiers, learning that Fez would not support them, abandoned their city (destroying and carrying off as much as possible) without a fight. The city of Al-A`rā'ish (Larache) was also abandoned by its inhabitants.

After capturing Arzila and occupying Tangiers, D. Afonso V changed his title to "*Rei de Portugal e dos Algarves d'aquem e d'alem mar*" (King of Portugal and the Algarves, both here and across the sea), a title maintained by subsequent monarchs. The papacy rewarded D. Afonso generously for his battles against the infidel by reducing the amount of the tithe owed to Rome so that the king could afford his debt payments. Thus, in 1471, the Portuguese conquest of cities in northern Morocco was complete.[15] In 1476, D. Afonso's foolish war with Castile nearly cost him Ceuta when the forces of al-Sheikh joined with Castilian troops to besiege the city. The *capitão* (governor) of the city, Rui Mendes de Vasconcellos, was able to resist the attack and break the siege.[16]

The next thirty years were mostly peaceful ones for the Portuguese in North Africa; it was an era of treaties. In 1479, near the end of D. Afonso V's reign, the king concluded his war with Castile by the signing of the Treaty of Alcáçovas. Additionally, this treaty recognized Portugal's right to conquer Fez, a goal the Portuguese took seriously. In fact, Diogo de Gouveia, the great Portuguese theologian, stated that one of the reasons King D. João II (1481-1495) sent him to Paris to study theology was so that he might one day celebrate the Mass in the great mosque of Fez.[17]

---

[15] Unless otherwise noted, the discussion of the years 1437-1471 comes from Braga, "A expansão," 256-86.

[16] "Introduction," in *SIHMP*, 1:XIII.

[17] Farinha, *Portugueses em Marrocos*, 27; Marcel Bataillon, "La rêve de la conquête de Fès et le sentiment imperial portugais au XVIe siècle," in *Études sur le Portugal au temps de l'humanisme* (Coimbra: University of Coimbra Press, 1952), 101-107.

Historical Background

The conquest of Fez by Muhammad al-Sheikh, now the first Wattasid sultan, in 1472, combined with the increasing Portuguese presence on the Moroccan littoral brought much confusion and danger to Moroccan politics. In addition to the Portuguese conquests, the Spanish had increased their raiding activity on the Atlantic coast of Morocco. In this climate, many of the southern Moroccan coastal cities, hoping to please whom they viewed as the strongest of their potential enemies, asked the Portuguese for protection. According to the Treaty of Toledo (1480), a companion treaty to that of Alcáçovas, the Castilians were required to respect the Portuguese sphere of influence in Morocco, which would be extended by any accords with other cities.

During this second half of the fifteenth century, Portuguese ships often stopped in southern Morocco, mainly at the cities of Azamor and Safi, in order to trade for various items, including grain for export to Portugal and cloth that they later used to trade for slaves in western Africa.[18] During the latter part of his reign, D. Afonso V concluded a treaty of protection and trade with Safi; this accord was confirmed by D. João II in 1488. We know little of the conditions of this accord, though by at least 1479 a Portuguese *feitoria* (factory) was active in the city and a small chapel had been constructed by 1491. The *alcaide* (Portuguese-approved Moroccan leader) of Safi was to pay tribute of 300 *miticais* per year, either in cash or in kind, and two good horses. He must protect the *feitor* (factor) and all Portuguese living in the *feitoria*. In return, the Muslim citizens of Safi could sail to Portugal in Portuguese ships and engage in commerce, paying only the duties that Portuguese subjects themselves would pay.[19]

Before renewing his father's treaty with Safi, D. João II concluded his own treaty with Azamor in 1486. The city of Azamor was to pay 10,000 shad in tribute each year, to charge no taxes on royal ships, to allow the Portuguese to buy horses, and to allow the construction of a *feitoria* and the residence of a *feitor* in the city. Not everyone near Azamor agreed with this treaty, leading D. João II to dispatch a force of about 1,200 men to compel local *dawwārs* (tent-based encampments of nomadic tribesmen) to pay tribute. After a

---

[18] See chapter five for more on trade.

[19] "Letter Patent of D. Manuel," Lisbon, 9 December 1500, *SIHMP*, 1:60-62.

brief but bloody fight, in which 900 Moroccans were killed and 400 captured, they submitted and paid tribute.[20] In the contested space of the Moroccan frontier, violence or the threat of violence was often used to advance Portuguese aims.

During this period of treaties, only one serious attempt was made to extend the territory held by direct Portuguese occupation. In 1486, D. João II, like his father before him, secured a papal bull of crusade, *Orthodoxae fidei*, which granted to all who participated in war against the infidels a plenary remission of sins and indulgence.[21] Then, in 1489, D. João II dispatched D. Gaspar Jusarte to build a fortress called Graciosa, fifteen kilometers up the Wadi Lukkus from the abandoned Moroccan city of Al-A`rā'ish (Larache). Muhammad al-Sheikh, seeing the obvious threat that this new fortress would produce, surrounded the construction zone and periodically bombarded the workers. Within a few months, the Portuguese king recognized the impossibility of completing the fortress and concluded a peace so that his men could retreat without being harmed. Included in the terms of this peace was a ten-year extension on the truce with the Wattasids, first agreed to in 1472.[22]

In the late fifteenth and early sixteenth centuries, the Castilians living on the Canary Islands continually traded with southern Morocco. This angered the kings of Portugal who saw this as a violation of their privileges. In 1505, King D. Manuel (1495-1521), apparently short on capital due to his attentions to Brazil and India, granted João Lopes de Sequeira the right to build a fortress in Agadir in order to prevent Castilian trade in the region. The fortress was in fact built with money from the dowry of his wife, D. Beatriz. Although Sequeira faced opposition from members of the local Qsima tribe, he was supported by the stronger Massa tribe who were allies of the Portuguese, and so

---

[20] "La conquête de Safi par les Portugais, 1508," in *SIHMP*, 1:151-161; "L'Établissement de la suzeraineté portugaise sur Azemmour, 1486," in *SIHMP*, 1:1-3; and Farinha, *Portugueses em Marrocos*, 26-27. For the treaty with Azamor, see *SIHMP*, 1:4-24. For more on the alliances with Safi and Azamor and other Moroccan political entities, see chapter six.

[21] Note that ever since Innocent IV (1243-1254), popes had maintained that only they – not secular leaders – had the right to authorize the invasion of infidel lands. James Muldoon, *Popes, Lawyers, and Infidels: The Church and the Non-Christian World, 1250-1550* (Philadelphia: 1979), 12.

[22] Farinha, *Portugueses em Marrocos*, 27-8 and Cook, 117-118.

the construction was able to proceed. The fortress came to be known as Santa Cruz do Cabo de Gué.[23]

The success of Santa Cruz and the threat of increased Castilian involvement in North Africa increased the pace of Portuguese expansion. In 1506 D. Manuel ordered Diogo de Azambuja, the same man who had built São Jorge da Mina in Guinea in 1482, to construct the fortress of Mogador (also known as Castelo Real). Early in 1507, while Mogador was still under construction, Azambuja marched to the nearby tributary city of Safi (Âsafî) in order to control rioting, and in 1508 conquered the city outright because its leadership was increasingly uncooperative.[24] The Portuguese also launched a diplomatic initiative with the Castilians that lead to the Treaty of Sintra in 1509. This gave the Portuguese the exclusive right to conquer Morocco from west of Velez de la Gomera all the way to Capes Bojador and Nun.[25] After fighting off a severe siege of Safi by Moroccan forces at the end of 1510, Portuguese control of Safi went unchallenged for nearly three decades. Shortly before this siege, the less important fortress of Mogador was abandoned by the Portuguese, who chose to focus their efforts on retaining the richer, established city of Safi.

D. Manuel extended his personal hold on North Africa greatly during 1513. First, he purchased the fortress of Santa Cruz from João Lopes de Sequeira and his wife, D. Beatriz, for 5,000 *cruzados* and a yearly pension of 100,000 *reis*.[26] The king next turned his attention to the conquest of the tributary city of Azamor during the same year. Due to repeated treaty violations on the part of the Moroccans, relations between Portugal and Azamor had been worsening since 1502. In one instance, a group of Portuguese ships ran aground in the river near

---

[23] Pierre de Cenival, "Introduction," in *CSC*, 15; Farinha, *Portugueses em Marrocos*, 29; *HP*, 3:453.

[24] Although this is the official date of conquest, effective Portuguese control of Safi might be dated to late 1498 when the Portuguese assisted `Abd al-Rahmān and his faction to gain power in the city over Yahya al-Zayyāt, who planned to ally with the Castilians and expel the Portuguese from the city. This act precipitated the papal declaration of the diocese of Safi in a bull dated 17 June 1499 ("La conquête de Safi," 1:152-153).

[25] "Le partage des conquêtes entre l'Espagne et le Portugal, au Maroc et sur la côte au sud du Maroc," in *SIHMP*, 1:211.

[26] "Alvará of D. Manuel," Evora, 25 January 1513, *SIHMP*, 1:374-377.

Azamor, and all of the merchandise in these ships was stolen under the direction of Azamor's leaders.[27]

Conquest had not always been the king's preferred option. In 1504, he sent Sancho Tavares to negotiate with Azamor's leaders in the hope of normalizing relations.[28] By 1507, however, the king had grown tired of constant problems with the treaty and ordered a naval expedition to map the sand bar in front of Azamor, as well as to map other locations along the Moroccan coast. In 1508, the same year as the outright seizure of Safi, a Portuguese force had landed with the intention of capturing Azamor, but was driven off. According to an anonymous Portuguese chronicler, the battle lasted seven hours, with twenty-two Portuguese killed and 1375 Moroccans killed.[29] By 1509, following negotiations in Lisbon between the king and Ahmed bin `Ali, the representative of Azamor's leader, Mawlay Zayyan, the Portuguese *feitoria* was once again in operation.[30]

In fact, Azamor remained loyal to Portugal when Safi was besieged in 1510, though Mawlay Zayyan had reportedly begun to threaten Portuguese living in the city.[31] It was at this time that D. Manuel gave his nephew, D. Jaime, the Duke of Bragança, the commission to conquer the city. In 1512, the *contador* of Safi, Nuno Gato, advocated the capture of Azamor, claiming that it would make the region very peaceful and it would be safer to travel from Safi to Azamor than from Lisbon to Santarém.[32] The conquest did not take place until 1513, when Mawlay Zayyan had violated the terms of the

---

[27] *HP*, 3:509.

[28] "Instructions for Sancho Tavares," Lisbon, 22 April 1504, *SIHMP*, 1:87-91 and "Letter from D. Manuel to the Inhabitants of Azamor," Lisbon, 22 April 1504, *SIHMP*, 1:92-102.

[29] *SIHMP*, 1:167. While the Portuguese often killed many more than their own forces lost, this discrepancy seems too large to hold as credible.

[30] *HP*, 3:511.

[31] "Letter from Diogo de Alcáçova to D. Manuel," Azamor, 3 November 1510, *SIHMP*, 1:248; *HP*, 3:511.

[32] "Letter from Nuno Gato to D. Manuel," Safi, 12 May 1512, *SIHMP*, 1:303. In fact, once the conquest of Azamor was complete, Nuno Fernandes de Ataíde, the *capitão* of Safi, used this same comparison to describe how easy travel was in the land, though he advocated people still travel with a strong guard or with interpreters and guides (*alformas*) who knew the area ("Letter from Nuno Fernandes de Ataíde to D. Manuel," Safi, 29 October 1513, *SIHMP*, 1:444).

Historical Background

1486 treaty and its subsequent reconfirmations by conclusively expelling Portuguese merchants from the city.[33] D. Jaime, eager to rehabilitate his reputation after murdering his wife and her alleged lover, conquered the city on 3 September 1513 after two days of fighting, assisted by 2,000 cavalry and 8,000 infantry who had arrived from Portugal in 500 ships.[34] In addition to avenging the humiliating defeat of 1508, the conquest of Azamor established another base for the desired Portuguese conquests of Fez and Marrakech, at least this is what D. Manuel suggested to the Pope.[35] The king's confidence knew no bounds following the conquest of Azamor: "Now [Morocco] is almost completely conquered by our people, and we must hope in Our Lord that very soon all of the conquests will be finished."[36]

Within weeks of the conquest of Azamor, Moroccans from the surrounding areas, including the cities of Almedina and Tit and the tribes from the region of Shawiyya, came to negotiate peace treaties with D. Jaime.[37] Almedina had nominally been allied with the Portuguese since their conquest of Safi, but often refused to pay its tribute in a timely manner.[38] They now knew that it was impossible to stop the influence of the Portuguese, pragmatically resigning themselves to working with them for the time being. The people of

---

[33] José Alberto Rodrigues da Silva Tavim, *Os judeus na expansão portuguesa em Marrocos durante o século XVI: origens e actividades duma comunidade* (Braga: Edições APPACDM Distrital de Braga, 1997), 213-214; "Letter from Diogo de Alcaçova to D. Manuel," Azamor, 3 November 1510, *SIHMP*, 1:248; and "Letter from `Ali bin Sa`īd to D. Manuel," Azamor, 3-12 November 1510, *SIHMP*, 1:249-254.

[34] "La conquête d'Azemmour, 3 septembre 1513," *SIHMP*, 1:394-402; "Letter from Jorge Pires to Fernando de Castro," Azamor, 4 September 1513, *SIHMP*, 1:403-409; "Letter from the Duke of Bragança to D. Manuel," Azamor, approx. 6 September 1513, *SIHMP*, 1:410-429; and "Account of the seizure of Azamor," n. 1., before 19 September 1513, *SIHMP*, 1:430-433.

[35] *HP*, 3:511 and n.5. See also, Bataillon, "Le rêve de la conquête de Fès," 101-107. Portuguese nobles shared these dreams. In 1507, Diogo de Azambuja had advised D. Manuel to have many sons so that one of them might be the king of Marrakech some day ("Letter from Diogo de Azamobuja to D. Manuel," Safi, 13 December 1507, *SIHMP*, 1:142).

[36] José Ramos Coelho, ed., *Alguns documentos do Archivo Nacional da Torre do Tombo acerca das navegações e conquistas portuguezas* (Lisboa: Imprensa Nacional, 1892), 293-294 and *HP*, 3:516-517.

[37] *HP*, 3:516.

[38] "Account of the seizure of Azamor," n. l., before 19 September 1513, *SIHMP*, 1:433; *HP*, 3:484-5.

Almedina had, however, abandoned their city for fear the Portuguese would come against it, and so were negotiating from encampments.[39] The people of Tit also abandoned their city, but soon returned and negotiated a tribute agreement with the Portuguese. The Wattasid sultan, Muhammad al-Burtughālī (1501-1526), son of Muhammad al-Sheikh, demonstrating his still substantial power, attacked and destroyed Tit during the first-half of 1514.[40]

Azamor is located two kilometers up the Umm al-Rabi` river, so the Portuguese thought it best to fortify the nearby coastline at Mazagão (modern al-Jadīda), about ten km south of the mouth of the Umm al-Rabi` river. As early as 1502 a Moroccan named Selim bin `Umar had proposed Mazagão as a site for a Portuguese fortress, with the hope that he and other local leaders would benefit from Portuguese commerce and monetary incentives. Although the Portuguese did not immediately endorse this plan, Selim's suggestion was not discarded. In 1505, D. Manuel gave permission to Jorge de Melo to erect a fortress in Mazagão at his own expense, as he had granted to João Lopes de Sequiera in the same year at Santa Cruz. D. Manuel, in his letter patent to Melo, specifically mentioned that Mazagão had long been a source of grain for Portugal and that a good profit in commerce could be made there.[41] Although Melo never built the fortress, the Portuguese did not forget about Mazagão. They continued trading there and maintained good relations with the local tribal leadership. Rabbi Abraham Rute, the *rabi mor* (head Rabbi) of Safi, reported that the Muslims of Mazagão were ready in late 1510 and early 1511 to ally with the Portuguese in an attack on Azamor because of their hatred for the city's *qā'id*, Mawlay Zayyan.[42] In 1514, one year after the conquest of Azamor, construction began on a royally-financed fortress at Mazagão.[43]

D. Manuel's final major attempt to create from scratch a Portuguese settlement in Morocco came in 1515, with the attempt to construct the fortress of São João da Mamora (Ma`mūra) at the mouth

---

[39] "Letter from Nuno Gato to D. Manuel," Azamor, 5 December 1513, *SIHMP*, 1:454.

[40] *HP*, 3:484.

[41] "Letter Patent of D. Manuel," Santarém, 21 May 1505, *SIHMP*, 1:109.

[42] "Letter from Rabbi Ibrahim bin Zamiro to D. Manuel," Safi, 3 January 1511, *SIHMP*, 1:283.

[43] *HP*, 3:530-533.

of the Wadi Sebu. In 1514, after receiving yet another papal bull of crusade to help fund the expedition and construction, D. Manuel sent Estêvão Rodrigues Berrio and João Rodrigues to study the location in order to determine its suitability for a fortress. In spite of a strong river current and a tricky sand bar, they recommended the location.[44] It seems that Portuguese pride overrode clearer heads. For instance, Diego de Medina, a Castilian assisting in the survey, said that the project should be scrapped and the site abandoned because, among other things, it seemed obvious to him that the location would be underwater during the winter floods. He was told to "keep quiet" because the same architect who had built the Jeronymos Monastery in Lisbon, Mestre Boytac, was there and could make it work.[45] Although the fortress was completed in early August, a terrible disaster occurred. The Wattasid sultan attacked, forcing the Portuguese to abandon the location after the loss of 4,000 Portuguese lives and substantial sums of money.[46] Although a fortress, to be built by D. Nuno Mascarenhas, was also planned for Al-Anfa, the disaster of Mamora ended these plans.[47]

There are also vague references to an attempt at building a fortress at Aguz around 1520. All that is known with certainty is that a garrison was sent there and construction was completed on a small walled compound (130 *braças*, only 286 meters of wall) with a small

---

[44] "Instructions for Estêvão Rodrigues Berrio and João Rodrigues," Lisbon 27 September 1514, *SIHMP*, 1:638-641. For more on the Mamora expedition, see "Letter from Master Duarte [Gonçalves] to D. Manuel," Villa Nova de Portimão, 19 July 1515, *SIHMP*, 1:703-706; "Letter from D. António de Noronha to D. Manuel," São João da Mamora, 30 July 1515, *SIHMP*, 1:707-712; "Letter from Diego de Medina to D. Manuel," São João da Mamora, 1 August 1515, *SIHMP*, 1:713-716; "Letter from D. António de Noronha to D. Manuel," São João da Mamora, 3 August 1515, *SIHMP*, 1:717; "Letter from D. António de Noronha to D. Manuel," São João da Mamora, 4 August 1515, *SIHMP*, 1:718-720; "Letter from Álvaro de Noronha to D. Manuel," São João da Mamora, 5 August 1515, *SIHMP*, 1:726-727; and "Account of the Expedition to Mamora," n. l., after 10 August 1515, *SIHMP*, 1:728-731.

[45] "Letter from Diego de Medina to D. Manuel," São João da Mamora, 1 August 1515, *SIHMP*, 1:714.

[46] Farinha, *Portugueses em Marrocos*, 29-31; "Mogador," in *SIHMP*, 1:120-127; *HP*, 3:533-536;"La conquête de Safi," 1:151-161; *CDM*, 2:57-64; "Le conquête d'Azemmour, 3 septembre 1513," in *SIHMP*, 1:394-402; "L'Expédition de la Mamora (juin-août 1515)," in *SIHMP*, 1:695-702. See Cook, 148-149, for details of the fighting at Mamora.

[47] "Letter from D. António de Noronha to D. Manuel," São João da Mamora, 3 August 1515, *SIHMP*, 1:717n1; *HP*, 3:536-537.

fortress and a church. Aguz came under almost immediate attack by Sa`adid forces. At the expense of hundreds of men, the Portuguese were able to prevent the fortress from falling. In 1525, however, D. João III appears to have agreed to abandon and destroy the fortress as part of a peace agreement with the Sa`adid leader.[48] Portuguese fortress building was at an end. Now, they needed to hold on to them.

Despite numerous and repeated attacks by the Wattasids, the Sa`adids, and the Hintati along with various tribal confederations, the Portuguese succeeded in expanding their sphere of influence in Morocco until about 1520, the beginning of a decade-long stalemate. They were especially successful in the Dukkala region around Safi and Azamor due to the assistance of a Berber *qā'id*, Yahya-u-Ta`fuft (d. 1518).[49] Nevertheless, the rise from about 1510 of the Sa`adid Sharif, Muahmmad al-Qā'im, in the Sus region of Morocco began to push the Portuguese back. Military encounters with small Sa`adian raiding forces near Santa Cruz began as early as 1511.[50] The Sa`adids increased their power rapidly. By 1525, the *capitão* of Santa Cruz could only claim to control three leagues of land around his fortress. Beyond that, the Sa`adids held sway.[51] It was, in fact, the Sa`adids who would force the Portuguese to abandon most of what they had gained in southern Morocco and cause the destruction of the Wattasid sultanate in 1549.

In late 1524 or early 1525, the Sa`adids accomplished what the Portuguese had hoped to but could not: the conquest of Hintati Marrakech.[52] Not only did this conquest give the Sa`adids a base of

---

[48] Incredibly, this fortress left few traces in the documentary record despite what seems to have been a five-year existence. "Letter from D. Nuno Mascarenhas to D. Manuel," Safi, 22 May 1519, *SIHMP*, 2:243-246, 244n2; "Letter from the Bishop of Safi to D. Manuel," Azamor, 11 August 1519, *SIHMP*, 2:252; "Presentation Letter for Duarte Fogaça," Évora, 11 October 1520, *SIHMP*, 2:280-281; *SIHMP*, 2:297n2; "Letter from D. João III to Gonçalo Mendes Sacoto," n.l., June or July 1523, *SIHMP*, 2:309-310; "Letter to D. João III from Six Portuguese Prisoners," n.l., September 1523, *SIHMP*, 2:326.

[49] Matthew T. Racine, "Service and Honor in Sixteenth-Century Portuguese North Africa: Yahya-u-Ta`fuft and Portuguese Noble Culture," in *Sixteenth Century Journal* 35 (2001): 67-90. Yahya-u-Ta`fuft is mentioned throughout this study.

[50] "Declaration of Knighthood," Santa Cruz, 8 July 1512, *SIHMP*, 1:334.

[51] "Letter from António Leitão de Gamboa to D. João III," Santa Cruz, 16 January 1525, *SIHMP*, 2:335.

[52] The city itself was controlled by Al-Naser al-Hintati until 1520 and then by Muhammad Bu Shantuf al Hintati until 1524/5, called the King of Marrakech by the

operations within 150 kilometers of Safi, it also bolstered their image among Moroccans as successful defenders of the faith against the Christian infidels.[53] After 1525, Wattasid influence was absent from Dukkala and restricted to the northern half of Morocco.

Even before this stunning victory, the Portuguese leadership in Morocco had recognized the danger posed by the Sa`adids, now led by brothers and co-rulers, Ahmed al-A`raj and Muhammed al-Sheikh (who should not be confused with the fifteenth-century Wattasid sultan), who had succeeded their father. Consequently, the Portuguese sought a peace with the Sa`adids in order to both slow the Sa`adids' expansionist activities and strengthen their own defensive position. In September 1523, the Portuguese and the Sa`adids concluded a three-month truce. The two parties agreed that this short cease-fire would be used as a window in which to negotiate a longer, more definitive peace. Such a peace was concluded sometime in 1524, and seems to have held, albeit tenuously, until at least the second half of 1526.[54] The Sa`adids used this respite to concentrate on their war against the Wattasids.

By the 1530s, it became clear to many Portuguese that while their control of the Moroccan coastline seemed unassailable, the Sa`adids controlled most of inland southern Morocco. The years between the expiration of the peace in 1526 and the late 1530s were not kind to the Portuguese. The Sa`adids and their allies constantly attacked the groups allied to the Portuguese that lived on the fringes of the Portuguese zone of control in Dukkala. In 1533, Sharif Muhammad al-Sheikh besieged and almost captured Santa Cruz. By 1536, both groups again sought a respite from the constant warfare. In retrospect, it was clear that the Portuguese needed a chance to lick their wounds, while the Sa`adids were buying time in which to strengthen their armies as well as continue their attacks on the Wattasids.[55]

Portuguese, and the mountains near the city were controlled by his cousin, Muhammad al-Hintati, called the Lord of the Mountains by the Portuguese.

[53] Farinha, *Portugueses em Marrocos*, 40.

[54] "Letter from Mawlay Ahmed al-A`raj to D. João III," n. l., 10 December 1525, *SIHMP*, 2:351-353 and "Letter from Mawlay Ahmed al-A`raj to Garcia de Melo," n. l., 10 September 1526, *SIHMP*, 2:357-358.

[55] For those interested in a detailed account of the military campaigns and development of the Sa`did Sharifs, see Cook, *passim*.

A four-year truce was concluded in 1537. The years from 1537 to 1541 were ones of peace for Safi, Mazagão, and Azamor, thanks to a treaty concluded between D. Rodrigo de Castro, *capitão* of Safi, and Sharif Ahmed al-A`raj. Santa Cruz had negotiated a separate truce in 1537, set to expire in September 1540. In that month, Sharif Muhammad al-Sheikh began a punishing siege of Santa Cruz that ultimately resulted in his conquest of the city on 12 March 1541, and subsequent capture of a large portion of the Portuguese living there.[56] Brimming with confidence, the Sa`adids launched smaller-scale assaults on both Safi and Azamor in the same year. These attacks were easily beaten back by the Portuguese. Nevertheless, King D. João III (1521-1557) decided to abandon these two cities beginning in October 1541, maintaining only Mazagão.[57]

In 1538, the Portuguese had concluded a peace with their long-time adversary, the Wattasid sultan of Fez. The Wattasids were so afraid of the Sa`adids that they declared a ten-year peace with the Portuguese in order to form a defensive alliance with them against their mutual adversary. Nevertheless, Sharif Muhammad al-Sheikh, now the sole Sa`adid ruler after arresting his brother in 1544, conquered Fez in 1549, causing D. João III to abandon Arzila and Alcácer Ceguer.[58] Thus, by 1550, the Portuguese only maintained Mazagão, Tangiers, and Ceuta. A massive siege in 1562 almost cost Mazagão, but the Portuguese were able to withstand it.[59]

From 1550 onward, the history of the Portuguese in Morocco is mainly that of trading enclaves. These outposts faced periodic raids and sieges, though were still able to trade with local merchants. Only one more great military campaign was undertaken by a Portuguese monarch in Morocco. The famous battle of Alcácer Kebir in 1578,

---

[56] Cenival, "Introduction," in *CSC*, 18 and Farinha, *Portugueses em Marrocos*, 40. For an account of this siege, see chapter seven. The fate of the Portuguese captives from Santa Cruz is discussed in chapter eight.

[57] The abandonment of the Moroccan fortresses and the decision-making process leading up to the abandonment is discussed in detail in the concluding chapter of this book.

[58] Farinha, *Portugueses em Marrocos*, 41.

[59] For a first-hand account of the siege, see Agostinho de Gavy de Mendonça, *História do Cerco de Mazagão* (Lisbon: Bibliotheca de Classicos Portuguzes, 1890). This has been translated into English in John R. C. Martyn, *The Siege of Mazagão: A Perilous Moment in the Defence of Christendom against Islam* (New York: Peter Lang, 1994).

which cost the life of King D. Sebastião (1557-1578), who died without an heir, and sent hundreds of Portuguese nobles into captivity. While no more fortresses were lost as a result of this foolish endeavor, the entire kingdom of Portugal passed into the hands of the Spanish in 1580.[60]

When the Portuguese regained their independence from Spain in 1640, Ceuta remained loyal to the Spanish and remains a Spanish possession to this day. Tangiers and Mazagão returned to their former masters. In 1661, Tangiers was given to the English as a dowry when King D. João IV's daughter, D. Catarina of Bragança, married King Charles II of England. Due to constant attacks by Moroccan forces under the `Alawite sultan, Mawlay Isma`il, the English eventually abandoned the city in 1684, without ever asking the Portuguese if they might want the city back.[61] Mazagão remained a Portuguese possession until 1769, when it was besieged by sultan Sidi Muhammed bin `Abd Allah. The Portuguese prime minister, the Marquês de Pombal, concluding that the fortress was a useless relic of times past, secured a truce with the sultan and ordered the enclave evacuated. The residents of Mazagão were quartered in Lisbon for two years until they were ordered to settle in a remote section of the Amazon. There they founded the Vila Nova de Mazagão.[62]

The abandonment of the Portuguese possessions in Morocco in 1541, 1550, and finally in 1769 were decisions based on sound reasoning. It would have been fiscal and military suicide for the Portuguese to have attempted to maintain a strong position in Morocco while at the same time seeking to expand their empire elsewhere. Still, some Portuguese nationalists during the Scramble for Africa in the late 1800s bemoaned what they termed the short-sightedness of Portugal's past leaders. It pained them greatly to see France and Spain seizing

---

[60] For a brief account of this battle, see Cook, 241-272, while a more detailed account can be found in E. W. Bovill, *The Battle of Alcazar* (London: Batchworth, 1952). Discussions of the succession crisis leading to Philip II of Spain becoming Philip I of Portugal can be found in any competent survey of Portuguese or Spanish history. See, for example, José Mattoso, *História de Portugal* (Lisbon: Editorial Estampa, 1997), 3:465-479 and John Lynch, *Spain, 1516-1598: From Nation State to World Empire* (Cambridge, Mass: Blackwell, 1991), 429-439.

[61] C. R. Boxer, "'Three Sights to be Seen': Bombay, Tangier, and a Barren Queen, 1661-1684," *Portuguese Studies* 3 (1987): 77-83.

[62] Abun-Nasr, *History of the Maghrib*, 239 and Farinha, *Portugueses em Marrocos*, 84-85.

control of what they felt should still be theirs.[63] If they had paid attention to their history instead of their jingoistic emotions, they would have been able to warn their fellow Europeans against attempts to impose a foreign political control on North Africans.

---

[63] See, for instance, the shrill introduction, written anonymously, to Gavy de Mendonça, *Historia do cerco de Mazagão*, 5-10.

Chapter Two: The Portuguese (and European) Population in Portuguese Cities in Southern Morocco

THROUGHOUT the period covered by this study, the non-Moroccan population within the Portuguese cities was in constant flux. As is the case with many frontiers, merchants and soldiers are among the first to arrive. In the case of Portuguese Morocco, merchants arrived with *feitorias* or simply on their own to trade with Moroccans before any direct military conquest of southern Moroccans cities. During the initial conquest phases, the cities were, not surprisingly, filled almost entirely with soldiers. Within a few weeks or months, however, members from nearly every portion of Portuguese society arrived, colonizing the newly acquired territory.

The Portuguese population consisted of two main groups: *fronteiros*, who were a rather fluid population, and *moradores*, a more permanent group. *Fronteiros* were typically nobles, normally serving in a military capacity, who had come to Morocco to "earn their spurs" fighting against Islam. *Fronteiros*, like Portuguese of all social levels, brought their wives and daughters with them to Morocco. While some of these men, notably high-ranking government officials, might stay in Morocco for many years, a vast majority remained only long enough to gain some wealth and enhance their reputation as warriors.

By contrast, the *moradores* (residents) were just about everyone else who resided in the city, including non-noble soldiers, women outside of the noble class, artisans, physicians, laborers, and others.[1] The total population of Portuguese residing in a Portuguese-controlled city was typically between 500 and 2,500, though as low as 200 and as

---

[1] Paulo Drumond Braga, "A expansão no norte de África," in *A expansão quatrocentista*, ed. A. H. de Oliveira Marques (Lisbon: Editorial Estampa, 1998), 297-300.

high as 4-5,000 (see Table 2.1). Because Jews and Moroccan Muslims also lived in these cities, the overall population was higher.[2]

Royal Officials

Royal officials formed the administrative structure, both civil and military, of each fortress. The highest-ranking of these officials was the *capitão*, or governor, of the city. His political authority was absolute over the city and the surrounding subjected territory. He had jurisdiction of nearly all aspects of life in the fortress, including criminal, economic, and military.[3] Religious matters were handled by the clergy, and civil disputes were handled by the courts, though the *capitão* had the right to overrule judicial decisions (see below). If one did not like the *capitão's* decisions, the only appeal was to the king himself.

For instance, when King D. Manuel named Diogo de Azambuja as the first the *capitão* of Safi, the king gave him the right to dispense justice in civil and criminal cases involving people "of whatever condition or quality that they may be." D. Manuel made a point to order all of the "nobles, knights, and squires" to obey Azambuja as if the king himself were there in person and had given the order.[4] D. Francisco de Castro, the first royally-appointed *capitão* of Santa Cruz, was given "the powers and the civil and criminal jurisdiction that the other *capitães* of overseas fortresses have."[5]

But the authority granted to this office came at a price, in that the *capitão* might spend huge quantities of his own money while the king refrained from reimbursing him in anything resembling a timely manner. Azambuja, in a particularly anguished plea, asked D. Manuel for money and begged him, "Do not let me lose everything." Similar

---

[2] Exact numbers will likely remain unknown. For a discussion of these groups, see chapter three.

[3] António Vasconcelos de Saldanha, *As capitanias do Brasil: antecedentes, desenvolvimento e extinção de um fenómeno atlântico* (Lisbon: CNCDP, 2001), 141-148; Maria Augusta Lima Cruz Fagundes, "Documentos inéditos para a história dos portugueses em Azamor," in *Arquivos do Centro Cultural Português* 2 (1970): 115.

[4] "Letter Patent of D. Manuel," Abrantes, 27 June 1507, *SIHMP*, 1:131.

[5] *CM*, 15, f. 148. For other examples of these privileges see *CM*, 15, f. 148v and *CJ*, 26, f. 156v, published in Joaquim Figanier, *História de Santa Cruz do Cabo de Gué (Agadir) 1505-1541* (Lisboa: Agência Geral das Colónias, 1945), 310-312 and 337-338.

expenses drove D. Rodrigo de Castro, the *capitão* of Safi in 1537, to such a state that he asked King D. João III to pay for his two daughters to enter a convent in Odivelas as he could neither afford their upkeep nor pay for a suitable marriages.[6]

These pleas came despite the fact that *capitães* throughout Portuguese Morocco earned an annual stipend of 114,000 *reis*, in addition to profits from any business transactions – especially slave trading – in which they might engage as well as their right to take one-fifth of all seized booty.[7] Actual income is difficult to estimate because it undoubtedly fluctuated depending on the number of raids in a given year and whether peace or war prevailed. For example, if a raiding party returned to the city with one hundred captives, not an uncommon number, and sold them at auction for an average price of 1,000 *reis*, the total amount realized would be 100,000 *reis*. From this, the *capitão* would gain 20,000 *reis* for his personal wealth. Five of six such prosperous raids annually, and the *capitão* could double his annual income.

The *capitão*, like other high-ranking officials, had the ear of the king, and could ask for his family or retainers to be promoted to positions of power and prestige, where wealth could be made. Azambuja, in fact, asked D. Manuel, when the king began filling offices in Safi, to remember that he had many "nephews and retainers" who served the king well and who deserved an appointment. Azambuja specifically named Francisco de Almeida as a candidate for *adail* and Francisco de Abreu for *alfaqueque*.[8]

The *capitão* was head of military operations, and normally fought with his men, both in the defense of his fortress and during

---

[6] ANTT, CC I, 59, 53. In 1540, the *capitão* of Santa Cruz asked the king to place his unmarried daughter, who lived in Portugal with her widowed sister, in a convent at royal expense ("Letter from D. Guterres de Monroi to D. João III," Santa Cruz, 1 June 1540, *SIHMP*, 3:243).

[7] ANTT, NA 597, f. 2 and "Order of Payment from D. Guterres de Monroi," Santa Cruz, 24 November 1533, *SIHMP*, 2:598.

[8] "Letter of Diogo de Azambuja to D. Manuel," Safi, 13 December 1507, *SIHMP*, 1:142-143. Almeida never held important office in Safi, but he did serve as *adail* of Azamor from 1513 until his death in 1516, when he was replaced by António Fernandes de Cadros (*CM*, 42, f. 125 and 25, f. 154v). Abreu did not receive the office of *alfaqueque*, though he remained in Safi until at least 1511 and was of sufficiently high status to receive command of an *estancia* during the siege of 1510 ("Letter from Nuno Gato to D. Manuel," Safi, 3 January 1511, *SIHMP*, 1:279).

offensive raids. For example, during the 1510 siege of Safi, *capitão* Nuno Fernandes de Ataíde would move with a group of troops to the weak spots on the walls or to the locations of heaviest combat. Just as soldiers often became more determined when their king led them into battle, the appearance of the *capitão* gave tired and frightened men a second wind and led them to greater martial deeds.[9] Literally hundreds of examples of Portuguese *capitães* leading or coordinating raids in the Moroccan countryside might be cited.[10]

In one instance, and only for one year, did D. Manuel attempt to separate the functions of *capitão* among two men. From 1513 to 1514, Rui Barreto acted as the *capitão da cidade* (city governor) of Azamor, while D. João de Meneses acted as the *capitão do campo* (field governor). The illogical separation of urban and rural jurisdictions in the highly militarized setting of the Moroccan frontier led to constant bickering between the two men, over matters both important and insignificant. When Meneses sickened and died in May 1514, D. Manuel relieved Barreto of his duties and appointed a new *capitão*, D. Pedro de Sousa, later the first conde do Prado, who unified the positions.[11]

Another role of the *capitão* was as the local arbiter of prestige. He was permitted to reward people for outstanding performance of duties. In one case, João Lopes de Sequeira, the *capitão* of Santa Cruz, granted João Pessoa the status of knight (*cavaleiro*) as a result of the valor he displayed against Moroccan soldiers during a siege that began on 18 August 1511 and lasted for "some days."[12] A *capitão* might also be called on to write a letter of certification in order to verify a man's deeds in North Africa so that he might be rewarded, with money and/or titles, by the Portuguese court. D. Pedro de Sousa vouched for one Mateus Pires, a crossbowman, saying that he had been involved in several raids, including one where he killed one Muslim and wounded

---

[9] "Letter from Nuno Gato to D. Manuel," Safi, 3 January 1511, *SIHMP*, 1:279.

[10] For a few examples, see chapter seven.

[11] *CDM*, 3:51, 201-202; *SIHMP*, 1:461n1; "Letter from D. João de Meneses to D. Manuel," Azamor, 18 February 1514, *SIHMP*, 1:487; "Letter from Rui Barreto to D. Manuel," Azamor, 21 February 1514, *SIHMP*, 1:493; "Letter from D. Manuel to D. João de Meneses," Lisbon, 24 May 1514, *SIHMP*, 1:559-560; *HP*, 3:521.

[12] "Declaration of Knighthood," Santa Cruz, 8 July 1512, *SIHMP*, 1:334. See also, "Alvará of D. Manuel," Lisbon, 15 July 1521, *SIHMP*, 2:289-290.

another and captured twelve horses.[13] *Capitães* also dispensed material rewards, often houses (both confiscated from Moroccans and newly built) and land, for important services rendered and were empowered to assign houses to royal officials of all types. For instance, D. Álvaro de Noronha gave houses to each of the river pilots (*pilotos da barra*) in Azamor in 1519.[14]

Since the responsibility of a *capitão* was so great, it was never a first assignment for a Portuguese noble. Appointees normally had proven themselves either as warriors or administrators before they were given their positions. For example, D. Nuno Mascarenhas was a descendant of a distinguished family that had served the kings of Portugal since the mid-fifteenth century. D. Nuno himself had received the commandry of Almodôvar in the Order of Santiago. He went on to serve valiantly in North Africa. In 1512, he commanded 100 lancers in Safi, and he participated in the conquest of Azamor the next year. He then served in the ill-fated expedition to build a Portuguese fortification at Mamora in 1515. His exemplary service and his family's history culminated in his appointment as *capitão* of Safi at the young age of twenty-six, serving in that capacity from 1516 until 1522.[15] Garcia de Melo, the *capitão* of Safi from 1525 to 1529, had previously served as the *alcaide mor* (military governor) of Castro Marim in southern Portugal on the border with Castile.[16] António Leitão de Gamboa, the *capitão* of Santa Cruz from 1522 to 1525 and again from 1528 to 1529, gained notice as the son of Pero Leitão, who had served as *adail* of Tangiers and then as *adail mor* of Portugal. Due to his family

---

[13] "Certification delivered by Pedro de Sousa," Azamor, 28 April 1516, *SIHMP*, 1:774-775.

[14] These pilots were precursors to modern tugboat captains. They guided large ships along the shallows of the Umm al Rabi` River to Azamor's docks. *CM*, 39, f. 106; *SIHMP*, 2:266n3; ANTT, *Livro das Ilhas*, fol. 128, published in José Alberto Rodrigues da Silva Tavim, *Os judeus na expansão portuguesa em Marrocos durante o século XVI: origens e actividades duma comunidade* (Braga: Edições APPACDM Distrital de Braga, 1997), 528. The king might also assign houses to individuals (*SIHMP*, 2:242n1, 267n2) and was always able to veto any housing and land gifts from *capitães*. For more on housing, see chapter four.

[15] Francis A. Dutra, "As ordens militares," in *O tempo de Vasco da Gama*, ed. Diogo Ramada Curto (Lisbon: CNCDP, 1998), 232-233 and "Letter from D. João Mascarenhas," n. l., 31 October 1540, *SIHMP*, 2:295-296. Twenty-five was, in fact, the age of majority for Portuguese males during this period.

[16] *SIHMP*, 5:215.

connections at court and his service as a soldier in the king's galleys in the Straits of Gibraltar and off the Guinea coast, António was made *adail mor* of Portugal in 1520.[17]

The second-ranking official in Portuguese cities in Morocco was the *contador*, who oversaw all matters relating to the king's treasury. The annual salary for this official was 12,000 *reis*.[18] In the event of the *capitão*'s absence or death, the *contador* normally assumed the position of *capitão* until he returned or the king named a replacement.[19] The hierarchy clearly shows that one of the top priorities for Portuguese monarchs in North Africa was to maintain order and generate income. At least one *contador*, Nuno Gato of Safi, was also the *alfaqueque mor*, in charge of the ransoming of Portuguese captives.[20] While another *contador*, António Leite, became the *capitão* of Mazagão (1520-1529) and then of Azamor (1529-1530).[21]

Beneath these two men was a military and financial hierarchy that enabled them to perform their tasks. The second-in-command of the military was the *adail* who, along with the *capitão*, commanded both offensive and defense operations. Despite what seems like the great responsibilities of an *adail*, these officials were paid only 3,600 *reis* per year.[22] But, like all Portuguese soldiers, they could supplement their

---

[17] *CM*, 38, f. 112v; *CM*, 37, 67v; *CJ*, 14, f. 62v, published in Figanier, 312-313 and 316-317. It should be noted that while military considerations had highest priority within the Portuguese fortresses, there appears to have been an attempt to reproduce a municipal civilian governing structure similar to that in Portugal. There are hints that there was a city council (*câmara*) in each of the southern fortresses, but nothing is known about their accomplishments ("Letter from Mestre Rodrigo to D. João III," Azamor, 12 January 1528, *SIHMP*, 2:427). Ceuta, the best-studied of the Portuguese fortresses, had a *câmara* for much of its existence under the Portuguese, though little is known about it. For example, the only year for which the composition of the *câmara* is known is 1648, when it consisted of one judge, one *almotacé* (overseer of weights and measures), one secretary of the *câmara*, and six deputies. The names of these people remain a mystery. Isabel M. R. Mendes Drumond Braga and Paulo Drumond Braga Braga, *Ceuta Portuguesa (1415-1656)* (Ceuta: Instituto de Estudios Ceutíes, 1998), 101.

[18] ANTT, NA 597, f. 120 and *CM*, 10, f. 142, published in Figanier, 315. It was typical that all royal officials padded their pockets through business deals, graft, and other means. Exact income figures for these men will never be known.

[19] Fagundes, "Documentos," 115.

[20] "Letter from Nuno Gato to D. Manuel," Safi, 14 May 1512, *SIHMP*, 1:309-310. See chapter eight for more on the role of the *alfaqueque*.

[21] *SIHMP*, 5:203.

[22] ANTT, NA 597, f. 123v and *CJ*, 40, f. 192v, published in Figanier, 341-342.

income through the capture of goods and people during raids and their subsequent sale. Beneath the *adail* were persons in charge of smaller groups of men or certain sectors of the town and surrounding area.[23]

The officials in charge of commerce were the *feitor* and *almoxarife*. The *feitor* was in charge of the *feitoria*, which oversaw the transfer and sale of all goods between the king and local merchants, whether they were Portuguese (or European), Jewish, or Moroccan. He also assessed necessary taxes and duties on these goods. Due to the importance of commerce to the Portuguese kings, *feitores* were paid well for their work. They received an annual salary of between 20,000 and 30,000 *reis* and 1-1.5 percent of the profits of royal merchandise sold to Moroccans.[24] The *feitor*, of course, had numerous functionaries working below him, including scribes, men in charge of receiving goods, those in charge of disbursing funds, etc.. *Feitores*, like *contadores*, might also serve as interim *capitães*. Lançarote de Freitas, having been replaced as *feitor* of Azamor in 1530, remained in the city and was appointed as interim *capitão* of Azamor for a few months during 1534.[25]

The *almoxarife* administered the *alfândega*, or customs house, which oversaw the flow of local goods into and out of the fortresses. He ensured that taxes and duties were collected on all non-royal trade goods that entered or left the city. This typically included agricultural and manufactured goods produced in the Moroccan countryside. An *almoxarife* typically earned between 10,000 and 15,000 *reis* per year as well as a monthly *moradia* (living allowance).[26]

The officials discussed above are the most high profile royal officials. However, men who worked for the king served in a myriad of capacities. Other royal officials, some of which are discussed in greater detail in other parts of this book, include judicial officials (*ouvidores*, *juízes dos orfãos*, bailiffs, jailers, and a whole host of scribes and notaries), economic and tax officials, and the ubiquitous *escrivães* (scribes). For instance, the *escrivão dos mantimentos* worked under the *recebedor dos*

---

[23] Fagundes, "Documentos," 116. See the "Soldiers" section below and chapter seven for a more detailed discussion of military positions.

[24] *CM*, 10, f. 78v and *CJ*, 19, f. 223-223v, published in Figanier, 314-315 and 334-335.

[25] *SIHMP*, 5:191; Fagundes, "Documentos," chart between pp. 124 and 125. For more on this topic, see chapter five.

[26] Figanier, 333-335 and *DCC*, 93-94.

mantimentos, recording the arrival of food and supplies to the city. Meanwhile, the *escrivão do anadel-mor dos besteiros* kept accounts on weaponry and ammunition and was responsible for ensuring that these supplies were replenished when necessary. The city of Azamor had an *escrivão da ribeira* whose task was to record the number of fish caught in the nearby Umm al-Rabi` River and collect taxes on the catch. Safi and Azamor each had an *escrivão do campo de El Rey* who collected fees for the use of grazing land that was controlled by the king near the Portuguese fortresses.[27]

Clergy

Portuguese clergymen seemed to have arrived in Moroccan cities either from the moment a *feitoria* was established there, as in the case of Azamor and Safi, or when construction on the city itself began, in the case of Santa Cruz and Mazagão. The existence of a Catholic chapel in Safi is mentioned in the quittance of *feitor* Rui Fernandes de Almada, who was *feitor* from July 1491 until June 1495. Lopo de Azevedo, *feitor* of Safi from 1 July 1495 until 15 February 1498, mentions in his quittance report that he imported various accoutrements for the Mass, including a painted altar cloth, a missal, and a triptych altarpiece painted with religious scenes.[28]

In 1511, there were eleven men identified either as clergy or friars living in Safi, and a twelfth, Gaspar de Villa Lobos, who apparently served as the personal priest (*vigário capelão da casa*) to the *capitão*.[29] By 1514, Safi had a Franciscan monastery (dedicated to St. Catharine) that was large enough for six or eight friars, though a larger building, that could house fifty friars, was already under construction. The guardian of the monastery, Frei Fernando, died in 1514. Consequently, Nuno Fernandes de Ataíde, the *capitão*, appointed the elderly Frei Vicente, who had been in Safi "a long time," as interim guardian. Because of Vicente's age, Nuno Gato, Safi's *contador*, requested that the king appoint a new guardian as soon as possible and

---

[27] ANTT, CC I, 71, 60; CC II, 46, 65; CC II, 73, 2, CC II, 108, 22.

[28] "Quittance of Lopo de Azevedo," Lisbon, 7 May 1499, *SIHMP*, 1:46-47. A quittance (*carta da quitação*) was a report that all *feitores* were required to file that listed the goods imported, exported, and sold through the *feitoria* during their time in office.

[29] ANTT, NA 597, ff. 62-64v, 122v.

send him to the city. Gato also claimed the good example that the friars exhibit was "very necessary" for the city.[30]

In contrast to the "good" friars in Safi, Rui Barreto, the *capitão* of Azamor in 1514, said that the few friars who were in Azamor wandered through the streets at night causing problems, mainly shouting and protesting the fact that no monasteries were being built for them. Furthermore, Barreto said that the friars in Azamor were of less than ideal character, because "they are those that in Portugal cannot remain orderly." Likely, they were sent to North Africa for punishment, probably as exiles (*degredados*). Because of a lack of money, both from a paucity of royal funds and from the low volume of alms contributions locally, no monasteries were under construction in Azamor. Barreto's concerns regarding clerical behavior may have been exaggerated because the number of clergy in Azamor was never great. In fact, the number of clerics in the city at any one time never exceeded seventeen. Barreto did, however, write to the king, telling him that if he truly wanted three monasteries in the city, as D. Manuel had suggested earlier, he needed to send money and materials to make it so, otherwise having friars wandering around the city will cause "a great disorder."[31] Disorder from the representatives of Christianity in a frontier fortress, located in a contested border where two great religious ideologies were confronting each other was not in the best interests of the Portuguese.

The clergy, of course, comforted the Christian residents of the Portuguese cities and ensured the continuation of the sacraments. The issues of death and burial are rarely mentioned in the sources, despite the fact that scores of Portuguese died each year, usually from battle, but also from sickness and age. Of the four wills extant from Safi, two of the testators requested that they be buried in the Franciscan monastery of St. Catherine and one in Safi's cathedral, while the fourth will is silent on this issue. Meanwhile all of the wills specify a certain

---

[30] "Letter from Nuno Gato to D. Manuel," Safi, 21 October 1514, *SIHMP*, 1:649-650. Frei Vicente may be the same "Frei Vicente, *frade*" who appears in ANTT, NA 597, f. 62.

[31] "Letter from Rui Barreto to D. Manuel," Azamor, 21 February 1514, *SIHMP*, 1:498 ("*estes sseram aqueles que em Portugall nom podem estar em ordem*") and Fagundes, "Documentos," 118. For more on exiles, see below. Chapter four discusses religious construction projects in more detail.

number of requiem masses to be sung.³² Many of the anonymous infantrymen and pages who served the schemes of Portuguese *fronteiros* were provided with a requiem mass at government expense.³³ D. João de Meneses, who died in Azamor only weeks after the deaths of two of his nephews during a raid in the countryside, was buried in the city's cathedral on 15 May 1514.³⁴

Undoubtedly, the clergy served to comfort the Portuguese in times of need. For example, Safi suffered a terrible shortage of grain between January and October 1540. The price of wheat was at the astronomical price of 300 *reis/alqueire* (26.8 *reis*/kg), and residents of the city were selling all of their possessions including furniture and clothing just to buy food. Women and children were reportedly sick and dying from malnutrition, and horses were dying as well. During this horrible situation, the clergy organized a procession on 5 August making a circuit of all of the city's Christian sites in order to ask for mercy from the Virgin Mary. The most startling spectacle of this procession were the malnourished and naked children who, in their wretchedness, implored the Virgin to be merciful and provide them with relief from their suffering.³⁵

Soldiers

Soldiers under Portuguese command could be Christians, Muslims, or Jews, with the vast majority consisting of Portuguese Christians and Moroccan Muslims. Moroccan soldiers were used extensively in raids and battles outside of cities, but do not seem to have been used in any significant numbers to defend the cities from besieging forces. Jews, however, rarely fought except in a defensive

---

[32] ANTT, CC I, 27, 52; CC II, 75, 150; CC II, 83, 57; CC II, 95, 136.

[33] ANTT, CC II, 48, 39.

[34] *SIHMP*, 1:559n1. Rui Barreto suggested that Meneses died of extreme despair following the deaths of his nephews (ANTT, CdGA, 97). Robert Ricard, "Les inscriptions portugaises de Mazagan," in Idem., *Études sur l'histoire des portugais au Maroc* (Coimbra: University of Coimbra, 1955), 411-412 mentions seven sepulchers dating from 1578-1721.

[35] "Letter from D. Rodrigo de Castro to D. João III," Safi, 24 June 1540, *SIHMP*, 3:248-250; "Letter from Álvaro de Moraes to D. João III," Safi, 27 August 1540, *SIHMP*, 3:259-261; "Letter from D. Rodrigo de Castro to D. João III," Safi, 13 September 1540, *SIHMP*, 3:262-264. The average price of wheat throughout the Portuguese occupation was about 60 *reis/alqueire* (see chapter four).

role during sieges.³⁶ Other than construction and maintenance of the fortresses, the monthly salaries (*soldos*) of soldiers were the largest expenses for the Portuguese kings. For example, during the final three months of 1511, the salary for all soldiers (*gente de ordenança*) in Safi alone amounted to 490,455 *reis*. The number of soldiers had decreased in Safi by 1517, for the amount needed to pay for the eighteen months from January 1517 until June 1518 was a mere 1,068,298 *reis* (or 178,050 *reis* every three months). Finally, the payroll for soldiers in Azamor during the first six months of 1522 totaled 761,533 *reis* (also see Tables 2.2, 2.3, 2.4).³⁷

The three largest categories by which soldiers were designated were cavalry, infantry, and artillerymen. The cavalrymen typically fought with lance and sword, though there were also large numbers of mounted crossbowmen (*besteiros*) as well as mounted matchlockmen (*espingardeiros*). Infantrymen (*gente de pé*) consisted largely of those who fought with swords and lances, with substantial numbers of crossbowmen and matchlockmen. Finally, artillerymen (*bombardeiros*) were important mainly for the defense of the fortresses, though small artillery pieces were sometimes taken on raids into the countryside.³⁸ Of the eleven artillerymen in Safi in 1511, at least three and perhaps six were non-Portuguese Europeans who had brought their expertise to Morocco. In Azamor in 1515, there were 32 German and 26 French mercenaries serving as soldiers.³⁹ Of great importance to the artillerymen was the *apontador* who calculated trajectories of weapons and computed correct amounts of gunpower needed to project the shot the appropriate distances.⁴⁰ Others who were considered essential auxiliaries to the military and were thus included in military payment

---

³⁶ In fact, other than the Moroccan soldiers mentioned later in this section, I have found no evidence of Moroccans assisting in the defense of a besieged Portuguese city. This lack of evidence, of course, does not mean that they never assisted. See also the discussion of Jewish combatants in chapter seven.

³⁷ ANTT, NA 597, f. 128; ANTT, CC I, 23, 99; Fagundes, "Documentos," 156-157. Determining the total expenditure for soldiers for each year that the Portuguese maintained four major fortresses in southern Morocco is difficult, but must have amounted to between 1 and 1.5 million *reis* per quarter, or 4 to 6 million *reis* per year.

³⁸ *CDM*, 3:196-197.

³⁹ ANTT, NA 597, ff. 125-127v and ANTT, CC II, 59, 163.

⁴⁰ ANTT, CC II, 59, 61 and ANTT, NA 597, f. 124. He recorded these measurements in his *livro de ponto* (ANTT, CC II, 97, 64).

rolls were trumpeters (*trombetas*), of whom there were three in Safi in 1511, drummers, and fife (*pifaro*) players.[41]

It should be noted that soldiers could hold more than one position and thus receive a salary for all of those positions. For example, João Rodrigues was both the *porteiro dos contos* (guardian of the treasury) and a crossbowman. As *porteiro*, he earned a stipend (*tença*) of 2,000 *reis* per year, while his salary as a crossbowman garnered him 750 *reis* per month or 9,000 *reis* per year, for an annual total of 11,000.[42] Luis Vaz and Mateus Fernandes were both crossbowmen, for which they earned 300 *reis* per month, and *atalaias da torre* (tower lookouts), for which they earned 400 *reis* per month, or a total of 8,400 *reis* per year.[43] Such situations, however, do not appear to have been very common.

While Moroccans often made up the majority of the soldiers in Portuguese raiding forces, few were on the Portuguese payroll. Rather they lived on one-time payments for specific actions or, more typically, from a share of booty seized on a raid. The seven who are mentioned on the 1511 payment roll for military personnel in Safi are exceptions. These seven Moroccan cavalrymen (*mouros de cavalo*) were Abu, Benamyra, Bulbarar, Masa'ud, Muhammad of Marrakech, Raho, and Riba. All of these men were paid 350 *reis* per month, the same rate as Portuguese Christian cavalrymen.[44] The only other Moroccan listed on the 1511 payroll was Yahya-u-Ta'fuft, the *alcaide dos mouros* for the surrounding region of Dukkala and thus of a different category entirely.[45] As many as twenty-one Moroccans may have been on the payroll in Azamor in 1517, as the *capitão* listed Sheikh Mimūn and his twenty men among the 800 soldiers in the fortress.[46]

---

[41] ANTT, NA 597, ff. 115-116. For an example of trumpeters in battle, see "Letter from Nuno Fernandes de Ataíde to D. Manuel," Safi, 4 January 1511, *SIHMP*, 1:286. Trumpeters, drummers, and fife players are mentioned in "Letter from D. Rodrigo de Castro to D. João III," Safi, 8 July 1541, *SIHMP*, 3:457.

[42] ANTT, NA 597, ff. 98v, 120v.

[43] ANTT, NA 597, f. 101v.

[44] ANTT, NA 597, ff. 33, 38-38v, 42, 83v.

[45] See the discussion of *alcaides dos mouros* and Yahya-u-Ta'fuft in chapter six.

[46] "Letter from Simão Correia to D. Manuel," Azamor, 20 May 1517, *SIHMP*, 2:86. Compare this with the use of Muslim soldiers by Christian rulers in medieval Iberia discussed in L. P. Harvey, *Islamic Spain, 1250 to 1500* (Chicago: University of Chicago Press, 1990), 138-150 and David Abulafia, "Introduction," in *Medieval Frontiers: Concepts*

Women

There were many Portuguese women in the North African fortresses. Without a doubt, in fact, there were more Portuguese women in Morocco than in Brazil, West Africa, or Asia during the sixteenth century.[47] These large numbers indicate that the Portuguese crown planned long-term settlements in Morocco rather than simply trading or military enclaves. During the reign of D. Afonso V, Alcácer Ceguer in northern Morocco had 100 women and children in a population of about 500, and by 1500, the population was 28 percent female and 11 percent children.[48] In fact, by 1516 in the northern Moroccan fortress of Arzila, the number of women and children was about one thousand.[49] Exact numbers for the southern fortresses are difficult to discern, though the percentages are likely similar, especially in Azamor and Safi. Santa Cruz and Mazagão were much smaller, and before 1540, Mazagão was little more than a transshipping point. Clearly, one should not assume that the only Portuguese women in North African fortresses were prostitutes, mistresses, and exiles.[50]

It is clear that among the elites, wives often came to Africa to live with their husbands and raise their children.[51] Some even brought Portuguese midwives and nannies. Nuno Fernandes de Ataíde's wife, D. Joana de Faria, and daughters were with him in Morocco while he served as *capitão* of Safi.[52] Nuno Gato, the *contador* of Safi, appears to have had his wife with him. The uncle of Gato's wife, Manuel da Silva,

---

and Practices, ed., David Abulafia and Nora Berend (Burlington, Vermont: Ashgate, 2002), 32.

[47] Charles R. Boxer, *Women in Iberian Expansion Overseas, 1415-1815: Some Facts, Fancies and Personalities* (New York: Oxford University Press, 1975), 11-16 and Braga and Braga, *Ceuta Portuguesa*, 53-60.

[48] Braga, "A expansão," 298.

[49] Ana Maria S. A. Rodrigues and Maria de Fátima Moura Ferreira, "Mulheres portuguesas em Marrocos: imagens do quotidiano feminino nos séculos XV e XVI," *O rosto feminino da expansão portuguesa* (Lisbon: Comissão para a Igualdade e para os Direitos das Mulheres, 1995), 1:419.

[50] This seems to be the implication in Timothy Coates, *Convicts and Orphans: Forced and State-Sponsored Colonizers in the Portuguese Empire, 1550-1755* (Stanford: Stanford University Press, 2001), 59-60.

[51] Braga and Braga, *Ceuta Portuguesa*, 54ff.

[52] "Letter from Nuno Fernandes de Ataíde to D. Manuel," 4 August 1515, *SIHMP*, 1:723 and *SIHMP*, 1:340n1.

came to Safi with one of his brothers and his wife.⁵³ D. Nuno Mascarenhas's wife, D. Beatriz da Silva, lived in Safi during his tenure as the city's *capitão* from 1516 to 1522.⁵⁴ Another woman who accompanied her husband to Morocco was the wife of Fernão Dias, whom the king had dispatched to Marrakech in order to attempt to negotiate a peace treaty in 1514. His wife stayed in Azamor while he was away on his diplomatic mission, and she was given 2,000 *reis* in order to pay her expenses.⁵⁵

Sometimes, however, getting the women to Morocco in the first place could be a challenge. In 1525, António Leitão de Gamboa, serving his first term as *capitão* of Santa Cruz, intended to marry a woman who was still living in Portugal. He hoped that she would join him in Morocco, but he claimed to have little money and asked the king to pay for her transportation. It appears that rather than send his fiancée to Morocco, D. João III recalled Leitão to Portugal, where he presumably married.⁵⁶ In 1541, only months before Safi would be evacuated, D. Rodrigo de Castro, the *capitão*, asked the king to send his wife to him as soon as possible because "there was no way" that he could maintain one household in Portugal and another one in Safi.⁵⁷

It should also be made clear that many married men did not bring their wives or families with them to North Africa. Apparently, this decision was not always wise. On 26 October 1536, D. Álvaro de Abranches, the *capitão* of Azamor, wrote to the king advising him that a large number of crossbowmen and matchlockmen had asked for his permission to return home to Portugal. They gave two reasons for this: their absence was prejudicial to their wealth (*fazenda*) and they missed

---

⁵³ "Letter from Nuno Gato to D. Manuel," Azamor, 5 December 1513, *SIHMP*, 1:454.

⁵⁴ *SIHMP*, 2:297n2.

⁵⁵ ANTT, CC II, 48, 80.

⁵⁶ "Letter from António Leitão de Gamboa to D. João III," Santa Cruz, 16 January 1525, *SIHMP*, 2:342. We can speculate that Leitão's wife did not accompany him to Santa Cruz when he returned in 1528 as *capitão*. In 1529, he raped a Moroccan woman, an act one hopes that he would not have committed were his wife in the fortress. He was then killed by a Moroccan man in revenge. See chapter four for details.

⁵⁷ "Letter from D. Rodrigo de Castro to D. João III," Safi, 8 July 1541, *SIHMP*, 3:462. I have been unable to determine if his wife ever arrived in Safi.

their wives.[58] Abranches relayed their request to have replacements sent from Portugal so that they could leave.[59] The need for replacements prior to the departure of these men implies that a large enough proportion of soldiers were without wives that to let them go would have compromised defense. In other words, of all the groups in the Moroccan fortresses, it was the non-noble soldiers who were least likely to have wives with them.

Women remained in the southern fortresses until just before they were abandoned, with the exception of the women in Santa Cruz who were captured when it fell to Sa`adid forces.[60] Women stayed in Azamor until early October 1541, when all of the women and children living in the city were placed on boats and sent to Portugal. Although the number of evacuees is unknown, it must have been quite large because Jorge Fernandes, a "laborer" (*trabalhador*), worked continuously for seven days dispensing and packaging enough hardtack for the people to take on the ship for their return voyage.[61] The evacuation of women and children resulted from the fear that the Sharif might attack and even capture Azamor and Safi as he had Santa Cruz.

Women's Civil Status

Portuguese women in the Moroccan fortresses were almost always married. Those who were single, not widows, and without a family for protection or employment as a servant were often prostitutes or mistresses. In fact, some of the previously unmarried single women had been exiled to Morocco as punishment for crimes such as concubinage continued to commit the same offenses once overseas.[62] Among those who kept a mistress was Simão Gonçalves da Costa, *capitão* of Santa Cruz, who maintained his mistress in her own

---

[58] Although these men may truly have missed their wives, their desire to return to Portugal may have had more to do with the fact that a truce had recently been concluded with the Sa`adids. Consequently, raiding activity was forbidden to the Portuguese, thus cutting off their main avenue to wealth and making their stay in Azamor much less profitable than they had hoped.

[59] ANTT, CC I, 57, 122.

[60] See Chapter Eight for an account of this Santa Cruz captivity.

[61] Fagundes, "Documentos," 168. Fernandes earned 30 *reis* per day for his efforts.

[62] Rodrigues and Ferreira, "Mulheres portuguesas," 420.

quarters.⁶³ Women who became single as the result of being widowed and who had no family in Morocco to support them, might depart for Portugal, remarry quickly for safety, or remain in Morocco in the hope of receiving a pension or working to support themselves. If this pension were large enough, they might delay marriage for a time or, perhaps, altogether.⁶⁴

The role of wife was the most common one for women. For those unmarried women who arrived in Morocco and sought a husband, there were several choices. She could marry a Portuguese or European man or, in extremely rare cases, a Moroccan ally of the Portuguese who had converted to Christianity.⁶⁵ There is some evidence that Portuguese men may have married Moroccan women, and although it is unclear if these women had converted to Christianity, one would assume it would be necessary. For example, Luís de Sacouto, *capitão* of Santa Cruz, was married to a Moroccan woman, for his brother-in-law was described as a "*mouro*."⁶⁶

When a Portuguese was captured and if his wife or the local *alfaqueque* could not raise the money to pay his ransom, she became one of the "*viúvas de vivos*" (widows of the living).⁶⁷ On 2 September 1522, the wives of Domingos Martins and Álvaro Vicente, soldiers who had been captured while fighting near Azamor, were paid the 2,800 *reis* that their husbands were owed for eight months service as cavalrymen.⁶⁸ The wife of João Dias was paid the 3,900 *reis* on 13 May 1523 that he had earned before being captured.⁶⁹ Others, like Beatriz da Fonseca of Azamor, whose husband, João Rodrigues, had been captured in 1531,

---

⁶³ *CSC*, 62-64.

⁶⁴ ANTT, CC I, 42, 57. For a general account of prostitution in Portugal during this period, see Maria Ângela V. da Rocha Beirante, "As mancebias nas cidades medievais portuguesas," in *A mulher na sociedade portuguesa: visão histórica e perspectivas actuais* (Coimbra: Coimbra Editora, 1985), 1:221-241.

⁶⁵ Rodrigues and Ferreira, "Mulheres portuguesas," 421 and Braga and Braga, *Ceuta Portuguesa*, 56. See the example of the Moroccan *mourisco* Henrique de Noronha discussed in chapter three.

⁶⁶ *CSC*, 50.

⁶⁷ Rodrigues and Ferreira, "Mulheres portuguesas," 420.

⁶⁸ ANTT, CC II, 103, 107 and CC II, 103, 108. The standard pay rate for a cavalryman in the first half of the sixteenth century was 350 *reis* per month.

⁶⁹ ANTT, CC II, 108, 8.

were provided with grain rations instead of money.[70] It is unclear how long these payments were made to these women. If, as was often the case, these men were not ransomed for years, then a one-time payment would provide only short-term financial relief, leaving the women in an untenable economic situation since they could not remarry.

True widows, especially those from the lower orders, often faced a dire future when their husbands died. Remarriage, return to Portugal, or assistance from family and friends were normally their only options. The kings of Portugal typically denied these women any financial assistance, though occasional *esmolas* (alms) were forthcoming. One such instance was in Safi in 1517, when it seemed that everyone in the fortress needed a helping hand: "The money that you [the king] sent to pay the living allowances and the salaries was another very great beneficence, like that which you did for the widows."[71]

Minor children whose fathers had died were considered "orphans" because it was extremely difficult for a non-elite single woman in Morocco to provide for her children. For instance, Simão Gonçalves da Costa, the *capitão* of Santa Cruz, wrote to the king explaining that he was providing, with funds from the royal treasury, for the maintenance of ten to twelve "orphans" and their mothers so that they would not "die of starvation." Gonçalves added that the king would "gain merit before God" for this kind act.[72] As true widows, however, these women were free to remarry and likely did so.

Widows of knights and government functionaries, on the other hand, were usually given pensions of some amount, though often, so they claimed, not enough to cover the expense of the lifestyle to which they had grown accustomed. Nuno Fernandes de Ataíde, in a letter to D. Manuel, described the battle death of Afonso Vaz and asked the king to provide for the dead man's wife and children.[73] While it is unclear in the letter, it seems likely that Vaz's family was living in Safi.

---

[70] ANTT, CC II, 170, 90 and Isabel M. R. Mendes Drumond Braga, *Entre a Cristandade e o Islão: cativos e renegados nas franjas de duas sociedades em confronto* (Ceuta: Instituto de Estudios Ceutíes, 1998), 70.

[71] "Letter from D. Nuno Mascarenhas to D. Manuel," Safi, 29 July 1517, *SIHMP*, 2:126.

[72] "Letter from Simão Gonçalves da Costa to D. João III," Santa Cruz, 15 September 1529, *SIHMP*, 2:485.

[73] "Letter from Nuno Fernandes de Ataíde to D. Manuel," Safi, 5 December 1510, *SIHMP*, 1:267.

In another example, D. Rodrigo de Castro asked that the king give a stipend to the infant son of Safi's *almocadém* (military scout or guide), João Lopes, who had recently been killed in battle. In effect, this was a stipend for the boy's mother as well.[74]

If payment for services was owed to a man who had been killed in battle, then his widow and any other heirs received that payment. Near the end of 1522, the widows of João Riscado and Pedro Gago, who were living in Azamor, received their husbands' salaries and their rations of wheat.[75] An elite status woman often recovered more than just back wages. For example, she might receive a one-time payment or "gift of alms" (*esmola*) in the event of her husband's death. The widow of João da Costa, the *adail* of Santa Cruz, received alms in the amount of 2,000 *reis* from D. Infante Cardeal Henrique in 1539.[76] Other widows of the elite, whose husbands had amassed large debts, might have them forgiven by royal order. For example on 13 August 1524, D. João III ordered the *feitor* of Safi not to hold the wife and heirs of D. Garcia de Eça responsible for the 12,740 *reis* that D. Garcia owed the royal treasury.[77] Inez de Aguiar, the widow of João Fernandes, a knight killed in 1532 while serving in Santa Cruz, was excused from paying a debt of 3,500 *reis* that he had incurred with the *feitoria*.[78] Debt-forgiveness likely precluded the additional receipt of alms from the king.

For some women, widowhood created an especially complex situation. Catarina Gonçalves was widowed when her husband, João Jorge, was killed near Azamor. João had previously been married and had one daughter, who lived in Portugal, by his first wife. Consequently, both Catarina and the daughter were his heirs. Catarina wanted to keep all 12,000 *reis* of his wealth in order to help her find a new husband in Azamor, but João's daughter also petitioned for the

---

[74] "Letter from D. Rodrigo de Castro to D. João III," Safi, 8 July 1541, *SIHMP*, 3:462.

[75] ANTT, CC II, 104, 45 and CC II, 105, 32.

[76] ANTT, CC I, 64, 64.

[77] ANTT, CC II, 118, 27.

[78] ANTT, CC I, 48, 74.

wealth. On 23 February 1540, the *capitão* of Azamor decided to split the baby, awarding 6,000 *reis* to each woman.[79]

These examples are not meant to demonstrate that Portuguese women in Moroccan fortresses were helpless and unable to control property and wealth. On the contrary, many women controlled sizeable amounts of wealth. Perhaps the most famous example is D. Beatriz, the wife of João Lopes de Sequeira, whose dowry funded the construction of the fortress at Santa Cruz. When the couple sold Santa Cruz to the king in 1513, D. Beatriz was acknowledged as an equal partner in the sale with her husband.[80] Other husbands shared control of their wealth with their wives. In June 1519, for example, one Luís Fernandes, a resident of Safi, gave his wife, Inês Gil, who remained in Portugal, the power of attorney over any goods he might accumulate while in Safi. Thus, in the event of his death, she would be able to dispose of their wealth as she saw fit.[81] Still other women are mentioned as sole owners of property. One Inês Amada owned several houses in Safi in 1541.[82] Furthermore, of the four wills extant that refer to residents in Morocco, two were written by women. Isabel Faiscas, who died in 1518, bequeathed 400 *reis* to Rodrigo Luís, 200 *reis* to the "wife of Francisco Álvarez," and 100 *reis* to Isabel Gonçalves. Brites Correia donated all of her goods to the Monastery of St. Catherine in Safi upon her death in 1519.[83]

Occupations of Women

The wives of *capitães*, known as *capitoas*, often had an important role in the politics of the fortresses. When their husbands were gone, typically in combat, they might exercise control of the city. In a unique and particularly notable case from northern Morocco, D. Maria de Eça governed Ceuta from January or February 1548 until August or

---

[79] ANTT, CC I, 67, 25. In Portugal, these decisions were normally made by the *juiz das justificações*, but in this case, the decision was made by the *capitão*.

[80] "Alvará of D. Manuel," Évora, 25 January 1513, *SIHMP*, 1:374-377.

[81] ANTT, CC II, 82, 76.

[82] "Letter from Inácio Nunes to Francisco de Lemos," Safi, 17 June 1541, *SIHMP*, 3:443.

[83] ANTT, CC II, 83, 57 and CC II, 75, 150. The other two wills are for Alonso de Subida (ANTT, CC I, 27, 52), and João Gonçalves (ANTT, CC II, 95, 136).

October 1549, while her husband, D. Afonso de Noronha, was in Portugal. By all accounts, she performed the office well.[84]

Although there is no evidence that D. Joana de Faria, the wife of Nuno Fernandes de Ataíde, ever administered the city of Safi in her husband's absence, she seems to have taken an active role in some of the treaty negotiations. Her motivation, however, may have been greed more than anything else, for she requested that the Awlad `Amran discani tribe include in their tribute three horses to be delivered to her personally.[85] *Capitoas* could also face the wrath of residents of the cities, such as that faced by the *capitão* of Safi, D. Rodrigo de Castro, and his wife who were accused of causing numerous problems because of their alleged vindictiveness.[86]

Elite women organized banquets and parties for the other members of the elite to celebrate religious holidays. They also commemorated great victories, important for their symbolic value to maintain Christian morality, to reenforce Portuguese solidarity, and to assert the legitimacy of elites as rulers. When men returned from a victorious battle, it was a joyous occasion. Along with the clerics, the women of all social levels marched outside the city gates to welcome the men and bring them wine, meat, and fruit.[87] Elite women marked their status in other ways. Most, if not all, of them had Portuguese maids, who served them as they would serve any ladies in Portugal. Furthermore, elite women typically acquired several female Moroccans slaves who became their servants. Some of these slaves subsequently converted to Christianity.[88]

---

[84] Paulo Drumond Braga, "D. Maria de Eça, capitoa de Ceuta nos meados do século XVI," in *O rosto feminino da expansão portuguesa* (Lisbon: Comissão para a Igualdade e para os Direitos das Mulheres, 1994), 433-437.

[85] "Letter from Nuno Fernandes de Ataíde to D. Manuel," 4 August 1515, *SIHMP*, 1:723; *SIHMP*, 1:340n1. For more on the Awlad `Amran discani, see chapter six.

[86] ANTT, CC I, 68, 79. It should be noted that these accusations were made in the autumn of 1540 in the midst of a great supply shortage that threatened many in Safi with starvation or bankruptcy. See note 117 above regarding the procession of naked children during this period.

[87] *CDM*, 3:199; Matthew T. Racine, "Service and Honor in Sixteenth-Century Portuguese North Africa: Yahya-u-Ta`fuft and Portuguese Noble Culture," *Sixteenth Century Journal* 32 (2001): 79; Rodrigues and Ferreira, "Mulheres portuguesas," 423, 425.

[88] Boxer, *Women*, 13 and Rodrigues and Ferreira, "Mulheres portuguesas," 423.

Evidence that women of the middle and lower classes performed any sort of professional activities, other than prostitution, on their own is scarce. Men even worked in the fields surrounding the cities because it was considered too dangerous for women to venture very far beyond fortress walls. Consequently, some tended gardens and grapes growing against the walls, but nothing more. One widow in the northern Moroccan fortress of Arzila, Isabel Marim, is mentioned as having supported herself and her children through her needlework.[89] Baking may have been a way for women to earn income. There is at least one reference to a female baker (*padreira*) in Mazagão in 1542.[90] Another common profession may have been that of vendor (*regateira*). In 1515, one Margarida Fernandes is described as a *regateira* in Azamor.[91] There is a reference to a woman in Ceuta who owned a lime oven (*forneira de cal*). Such property likely turned a handsome profit as walls and buildings were in constant need of repair, and lime was needed for mortar.[92]

Domestic chores, such as making bread, occupied most married women, though even this was not without danger. In Arzila, one woman, while going to fetch water with a black female slave, was attacked by Moroccan slaves attempting to escape.[93] It seems, in fact, that slaves performed many of the daily chores and household tasks. The abundance of captured Moroccans may have enabled even plebeian women to have a relatively leisurely existence, a common occurrence in colonial situations.

One could argue that except for the elite women, Portuguese women lived materially better lives in Morocco than they would have in Portugal and were provided an opportunity to rise in the social hierarchy that simply did not exist in Portugal.[94] Despite this, those

---

[89] *AA*, 1:298.

[90] "Letter from Luís de Loureiro to D. João III," Mazagão, 15 December 1542, *SIHMP*, 4:115.

[91] ANTT, CC II, 60, 77.

[92] "Order of D. Nuno Álvares Pereira," Ceuta, 1 May 1532, *SIHMP*, 2:576. It is unclear how this woman came to own a lime oven. One possibility is that her husband may have owned it and then she became the proprietress upon his death.

[93] *AA*, 1:246.

[94] Rodrigues and Ferreira, "Mulheres portuguesas," 422, 424.

women who did not have enough money to purchase slaves and who did not have a husband or family to provide for them often lived a difficult existence.

Medical Personnel

Physicians (*físicos*) and surgeons (*cirurgiões*), as well as the less-skilled barbers (*barbeiros*), were very important in cities where warfare was a semi-permanent state of affairs. Medical care, even of a level that we today would call primitive, could save the lives of soldiers wounded in battle. Barbers may have been in the Portuguese *feitoria* in Safi as early as 1495. In his letter of quittance, summarizing the accounts of the *feitoria* during his tenure, Lopo de Azevedo, *feitor* of Safi from 1 July 1495 until 15 February 1498, mentions having received one grindstone (*moo de barbeiro*) for sharpening razors and knives.[95] Of course, he could have sold this to a non-Portuguese, but the fact that only one came to the city makes this seem unlikely. In December 1507, when Safi had yet to be conquered, there was already a physician and a barber in the city.[96] The barber mentioned was named Samuel, a Jew, who had been in Safi since at least November 1507 and who earned 600 *reis* per month. He was still the city's barber as of August 1510.[97] By 1508, Safi had a surgeon, Mestre Marcos, a New Christian.[98]

In December 1513, only three months after the conquest of Azamor, D. João de Meneses, the *capitão do campo* of Azamor, complained that the city had neither a physician nor a surgeon and "men die for lack of them."[99] In 1520, *capitão* D. Álvaro de Noronha wrote to the king asking him to send a physician to Azamor because the city was in dire need of one.[100] Appeals to the king were necessary

---

[95] "Quittance of Lopo de Azevedo," Lisbon, 7 May 1499, *SIHMP*, 1:46.

[96] "Letter of Diogo de Azambuja to D. Manuel," Safi, 13 December 1507, *SIHMP*, 1:142-143.

[97] ANTT, CC II, 16, 117; CC III, 4, 31; Tavim, *Os judeus*, 388

[98] ANTT, CC II, 16, 65. New Christians were Jews who had converted, often forcibly, to Christianity. See chapter three for more information.

[99] "Letter from João de Meneses to D. Manuel," Azamor, 1-9 December 1513, *SIHMP*, 1:465.

[100] "Letter from D. Álvaro de Noronha to D. Manuel," Azamor, 18 April 1520, *SIHMP*, 2:274.

because it was the king's prerogative to appoint the physicians and surgeons.[101] Even when a physician was present in the fortress, his quality could be in question. Afonso Rodrigues, *feitor* of Santa Cruz, asked D. Manuel to send a replacement for the town's current physician who was "a New Christian who does not know anything."[102]

It was, in fact, typical that medical personnel in Portuguese North African fortresses were either Jews or New Christians, though, unlike the physician in Santa Cruz, most of them were skilled at their professions.[103] Rabbi Abraham Rute, the head rabbi (*rabi mor*) of Safi, was also a physician. As a reward for his services, both medical and political, D. Manuel confirmed on 7 April 1510 Rute's ownership of several houses, a small shop (*tenda*), and a market garden in Safi that had been granted to him earlier by Diogo de Azambuja.[104] From 1521 until at least 1528, when he was seventy-one years old, Mestre Rodrigo, a New Christian, served as the physician of Azamor. In this capacity he earned a stipend (*tença*) of 2,600 *reis* per year.[105] Nevertheless, not all doctors who served in Portuguese Morocco had a Jewish background. One of the doctors in Azamor in 1523 was João de Sá Carreira, a Portuguese Christian. In fact, he was once paid three *cruzados* (1,200 *reis*) for treating Sa`id Muhammad, an ambassador from Mawlay al-Naser, the Wattasid viceroy.[106]

---

[101] Francis A. Dutra, "The Practice of Medicine in Early Modern Portugal: The Role and Social Status of the *Físico-mor* and the *Surgião-mor*," in *Libraries, History, Diplomacy, and the Performing Arts. Essays in Honor of Carleton Sprague Smith*, ed., Israel J. Katz (Stuyvesant, NY: Pendragon Press, 1991), 135 and Lopes, *A expansão*, 44. For a brief discussion of the practice of medicine in Portugal during the sixteenth century, see Isabel M. R. Mendes Drumond Braga and João Carlos Oliveira, "A saúde," in *Portugal do Renascimento à crise dinástica*, ed. João José Alves Dias (Lisbon: Editorial Presença, 1998), 644-657.

[102] "Letter from Afonso Rodrigues to D. Manuel," Santa Cruz, 24 December 1513, *SIHMP*, 1:475.

[103] Tavim, *Os judeus*, 384-388.

[104] ANTT, *Livro das Ilhas*, f. 128, published in Tavim, *Os judeus*, 528.

[105] "Letter from Mestre Rodrigo to D. João III," Azamor, 15 November 1527, *SIHMP*, 2:418-424; "Letter from Mestre Rodrigo to D. João III," Azamor, 12 January 1528, *SIHMP*, 2:425-428.

[106] ANTT, CC II, 112, 7. In 1530, a New Christian physician, Mestre Francisco, traveled from Azamor to Tadla in order to treat the nephew of Al-`Attar, a Portuguese ally ("Letter from D. Pedro Mascarenhas to D. João III," Azamor, 9 June 1530, *SIHMP*, 2:527).

Another member of the healthcare profession who is rarely mentioned in correspondence but who appears on payment rolls is the apothecary or pharmacist (*boticário*). One pharmacist in Azamor earned 4,000 *reis* per year.[107] Pharmacists, and perhaps all medical professionals, were when necessary reimbursed by the royal treasury for their expenses, as was Mestre João who was paid 600 *reis* for the remedies (*mezinhas*) that he gave to some sick people in Azamor in 1524.[108]

In addition to the obvious need to treat common illnesses and soldiers wounded in combat, epidemics were also of concern for the Portuguese. At least two unspecified plagues broke out in Fez, one in 1519 and another in 1537. Portuguese leaders feared these might spread to the southern fortresses, though it does not appear they spread beyond Fez in those years.[109] Nevertheless, plagues did hit Portuguese cities. A plague hit Santa Cruz in 1528, but there are no further details about the incident.[110] There may have been some sort of epidemic in Safi in 1521, for Alonso de Subida described himself in his will as "sick from the sickness" (*enfermo da enfermidade*).[111]

Professionals, Artisans, and Merchants

Notaries public (*tabelião*, pl. *tabeliães*) were in every Moroccan fortress. They recorded contracts, judicial proceedings, and all legal transactions. D. Manuel appointed Artur Golayo as notary public of Azamor on 14 October 1513, about six weeks after the city was taken.[112] In Azamor in 1523, there was a notary for the courts (*tabelião*

---

[107] Fagundes, "Documentos," 110. ANTT, CC II, 60, 91.

[108] ANTT, CC II, 113, 112.

[109] "Letter from D. Nuno Mascarenhas to D. Manuel," Safi, 22 May 1519, *SIHMP*, 2:247 and "Letter from Estêvão Ribeiro de Almeida to D. João III," Azamor, 16 January 1537, *SIHMP*, 3:84.

[110] "Alvará of D. João III," Lisbon, 5 June 1529, *SIHMP*, 2:466.

[111] ANTT, CC I, 27, 52. While plague does not appear to have been a major problem in the southern fortresses, the northern ones were indeed affected. In 1521, Arzila suffered a plague that killed "*tanta gente.*" The origin of this plague allegedly was three infected Moroccans who had been captured during a raid and, despite being obviously sick, were brought into the city by greedy Portuguese who wanted to sell them for profit (*AJ*, 1:89).

[112] *CM*, 42, f. 129v.

do judicial) and a notary for the king (*tabelião por el rei*), both of whom worked together to record civil cases that touched on the king's treasury.[113] João Álvares, the notary for Santa Cruz, was paid 880 *reis* for an investigation that he conducted in 1531 of the books kept by the *feitor* of Santa Cruz, Vicêncio Ambrum.[114] Gonçalo Pires, royal notary in Safi in 1537, recorded the proclamation of peace between the Sharif and the *capitão* of Safi.[115] Notaries could hold their positions for many years. João Godinho was a judicial notary in Azamor from 1517 until at least 1523.[116]

Numerous artisans, especially those associated with construction and warfare, were present in Portuguese North Africa. Historian Maria Augusta Lima Cruz Fagundes lists the most common professions in Azamor based on sources from 1521-22 and 1537-38. In declining order, they are: carpenter, mason, cobbler, butcher, barber, blacksmith, market-gardener, merchant, persons who made mud walls, steward, tile maker, sawyer, goldsmith, locksmith, arms maker, rope maker, physician, pharmacist, and surgeon.[117] Unfortunately, such comprehensive sources for other southern Moroccan Portuguese cities do not seem to exist, so any direct comparisons are impossible. Perhaps similar ratios existed.

Sources rarely discuss these men who were so crucial to the success of the Portuguese enterprise in Morocco except when they are directly involved in politics, military preparations, or construction. For example, in 1514 João Gonçalves, a cobbler in Azamor, made four pairs of shoes, for which he was paid 400 *reis*, to be given as gifts to Muhammad al-Hintati, the so-called, "Lord of the Mountains" near Marrakech. These gifts were given during a process of peace

---

[113] ANTT, Gaveta XX, 5, 16, published in *GTT*, 10:421-424.

[114] ANTT, CC II, 169, 113, published in Tavim, *Os judeus*, 547. Although Ambrum was originally convicted of financial malfeasance in 1531 and sentenced to four years' exile in sub-Saharan Africa, he was eventually pardoned and reinstated as *feitor* and *almoxarife* of Santa Cruz in 1533 (see ANTT, CC I, 43, 42; *CJ, Perdões e legitimações*, 9, f. 219v; *CJ*, 19, 223-223v, published in Figanier, 324-325 and 333-335).

[115] *SIHMP*, 3:96-102.

[116] *CM*, 10, f. 119 and ANTT, Gaveta XX, 5, 16, published in *GTT*, 10:421-424.

[117] Fagundes, "Documentos," 110: *carpinteiro, pedreiro, sapateiro, carniceiro, barbeiro, ferreiro, hortelão, mercador, taipeiro, adegueiro, telheiro, serrador, ourives, serralheiro, armeiro, cordeiro, físico, boticário,* and *cirurgião*.

negotiations that eventually failed.[118] Lourenço Fernandes was employed at least twice, once in 1515 and again in 1517, as a painter to create military banners to be flown from Azamor's ramparts. In 1515, he was paid 3180 *reis* to paint 106 banners in anticipation of an assault by the Wattasid sultan. In 1517 he only needed to paint forty banners.[119] While in 1514 an unnamed artisan made five embroidered banners, at a cost of 160 *reis* each, to be displayed by Moroccan allies.[120]

Carpenters were also extremely important, both for construction and repairs, and their high pay scales reflected their skills and necessity. For instance, in 1521 João Gonçalves and João Lopes, carpenters in Azamor, were paid 360 *reis* to repair boat docks along the river. Later that year, João Lopes earned another 400 *reis* for repairing the ferry (*barca da passagem*). Afonso Lopes and his two assistants were paid 3240 *reis* for eighteen days of work to repair the gates of Azamor's keep and construct another gate.[121] Masons were also paid well. Jorge Dias was paid 600 *reis* for minor repair work on a doorway in the customs house of Azamor. Another mason in Azamor was paid 120 *reis* for making 60 stone balls for use as ammunition in bombards.[122] Gonçalo Carneiro, a blacksmith (*ferreiro*) earned 8,715 *reis* for making enough nails to build a new ferry for Azamor in 1524. Because Cristóvão Rodrigues earned 492 *reis* for making 112 nails, Carneiro appears to have made nearly 2,000 nails.[123] Bento Fernandes, a metalworker (*serralheiro*), earned 1,000 *reis* in 1521 for making 300 nails for the boat docks in Azamor. Another metalworker, António Dias, earned 848 *reis* in 1522 for making locks and hinges for some doors in Azamor's keep and 810 *reis* in 1524 for making a number of keys.[124]

---

[118] ANTT, CC II, 54, 107. A normal pair of shoes cost around 50 *reis* (ANTT, CC II, 55, 96).

[119] ANTT, CC I, 66, 28; CC II, 59, 42; *SIHMP*, 1:704n3.

[120] ANTT, CC II, 49, 162.

[121] ANTT, CC II, 94, 149; CC II, 98, 1; CC II, 98, 2. The ferry was likely used to cross the Umm al-Rabi` river to the north to engage in trade or raiding activity.

[122] ANTT, CC II, 96, 103 and CC II, 119, 110.

[123] ANTT, CC II, 113, 167 and CC II, 94, 137. See also ANTT, CC II, 98, 5; CC II, 98, 144; CC II, 97, 98.

[124] ANTT, CC II, 94, 172; CC II, 102, 31; CC II, 119, 99. See also, ANTT, CC II, 94, 111; CC II, 97, 130; CC II, 108, 23.

Meanwhile, in 1535 an unidentified blacksmith earned 260 *reis* for making 26 pairs of shackles used to restrain captives taken during raids.[125]

Merchants in the Portuguese cities ranged from the small storekeeper, market-gardener, baker, or tavern keeper to those involved with small- and large-scale trading, particularly agricultural goods and textiles. Merchants who lived within the Portuguese cities were mainly Portuguese, Jews, or other Europeans. What and how these merchants traded is discussed in chapter five. But merchants were not exclusively traders. Portuguese leadership in the cities often relied on merchants to assist in peace negotiations. Merchants were periodically required to provide lodging, food, and even gifts for Moroccan leaders or their diplomats. Although the sources for this are scarce, it seems that Jewish merchants were asked to do this much more often than their non-Jewish counterparts.[126] Merchants were also a source of loans for various purposes. For example, Diogo de Azambuja borrowed 12,000 *reis* from the Jewish merchant, Isaac Benzamiro, to meet unspecified expenses. Other merchants provided loans to help pay the ransom for certain Portuguese captives.[127]

Foreigners

As previously mentioned, foreigners, mainly German and French, were a large percentage of the artillerymen in Safi and provided a sizeable number of soldiers in Azamor. In 1526, the Italian, García "da Bologna," became the *mestre das obras* in Safi, replacing the Portuguese stonemason, Luís Dias.[128] Benito Maça, from Genoa, lived

---

[125] "Order of Payment from D. Garcia de Noronha," Safi, 2 January 1535, *SIHMP*, 3:16.

[126] For some examples of this, see ANTT, CC II, 48, 07, CC II, 108, 111; "Order of Payment from D. Álvaro de Abranches," Azamor, 3 July 1536, *SIHMP*, 3:41; "Order of Payment from António Leite," Azamor, 26 November 1537, *SIHMP*, 133-134;"Order of Payment from António Leite," Azamor, 20 December 1537, 3:135-136; "Order of Payment from António Leite," Azamor, 4 August 1539, 3:207-208; "Order of Payment from António Leite," Azamor, 12 November 1540, *SIHMP*, 3:277-278. The case of Ya`qub Daroque discussed in chapter eight.

[127] ANTT, CC II, 15, 108; CC I, 43, 99; "Letter from Sebastião Gonçalves to D. João III," Tarudante, 9 March 1543, *SIHMP*, 4:121-123. See chapter eight for one account of loans offered to free a captive.

[128] Vergilio Correia, *Lugares d'Além: Azemôr, Mazagão, Çafim* (Lisbon, 1923), 80-83 and *SIHMP*, 2:48n2. Although Correia states that García da Bologna replaced João Luís,

in Safi for a number of years until he became the *feitor* and *almoxarife* of Azamor, serving in that capacity from 1520 until 1524.[129]

It was, however, Castilians, normally as soldiers or merchants, who were the largest group of foreigners in the Portuguese fortresses. Many of them were a transient population, coming to Morocco as reinforcements during sieges or particularly worrisome moments when Portuguese leaders appealed for military assistance. For example, during the December 1510 siege of Safi, Diego Sanchez arrived from Andalusia with fifty-one crossbowmen, while Álvaro Fernandez arrived with 100 matchlockmen.[130]

It seems that the foreigners formed associations with each other, when possible. In the midst of a severe illness, Alonso de Subida composed his will while in the home of a fellow Castilian, Diego. João Gonçalves of Galícia named Diego Fernandez of Seville as the executor of his will.[131] This is not to say that extended relationships between Portuguese and foreigners were not possible. For example, D. Mécia, the daughter of D. Guterres de Monroi, the *capitão* of Santa Cruz, was married to Rodrigo de Carvajal, a Castilian.[132]

Other foreigners lived in Moroccan cities not under control of the Portuguese and this caused much anger on their part. Many foreign merchants, especially those from Castile and Genoa, lived in Tarkuku, twenty kolometers north of Santa Cruz, and were accused by the *feitor* of Santa Cruz of stealing business from the Portuguese as well as selling war materiel to Moroccan Muslims.[133]

Exiles and Fugitives

The mainland Portuguese judicial system provided a small but steady source of population for the North African fortresses. Both those who had been convicted and sentenced to exile (*degredados*) and

---

who had served as *mestre das obras* from 3 June 1513 until 13 November 1524. It seems, in fact, that João Luís was replaced by one Luís Dias.

[129] ANTT, Fragmentos, caixa 8, doc. 130, published in Tavim, *Os judeus*, 536 and Fagundes, "Documentos," table between pages 124 and 125.

[130] *CDM*, 3:55.

[131] ANTT, CC I, 27, 52 and CC II, 95, 136.

[132] *CSC*, 100.

[133] *HP*, 3:455. See chapter five for more details.

those who were fugitives from justice seeking asylum (*homiziados*) often found their way to Morocco. Criminal exile was a common technique used by European countries into the nineteenth century to force criminals to reside in locations that could not always attract sufficient voluntary immigrants. Although it was not until the late sixteenth century that King D. Sebastião had issued a decree detailing the system of transportation for exiles to colonies, criminals were exiled to Portugal's overseas possessions already in the first half of the fifteenth century. In fact, according to laws collected in the *Ordenações Manuelinas*, any male serving a sentence of exile within Portugal would have his sentence reduced by half if he agreed to serve in a North African fortress. Furthermore, a decree of 1519 ordered judges to no longer sentence exiles to a specific place, but rather to somewhere on the other side of the Straits of Gibraltar, i.e., to North Africa. The lack of specificity allowed exiles to be sent to whichever city most urgently needed the manpower.[134]

Fugitives who fled to Morocco in order to gain immunity from prosecution were following a precedent established in the medieval period and based upon Roman and Visigothic law. At the beginning of the 1300s, the Portuguese Crown established a system of asylum cities (*coutos*) in order to relocate populations to frontier and border regions that remained lightly populated. Towns and cities deemed in most need of extra population were designated as places of asylum for all criminals except for those guilty of counterfeiting or treason or, if female, adultery. One location where the use of *homiziados* was especially effective was in the Algarve, in southern Portugal, along the border with Castile.[135] Not surprisingly, with Morocco in need of Portuguese colonists, fugitives were permitted asylum there.

The exiles and fugitives made up a small but noticeable portion of the population of Portuguese fortresses. For example, in Arzila in

---

[134] Coates, xv-xvii, 29-41, 59. *Ordenações Manuelinas*, 5 vols. (Lisbon: Calouste Gulbenkian Foundation, 1984), 5, t. 107, 4, also cited in Coates, 55. The decree of 1519 is published in José Anastásio de Figueiredo, *Synopsis chronologica de subsidios ainda os mais raros para a historia e estudo critico da legislação portuguesa* (Lisbon: Academia Real das Sciencias, 1740), 1:234 and cited by Coates, 59.

[135] Coates, 50; Luís Miguel Duarte, "Garcia de Melo em Castro Marim (A actuação de um alcaide-mor no início do século XVI)," in *Actas da III jornadas de história medieval do Algarve e Andaluzia* (Loulé: Câmara Municipal de Loulé, 1989), 218-219; Joaquim Veríssimo Serrão, *História de Portugal* (Lisbon: Editorial Verbo, 1980), 2:250-252.

1498, of the 414 men who received a salary nineteen, or 4.5 percent, were exiles.[136] Once in the overseas colonies, exiles were not to be treated harshly; it was permitted neither to detain them nor to beat them, simply because of their status as exiled criminals. In 1534, D. João III issued a decree that specifically forbid beating exiles and ordered that they should be treated in the same manner as everyone else.[137]

Exiles could be sent to North Africa for a variety of crimes, with the duration of their exile dependent on the type of crime committed. For example, opening letters written by nobles, maintaining a private prison, participating in brawls, witchcraft, and even manslaughter would earn sentences of exile lasting from one to five years. Adulterous men could earn seven years, the length of the term for gambling was imposed at royal discretion, while the knowing use of counterfeit money was punishable by perpetual exile.[138] In 1487, Duarte Fernandes, who patrolled the streets of Setúbal at night in order to prevent crime, was charged with using his position to commit numerous sexual crimes against women and even committing incest. He was able to avoid prison, or more likely execution, by agreeing to be exiled to Tangiers for four years.[139] In this example, the punishment of exile was a better alternative to the standard judicial punishment.

Exiles were not necessarily from the lower levels of society. In fact, the punishment of exile was theoretically restricted to the nobility, while the non-noble would be forced to provide manpower for the royal galleys, though in practice, people from all levels of Portuguese society were exiled.[140] Nuno Fernandes de Ataíde's nephew, Álvaro

---

[136] Braga, "A expansão," 304.

[137] Coates, 35.

[138] Braga, "A expansão," 302-303 and Braga and Braga, *Ceuta Portuguesa*, 62-64. For more information see Maria Ângela Beirante, "Ceuta nas ordenações Afonsinas," 87-100 and Paulo Drumond Braga, "Transferências de degredos: de e para Ceuta (Portugal, meados do século XV)," 145-153, both in *Ceuta Hispano-Portuguesa* ed. Alberto Baeza Herrazti (Ceuta: Instituto de Estudios Ceutíes, 1993); Humberto Baquero Moreno, "Elementos para o estudo dos coutos de homiziados instituídos pela coroa," in *Os municípios portugueses nos séculos XIII a XVI. Estudos de História* (Lisbon, 1986), 93-138; Coates, 24-25.

[139] Beirante, "As Mancebias," 1:223.

[140] Coates, 11-12, 23.

Mendes Cerveira had served in Tangiers and Arzila for seven years before coming to Safi. After his first two years in Safi, he was made a *degredado*, perhaps due to an infraction committed in the past, in Safi, or in Portugal during a trip there. Cerveira's crime must have been severe, since his exile was permanent. Ataide, however, describing his cousin as a "valiant man," asked the king to remove Cerveira's *degredado* status after two years, a request made both because Cerveira had served the king well in battle and because his status as an exile had impoverished him.[141] Indeed, requesting pardons as the result of noteworthy service to the crown was not uncommon throughout the Portuguese Empire, providing an incentive for disgraced people to perform well in exile.[142]

According to the payroll of soldiers in Safi in 1511, there were eight fugitives and thirty exiles, out of a total of 524 soldiers on the payroll, or about seven percent of the total. (This ratio is similar to that given earlier for Arzila, especially if one considers that non-soldiers are not included in the Safi numbers.) Unfortunately, the reasons for their flight or exile are not given. There is, however, additional information for two of the exiles, Pero Bras and João Fernandes, whose trades are listed as cobbler and blacksmith, respectively.[143] It seems likely that they would have practiced these trades in Safi, especially to supplement their meager *degredado* income of 85 *reis* per month. Although some of these people might be undesirables, some of them at least arrived with useful skills.[144]

Officials in the fortresses were not routinely given information about exiles' sentences. Legally, exiles were required to inform officials of the terms of their sentences, but João Rodrigues, *porteiro dos contos* of Safi, said many did not do so. Consequently, some were able to earn salaries when their crimes prohibited it. For instance, exiles were forbidden to work in the government bureaucracy.[145] Rodrigues gives

---

[141] ANTT, Gaveta XX, 2, 61, published in *GTT*, 10:305.

[142] Coates, 104.

[143] ANTT, NA 597, f. 67-77. See f. 72v for "pero bras çapateiro" and f. 73v for "joão fernandes ferreiro."

[144] See also, ANTT, CC II, 108, 108. In 1586, a visitor to Ceuta recommended that exiles should be encouraged to learn artisanal skills because they seemed to be extremely reluctant to serve in any military capacity and were therefore useless (Braga and Braga, *Ceuta Portuguesa*, 64).

[145] Coates, 35.

the example of a Castilian, Afonso Barracho, who lived and worked in Safi for four years despite having been sentenced to exile outside of Portugal and all its dominions for life. It was, in fact, common practice that foreigners not be sent overseas, but rather simply banished from Portugal.[146] Although this example shows that criminal acts by *degredados* were at times a problem, it also shows that the colonial bureaucracies had a difficult time keeping track of all the exiles. Consequently, those among them who were skilled and willing could effectively remove their exile status if they could relocate.

Conclusion

The Portuguese and European population within the Portuguese-controlled Moroccan cites was like that of any urbanized area of Portugal in the early sixteenth century, with three notable exceptions. First, the percentage of men employed by the military was much higher. Such a high rate of militarization was consistent with the danger and instability inherent in the contested space of a frontier setting. Second, exiles and fugitives were present in greater percentages than in any Portuguese cities except perhaps those near the border with Castile which had served as the main outlet for these people before the Portuguese push across the Mediterranean and around the globe. Exiles and fugitives, especially the men, provided an inexpensive way to fill out fortress garrisons. Third, the percentage of women and children in the overseas fortresses was smaller. Moreover, women and children normally faced a precarious existence without a man to provide for them. The reduced presence of women and children in the population as well as the instability that often affected them reflects a typical frontier situation.

---

[146] ANTT, CdGA, 334 and Coates, 23.

Table 2.1: Total Population of Portuguese in Southern Moroccan Fortresses[147]

YEAR	AZAMOR	MAZAGÃO	SAFI	SANTA CRUZ
1507			50	
1513	3,000			
1521	599			
1522	621			
1530	618			
1536		c. 200		
1537-38	448 (?)			
1540			c. 4-5,000[148]	
1541	2,600	> 2,000		1,400
1542		c. 1,200		

---

[147] Sources for Table 2.1: Durval R. Pires de Lima, *História da Dominação Portuguêsa em Çafim (1506-1542)* (Lisbon: 1930), 26; Fagundes, "Documentos," 113; "Letter from D. Pedro Mascarenhas to D. João III," Azamor, 9 June 1530, *SIHMP*, 2:528-529; "Letter from Manuel de Sande to D. João III," Mazagão, 21 September 1536, *SIHMP*, 3:64; "Letter from D. Rodrigo de Castro to D. João III," Safi, 13 September 1540, *SIHMP*, 3:263; "Letter from D. João III to the Count of Castanheira," Almeirim, 23 February 1541, *SIHMP*, 3:309; "Letter from Luís de Loureiro to D. João III," Mazagão, 15 December 1542, *SIHMP*, 4:114-115; ANTT, CC I, 70, 66.

[148] Based on numbers in other cities, this seems high. Nevertheless, the words of D. Rodrigo de Castro, the *capitão* of Safi in 1540, described the population as "*quatro ou cinco mil almas*" (3:263).

Table 2.2: Payroll for Soldiers in Southern Moroccan Fortresses[149]

YEAR	LOCATION	DURATION	AMOUNT (*REIS*)	APPOX. ANNUAL COST (*REIS*)
1511	Safi	3 months	490,455	1,961,820
1517-18	Safi	18 months	1,068,298	712,199
1522	Azamor	6 months	761,533	1,523,066

Average payroll per year in all fortresses: 1,399,066 *reis*.

---

[149] Sources for Table 2.2: ANTT, NA 597, 128; ANTT, CC I, 23, 99; Fagundes, "Documentos," 156-157.

Table 2.3: Monthly salaries for soldiers (Salary given in *reis*)[150]

POSITION	AZAMOR	MAZAGÃO	SAFI	SANTA CRUZ
Cavalry	350	350	350	350
page on horseback	195		185	
page without horse			135	
Lancers	137.5	350[151]		183
Escutas[152]	555			
Atalaias			577	
crossbowman, mounted	500		300 or 500[153]	
crossbowman			300 or 750	175
matchlockmen			400, 500, 900, or 1000	183 or 500
artilleryman	1000		1000	
Patrão de fusta[154]	1000			
ajudantes de fusta[155]	600			

---

[150] Sources for Table 2.3: ANTT, NA 597; Fagundes, "Documentos," 111; "Letter from Luís Sacoto to D. João III," Santa Cruz, 14 March 1527, *SIHMP*, 2:396-397.

[151] Luís Sacoto, the *contador* of Santa Cruz, claimed that this was the pay rate for lancers in Mazagão. I have not been able to confirm this with any other source (*SIHMP*, 2:397).

[152] These men were typically sent on reconnaissance missions shortly before the Portuguese raided into a certain location.

[153] For this and other positions with varied pay rates, I have been unable to determine the rationale behind the differences in pay. Perhaps it related to one's experience or one's connections.

[154] Captain of a boat similar to a galley but smaller (Coates, 47).

[155] Assistants to *fusta* captain.

Position	Azamor	Mazagão	Safi	Santa Cruz
homens do batel da barra[156]	500			
Trumpeters			780	
exiles[157]	85		85	

---

[156] Men who sailed in small boats to alert ships as to the location of the sand bar near Azamor in the Umm al-Rabi` River.

[157] This only applied to exiles serving as soldiers. Compare to Coates, 36.

Table 2.4: Annual Stipends (*Tenças*) Paid in Safi in 1511 (in *reis*)[158]

NAME	POSITION	AMOUNT
Lopo Barriga	*adail*	3,600
Yahya-u-Ta`fuft	*alcaide dos mouros*	16,000 (paid as 50 ounces of silver)[159]
Nuno Gato	*alfaqueque*	2,000
Diogo Lopes	*almocadém*	4,000
Felipe [last name illegible]	*apontador*	2,000
Ruy Fernandes	*armario*	4,000
Nuno Fernandes de Ataíde	*capitão*	114,000
Frei Diogo Lopes	*clerigo d'capelão d'alcaçava*	8,000
Nuno Gato	*contador*	12,000
Bras de Pina	*escrivão dos contos*	3,000
Pero Annes	*ferrador*	2,000
Moses Dardeiro	*lingua*	6,400[160]
Isaac Benzamiro	no title	6,000
Ameto (a Jew)	no title	5,000
João Rodrigues	*porteiro dos contos*	2,000
Rabbi Abraham Rute	*rabbi mor dos judeus*	12,000
Gaspar de Villa Lobos	*vigário da capelão da casa*	12,000

---

[158] Sources for Table 2.4: ANTT, NA 597, f. 120-124 and *SIHMP*, 1:599n2.

[159] In 1516, when Yahya returned to Safi after his semi-exile in Portugal, his yearly stipend was raised to 300 ounces, or 96,000 *reis* per year.

[160] Dardeiro had held this position since 1509 and maintained it until his murder in December 1512. See ANTT, CC II, 19, 13 and CC II, 21, 6; these documents are also cited in Tavim, *Os judeus*, 376n900 and 901.

Chapter Three: Non-Christians and New Christians in Portuguese Cities in Southern Morocco

AS FRONTIER outposts, the Portuguese-controlled cities served both as the spearheads for the Portuguese military's thrust into Morocco and as centers of trade. Because these cities were the most populous urban areas in the Moroccan frontier zone, they attracted representatives of all peoples and religions that existed in sixteenth-century Morocco. That is, these cities demonstrated the cultural interaction and porosity common in all frontier environments. One of the most startling features of the Portuguese presence in Morocco was the large numbers of non-Christians who lived in or near Portuguese-controlled cities. It is startling because the Portuguese had expelled all non-Christians who refused to convert to Christianity from Portugal in 1497, and scarcely one decade later, they were compelled to develop working relationships with some of these same groups in order to ensure the success of their program of expansion in Morocco.

Non-Christians outnumbered Christians in North Africa by a sizeable margin. Even within the general confines of Safi and Azamor, Muslims were the overwhelming majority. Previous Portuguese experiences administering minority Jewish and Islamic populations within their borders provided them with a blueprint for administering these groups in Morocco. Muslims and Jews were given a measure of autonomy to decide legal issues among themselves by their own laws and customs and under the leadership of a member of their own religious community. The only religious restriction placed on members of either faith was a prohibition of proselytizing Christians.

Urban residential geography for the three religious groups in Portuguese-controlled cities was quite simple. The Portuguese and other Christians lived in the most highly fortified portion of the city, the area in and around the keep (*torre de menagem*). The keep housed government and financial offices and served as a refuge for the

Christian population in the event of an attack on the city. The Jewish communities were able to secure housing either inside this central area or just outside it. Their neighborhood was known to the Portuguese as the *judiaria*. The Muslim population lived either in the older, less fortified portion of the city, or just outside the city walls, moving inside or fleeing to the countryside in the event of an attack.

In addition to Jews and Muslims, there existed liminal religious actors: New Christians and *mouriscos*. New Christians were Jews who had converted to Christianity, while *mouriscos* were Christians who had once been Muslims. Many of these converts had been forcibly converted in Portugal in 1497. Some of the *mouriscos*, however, were Moroccan Muslims who had, for varying reasons, chosen to become Christians.

This chapter does not pretend to exhaust all possible information about the Jews, New Christians, Muslims, and *mouriscos* who lived in Portuguese-controlled cities in southern Morocco. Rather, the goal here is to give a brief overview of the types of people and interactions that took place between the various groups. Other chapters in this book contain more detailed accounts of specific interactions that will expand upon the basic principles discussed here.

Jews

Although there had been a population of Jews in Morocco for many centuries, the Jews with whom the Portuguese dealt and to whom they gave important positions within their cities were almost exclusively Jews who had, until the late fifteenth century, lived in either Spain or Portugal. These Iberian (or Sephardic) Jews lived separately from the native Moroccan Jews, retaining their own customs and, because many could speak Arabic in addition to Portuguese or Spanish, assumed positions as power brokers inside Portuguese fortresses.[1]

Such high status was possible because Jews in Portuguese North Africa were treated much better than they had been in Portugal, at least in the latter part of the fifteenth century. The Jewish communities in the Portuguese fortresses were given great privileges because they were of use in diplomatic, supply, and commercial

---

[1] José Alberto Rodrigues da Silva Tavim, *Os judeus na expansão portuguesa em Marrocos durante o século XVI: origens e actividades duma comunidade* (Braga: Edições APPACDM Distrital de Braga, 1997), 198-199.

activities. Their linguistic and cross-cultural skills made them integral as interpreters, diplomats, and *alfaqueques* (ransom negotiators). Their commercial ties made them essential to the flow of food and goods from the Moroccan hinterland to the coastal cities.[2]

Both Safi and Azamor had sizeable Jewish communities, numbering in the hundreds of families, before the Portuguese conquered the cities. The size of these communities swelled in 1492, as expelled Spanish Jews sought refuge, and again in 1497, as their Portuguese brethren followed suit.[3] In fact, evidence indicates that Portuguese Jews were especially attracted to Safi and formed an important part of the Jewish community in the city after 1497. There was another surge in the Jewish population during the first half of the sixteenth century as Portuguese New Christians were forced to leave Portugal because of their religious irregularities. Once they arrived in North Africa, they often reverted openly to Judaism.[4]

Unfortunately, due to the lack of surviving historical sources, exact population figures will likely never be known. Nevertheless, rudimentary estimates can be made for Safi and Azamor. During the siege of 1510, Safi's Jews were charged with defending one section (*estancia*) of the city walls. As there were fourteen *estancias* divided among 900 fighting men, this gives a loose estimate of about sixty-four men per *estancia*. The *capitão* of Safi, in fact, describes the number of Jewish soldiers as "a lot." Assuming at least half of these men had wives and children, there may have been anywhere from 160 to 300 Jews in the city.[5] In Azamor, there were approximately 100 Jewish men who were listed as part of the city's garrison in 1517. Using the same calculation as in the case of Safi, the Jewish population was probably

---

[2] Tavim, *Os judeus*, 204. For more on their roles as merchants, see chapter five. *Alfaqueques* are discussed in detail in chapter eight.

[3] Tavim, *Os judeus*, 195-196.

[4] Tavim, *Os judeus*, 198.

[5] "Letter from Nuno Gato to D. Manuel," Safi, 3 January 1511, *SIHMP*, 1:271-280 and "Letter from Nuno Fernandes de Ataíde to D. Manuel," Safi, 4 January 1511, *SIHMP*, 1:285-286, 288. Jerónimo Mendonça, in his *Jornada de África* (Lisbon, 1607), suggested that approximately 200 Jewish men sailed from Azamor to Safi to participate in the siege defense (f. 90). No contemporary documentation supports this claim (Tavim, *Os judeus*, 394).

somewhere between 250 and 400 people.[6] If these numbers are correct, and if we exclude Muslims in the population figures for those residing within the city walls, Jews may have comprised between ten and twenty percent of the population of Azamor and Safi.[7]

Santa Cruz and Mazagão had much smaller Jewish communities, as neither city existed prior to the arrival of the Portuguese and therefore neither city contained an indigenous Jewish community. By the 1530s, there was a small, but flourishing Jewish community, with its own rabbi, living in Santa Cruz.[8] Mazagão was home to a contingent of Jews before 1541, though it may only have been a handful, for the population of the entire fortress was quite small. For example, in 1536, the *capitão* of Mazagão, Manuel de Sande, said that there were no more than 120 men in the entire fortress, including "boys, elderly men, clerics, and Jews."[9]

The Jews in Portuguese fortresses were governed by the *rabi mor* (head rabbi), a position replicated from the former *judiarias* in Portugal. He had jurisdiction over all civil and criminal cases between Jews, whom he was to judge based on Mosaic law, with the only appeal for any who felt aggrieved being to the *capitão* of the city or the king of Portugal himself. Jews who were sentenced to prison were to be kept in a separate jail located in the Jewish quarter of the city.[10] It is unclear if the Jews were locked into the *judiaria* at night as they had been in Portugal, and there are no references to gates or curfews in any documents. The importance of the Jews to the success of the Portuguese may have prevented such regulations from being implemented and may have prevented any overzealous anti-Semites from attacking the Jews in their homes. Unlike the history of the Jews in Portugal, there is no evidence that Jews in Portuguese-controlled

---

[6] "Letter from Simão Correia to D. Manuel," Azamor, 20 May 1517, *SIHMP*, 2:86

[7] This is a much greater percentage than the one and one-half to six percent of the population that Jews comprised in urban areas of Portugal before their expulsion. A. H. de Oliveira Marques, *Portugal na crise dos séculos XIV e XV* (Lisbon: Editorial Presença, 1987), 38-9

[8] Tavim, *Os judeus*, 193-194.

[9] "Letter from Manuel de Sande to D. João III," Mazagão, 21 September 1536, *SIHMP*, 3:64 and Tavim, *Os judeus*, 247.

[10] "Carta de mercê e confirmação do ofício de rabi-mor dos judeus de Safim a Rabi Abraão," ANTT, Livro da Ilhas, fols. 128-129, published in Tavim, *Os judeus*, 528-529.

Morocco were ever singled out for attack based solely on their religion.[11] The need for accommodation of difference along the frontier can be seen clearly in the Portuguese-Jewish relations.

While the Portuguese kings considered it very important to keep as many Jews as possible in their Moroccan cities, four families received a majority of important offices. In fact, we know very little about any other Jews specifically. These families were the Rute, Benzamiro, and Levi of Safi and the Adibe of Azamor. Abraham Rute was appointed the *rabi mor* of Safi in 1510, and both Rute and Isaac Benzamiro were given the right to enter Portugal, a privilege that assisted them greatly with their commercial endeavors.[12] Abraham Benzamiro, Isaac's brother, served as the official interpreter of Mazagão from October 1527 and then as *rabi mor* of Safi from 1537 until his death in 1540.[13] The Benzamiro were a powerful commercial family with contacts in all Portuguese-controlled Moroccan cities, Muslim-controlled Morocco, and even Lisbon (see chapter five).

Meyer Levi, a textile merchant who had valuable contracts with the Portuguese, was killed by Sa`adid forces in the 1520s as he attempted to warn Santa Cruz of an impending attack. Levi's brother was captured by the Sa`adids and later became a trusted advisor to the Sa`adid leader, Muhammad al-Sheikh. Meyer Levi's son, Yusef, served as the official interpreter and Arabic scribe in Safi from an unknown date until the evacuation of the city in 1541.[14]

The Adibe family dominated the political and religious power among the Jews of Azamor, maintaining a virtual monopoly on the office of *rabi mor* throughout the Portuguese dominion.[15] This office provided access to other avenues of power. For instance, José Adibe

---

[11] Joaquim Veríssimo Serrão, *História de Portugal* (Lisbon: Verbo, 1978), 2:256-263; Oliveira Marques, *Portugal na crise*, 398; Maria Filomena Lopes de Barros, *A comuna muçulmana de Lisboa (Séculos XIV e XV)* (Lisbon: Hugin, 1998), 14.

[12] Tavim, *Os judeus*, 203, 204, 211, 320 and ANTT, *Livro das Ilhas*, f. 128-129, published in Tavim, *Os judeus*, 528-529.

[13] *SIHMP*, 2:352n1; Tavim, *Os judeus*, 474-475.

[14] "Letter from Heitor Gonçalves to D. Manuel," Safi, 18 June 1512, *SIHMP*, 1:333; "Letter from Meyer Levi to D. Manuel," Safi, 14 November 1514, *SIHMP*, 1:653-654; "Letter from D. Henrique de Noronha to D. João III," Safi, 4 June 1541, *SIHMP*, 3:418-422.

[15] Tavim, *Os judeus*, 214-218.

was named *rabi mor* on 23 June 1514 and the next day named *corretor* (broker) of the *feitoria*. In September of that year, his son, Yahya, was named the official interpreter (*lingua*) of Azamor, earning an annual stipend of 4,000 *reis*. Yahya received the post of *rabi mor* upon the death of his father in March 1522. Following Yahya's death in October 1534, the office was passed on to his younger brother, Ya`qūb, who retained the post until Azamor was abandoned in 1541.[16]

While certain families won the greatest privileges, the Jewish communities in general were treated well by royal proclamations. In 1509, D. Manuel promised the Jews of Safi that they would never be compelled to become Christians or expelled from the city against their will without a minimum of two years' notice, at which time they could remove all their belongings with them. This agreement ensured the Jews that they would not suffer the dislocations that they had in Iberia in the 1490s.[17] Three years later, D. Manuel promised Safi's Jews more freedom of movement, giving them the right to leave the city with all their goods and their families whenever they wished. The king hoped that by giving them such freedom he could attract Jews to Safi who would then pay taxes and engage in commerce from their new headquarters.[18]

Meanwhile in Azamor after June 1514, Jews were required to pay only an annual tribute of 320 *reis* per household and were exempted from paying the ten percent duty on merchandise entering or leaving the city by land, though they were still required to pay this for goods entering or leaving by sea.[19] In 1516, there were negotiations regarding the location of the *judiaria* in Azamor. Yahya Adibe, who negotiated with the *capitão*, Simão Correia, was given three streets near the central

---

[16] Tavim, *Os judeus*, 239, 487. Jews were also important servants to the Sa`adid Sharifs. In particular, the Cabeça family, originally from Spain, served the Sharif from the 1530s until at least 1557. Abraham Cabeça, in fact, served as a confidential advisor (*privado*) to Sharif Muhammad al-Sheikh. See Diego de Torres, *Relación del origen y suceso de los xarifes y del estado de los reinos de Marruecos, Fez, y Tarudante*, ed. and intro. Mercedes García-Arenal (Madrid: Siglo Veintiuno de España, 1980), 150, 183, 199 and Julio Caro Baroja, *Los judios en la España moderna y contemporanea* (Madrid: Ediciones Arion, 1961), 1:214.

[17] "Letter Patent of D. Manuel," Évora, 4 May 1509, *SIHMP*, 1:174-176 and Tavim, *Os judeus*, 201.

[18] Tavim, *Os judeus*, 211-212. See "Letter of privilege for the Jews that live in the city of Safi," Lisbon, 20 April 1512, Tavim, *Os judeus*, 532-533.

[19] Tavim, *Os judeus*, 239.

keep. This location was important to the Jews, whose homes could be defended by Portuguese artillery in the event of an attack, while the keep provided a safe refuge in the event of a breach of the city walls. Moreover, it was near the commercial center: the *feitoria*. The king approved the results of the negotiation and even requested that the *judiaria* be built inside the fortress, moving outside the fortress only should the space not be large enough. It appears that, other than his Portuguese subjects, D. Manuel felt that the Jews were the most valuable group to protect in each fortress.[20]

Most Jews, once settled in a Portuguese city, remained there, and the Portuguese looked after them. In 1541, when the Portuguese were abandoning their fortresses in Dukkala, they evacuated all the Jews from the area to the Portuguese cities of Mazagão or Tangiers and Arzila in northern Morocco.[21] Nevertheless, not all Jews were happy with their circumstances under the Portuguese. At least thirty Jewish families moved from the city of Safi in 1518; their reasons are unclear, and the sources do not reveal their destination.[22]

In addition to their involvement in regional commerce (see chapter five), Jews were permitted to own property within Portuguese fortresses. While many of these properties were purchased, others were granted to prominent Jews in return for their service to Portugal. For example, Diogo de Azambuja, in his capacity as *capitão* of Safi, granted Rabbi Abraham Rute "some houses," a shop, and a market garden in 1508. This grant was confirmed and approved by the king in April 1510.[23] Jewish property owners were cause for concern in Azamor during the 1520s. Mestre Rodrigo, the New Christian physician of Azamor, reported that Jewish landlords had been charging increasingly exorbitant rents during the years 1524 to 1527, a period when Azamor experienced an economic slow down. In specific, he

---

[20] Tavim, *Os Judeus*, 240-241 and "Letter from Simão Correia to D. Manuel," Azamor, 3 October 1516, *SIHMP*, 2:40.

[21] "Letter from D. João III to António Leite and D. Manuel Mascarenhas," Lisbon, April 1541, *SIHMP*, 3:352-355; "Letter from D. João III to D. Fernando de Noronha," Lisbon, 2 September 1541, *SIHMP*, 3:516-517; Tavim, *Os judeus*, 475.

[22] "Letter from D. Nuno Mascarenhas to D. Manuel," Safi, early 1519, *SIHMP*, 2:224.

[23] See ANTT, *Livro das Ilhas*, f. 128, published in Tavim, *Os judeus*, 528.

said that one member of the Benzamiro family had been raising rents every six months.[24]

Jews, serving as interpreters, negotiators, and couriers, were of central importance for the execution of Portuguese political and expansionist policies. Persons able to function effectively in all the cultures in a frontier zone are among the most valuable in that zone. Moses Dardeiro, for example, served as the head interpreter in Safi from 1509 until his murder in December 1512.[25] Rabbi Abraham Rute and the Benzamiros were active in negotiating treaties and captive releases. Yahya Adibe traveled from Azamor to Lisbon in 1514 and was given gifts of clothing and symbols of power to deliver to Moroccan Muslim allies of the Portuguese.[26]

Serving the Portuguese was not without risk. In May 1541, after the conquest of Santa Cruz, a Jew named Bregis delivered a letter from the king of Portugal to Mawlay Idris, the father-in-law of Sharif Ahmed al-A`raj, who administered the territory near Marrakech. The letter apparently claimed that some of the local Arab tribes were going to side with the Portuguese and the Wattasid sultan against the Sharif who was increasing his hold on the Dukkala region. In what seems to have been an object lesson to anyone who would dare ally with the king of Portugal, Idris killed the messenger. Bregis's body was then taken to the Sharif, who was in Marrakech. The Sharif ordered that the body be cut into pieces.[27]

Portuguese leaders often requisitioned food and goods from Jewish merchants to assist in their negotiations with Moroccan Muslim leaders and their representatives. The merchants were always

---

[24] "Letter from Mestre Rodrigo to D. João III," Azamor, 15 November 1527, *SIHMP*, 2:420-421.

[25] Tavim, *Os judeus*, 376-378; ANTT, CC II, 19, 13. For more on this murder, see chapter four and Matthew T. Racine, "Service and Honor in Sixteenth-Century Portuguese North Africa: Yahya-u-Ta`fuft and Portuguese Noble Culture," *Sixteenth Century Journal* 32 (2001): 77-78.

[26] ANTT, CC I, 16, 12; "Alvará of D. Manuel," Lisbon, 28 August 1514, *SIHMP*, 1:609-610 and 609n1. For more on Jews as diplomats, see chapter six and Tavim, *Os judeus*, 397-427.

[27] "Letter from Inácio Nunes Gato to D. João III," Safi, 30 May 1541, *SIHMP*, 3:408-409; "Letter from Vicente Rodrigues Evangelho to D. João III," Azamor, 10 April 1530, *SIHMP*, 2:512; Baroja, *Los judios*, 1:214. Death for acting as a courier was an extraordinary event. Usually, such danger was minimal, see "Letter from Bastião Vargas to D. João III," Azamor, 6 March 1538, *SIHMP*, 3:137.

reimbursed. Records indicated that these requisitions occurred in Azamor, Safi, and Santa Cruz, throughout the entire period of Portuguese occupation. Of the fifty-five requests located, forty-eight of them were made in Azamor and of those forty-eight, twenty-nine were made to Ya`qūb Daroque. Daroque's name does not appear in records until 1536, indicating that he may have arrived in Azamor only in that year, though he was obviously a powerful merchant with the ability to secure large amounts of grain. The size of these food requisitions varied from the small (less than 100 *reis* worth) to the massive (over 25,000 *reis*), though 1-2,000 *reis* was most typical. Of these fifty-five requests, five of them included requests for cloth and clothing worth nearly 6,000 *reis*.[28]

Jews periodically pledged money to assist in the completion of Portuguese construction projects. These donations may have been a means for members of the Jewish community to ingratiate themselves with Portuguese leadership and to prevent higher taxes from being levied on them as a community. For example, in 1513 rabbi Abraham Rute gave the Portuguese 25,000 *reis* collected from the entire Jewish community to assist with the costs of various construction projects in Safi.[29] The Jews in Azamor gave between 600 and 700 *cruzados* (over 240,000 *reis*) to fund construction of a bridge over the Umm al-Rabi` River in 1519.[30] As one of the reasons for construction of this bridge was to make trade easier, commercial motives may have been at the heart of this donation.

Completely ignored in the sources are what must have been a large number of Jewish women. All we know is that they did exist, as families and marriages are mentioned occasionally in historical sources.[31] Even Portuguese historian José A. R. da Silva Tavim in his important and thorough study, *Os judeus na expansão portuguesa em*

---

[28] "Payment Order from António Leite," Azamor, 10 March 1540, *SIHMP*, 3:240; Tavim, *Os judeus*, 274-276, 400-402, 426-428; ANTT, CC II, 71, 100; CC II, 108, 111. Portuguese merchants were also asked, though it does not seem they were asked as often, to supply food and goods for visiting diplomats (e.g., ANTT, CC I, 68, 108).

[29] *SIHMP*, 1:300n1.

[30] "Letter from D. Álvaro de Noronha to D. Manuel," Azamor, 11 July 1519, *SIHMP*, 2:248. For more about this bridge, see chapter four.

[31] For example, see "Letter from D. João III to António Leite and D. Manuel Mascarenhas," Lisbon, April 1541, *SIHMP*, 3:353.

Marrocos durante o século XVI, makes no mention of Jewish women other than through sporadic references to Jewish "families."

New Christians

New Christians (*cristãos novos*) is the label applied to Jews who had converted (usually forcibly) to Christianity in order to escape persecution and expulsion at the hands of the Portuguese and Spanish crowns in the late fifteenth century. Because most "Old" Christians viewed the sincerity of these conversions with suspicion, New Christians were often the targets of rumor and accusation. Many fled Iberia in the early sixteenth century and settled in Jewish communities in Morocco, often with Jewish relatives. Once in Morocco, many were accused, not always without merit, of returning to their Jewish ways. Still, there were no anti-Jewish riots or massacres of New Christians in Portuguese North Africa the way there had been in Lisbon in 1506, when 1,500-2,000 New Christians were killed.[32]

New Christians, for some reason, seem to have been especially attracted to Azamor after 1513.[33] Immediately following the conquest of Azamor, there were over three hundred people in Lisbon who volunteered to go to the city and populate it. The majority of these people were New Christians, which raised some cautionary eyebrows among Portuguese leaders. The prior of Azamor, Gonçalo de Almeida, suggested to D. Manuel that he forbid New Christians from relocating to Azamor, for fear they might return to Judaism. D. Manuel forbade this exodus, and told the *capitão* of Azamor, Rui Barreto, that it was not his wish that New Christians lived in Azamor. As of December 1513, there were only four New Christian men (and, possibly, their families) living in Azamor. Two months later, Barreto wrote that only ten New Christian men lived there and that nearly all of these were essential to the functioning of the city and that there did not exist Old Christians to replace them. Among these New Christians were one candle maker (*cerieiro*), one dyer (*tintureiro*), two tailors, one shearer (*tosador*), one metal

---

[32] Yosef Hayim Yerushalmi, *The Lisbon Massacre of 1506 and the Royal Image in the Shebet Yehudah* (Cincinnati, Ohio: Hebrew Union College, 1976).

[33] Tavim, *Os judeus*, 218-219.

worker (*serralheiro*) and four merchants.³⁴ This slow increase seems to indicate that D. Manuel's decree was enforced laxly, if at all.

As Christians, even with the taint of Judaism, New Christians were not surprisingly permitted to own property in the Portuguese fortresses. This included houses. A documentary fragment of a house sale provides some interesting information. On 21 December 1518, Meymam Belleames and his wife, Ariqua, both New Christians, sold their house on the *Rua de Gonçalo Dias* in Safi to Joce bem Myara and his wife Solltana, also New Christians. The boundary of this house was delimited by a city wall and a house owned by Cymbealla Menagullo, another New Christian.³⁵ What this indicates, other than an inability of the Portuguese to transliterate non-Portuguese names, is that New Christians appear to have lived together in the same neighborhood. This makes sense as it would be easier to avoid potential problems caused by overzealous Portuguese Christians.

New Christians were constantly under suspicion for any possibility that they might return to their former religion. This occurred whether they resided in North Africa or simply traveled there. One case involved a New Christian who lived in Beja, Portugal, and often traveled to Safi and Azamor for business (his trade is never described). While in Azamor in 1527, a rumor started that he planned to bring his family to Morocco and defect to territory controlled by Moroccans in order that he and his family might openly return to their Jewish ways. Jorge Viegas, the *capitão* of Azamor, had the man arrested and threatened to whip him unless he paid a fine of twenty *cruzados*. The man was only able to pay ten, while Azamor's New Christian community, including Mestre Rodrigo, the city's physician, paid the remainder of the "fine" – which Rodrigo viewed as a bribe to prevent the false apostasy charges – in order to free the man. Mestre Rodrigo,

---

[34] "Letter from D. João de Meneses to D. Manuel," Azamor, 1-9 December 1513, *SIHMP*, 1:462; "Letter from Rui Barreto to D. Manuel," Azamor, 21 February 1514, *SIHMP*, 1:497; Tavim, *Os judeus*, 226.

[35] ANTT, Fragmentos, caixa 8, doc. 130, published in Tavim, *Os judeus*, 537. Unfortunately, this document is incomplete and does not list a total price for the house, though 2,500 *reis* was part of the payment.

in fact, wrote D. João III and told him that the man would never desert Portugal or Christianity and that the king could trust him.[36]

Following the establishment of the Portuguese Inquisition in 1536, those suspicious of New Christians had a new tool. In 1537, Estêvão Ribeiro de Almeida, the prior of the church in Azamor since 1532, asked that the king send a representative of the Portuguese Inquisition to Azamor in order to investigate the New Christians and *mouriscos* who had apostatized and married Jewish and Muslim women, respectively. Almeida made this request despite the fact that D. Álvaro de Abranches, Azamor's *capitão*, had previously written to D. João III about the situation, and the king had ordered him to leave the apostates in peace, likely because of their commercial influence.[37] In fact, the Inquisition never made a visitation to the southern Moroccan cities and never appears to have required anyone from those cities to appear before it. The apostasy of New Christians, in other words, was not something to be overly concerned with outside of Portugal, at least not during the first half of the sixteenth century.[38]

Muslims

Muslims were the largest population group in Morocco as well as in and around the Portuguese cities. For them, the transition to

---

[36] "Letter from Mestre Rodrigo to D. João III," Azamor, 15 November 1527, *SIHMP*, 2:423-424. Suspicion was such that when a Jewish merchant from one of the Portuguese cities traveled to Lisbon on business, he was accompanied by a guard to prevent him from talking with any New Christians on the pretext that he might convince them to become Jews once again. Bastião de Vargas, D. João III's ambassador to the Wattasid court in Fez, suggested that a reverse regulation should be put in place to keep a guard with any New Christian who visited Morocco in order to prevent him from having conversations with Jews while there ("Letter from Bastião de Vargas to D. João III," Fez, 6 June 1542, *SIHMP*, 4:56).

[37] "Letter from Estêvão Ribeiro de Almeida to D. João III," Azamor, 16 January 1537, *SIHMP*, 3:83-84. D. João III established the Portuguese Inquisition in 1536. For more on the Portuguese Inquisition, see the classic Alexandre Herculano, *History of the Origin and Establishment of the Inquisition in Portugal* (New York: KTAV Publishing Group, 1972) and Francisco Bethencourt, *História das Inquisições: Portugal, Espanha, e Italia* (Lisbon: Tema e Debates, 1996).

[38] This seems to have been the case throughout the Portuguese empire. The case of Garcia da Horta (1501-68), the famed New Christian physician and botanist who lived a prosperous life in Goa, illustrates this. It was only in 1580, twelve years after his death, that his bones were exhumed by the Goan Inquisition and burned for alleged apostasy. See José Mattoso, ed., *História de Portugal* (Lisbon: Editorial Estampa, 1997), 3:353-356.

Portuguese rule was likely the most traumatic. The Jews were used to being subject to rulers of another religion, while Moroccan Muslims were not. Robert I. Burns argues similarly with respect to Valencian Muslims who, during the thirteenth century, came under the control of the Christian King James I:

> The very act of conquest . . . was a traumatic blow to the entire body social. Islam is not a church, separately structured, but a function, or better the informing soul, of a sociopolitical order. To destroy its central authority, leaving only local control, is to unroof the Muslim. To place an infidel society in supreme command, with its garrisons and representatives on every hand, with alien communities infiltrated at strategic cities, is to remake his world and wrest it from his control.[39]

Furthermore, from the mid-thirteenth century on, the Portuguese had become accustomed to having unquestioned dominion over Muslims in their kingdoms. Muslims in Portugal were subservient, the majority working as field hands in the agricultural regions of Portugal. In fact, as the years advanced from the final military conquest of Islamic political entities within Portugal in 1249, the numbers of Muslims within Portugal decreased as they were increasingly assimilated into the Portuguese Christian majority. In short, the Portuguese viewed Muslims as people to be conquered and ruled.[40]

Portuguese militarism in Morocco did little to alter this opinion. Moreover, the Portuguese conquests of Azamor and Safi were violent, and the Portuguese relationship with Muslims always had an undercurrent of violence. For example, when the Portuguese seized Safi in 1508, many of the Muslim residents sought refuge in the city's mosques. The Portuguese attacked them mercilessly, killing scores before accepting their surrender. Once the bodies were removed, the Portuguese converted the largest of these mosques to churches and

---

[39] Robert I. Burns, "Spanish Islam in Transition: Acculturative Survival and its Price in the Christian Kingdom of Valencia, 1240-1280," in Idem, *Moors and Crusaders in Mediterranean Spain* (London: Variorum, 1978), XIII:94.

[40] Serrão, *História*, 2:254-256; Barros, *A comuna muçulmana, passim*. The idea of Portuguese dominance over Muslims as an underlying and fundamental Portuguese belief is discussed in detail in chapter six.

barracks.⁴¹ Because Mazagão and Santa Cruz were built by the Portuguese, the desecration of Islamic holy sites in these cities was not an issue. Nevertheless, the land on which the Portuguese built Santa Cruz was seized only after fighting with local tribes, and construction on the fortress of Mazagão did not begin until a few months after Azamor was taken.⁴²

Muslims who were subject to Portuguese control (i.e., *mouros de pazes*) were administered by the Portuguese-appointed *alcaide dos mouros*. This position was held exclusively by Moroccan Muslim men. These men were typically in charge of a large and diverse geographical area and were charged by the Portuguese to maintain order among the subject communities. The *alcaide dos mouros* furthermore was required to apply Islamic law and Moroccan custom to all juridical decisions. Although the Portuguese allowed traditional laws and customs to remain, the Portuguese reserved the right to enforce their own laws above all others. A graphic example of this was the hanging of four Muslim criminals, two for robbery and two for attempting to sell illegally-captured slaves.⁴³ Muslims convicted of lesser crimes and imprisoned within Portuguese cities were kept in separate prisons, like the Jews, and at least some of the inmates were fed at Portuguese expense.⁴⁴

The Islamic population of Morocco should not be mistaken as monolithic. It consisted of two ethnic groups: Berbers and Arabs. Berbers (called *barbaros* in Portuguese sources) tended to be settled agriculturalists, living sedentary lives in villages and cities, while the Arabs (*alarves*) tended to be nomadic, living in a group of from fifty to one hundred tents known in Arabic as a *dawwār*.⁴⁵ It seems that the

---

⁴¹ *CDM*, 2:63-64.

⁴² For more on the theme of violence, see chapters six and seven.

⁴³ "Letter from D. Nuno Mascarenhas to D. Manuel," Safi, 11 March 1517, *SIHMP*, 2:65. For more on *alcaides dos mouros*, see chapter six. Allowing Islamic laws and customs to remain after the conquest of an Islamic polity was a common trait of Christian kings in Iberia, see Burns, "Spanish Islam," 92-93.

⁴⁴ ANTT, CC II, 97,30 and CC II, 98, 16.

⁴⁵ Maria Augusta Lima Cruz Fagundes, "Documentos Ineditos para a Historia dos Portugueses em Azamor," *Arquivos do Centro Cultural Portugues* 2 (1970), 112-113 and *HP*, 3:485. Technically, the plural of *dawwār* is *adwār*, though to avoid confusion, I will use the form *dawwārs*.

majority of Muslims living in Safi and Azamor at the time of the Portuguese conquest were Arabic-speaking Berbers.

Despite the fact that Muslims made up the majority populations in Azamor and Safi, documentation referring to their activities within these cities is scarce. This lack of data is remedied somewhat for the elite Muslims who were normally mentioned because they often had direct interaction with the elite among the Portuguese. Consequently, the information that follows here will be at best a sketch of the lives of Muslims living in Portuguese fortresses.

Muslims contributed a great deal to the functioning of the Portuguese fortresses with their labor (both as paid laborers and slaves), their commercial and trade activities, and their service as soldiers. The Portuguese employed Muslims in a variety of tasks. There are many instances of Muslims being used as messengers. In 1514, a Muslim delivered a letter from Azamor to Almedina, earning 400 *reis* for the job. The following year, a Muslim living near Azamor was used twice by the *capitão* to deliver messages – it is unclear to whom or to where – and was paid 690 *reis* for his efforts.[46] Other Muslims served as guides (*alformas*, from the Arabic *al-ḥurma*) for merchants and diplomats. Still others, like Selim in Safi in 1511, served as military guides (*guias*). Selim earned 378 *reis* per month.[47]

As laborers, Muslims helped construct walls and buildings, making lime (*cal*) for mortar, carrying stones, and serving as masons. For example, within weeks of the conquest of Azamor, many of the former residents, having fled the initial invasion, returned to the city and asked to have a separate part of the city to live in, near the Jewish quarter. That way, they could return to their previous lives as fishermen, lime (*cal*) makers, merchants, laborers, and artisans and participate in the rebuilding of the city.[48]

Without help from Moroccan Muslims, construction projects could not be completed in a timely manner or, perhaps, even at all. For instance, a group of Arabs who had been encamped near Mazagão was

---

[46] ANTT, CC II, 49, 106 and CC II, 60, 131. See also ANTT, CC II, 24, 115; CC II, 52, 160; CC II, 98, 12; CC II, 101, 8.

[47] ANTT, CC I, 2, 54; CC I, 2, 57; *SIHMP*, 1:74n4; "Letter from Nuno Fernandes de Ataíde to D. Manuel," Safi, 29 October 1513, *SIHMP*, 1:444; ANTT, NA 597, f. 95.

[48] "Letter from Lud," n. l., c. 5 December 1513, *SIHMP*, 1:458.

being paid to make lime at that location. Upon hearing word that D. João de Meneses was recruiting soldiers for a raiding expedition, they quit working, as had their colleagues near Azamor, and joined the expedition in search of the quick wealth to be had through the seizure of booty. Consequently, lime production slowed dramatically and so did construction on Mazagão and Azamor.[49] This also shows how vital having a substantial local labor base was to the Portuguese.

Slaves were ubiquitous in Portuguese fortresses and were almost entirely comprised of Moroccan Muslims, though there is evidence of black slaves, both those transported to Morocco by Portuguese ships and those owned by or captured from Moroccans.[50] The majority of these slaves were captured as the result of warfare and raids, though some were purchased from Moroccans, despite royal prohibitions against this practice. The male slaves were given heavy tasks and were locked in irons during the night so that they could not escape or commit acts of violence against their masters. Female slaves were typically engaged in domestic tasks during the day and then were locked in a room at night to prevent escape. Unlike male slaves, the relatives of these women sometimes would attempt to recapture them.[51]

Muslims were involved in all forms of commerce, both local and international. Agricultural goods and textiles were the main areas of participation. Towns, villages, and *dawwārs* sold grain, vegetables, hides, horses, and beeswax, among other things, to Portuguese and Jewish merchants.[52] Muslim merchants participating in the textile industry benefited from family and business connections both in

---

[49] "Letter from Vasco da Pina to D. Manuel," Azamor, 30 March 1514, *SIHMP*, 1:524 and "Letter from Francisco and Diogo Arruda to D. Manuel," Azamor, 31 March 1514, *SIHMP*, 1:528.

[50] "Letter from Lopo Barriga to D. Manuel," Safi, 22 August 1515, *SIHMP*, 1:747, refers to a black slave who had escaped from the King of Fez's camp and gave the Portuguese news of the King's location. There is no word about what happened to this man afterward. D. Guterres de Monroi, the final *capitão* of Santa Cruz, owned at least two black slaves, one male and one female (*CSC*, 152).

[51] Ana Maria S. A. Rodrigues and Maria de Fátima Moura Ferreira, "Mulheres portuguesas em Marrocos: Imagens do quotidiano feminino nos séculos XV e XVI," in *O rosto feminino da expansão portuguesa* (Lisbon: Comissão para a Igualdade e para os Direitos das Mulheres, 1995), 422. (For more on slavery, see chapter eight).

[52] For an overview, see Duarte Pacheco Pereira, *Esmeraldo de Situ Orbis* ed. Damião Peres (Lisbon, 1988), chaps. 15-21 and chapter five of this book.

Portuguese cities and in Moroccan-administered cities such as Almedina and even Marrakech.[53]

With the available sources, it is possible to produce a small case study that addresses all of these themes. Just outside the southern gate of Safi was the town of al-Khemis (called alternately Gormiz, Guarniz, Guamiz, by the Portuguese). On two of its edges, al-Khemis was bordered by the sea and a small freshwater lake. Given the proximity to Safi, the residents of this town had little choice but to ally with the Portuguese or flee. Most of them stayed and provided the Portuguese with tribute and military assistance. In fact, although the population of the city had been almost exclusively Berber in 1508, by 1519 numerous Arab tribes of *mouros de pazes* had moved their encampments to al-Khemis, making it into a sort of boomtown. The residents of this city raised grain in nearby fields, paying an unknown portion of it to the Portuguese each year as tribute. They also gathered and sold firewood to the Portuguese for use in the lime ovens. In December 1516, for instance, al-Khemis provided Safi with 2,000 loads of wood.[54]

Alliance required more than just tribute. The Portuguese were obligated to treat the residents of al-Khemis well, and the Moroccans living in al-Khemis were required to provide military assistance. The Portuguese offered protection in various ways. For instance, their artillery and soldiers prevented anyone from attacking al-Khemis without also attacking Safi. The Portuguese also protected al-Khemis' crops and livestock. Once, a Portuguese patrol observed some Moroccan thieves stealing cattle from the al-Khemis herd. The Portuguese rode after the thieves, chasing them away and retrieving the stolen cattle.[55]

As part of their alliance with the Portuguese, the men of al-Khemis were required to serve the Portuguese in a military capacity

---

[53] "Letter from D. Álvaro de Noronha to D. Manuel," Azamor, 18 April 1520, *SIHMP*, 2:274.

[54] "Letter from Nuno Gato to D. Manuel," Safi, 3 January 1511, *SIHMP*, 1:273 and n1, 279; "Letter from Nuno Gato to D. Manuel," Safi, 4 July 1516, *SIHMP*, 2:12 and n4; "Letter from D. Nuno Mascarenhas to D. Manuel," Safi, 9 December 1516, *SIHMP*, 2:48; "Letter from D. Nuno Mascarenhas to D. Manuel," Safi, early 1519, *SIHMP*, 2:223; "Letter from Francisco Lopes Girão to D. João III," Safi, 20 April 1529, *SIHMP*, 2:456 and n3.

[55] "Letter from D. Nuno Mascarenhas to D. Manuel," Safi, 9 September 1517, *SIHMP*, 2:169.

when called upon. In June 1518, for example, the town provided ten cavalrymen to accompany a Portuguese raiding party. While in 1519, it provided fifty infantrymen to assist in another campaign. The people of al-Khemis celebrated victories for Portuguese arms as well. They held a particularly massive celebration following a resounding defeat of Sa`adid forces in 1517 by a contingent led by Yahya-u-Ta`fuft, the *alcaide dos mouros* of Dukkala.[56]

The loyalty of the residents of al-Khemis did not mean that the Portuguese could simply order them to do whatever they felt best. Fair treatment was essential. For example, residents of al-Khemis seem to have been enslaved illegally, both by Portuguese and by fellow Moroccans, and then sold to Castile. In 1517, King D. Manuel put a stop to this with a royal order requiring the execution of anyone convicted of illegally enslaving Muslims. The *capitão* of Safi, D. Nuno Mascarenhas, vigorously enforced this decree. As a result, the residents of al-Khemis were joyous, and as Mascarenhas reported to his king, "There is not a single Muslim in al-Khemis who has not stopped by to offer me his thanks." In 1519, D. Manuel considered appointing a Christian *alcaide dos mouros* for al-Khemis. Mascarenhas advised the king that this would be a horrible idea, resulting in a flight of people from al-Khemis. The king reconsidered.[57]

Muslim Women

The only Muslim women about whom any details are known are those living in Portuguese cities. More specifically, these women were hostages, the wives or mothers of hostages, or the wives of allied Muslim leaders. In short, all of these women were from the Moroccan elite, as hostages given to guarantee treaty agreements were normally related to the male Moroccan leaders who had negotiated these agreements (see chapter six).

---

[56] "Letter from D. Nuno Mascarenhas to D. Manuel," Safi, 30 June 1518, *SIHMP*, 2:200; "Letter from D. Nuno Mascarenhas to D. Manuel," Safi, early 1519, *SIHMP*, 2:223; "Letter from D. Nuno Mascarenhas to D. Manuel," Safi, 3 April 1517, *SIHMP*, 2:75.

[57] "Letter from D. Nuno Mascarenhas to D. Manuel," Safi, 11 March 1517, *SIHMP*, 2:65; "Letter from D. Nuno Mascarenhas to D. Manuel," Safi, early 1519, *SIHMP*, 2:224.

The wives of Muslim allies were often given maintenance and gifts in the absence of their husbands. For instance, in January 1516, Nuno Fernandes de Ataíde, the *capitão* of Safi, purchased two sweets (*ambrosias*) at the cost of 200 *reis* for the wives of a loyal Moroccan ally.[58] Just as the Portuguese king favored elite Portuguese women should their husbands die in battle, so too did he reward elite Muslim women for the risks taken by their loyal husbands. On 19 August 1521, D. Manuel ordered the *feitor* of Azamor to give Myra, the wife of Mawlay Fares, two *moios* (1324 kg) of wheat and twenty ounces of silver in order to maintain herself and her servants.[59] Twenty ounces of silver was equivalent to 6400 *reis*, an amount greater than the yearly salary of most Portuguese officials.[60] When Fares and his brother, Mawlay `Abd al-Rahman bin Haddu, who had served as the *alcaide dos mouros* in Sharquiyya, were captured and executed by the Wattasid sultan on 14 March 1522, D. João III gave Myra another twenty ounces of silver and Maryam, the wife of `Abd al-Rahman, thirty ounces.[61] Both were granted this large sum of money in recognition of the service and loyalty of their husbands and to sustain them financially. Note that Maryam, as the wife of a more important official, received a larger death benefit.

Many of the elite Moroccan Muslim women who were in Portuguese cities were there as hostages to guarantee treaties and alliances that the Portuguese had made with their husbands or fathers. Typically, it seems, these women were held as hostages along with their children, both male and female, and servants. While hostages, they were generally treated very well. After all, if something were to befall them while in Portuguese hands, it would lead to problems with their allies. For instance, a group of women held hostage in Azamor in 1521 received six oxen and twenty-eight goats from the Portuguese in order to feed them and their dependents.[62]

---

[58] ANTT, CC II, 62, 165.

[59] ANTT, CC I, 27, 44. Cited in *SIHMP*, 2:285n2.

[60] ANTT, NA 597, f. 120v and Table 2.3 in this book.

[61] ANTT, CC I, 27, 118. Cited in *SIHMP*, 2:285n2.

[62] ANTT, CC II, 98, 33. For an extended discussion of hostages, see chapter six.

Elite Muslim women in a position of trust could be important sources and conduits of information. In one instance, the wives of four of the sheikhs of the Awlad `Amran lithali tribe traveled to Safi in order to visit their children, who were presumably being held as hostages, and to speak with the *capitão*, Nuno Fernandes de Ataíde. In addition to seeing their children, they also reported to Ataíde a rumor about the usurpation of power by Yahya-u-Ta`fuft, the *alcaide dos mouros* of Dukkala, as well as the fact that Bin Yehuda, a notable among the Gharbiyya tribe, had addressed Yahya as "king."[63] They showed a motherly concern as well as the necessary status to speak about politics with Ataíde. Although they may have been giving information to Ataíde in good faith, their position as the wives of elite men of the periodically hostile Awlad `Amran tribe points to the possibility that they may have been attempting to destabilize Portuguese power in the region by sowing dissension.[64]

Information intended for Moroccan Muslim leaders was entrusted to their wives without hesitation. For instance, letters from the Portuguese king addressed to Yahya-u-Ta`fuft were left with his wives to be delivered to him.[65] Yahya's wives apparently knew much of his business, for it was through them that D. Nuno Mascarenhas, the *capitão* of Safi, first learned of a possible peace agreement negotiated by their husband and the Sa`adids in 1517, after he had summoned the women to discover if they knew anything. This report later turned out to be premature and no agreement was concluded.[66]

Mouriscos

Unlike in Spain, where Muslims converted to Christianity were called *nuevos convertidos* until the middle of the sixteenth century,[67] the term *mourisco* can accurately be used in the Portuguese context. The

---

[63] "Deposition against Yahya-u-Ta`fuft," n. l., early 1513, *SIHMP*, 1:378-379.

[64] For details on the Awlad `Amran, see the case study in chapter six. Yahya-u-Ta`fuft was, in the main, a trustworthy ally (Racine, "Service and Honor," *passim*).

[65] "Letter from D. Nuno Mascarenhas to D. Manuel," Safi, 11 March 1517, *SIHMP*, 2:66.

[66] "Letter from D. Nuno Mascarenhas to D. Manuel," Safi, 10 August 1517, *SIHMP*, 2:148-149.

[67] L. P. Harvey, *Islamic Spain, 1250 to 1500* (Chicago: University of Chicago Press, 1990), 2-3.

term was in common use by 1500 and was employed by the Portuguese to refer to any Muslim who had converted to Christianity, whether in Portugal, Morocco, or elsewhere. In Morocco, the majority of people called *mouriscos* appear to have been Portuguese Muslims who had converted to Christianity in 1497 while still in Portugal and then had somehow traveled to the fortresses in Morocco. By the 1530s, all *mouriscos* had to ask permission to enter or leave Portugal or travel between the kingdom and any of the Portuguese colonies. A smaller number of converted Muslims were Moroccans who, with varying levels of sincerity, chose to abandon the religion of their birth and become Christians.

Most Portuguese viewed *mouriscos* with suspicion, the belief in their inherently treacherous nature extending back to at least the fourteenth century.[68] In this respect, they occupied a place similar to the formerly Jewish New Christians. In fact, the term "New Christian" was at times applied to *mouriscos*. For example in 1529, António Leite, *capitão* of Azamor, wrote to the king to complain about the "many New Christian *mouriscos*" who lived in Azamor and who had shunned all Christian practice and now lived by Islamic law. He furthermore claimed that on two separate occasions, these *mouriscos* had requested that the Sharif and the Wattasid sultan come to Azamor and help them escape and become Muslims again. Both times the city had come under attack. (In all likelihood, Leite had committed a *post hoc ergo propter hoc* fallacy, for it is unlikely that *mourisos* would have such influence over either the Wattasid or Sa`adid leadership.) In order to prevent further "treasons" caused by these *mouriscos*, Leite suggested to the king that they, "with all their wives and children," be relocated to some uninhabited island that they could populate and where they could be instructed in the ways of Christianity without the undue influence of living surrounded by Muslims.[69] The Portuguese king rejected this policy of population transfer out of hand.

---

[68] Barros, *A comuna muçulmana*, 18.

[69] "Letter from António Leite to D. João III," Azamor, 10 September 1529, *SIHMP*, 2:479. Compare Leite's suggestion to the fate of the approximately two thousand Jewish children under the age of eight who were taken from their parents in the 1490s, forcibly baptized, and then shipped to the island of São Tomé (in the Gulf of Guinea) in order to populate it as Christians. Most of these children died before reaching adulthood. See Timothy J. Coates, *Convicts and Orphans: Forced and State-Sponsored*

Luís de Loureiro, the *capitão* of Mazagão, echoed the belief in the treasonous nature of *mouriscos*. In 1542 he reported that three *mouriscos*, who had fled Safi when it was evacuated, were now living in Mazagão. He was unhappy with this circumstance and asked the king to prevent any more *mouriscos* from coming to his city because "in a thousand, there is not one who is loyal."[70] This accusation was not without some merit. An unidentified *mourisco* fled Azamor in 1521 in hopes of returning to his home and to Islam. He was tracked down by Canumaconde [?], a Moroccan Muslim bounty hunter, who was paid 1280 *reis* for capturing him.[71] In 1531, the harvests in Dukkala were small, and many Muslims came to Mazagão and converted to Christianity. There they remained for many months, eating food provided by the Portuguese government. Later, they fled Mazagão and returned to their Islamic ways.[72] Perhaps the most treacherous *mourisco* of all was Diogo, a trusted servant of Simão Gonçalves da Costa, the *capitão* of Santa Cruz. In 1533, Diogo opened the gates of the city to Sa`adid forces, resulting in the *capitão's* death and the near loss of the fortress.[73]

Still, not all *mouriscos* were distrusted. At least one, described as a "knight" and a "good Christian," lived in Santa Cruz in 1533, when he was killed by Sa`adid forces when they breached the fortress for a few hours.[74] Another *mourisco* named João was paid 100 *reis* and given 150 *reis* worth of olive oil as payment for his services to the Portuguese in Santa Cruz in 1537.[75] It is unclear if these *mouriscos* were of Portuguese or Moroccan origin.

Colonizers in the Portuguese Empire, 1550-1755 (Stanford: Stanford University Press, 2001), 61.

[70] "Letter from Luís de Loureiro to D. João III," Mazagão, 15 December 1542, *SIHMP*, 4:114.

[71] ANTT, CC II, 94, 187.

[72] *SIHMP*, 5:120. Afonso Vaz, the man who reported this incident to the Portuguese Inquisition in 1537, accused the *capitão* of Mazagão, António Leite, of permitting the *mouriscos* to leave with the knowledge that they would apostatize. Unfortunately, I have been unable to locate further information about this incident; however, these accusations may stem from Leite's attempts to stop the illegal enslavement of Muslims and *mouriscos* in the late 1520s (see below).

[73] See chapter six for a detailed account of this episode.

[74] *CSC*, 62.

[75] "Payment Order from Luís de Loureiro," Santa Cruz, 30 May 1537, *SIHMP*, 3:103.

The conversion of Moroccan Muslims to Christianity was viewed by the Portuguese kings as an occasion to be celebrated. Consequently, many, if not all, Moroccan Muslims who converted to Christianity were given some sort of reward. Two men who converted in Ceuta in the first half of the sixteenth century were each given 1,000 *reis*.[76] Another Muslim who came to Safi and converted to Christianity was rewarded for his conversion with 6,540 *reis* worth of clothing. As all converts were required to use a Christian name, this man took the name Henrique de Noronha, after Safi's *contador*, D. Henrique de Noronha. Furthermore, the *capitão* gave 4,000 *reis* in cash to the convert, who had been a stable master (*cevadeiro*) for the Sharif, in order to pay for his marriage to an unidentified Christian (Portuguese?) woman. The *capitão* hoped that this generous reward would set an example to other Muslims so that they too would convert to Christianity.[77]

Some *mouriscos* were able to live outside of Portuguese fortresses and did not appear to cause any problems. An unknown number of them were living with Moroccan Muslims in 1527 in the lands surrounding Mazagão and Azamor. It is likely, in fact, that these *mouriscos* had given up Christianity and were practicing Islam. Unfortunately for them, Jorge Viegas, the *capitão* of Azamor, had been enslaving both the *mouriscos* and the Muslims illegally, in spite of their alliance with the Portuguese. António Leite, the *capitão* of Mazagão, had taken in as many of these people as possible to prevent further seizures. Meanwhile, he wrote to D. João III asking him to reprimand

---

[76] Isabel M. R. Mendes Drumond Braga and Paulo Drumond Braga Braga, *Ceuta Portuguesa (1415-1656)* (Ceuta: Instituto de Estudios Ceutíes, 1998), 69.

[77] "Payment Order from D. Garcia de Noronha," Safi, 2 January 1535, *SIHMP*, 3:15-16; "Payment Order from D. Garcia de Noronha," Safi, 4 January 1535, *SIHMP*, 3:17; Isabel M. R. Mendes Drumond Braga, *Mouriscos e cristãos no Portugal quinhentista: duas culturas e duas concepções religiosas em choque* (Lisbon: Hugin, 1999), 54. Muslim allies might also be given wedding gifts. One such person was Lames [?], identified only as a "*mouro de pazes*," who had been married in Azamor and who was given a gift of clothing to celebrate the occasion (ANTT, CC I, 55, 130). Conversion might also be a long slow process. A married Moroccan Muslim couple abandoned the territory controlled by the Sharif in the 1530s and came to live in Santa Cruz. They stayed in the fortress for four years, remaining Muslims. Then, under unknown circumstances, they moved to the island of Madeira where they converted to Christianity. Eventually, the husband, Francisco, moved to Lisbon, apparently after the death of his wife (Braga, *Mouriscos e cristãos*, 93).

and punish Viegas.[78] The illegal enslavement of *mouriscos* was, in fact, a serious problem. In 1517, Simão Correia, the *capitão* of Azamor, was accused of selling a large number of Moroccan Christians to Castile. Among them was the "son of an honored sheikh" who had recently converted to Christianity. Unlike Viegas who retained his position as *capitão* until early 1529, Correia was replaced as *capitão* only four months later.[79]

Conclusion

It is typical of frontier settlers and colonialists to recreate conditions that resemble those of their homes. Iberians in the Americas are famous for their attempts to recreate the village and city life of their European origins. In effect, the Portuguese in Morocco attempted to recreate relationships with Jews and Muslims that resembled what had existed in Portugal until the late fifteenth century. These were relationships characterized by the dominance of Christianity and the submission of all other religions. Nevertheless, it is also a trait of those living in a frontier to adapt to the realities of their new situation. Consequently, faced with the need to attract the commercial and diplomatic skills of Jews to their fortresses and to maintain a calm Islamic population, the Portuguese made concessions to these groups that they would likely not have made had they resided within Portugal.

When the Portuguese chose to abandon all of their fortresses in southern Morocco, except Mazagão, one of the factors influencing the decision of which fortresses to abandon was the presence of a large Muslim population. After 1542, the only Portuguese fortress remaining in southern Morocco was Mazagão. As there was never a meaningful population of Muslims living within or near the fortress walls, it was easiest for the Portuguese to strengthen and retain that fortress. Safi and Azamor were abandoned because such massive cities would be difficult to defend from Sa`adid forces, both because of outmoded

---

[78] "Letter from António Leite to D. João III," Mazagão, 5 February 1527, *SIHMP*, 2:391-395.

[79] ANTT, CC I, 22, 55, published in Fagundes, "Documentos," 143. The reasons for Correia's quick dismissal and Viegas's retention are unclear. Perhaps the accusations against Viegas had little merit, perhaps Viegas had more influence at court than Correia, or perhaps D. João III had less tolerance for *mouriscos* than did D. Manuel.

defenses and the possibility of the local Muslim population rising against the Portuguese. Jews, on the other hand, were not feared and were allowed to live in Mazagão if they so desired, as some did. Others, as mentioned above, moved to the Portuguese cities of Arzila and Tangiers, while a number of Jewish families moved to cities administered by Moroccans.

A royal order of 30 August 1556, however, required all Jews to leave the remaining Portuguese fortresses throughout Morocco.[80] It is from this date – at the very latest – that the Moroccan littoral can no longer be considered a frontier zone between the Portuguese and Moroccans. After 1556, the three remaining Portuguese cities in Morocco – Mazagão, Tangiers, and Ceuta – are best described as enclaves. When not under attack by Moroccan forces, the Portuguese were able to trade with local Moroccans for food, textiles, and other raw materials. The extensive and pervasive interactions between these three religious groups would not occur again in Western Europe or Morocco until the colonialism of the nineteenth century.

---

[80] Tavim, *Os judeus*, 247.

Chapter Four: Food, Construction, and Justice: Logistics and Order on the Portuguese-Moroccan Frontier

ESTABLISHING a frontier outpost and ensuring that it functions both as a home for colonists and as a tool of occupation is a complex endeavor. First, a location must be seized, usually by force, and held militarily against a hostile enemy. Next, colonists must occupy this location, and they must be fed and housed. Construction projects of all dimensions need to be completed; structures must be repaired, modified, strengthened, or built. Finally, order needs to be guaranteed within the colonial outpost, just as in a metropolitan city, so that chaos and criminality do not interfere with occupation and colonization. In other words, for colonization to be successful, effective institutions and supply structures must be established, adequately funded, and properly maintained.[1]

Food Supply

The staples of the Portuguese diet have changed little since the sixteenth century. In fact, one observer reported that the three main items consumed in Azamor in the 1520s were bread, wine, and fish, a menu that would satisfy almost any modern Portuguese.[2] Food in the Portuguese fortresses was obtained in a variety of ways. Some of the food was grown locally by residents of the city. Livestock could be raised, fish could be caught in nearby rivers and the ocean, and wild animals could be hunted. Large amounts of grain were collected as tribute from subject Moroccans. Regional trade, utilizing traditional market locations, especially in Safi and Azamor, brought foodstuffs to

---

[1] Manuel González Jiménez, "Frontier and Settlement in the Kingdom of Castile (1085-1350)," in *MFS*, 52.

[2] "Letter from Mestre Rodrigo to D. João III," Azamor, 15 November 1527, *SIHMP*, 2:420.

the cities where the residents purchased it. During periods of scarcity, food, especially grain, was imported from beyond Morocco, mainly from Portugal and Andalusia. Finally, all manner of foodstuffs was seized during Portuguese raids against non-allied Moroccan tribes and villages.

Residents of Portuguese fortresses were able to grow a surprising amount of their own food, especially in times of peace, though never enough to supply all demands. For example, about a half-league outside of the walls of Safi there were groves of olive trees (*Zamujeiros*) that were seized by the Portuguese shortly after the conquest.[3] The proximity of olive trees probably meant that, in times of peace, Safi could supply its own olive oil. If the groves were large enough, Safi may have been able to lay up supplies to carry it through any extended siege. Also situated somewhere outside Safi's walls was a fig orchard owned in 1541 by one Afonso Eanes. Unfortunately, it is not clear if the Portuguese planted the orchard when they conquered Safi, or if they merely seized an extant orchard. The second possibility is most likely as it takes a long period of time to create a productive orchard.[4]

There is mention of gardens (*hortas*) outside the Almedina gate on the eastern side of Safi and others to the southeast in the shadow of one of the city's main towers.[5] Thus it appears that gardens abutted city walls for protection. Such locations may also have provided extra heat or shade for crops in order to extend their cultivation periods. What grew in these gardens and who tended the land? In the northern fortress of Ceuta, it seems as though the Portuguese themselves may have cultivated the gardens. This information coincides with evidence that market gardeners (*hortelões*) were among the most numerous residents of Azamor.[6]

---

[3] "Letter from Nuno Fernandes de Ataíde to D. Manuel," Safi, 5 December 1510, *SIHMP*, 1:266.

[4] "Letter from D. Rodrigo de Castro to D. João III," Safi, 8 July 1541, *SIHMP*, 3:456. The exact distance from the city is unclear.

[5] "Letter from Nuno Gato to D. Manuel," Safi, 3 January 1511, *SIHMP*, 1:278; "Letter from Nuno Fernandes de Ataíde to D. Manuel," Safi, 4 January 1511, *SIHMP*, 1:291; "Letter from Nuno Fernandes de Ataíde to D. Manuel," 4 August 1515, *SIHMP*, 1:722; *CDM*, 3:54.

[6] Isabel M. R. Mendes Drumond Braga and Paulo Drumond Braga, *Ceuta Portuguesa (1415-1656)* (Ceuta: Instituto de Estudios Ceutíes, 1998), 71 and Maria Augusta Lima

By 1516, the *capitão* of Azamor, Simão Correia was able to report to his king that significant areas of the old portion of the city had been demolished and, among other things, many vineyards, gardens, and orchards had been planted there. These areas were within the city's walls.[7] The Portuguese obviously intended on holding these cities indefinitely, as the creation of vineyards for a supply of wine especially attests. The Portuguese even managed, during some years, to plant small crops of wheat and barley near their fortresses. For example, in August 1517, D. Nuno Mascarenhas wrote to the king asking him to send 200 additional cavalrymen to Safi in order to protect their plantings near (*ao redor*) the city from a possible invasion by the Wattasid sultan. It is unclear if any were sent in 1517, but the king did provide troops to protect crops the following year.[8]

A ready source of meat was also important for the Portuguese. Consequently, at least near Azamor and Safi, the Portuguese maintained herds of livestock. Because these animals were frequently the target of Moroccan thieves and raiding parties, guards were posted to help prevent such theft.[9] This could be a dangerous job. In 1514, for example, Afonso do Amaral was killed by Moroccans while guarding the king's cattle (*gado de El Rey*) near Azamor. His widow was given the 1000 *reis* he was owed as pay "for the one month he had the job."[10]

These herds were likely substantial, at least during periods when the Portuguese had control over extensive territory in Dukkala. For example, in the autumn of 1514, D. Manuel granted Estêvão Rodrigues Berrio *twenty* cows from an unknown number of those held in the king's name in the city of Azamor. At about the same time in

---

Cruz Fagundes, "Documentos inéditos para a história dos portugueses em Azamor," *Arquivos do Centro Cultural Portugues* 2 (1970), 110.

[7] "Letter from Simão Correia to D. Manuel," Azamor, 3 October 1516, *SIHMP*, 2:39.

[8] "Letter from D. Nuno Mascarenhas to D. Manuel," Safi, 29 July 1517, *SIHMP*, 2:126; "Letter from D. Nuno Mascarenhas to D. Manuel," Safi, 5 August 1517, *SIHMP*, 2:146; "Letter from D. Nuno Mascarenhas to D. Manuel," Safi, 3 September 1518, *SIHMP*, 2:215.

[9] "Letter from Nuno Fernandes de Ataíde to D. Manuel," Safi, 5 December 1510, *SIHMP*, 1:265-268.

[10] ANTT, CC II, 50, 34. At 12,000 *reis* per year, Amaral's salary was on par with high-ranking government officials (see Table 2.3).

Safi, the royal herd was 100 head strong.[11] Another animal kept in herds was sheep. Pedro Álvares served as the shepherd in Azamor in 1514 and earned 400 *reis* per month. Sheep provided food, hides, and above all, wool. At least one sheep-shearer (João Rodrigues) lived in Azamor in 1514.[12] Pigs were also raised near some Portuguese cities. In addition to being a cultural insult to Moroccan Muslims, the pigs caused environmental problems. Both Moroccans and Portuguese complained that the stocks of pigs befouled lakes and streams, making the water unusable for other animals.[13] Chickens also appear to have been raised in large numbers within the fortresses.[14] Food animals required butchers, and there were at least two Portuguese butchers in Azamor in 1517.[15]

Hunting provided a useful source of meat, especially in the bountiful lands near Azamor. In 1519, the Bishop of Safi (i.e., of all southern Morocco), D. João Sutil, paid a visit to Azamor. In his honor, the bishop was taken on a hunting expedition into the nearby region of Shawiyya. According to the astounded bishop, he and his companions killed in a single day eighty pigs, a wild bull, some gazelles, and a number of partridges.[16] Animals taken during hunting expeditions near Azamor in the late 1520s were described as so numerous and varied that "one had to see it to believe it."[17]

Fishing was another crucial source of food for the Portuguese fortresses. One observer described the Umm al-Rabi` River near

---

[11] *DCC*, 125-126 and ANTT, CdGA, 364.

[12] ANTT, CC II, 49, 85 and CC II, 49, 127.

[13] "Letter from Bastião de Vargas to D. João III," Fez, 6 and 9 December 1540, *SIHMP*, 3:290. Such a problem continues in modern times with concentrated animal feeding operations (CAFOs).

[14] ANTT, CC II, 15, 137.

[15] The two butchers were Álvaro Gonçalves and Afonso Annes (ANTT, CC II, 69, 126). There were also likely separate butchers for the Jewish and Muslim inhabitants, in deference to their dietary laws, as there had been in the *judiarias* and *mourarias* in Portugal.

[16] "Letter from the Bishop of Safi to D. Manuel," Azamor, 11 August 1519, *SIHMP*, 2:253.

[17] "Letter from Mestre Rodrigo to D. João III," Azamor, 15 November 1527, *SIHMP*, 2:422: "*que ho nom crera senom quem ho vir*". There is also evidence that hunting was common near Ceuta, where rabbits and birds, including partridges, doves, and quails, were taken. Braga and Braga, *Ceuta Portuguesa*, 71.

Azamor in the following manner: "The richness and bounty of the river is such that I do not believe that there could be a better one in these parts."[18] All of the Portuguese fortresses were on the seacoast or a riverbank, primarily for access to trade, though with the added bonus of easy access to fisheries. The saga of Santa Cruz serves to illustrate this point. Upon purchasing the fortress in 1513, D. Manuel ordered that the fortress obtain a translator who spoke Arabic, a physician, and two fishermen in order to supply the residents with fish. After almost one and a half years, there were still no fishermen, and Afonso Rodrigues, the *feitor* of Santa Cruz, wrote to the king begging for the fishermen to be sent "because all the people here are dying of hunger."[19]

Fish were also a valuable source of royal revenue. The *contador* of Azamor announced to the residents of the city in 1518 that no one could export fish from the city, either by land or sea, without making it known to the *escrivão da ribeira*. This was necessary so that the fish could be counted and taxed.[20] Such taxes were high. For example, on 18 January 1526, 360 fish were caught near Azamor. Of these, 72 were taken as the royal fifth, while another 144 were given to the owners of the ships (*armadores*) used by the fishermen. This left the fishermen with 144 fish, only 40% of the initial catch.[21] For those fishermen who fished from shore, finding a prime spot was essential. Apparently, competition for these spots caused arguments, for the *contador* of Azamor proclaimed in 1518 that once someone pulled in his net, he had to surrender his spot immediately if another person was waiting to cast his own net.[22] This taxation and regulation implies that fishermen earned their income from what they sold, rather than a set stipend from the royal government. In addition to taxes, danger from storms and

---

[18] "Letter from Mestre Rodrigo to D. João III," Azamor, 15 November 1527, *SIHMP*, 2:422.

[19] "Letter from Afonso Rodrigues to D. Manuel," Santa Cruz, 24 December 1513, *SIHMP*, 1:475 and "Letter from Afonso Rodrigues and Francisco Fernandes to D. Manuel," Santa Cruz, 4 June 1514, *SIHMP*, 1:566-567. (Rodrigues is probably guilty of hyperbole here.)

[20] ANTT, CC II, 73, 2.

[21] Fagundes, "Documentos," 157 and ANTT, NA, 575.

[22] ANTT, CC II, 73, 73. These laws seem to have applied to Moroccans who fished from the banks as well.

currents, and fights over prime locations, Portuguese fishermen had to worry about Moroccan raiding parties. For example, five unfortunate Portuguese were fishing along the riverbank near Azamor in 1514 when they were captured by a Shawiyyan raiding force.[23]

Although it is clear that the Portuguese could provide themselves with large amounts of fish and small amounts of fruits, vegetables, meat, and grain, it was wheat that supplied the bulk of their calories. For this, as well as for other foods, the Portuguese relied heavily on tribute from and trade with Moroccans. Tribute payments provided an extraordinary amount of grain for the Portuguese. According to historian Ahmed Boucharb, the minimum tribute amount for allied Moroccans was 5 *alqueires* of wheat per household per year, while the maximum was 30 *alqueires* (the larger amounts were typically assessed against recently pacified groups). The median tribute amount was either 8 *alqueires* of wheat or 16 *alqueires* of barley per household per year. As the *alqueire* was a unit of volume equal to 14 liters, it is important to convert it to a weight measure. One *alqueire* of wheat weighs 11.2 kg, while one *alqueire* of barley weighs 7.42 kg. Consequently, the median tribute was either 89.6 kg of wheat or 118.72 kg of barley per household per year.

Boucharb calculated that the tribute from the Dukkala and `Abda (to the south of Safi) regions during the height of Portuguese power (i.e., 1515-1525) averaged 37,333 *quintals* (2,240,000 kg) of wheat and 37,100 *quintals* (2,226,000 kg) of barley per year. In comparison, the sixteenth-century Portuguese chronicler, Damião de Góis, gives numbers for the year 1511 that are 30-40% lower. He estimates the annual tribute during these years at 26,133 *quintals* (1,568,000 kg) of wheat and 21,875 *quintals* (1,312,500 kg) of barley. These lower numbers bear out Boucharb's higher numbers for later years as the Portuguese expanded their territorial control and collected increased tribute in the years after 1511. As much as 40,000 additional *quintals* (2,400,000 kg) of grain were sold annually in Safi and Azamor to both Portuguese and other European merchants. For example, in 1512, the king ordered the *contador* of Safi to purchase 3,000 *moios* (1,986,000 kg)

---

[23] "Letter from António Leite to D. Manuel," Azamor, 27 July 1514, *SIHMP*, 1:585. One of these men was probably Pero Eanes (Isabel M. R. Mendes Drumond Braga, *Entre a Cristandade e o Islão: cativos e renegados nas franjas de duas sociedades em confronto* (Ceuta: Instituto de Estudios Ceutíes, 1998), 32).

of Moroccan wheat and place it in the city's granary.[24] Boucharb estimates that tribute and trade took twenty percent of the region's harvest during fertile years.[25] The loss of such a huge portion of the harvest to the Portuguese must have devastated the economic futures of Moroccans farmers and created a generalized fear of food shortages, which did at times occur.[26]

Without this massive amount of grain, the Portuguese could not have fed themselves or their warhorses except at astronomical expense. For example, Azamor, in spite of massive tribute payments, had to import grain – most often from Iberia and Madeira – in at least thirteen of the thirty years that the city was under Portuguese control. Some of the annual import amounts exceeded 500,000 kg of grain, though they averaged between 100,000 and 150,000 kg (see Table 4.1).[27] There are about 8,929 *alqueires* in 100,000 kg. Even at the moderate cost of 42 *reis* per *alqueire* of wheat in 1514, 100,000 kg cost nearly 375,000 *reis* simply to purchase, plus approximately 3.3 *reis* per

---

[24] "Letter from Nuno Gato to D. Manuel," Safi, 29 May 1512, *SIHMP*, 1:311-312. Gato reported to the king that he would try to buy this amount of wheat "secretly" so as not to raise suspicions that it was for the king and thus drive prices up. Although much of this wheat would have to be purchased in the countryside, some could be purchased from Moroccan merchants in Safi's *sūq*.

[25] Vincent J. Cornell, "Socioeconomic Dimensions of Reconquista and Jihad in Morocco: Portuguese Dukkala and the Sa`did Sus, 1450-1557," *International Journal of Middle East Studies* 22 (1990): 388-398; *DIB*, 108, 267-268, 285-290; *CDM*, 3:62-63. One *quintal* is approximately 60 kg.

[26] See below. Bernard Rosenberger and Hamid Triki, "Faimes et Épidémies au Maroc aux XVI et XVII siècles," *Hespéris-Tamuda* 14 (1973): 109-176 and 15 (1974): 5-103 and Ahmed Boucharb, "Les conséquences socio-culturelles de la conquête ibérique du littoral marocain," in *Relaciones de la peninsula ibérica con el magreb (Siglos xiii-xvi): actas del coloquio*, ed. Mercedes García-Arenal and María J. Viguera (Madrid: Instituto Hispano-Árabe de Cultura, 1988), 487-521.

[27] The majority of these imports came from wheat purchased in Castile by the Portuguese *feitor* in Andaluzia. See "Les facteurs portugais d'Andalousie (1509-1588)," in *SIHMP*, 2:564-573. But how much grain did a city need? Based on a letter from António Leite, the *contador* of Mazagão, it is possible to estimate wheat consumption in Mazagão and Azamor during 1517. As of October of that year, Mazagão had 180 *moios* (119,160 kg) of wheat in its stores, while Azamor had 400 (264,800 kg). Leite estimated that these amounts would be sufficient for each city until the end of March 1518, or five full months. These numbers enable a few calculations. First, there were approximately double the number of people who depended on wheat in Azamor as in Mazagão. Second, Azamor used approximately 80 *moios* (52,960 kg) of wheat per month during this period while Mazagão used 36 (23,832 kg). See "Letter from António Leite to D. Manuel," Mazagão, 20 October 1517, *SIHMP*, 2:176-177.

kilogram for shipping charges from Iberia to Morocco that effectively doubled the cost of the wheat.[28] Barley, the other important grain, was given mainly as rations to cavalrymen to feed their horses, though if wheat were scarce or overpriced, it was consumed by humans. Wheat was given to some as part of their *moradia* (daily living allowance) or sold to bakers who provided the cities with bread.[29] In March 1518, for example, D. Nuno Mascarenhas said that there were three bakeries (*lojas de pão de venda*) operating within Safi.[30]

In addition to supplying grain through tribute, Moroccans sold excess produce to the Portuguese and their fellow Moroccans in the markets of the Portuguese-controlled cities. Detailed references to Moroccan food traders are, however, rare. Some traders from Gharbiyya were described as selling onions, turnips, and cucumbers in Safi.[31] One Portuguese observer reported large orchards of mulberry, loquat, and fig trees in the Shawiyya region to the north of Azamor.[32] Moroccans often brought dates, almonds, livestock, and chickens to sell in Portuguese markets.[33]

The distribution of food, as well as many trade goods, such as cloth, straw, and firewood, took place in the market squares of the

---

[28] Fagundes, "Documentos," 120-121 and Tables II and III; ANTT, CC II, 44, 98; CC II, 50, 33. Wheat prices in Morocco could fluctuate wildly. In 1508, the *capitão* of Safi purchased wheat from a Jewish merchant for 7.6 *reis*/kg (85 *reis*/*alqueire*). In November 1516, the *contador* of Safi purchased wheat from Moroccan traders for 2.2 *reis*/kg (24 *reis*/*alqueire*) and barley for 1.4 *reis*/kg (10 *reis*/*alqueire*). By December 1516, wheat was selling for 11.6 *reis*/kg (130 *reis*/*alqueire*) and barley for only 0.9 *reis*/kg (6.6 *reis*/*alqueire*) in al-Khemis, a suburb of Safi. In Azamor in 1525, wheat was valued for accounting purposes at 5.4 *reis*/kg (60 *reis*/*alqueire*). In August 1540, during a severe grain shortage in Safi that precipitated a famine, wheat sold for 26.8 *reis*/kg (300 *reis*/*alqueire*). ("Letter from D. Nuno Mascarenhas to D. Manuel," Safi, 9 December 1516, *SIHMP*, 2:49; "Letter from Álvaro Moraes to D. João III," Safi, 27 August 1540, *SIHMP*, 3:260; ANTT, CC II, 15, 157; CC II, 67, 42; CC II, I, 31, 120).

[29] A *moradia* was a stipend consisting of a monetary and a grain payment. The stipend was normally paid to nobles in order to make service in Morocco more financially attractive. Grain-only *moradias* consisting of barley or wheat rations were given to cavalrymen in order to feed their warhorses.

[30] "Letter from D. Nuno Mascarenhas to D. Manuel," Safi, 11 March 1518, *SIHMP*, 2:181.

[31] "Letter from Nuno Gato to D. Manuel," Safi, 4 July 1516, *SIHMP*, 2:13.

[32] ANTT, CC III, 5, 57, printed in Fagundes, "Documentos," 134-135.

[33] ANTT, CC II, 22, 58, printed in Fagundes, "Documentos," 146 and "Letter from Álvaro Moraes to D. João III," Safi, 27 August 1540, *SIHMP*, 3:260.

fortresses. The Portuguese in Morocco adopted the Arabic term of *sūq* (*çoquo* or *çoco* in documents) to refer to this location.³⁴ Because the market was in some sense a cultural- and status-neutral location within each city, where Christians, Muslims, and Jews, the wealthy and the poor gathered, it was used to make important announcements of consequence to the entire population. For instance, when peace agreements were reached with several "renegade" tribes in the summer of 1516, these agreements were read aloud in Safi's *sūq* so that the terms of the agreement would be known by all. There was also much fanfare with banners and trumpets. After all, there was reason to celebrate the aversion of war.³⁵ The *sūqs* of allied cities were also used to make proclamations, as was the case in Almedina in 1513.³⁶

In spite of the sizeable grain tribute and Moroccan willingness to sell food in the Portuguese cities, food could run short. In a supply system constantly subject to the contingencies of the frontier, this is not surprising. In 1514, Santa Cruz was short of wheat, and the situation was made worse by the need to feed forty Portuguese sailors who were rescued after their ships had foundered on the reefs just offshore. Ironically, these ships contained a supply of wheat that Santa Cruz's leadership had requested earlier.³⁷ In the summer of 1517, D. Nuno Mascarenhas complained that food was in short supply in Safi and some people were beginning to show signs of malnutrition and walked through the streets "shaking" with hunger. Mascarenhas asked the king to send some grain to help the population until the winter harvest.³⁸ In 1519, a severe famine hit the entire Dukkala region. In

---

[34] "Letter from Nuno Gato to D. Manuel," Safi, 12 May 1512, *SIHMP*, 1:301 and "Letter from the Duke of Bragança to D. Manuel,'" Azamor, 30 September 1513, *SIHMP*, 1:440.

[35] "Letter from D. Nuno Mascarenhas to D. Manuel," Safi, 11 March 1517, *SIHMP*, 2:64 and "Letter from Yahya-u-Ta`fuft to D. Manuel," Safi, 9 August 1516, *SIHMP*, 2:25. Announcements and ceremonies meant only for the Portuguese were conducted inside the city's cathedral. For example, when a new *capitão* took command of a city, the keys to that city were passed to him inside the cathedral and witnessed by all of the nobles and selected residents of the city (Fagundes, "Documentos," 134-135, 141).

[36] "Letter from Nuno Fernandes de Ataíde to D. Manuel," Safi, 29 October 1513, *SIHMP*, 1:444.

[37] *HP*, 3:459.

[38] "Letter from D. Nuno Mascarenhas to D. Manuel," Safi, 10 August 1517, *SIHMP*, 2:149.

Safi, the cost of bread was so high that people were selling everything in their houses to buy bread. Again, Mascarenhas begged the king to send grain to alleviate the crisis within the city.[39] During the winter of 1527-1528, Azamor suffered from a shortage of food due in large part to the "sterility" of the nearby land. Merchants in the city charged exploitative prices on food. Jorge Viegas, the *capitão* of the city, provided no relief for the citizens despite the allegedly large amount of grain stored in the city's grain cellar. In fact, the *capitão* was accused of accessing the grain stores for him and his close associates only. The only source of food for some citizens was what they could catch while hunting. As a result, some of the residents of Azamor rioted, looting and destroying the homes of several merchants.[40] The famine of the late 1520s spread throughout Dukkala and reached as far south as the lands around Santa Cruz.[41]

Finally, during both stable and instable periods, the Portuguese augmented their food supply by raiding Moroccan villages and encampments. Although the prime motivation for raiding activity was the capture of slaves, nearly every raiding party returned home with some livestock or grain. Occasionally, these seizures were spectacular. During one raid on a nomadic encampment in Shawiyya territory, the Portuguese claimed to have seized 150 captives, 6-7,000 head of livestock, and approximately 750 *moios* (450,000 kg) of wheat and barley.[42] Such an amount is difficult to believe, if only for the fact that so much grain in the possession of a nomadic group is mind-boggling, though the raid did come about three months after the harvest, meaning the nomads would have nearly full stores. Nevertheless, if the seizure was even one-third of this amount, it would have supplied the Portuguese in Azamor for several months and would likely have condemned to starvation any Moroccans who escaped this raid.

---

[39] "Letter from D. Nuno Mascarenhas to D. Manuel," Safi, 23 May 1519, *SIHMP*, 2:247.

[40] "Letter from Mestre Rodrigo to D. João III," Azamor, 12 January 1528, *SIHMP*, 2:426. These merchants are not indentified, but were probably mainly Portuguese, though some might have been Jews.

[41] "Alvará of D. João III," Lisbon, 5 June 1529, *SIHMP*, 2:466.

[42] "Letter from Duarte Lopes to D. João III," Azamor, 10 August 1523, *SIHMP*, 2:315.

Housing

Through the accident of documentary survival, almost all information regarding housing in Portuguese fortresses in southern Morocco relates to the city of Azamor. Still, assuming housing issues were like other things in Portuguese Morocco, what was true for Azamor was true in general for the other fortresses. Housing followed a theoretical model similar to that of landgrants. The king claimed all land conquered by the Portuguese and claimed the right to dispose of it as he saw fit. This follows settlement patterns used as Portugal pushed back the Islamic frontier in Iberia during the eleventh through the thirteenth centuries.[43]

Once Moroccan residents of the conquered cities fled or were expelled from their homes, the king could assign houses and land to Portuguese and allied individuals. For example, shortly after the conquest of Azamor, over 300 Portuguese requested that they be given houses.[44] The authority to distribute these grants was normally delegated to a royal official. Occasionally, this led to corruption. In June 1514, Gonçalo Ribeiro de Almeida, the prior of Azamor, reported unrest as a result of the distribution of houses and land. Diogo Ruis, described simply as a "scribe" (*escrivão*), was accused of taking bribes from the Jews in Azamor and giving them the best built and best located houses in the city. Meanwhile, the knights and "honored men" were living in "ruins" (*pardieiros*).[45]

In 1516, the king hoped to solve this problem by giving people in Azamor forty *cruzados* (about 16,000 *reis*) each to build a house on land that he granted to them within the castle walls of Azamor. A similar grant was made to the residents of Mazagão the same year. It is unclear if these grants were given to persons of any social status or if the grants were restricted to members of the elite. In exchange, the people receiving the money had to pledge to spend it only on building

---

[43] A. H. de Oliveira Marques, *História de Portugal* 13th ed. (Lisbon: Editorial Presença, 1997), 1:130-139. In medieval Portugal, much of this land was initially granted to military orders that protected it and began the process of settlement.

[44] "Letter from João de Meneses to D. Manuel," Azamor, 1-9 December 1513, *SIHMP*, 1:462.

[45] ANTT, CC III, 5, 57, printed in Fagundes, "Documentos," 134-135. This description was probably exaggerated, though many buildings in Azamor sustained artillery damage during the Portuguese conquest of the city and were not immediately repaired.

houses.⁴⁶ By September 1516, eight-one houses were under construction. Despite the fact that there were 200 masons in Azamor in 1516, Simão Correia, the *capitão*, reported that it would still take many months to complete work on both the walls and the houses. He advised that the king send more workers. In addition, Correia ordered each of the homeowners to pave the area in front of his house with stones, presumably to lessen the cost to the government for paving streets. Paving the streets in Azamor had largely been completed by October 1516.⁴⁷

Even after houses had been distributed, problems still arose. The king had granted Francisco de Almeida, the *adail* of Azamor from 1513 until his death in 1516, several "large and well built" houses. After his death, his wife, before returning to Portugal, gave these houses to João Fernandes, the *alfaqueque mor*, who, for an unstated reason, subsequently had them torn down. During the same period, a disused mosque "that housed Álvaro Carvalho with many people" was torn down, presumably on orders from Simão Correia, the *capitão*. The twelve signatories to the letter documenting these actions to the king stated that the destruction of these houses had violated a royal order preventing the destruction of buildings needed to house Portuguese.⁴⁸ Additionally, this letter shows that nearly four years after the conquest of Azamor, the issue of sufficient housing was far from solved.

The violation committed by the destruction of these buildings stemmed from the fact that until 1518, the houses in Azamor legally belonged to the king, rather than to the tenants who simply had

---

⁴⁶ ANTT, CC II, 66, 79; CC II, 71, 32; CC II, 71, 121. The 16,000 *reis* payment applied to Mazagão as well (ANTT, CC II, 71, 32) and, one would assume, Safi and Santa Cruz. It is unclear whether or not 16,000 *reis* was enough to pay for the entire construction process or if additional capital was needed. The payment seems to have been raised to 20,000 *reis* (50 *cruzados*) in 1517 (ANTT, CC II, 71, 121). I have been unable to uncover a description of what these houses may have looked like, though I would speculate that they were mostly one-story houses with brick and mortar walls and tile roofs, similar to houses found in the Alentejo and Algarve regions of Portugal even today.

⁴⁷ ANTT, CdGA, 359, mentioned in *SIHMP*, 2:38n2 and "Letter from Simão Correia to D. Manuel," Azamor, 3 October 1516, *SIHMP*, 2:39-40. Construction and repair of houses kept many people employed throughout the Portuguese presence. For example, Fernão Gonçalves earned 560 *reis* for making eight beams and two large doors for use in work on the *capitão* of Azamor's house in 1521 (ANTT, CC II, 98, 52). See chapter two for more examples.

⁴⁸ ANTT, CC I, 22, 58, printed in Fagundes, "Documentos," 145-147.

usufruct privileges. Consequently, no one except the king had the right to demolish them. For an unknown reason, though perhaps to spare himself from dealing with similar controversies, King D. Manuel issued an order on 23 July 1518, stating that any resident of Azamor who had been granted the right to live in a building and who had maintained that house in good condition was now the rightful owner of that house and could dispose of it any way he saw fit. The king ordered the *capitão* to proclaim this order publicly so that there would be no disagreements arising from any misunderstandings of the law.[49]

Even after this proclamation, the king remained in possession of substantial properties within the Portuguese-controlled cities. For example, D. Manuel granted a house to Álvaro do Cadaval, the *almoxarife* of Azamor, on 13 September 1518, while river pilots João Fernandes and João Cardenal were each given a house in October 1519. Meanwhile, João Álvares Frazão, a knight, received a house within the keep of Azamor in December 1519. In 1520, Martim Teixeira, a mason, received land that once housed a slaughterhouse before the Portuguese conquest of Azamor. He was granted permission to build a house there.[50]

Houses could build substantial wealth. In 1518, the sale of two houses recorded by the notary of Safi were for the prices of 2,500 and 4,000 *reis*.[51] Upon her death in 1534, Catarina Rodrigues owned several houses in Azamor worth more than 30,000 *reis*. Meanwhile in 1535, the brothers Afonso and Gregório Lopes owned houses in Azamor worth nearly 65,000 *reis*.[52] Homeowners could also earn money by renting out their property. João Rodrigues earned 7500 *reis* for a year's rent on five of his houses in Azamor in 1520, while in 1521 Álvaro Cabral earned 6,000 per year for four of his houses and Diogo Fragoso was paid 4500 per year for three of his houses.[53] It seems that, at least during the early

---

[49] *CM* 28, f. 35v, printed in Fagundes, "Documentos," 150-151.

[50] *CM* 39, f. 106v and *Livro das Ilhas*, f. 167, 230v, 232v. See also *SIHMP*, 2:242n1, 253n4, 266n3, 267n2. Martim Teixiera also served as the *mestre das obras* for the planned construction of a bridge across the Umm al-Rabi` River (see below).

[51] ANTT, Fragmentos, caixa 8, doc. 130, published in Tavim, *Os judeus*, 536-537.

[52] ANTT, CC I, 52, 103 and CC I, 55, 17.

[53] ANTT, CC I, 59, 84; CC II, 93, 15; CC II, 95, 32; CC II, 97, 138.

1520s in Azamor, the typical rental rate for a house was 1,500 *reis* per year or 125 per month.

Non-Military Construction

Although the greatest effort and expense went into building and maintaining defensive structures (see chapter seven), a sizeable amount of construction was necessary to ensure that the functions of government and religion could be carried out. Funding for this construction came almost entirely from the royal treasury. The first priority, however, was always defensive preparations, so government buildings and places of worship were built when time and money allowed, and always after walls and battlements were completed.

Governmental Construction

Construction projects conducted in the name of the king and at the king's expense were overseen by the *vedor das obras*. This man was in charge of acquiring the proper materials for the project, accounting for all expenses, and overseeing and paying the laborers. In fact, the *vedor's* responsibilities were so broad and wide-ranging that they extended to any workers who fell ill. Pedro Álvares de Faria, the *vedor das obras* in Safi in 1516, received three beds from Portugal to be used by any sick workers.[54]

Royal projects needed standard construction items, such as wood, nails, tile, glass, stone, and mortar. Requests for these goods are scattered throughout documentary sources.[55] Additionally, there was need for power. In order to haul heavy goods, the Portuguese used oxen. Vasco Henriques and Rui Pereira transported twenty-four oxen from Portugal to Azamor in 1514, at a cost of 36,000 *reis*.[56] For basic buildings, such as houses and shops, architectural planning appears to

---

[54] ANTT, CC I, 19, 6 and CC II, 63, 147. Among those working beneath the *vedor* was the *recebedor das obras*, who specifically directed the accounting, the *mestre da obra*, who was in charge of a specific project, and the *escrivão das obras* (*SIHMP*, 2:253n4; ANTT, CC I, 20, 105; CC II, 64, 83).

[55] Many examples are cited throughout this portion of the chapter, but other documents include: ANTT, CC I, 26, 63; CC II, 49, 184; CC II, 59, 149; CC II, 67, 24; CC II, 70, 14; "Letter from Afonso Rodrigues to D. Manuel," Santa Cruz, 24 December 1513, *SIHMP*, 1:473. Roof tile (*telha*) appears to have been relatively inexpensive, selling normally for one *real* each (ANTT, CC II, 111, 75).

[56] ANTT, CC II, 59, 164.

have been done by skilled masons and carpenters. More complex designs were executed by architects. For example, when Azamor needed a building in which to store grain (*celeiro*), the famous architect brothers, Francisco and Diogo Arruda, designed it in consultation with the *capitão* of the city, Rui Barreto.[57]

The amount of time and money spent on construction was monumental. For example, from March 1508 to January 1513, the Portuguese in Safi spent over 5,000,000 *reis* on defensive construction and the city's *feitoria*.[58] Despite such massive spending, many projects took years to complete. For example, in Safi in 1516, eight years after the city was first conquered by the Portuguese, the building serving as the courthouse (*audiencia*) was finally completed.[59] Meanwhile, for lack of funds, the *Casa dos Contos* (Treasury House) was still housed in a ruin that was so rickety that people refused to go inside of it during winter storms for fear that it would collapse on them. Nuno Gato, the *contador* of Safi, hoped the king would send money to fund the construction of a new *Casa*.[60]

Once buildings were constructed, they had to be maintained. The documentary record is filled with various indications of this. These include receipts for money paid for lime (*cal*) and for the labor of workers to use the lime to repair walls and buildings, payments for wood and nails, and payments to carpenters and masons.[61] Repairs were not infrequent. In addition to damage done to walls and buildings by periodic Moroccan attacks, especially in Santa Cruz, time and weather were enemies. Less than six years after its initial construction, the customs warehouse of Mazagão had to have its tile roof and

---

[57] "Letter from Rui Barreto to D. Manuel," Azamor, 21 February 1514, *SIHMP*, 1:499; "Letter from Nuno Gato to D. Manuel," Azamor, 5 December 1513, *SIHMP*, 1:455; "Letter from Francisco and Diogo de Arruda to D. Manuel," Azamor, 31 March 1514, *SIHMP*, 1:525-529. The Arrudas were also primarily responsible for initial defensive construction in Safi, Azamor, and Mazagão.

[58] *SIHMP*, 1:300n1.

[59] ANTT, CC II, 64, 88.

[60] "Letter from Nuno Gato to D. Manuel," Safi, 4 July 1516, *SIHMP*, 2:14-15. The envisioned building would be two stories, with a chimney and two windows looking out on the street and another window looking into the customs area where the tithe (the *dízima*) would be assessed. For ease of function, there would be a separate entrance and exit and a separate room in which to store money.

[61] ANTT, CC II, 112, 29; CC II, 58, 102; CC II, 60, 35.

wooden supports almost completely replaced. The supplies necessary came from Azamor's *feitoria*, where they had originally been imported from Portugal.[62]

The lack of proper buildings was common to the Portuguese fortresses. Santa Cruz was apparently in a state of advanced disrepair in late 1513 when Afonso Rodrigues, the new *feitor* arrived. He complained that every house leaked, and that he had to store flour in the church, "where it also rains like out in the street for lack of ceiling tiles." Rodrigues requested that tiles be sent to repair these leaks and that wood be sent to build or enlarge existing structures so that merchandise could be stored easily and Santa Cruz could take its place as an important regional trade center.[63] Even at the late date of 1541, the cathedral in Azamor had to be partitioned to create a granary in part of the nave. Lack of money for repairs to the city's leaky official granary made this the only affordable option.[64]

Docks and piers for boats and ships were another important construction project taken on by the Portuguese. Cities like Azamor and Safi already had preexisting docks that could be repaired and enlarged. In Mazagão and Santa Cruz, these had to be built from scratch. The largest docks were built as close as possible to the custom's house in order to facilitate ocean-going trade.[65] Because Azamor strove to have contacts with the Shawiyya region, to the north across the Umm al-Rabi` River, the city maintained a ferry boat (*barca da passagem*) at royal expense. The ferry was initially used to transport soldiers and horses across the river to conduct raids and, after a peace agreement was signed in 1522, to transport Moroccan traders from Shawiyya to Azamor where they could sell and buy goods. The boat itself was connected to a long rope (*maroma*) used to pull it across the

---

[62] ANTT, CC I, 26, 63. Some tiles may have been made locally in Morocco, but the overwhelming majority were imported from Portugal (see next paragraph).

[63] "Letter from Afonso Rodrigues to D. Manuel," Santa Cruz, 24 December 1513, *SIHMP*, 1:473, 475.

[64] "Order of António Leite," Azamor, 12 April 1541, *SIHMP*, 3:384-385.

[65] "Letter from Simão Correia to D. Manuel," Azamor, 3 October 1516, *SIHMP*, 2:39-40; ANTT, CC II, 94, 172; CC II, 94, 149; CC II, 97, 130.

river. The system of ropes was somewhat expensive. It was completely replaced in June 1523 for a cost of 6,400 *reis*.[66]

Evidently, this method of transportation had become tiresome as early as 1519, because the residents of Azamor considered building a bridge over the river. Upon his arrival in July 1519, the Bishop of Safi found the residents of the city so desirous of a bridge that he personally contributed 100 *cruzados* to the effort. The *capitão* gave another 100 *cruzados*, and many others contributed what they could, including 600 or 700 *cruzados* from the city's Jewish community.[67] In a letter to the king, the bishop argued that the bridge was essential, for with the bridge and two hundred more cavalry it would give the Portuguese the military striking force of five hundred or a thousand additional cavalry then without the bridge. By 1520, the king was convinced that the project was a good idea. He appointed Martim Teixeira as *mestre da obra da ponte* and dispatched excavators and masons to Azamor.[68] It is unclear how much work was actually completed on this bridge, but the project itself was definitively halted at the end of 1522 when the Portuguese concluded a peace agreement with the Shawiyyan tribes who lived across the river. The peace allowed boats to travel across the river in larger numbers and without fear of attack.[69]

Construction involved building things other than large structures. Especially important to life in a semi-arid region like coastal Morocco was a good system of cisterns and fountains. The cities captured by the Portuguese already had cisterns, but the Portuguese constantly needed to maintain them.[70] They also typically improved the

---

[66] ANTT, CC II, 113, 167; CC II, 98, 1; CC II, 98, 3; CC II, 98, 8; CC II, 98, 10; CC II, 99, 113; CC II, 108, 87; CC II, 108, 146; CC II, 113, 128. Most of these references are for payments to carpenters and caulkers (*calafates*; from Ar. a*l-qalafāt*) who repaired the ferry. I have been unable to determine what fee (if any) was charged for passage on the ferry.

[67] "Letter from D. Álvaro de Noronha to D. Manuel," Azamor, 11 July 1519, *SIHMP*, 2:248.

[68] "Letter from the Bishop of Safi to D. Manuel," Azamor, 11 August 1519, *SIHMP*, 2:250-254.

[69] "Peace Agreement with the Shawiyya," n. l., end of 1522, *SIHMP*, 2:303-307; *SIHMP*, 2:253n4.

[70] ANTT, CC II, 59, 149

water delivery system.[71] António Leite, supervising construction in Mazagão in 1517, suggested to the king a very interesting device. He argued that a chamber should be dug, at least 20 hands deep, into which sea water could run. The sea current could then be used to turn a water wheel, likely to be used for grinding grain.[72]

Religious Construction

Religious construction was the final priority for government funding after defensive construction and government buildings. Although God figured as the preeminent justification for expansion into Morocco, building houses for His worship was often ignored. Consequently, preexisting buildings were commandeered for religious use. In both Safi and Azamor, the cities' central mosques were converted into cathedrals immediately after the Portuguese conquests.[73] It was only in 1519, more than ten years after the Portuguese first took control of the city, that construction finally commenced on the cathedral of Safi. D. Nuno Mascarenhas, Safi's *capitão*, reported that financing for the project remained scarce despite its necessity. In the typically hyperbolic manner of a sixteenth-century bureaucrat seeking more funds, he claimed that the Portuguese in Safi "live more like heathens than Christians."[74] In Azamor, no new cathedral was ever built.

Although Portuguese kings did not always have enough money to fund religious construction, they ensured that the proper objects for the celebration of the Mass were supplied to each city. After all, the defense and promotion of Christianity were important duties of the

---

[71] The most famous example is from the northern Moroccan city of Tangiers, where, by the time the Portuguese handed the city over to the British in 1662, they had constructed a system whereby nearly every home and building had running water. See C. R. Boxer, "'Three Sights to be Seen': Bombay, Tangier, and a Barren Queen, 1661-1684," *Portuguese Studies* 3 (1987): 81.

[72] "Letter from António Leite to D. Manuel," Mazagão, 20 October 1517, *SIHMP*, 2:175.

[73] Fagundes, "Documentos," 118-119. There is no indication that the Portuguese modified the architecture of the mosques, rather they seem to have stripped away or covered any Islamic symbols and replaced them with Christian ones.

[74] "Letter from D. Nuno Mascarenhas to D. Manuel," Safi, early 1519, *SIHMP*, 2:224 and "Letter from the Bishop of Safi to D. Manuel," Azamor, 11 August 1519, *SIHMP*, 2:252.

Portuguese kings. This began even before the Portuguese conquered the southern Moroccan cities. Portuguese *feitorias* in allied Safi and Azamor were supplied with priests and religious paraphernalia.[75] After the conquests, the kings supplied the fortresses with numerous objects for the celebration of the Mass, vestments for the priests, curtains, and devotional objects.[76] In November 1514, for instance, King D. Manuel ordered a silk *palio* (a canopy carried over the Sacrament during processions) made in Lisbon to be shipped to the cathedral of Azamor.[77] Incense was supplied from Portugal. In 1517, for example, 20 *arrateis* of incense were delivered to Santa Cruz.[78] Religious objects could also wear out and need replacement, such as the six altar cloths delivered to Santa Cruz in 1534 and the liturgical vestments sent to the cathedral in Safi in the same year.[79] When the fortresses were abandoned, as many of the religious objects as possible were returned to Portugal so as not to be desecrated by Moroccan Muslims.[80]

In addition to churches, D. Manuel hoped to establish monastic communities in all his Moroccan possessions, though he concentrated his efforts in the two largest fortresses: Safi and Azamor.[81] By 1514, in Safi, there was a Franciscan monastery (dedicated to St. Catharine) that was large enough for six or eight brothers, though a larger building, that could house fifty friars, was already under construction.[82] Construction on the larger Franciscan monastery was still in the early stages by 1517. Nuno Gato, the *contador* of Safi, wrote the king asking if the building should be made of stone and lime or stone and clay. The king, wanting a more permanent structure, opted for the more costly stone and lime. Consequently, the

---

[75] "Quittance of Lopo de Azevedo," Lisbon, 7 May 1499, *SIHMP*, 1:46-47.

[76] Fagundes, "Documentos," 130-131 and "Alvará of D. Manuel," Lisbon, 8-23 August 1514, *SIHMP*, 1:598-600.

[77] *DCC*, 129-130.

[78] ANTT, CC I, 22, 74. Twenty *arrateis* is about nine kg.

[79] ANTT, CC I, 54, 24 and CC I, 53, 128.

[80] ANTT, CC I, 70, 115.

[81] By September 1532, the monastery of São Sebastião existed in Santa Cruz (ANTT, CC I, 49, 99 and CC I, 56, 119).

[82] "Letter from Nuno Gato to D. Manuel," Safi, 21 October 1514, *SIHMP*, 1:649-650 and ANTT, CC II, 45, 47.

king permitted Gato to take 60,000 *reis* from tribute receipts in order to fund the building expenses.[83]

D. Manuel had a more ambitious plan for Azamor. He wanted three monasteries. Due to the need to fund defensive and governmental construction, the first monastery, a Franciscan one, was not completed until the early 1530s. Before this, Augustinian and Franciscan monks lived in converted mosques. The Augustinians finally completed a monastery building of their own in 1539.[84] There was no monastery in Santa Cruz until the Franciscans completed one in the late 1520s.[85] Mazagão had no religious houses until after 1542.

Crime and Justice

Crime is a ubiquitous phenomenon in human relations, and the Portuguese-Moroccan frontier was in no way excepted from this truth. Although the *capitão* was the final arbiter of justice within each fortress, a rudimentary system of justice – based on that found in Portugal itself – was in place in these cities to deal with the majority of judicial concerns. The head of this system was the *ouvidor* (chief magistrate). *Ouvidores*, typically educated men of high social status, were appointed by the *capitão* of a city and later confirmed by the king. *Ouvidores* decided both criminal and civil cases and were empowered to order the execution of persons found guilty of capital crimes. Their decisions could be overruled by the *capitão*, but this rarely occurred.[86]

Another prominent judicial official was the *juíz dos órfãos*, a probate judge who also, as his title implies, had authority over orphans. He ensured that orphans received any due inheritance and that they were educated until age fourteen for boys and age twelve for girls. His permission was required should an orphan in his charge wish to marry, under eighteen for girls and under twenty-five for boys.[87] Because the Portuguese population in Morocco was rather small, the offices of

---

[83] "Alvará of D. Manuel," Lisbon, 11 January 1517, *SIHMP*, 2:57.

[84] "Letter from the Nobles and Residents of Azamor to D. João III," Azamor, 20 March 1540, *SIHMP*, 3:241-242.

[85] Robert Ricard, "L'Évêché de Safi (1487?-1542)," *SIHMP*, 3:81-82.

[86] *SIHMP*, 2:379n1. See also ANTT, CC I, 27, 68; CC I, 68, 94; CC II, 123, 112.

[87] See Coates, 122-124, for a discussion of the *juíz dos órfãos*.

ouvidor and *juíz dos órfãos* were often held by the same man.[88] Beneath these men was a group of bureaucratic officials. The most important were the notaries (*tabeliães*) and the scribes (*escrivães*) who recorded legal proceedings and legal documents.[89] There were also bailiffs (*meirinhos*), investigators (*inquiridores*), and jailers (*carcereiros*).[90]

Judicial positions were filled rapidly following the establishment of Portuguese control over a Moroccan city. João de Abreu was the *ouvidor* of Safi from at least October 1511.[91] By 1513, Safi had several "judges" in the city.[92] Martinho de Aguiar is listed as the *ouvidor* in Azamor on 26 September 1514.[93] Artur Golaio was confirmed as a notary in Azamor less than six weeks after the city was seized by the Portuguese.[94] When an official needed to be replaced, the *capitão* often appointed a prominent man already residing in Morocco. For instance, Luis Gonçalves Bocarro, a knight who had been serving in Safi from at least 1527, became the *ouvidor* of Safi by 1537.[95]

Crimes

The criminal activities in Morocco were, of course, both non-violent and violent. Examples of non-violent crimes are rare in the surviving documentation; perhaps they were viewed as not worth

---

[88] See the example of Diogo Fragoso in Azamor in 1517 (ANTT, CC I, 21, 100 and "Letter from Simão Correia to D. Manuel," Azamor, 20 May 1517, *SIHMP*, 2:87). This lack of population meant that the judicial system in Morocco was never articulated beyond this. This state of affairs is in contrast with Brazil where, in 1549, about 16 years after the first *ouvidores* were appointed in the captaincies, a royally-appointed *ouvidor geral* arrived in order to oversee the conduct of the local *ouvidores* (Harold Johnson and Maria Beatriz Nizza da Silva, *O império luso-brasileiro, 1500-1620* (Lisbon: Editorial Estampa, 1992), 364. In Morocco, either the *capitães* or the king himself conducted the oversight.

[89] See the section on notaries in chapter two. See also, ANTT, NA 883, 884; CC II, 169, 113; CC I, 57, 6. The subject of the role of notaries in Portuguese fortresses needs to be explored in greater detail.

[90] *GTT*, 10:424; ANTT, CdGA, 126; CC I, 68, 94; CC II, 52, 93; CC II, 65, 114.

[91] ANTT, NA 597, 22v.

[92] "Letter patent of D. Manuel," Lisbon, 2 July 1513, *SIHMP*, 1:393.

[93] ANTT, CC II, 51, 129.

[94] *CM* 42, f. 129v, mentioned in *SIHMP*, 1:401n3.

[95] "Letter from Garcia de Melo to D. João III," Safi, 9 July 1527, *SIHMP*, 2:409 and "Proclamation of the Peace of Safi," Safi, 25 April 1537, *SIHMP*, 3:100, 102.

reporting in most cases. One incident that was reported involved one Gomes Aranha and an unnamed accomplice who were caught making and selling forged documents (*certidões falsas*) of some sort. They were arrested in Azamor in 1514 and returned to Portugal for judgment. It was, in fact, fortunate they were caught because their counterfeiting was of "such subtle art."[96]

In 1523, Fernão Gonçalves, *ouvidor* of Azamor, heard a case to determine whether or not Francisco Gomes, the *recebedor de alfandega* (a customs official), should or should not be held liable for a debt, because the goods that he planned to sell in order to pay that debt were aboard a Portuguese ship that was robbed by French pirates. The conclusion of the court was that Gomes was the victim of malicious circumstance and that he would be excused from paying the debt until he could arrange another shipment of goods.[97]

The evidence of violent crime (since the Portuguese did not view their raiding activity as criminal) in Portuguese Morocco is not as strong as one might expect. Two reasons can be given for this: either the rate of violent crime was actually very low or, more likely, such crimes were simply common and normal, and therefore not commented on much in the available sources. The second possibility seems most likely, for the sources do hint at larger patterns of violence.

One of the most common violent acts was the rape of non-slave women.[98] For example, in 1529 a Muslim man named Asuya arrived at Santa Cruz with a "very beautiful" (*mutia fermoza*) Muslim woman, who does not seem to have been his wife and is described by the chronicler as having been "*furtada*" (stolen/kidnapped). The *capitão* of Santa Cruz, António Leitão de Gamboa, probably already planning the rape, did not allow the two to sleep in the same room, and later that

---

[96] "Letter from António Leite to D. Manuel," Azamor, 27 July 1514, *SIHMP*, 1:583; ANTT, CC II, 50, 31. Why they were not judged in Azamor is unclear, though it may have something to do with intense royal concern over counterfeiting of any sort. The *Ordenações Manuelinas* stated that those who counterfeited money were to be burnt and all their goods confiscated – this applied to all levels of society without exception – and those who knowingly used counterfeit currency would either be executed and have their goods confiscated or be exiled for life to São Tomé, depending on how much money they had spent before being caught.

[97] ANTT, Gaveta XX, 5, 16, published in *GTT*, 10:421-424.

[98] As seen in chapter eight, the sexual use of slave women was considered licit by both Portuguese and Moroccan societies.

night, he raped the woman. In the morning, the woman told Asuya what had happened, and he swore to kill the *capitão*. The next night, Leitão raped the woman again, but this time, after he had fallen asleep, she opened the door to his bedroom, and Asuya came in and stabbed him to death. After the murder, the two escaped and were never caught.[99]

Rape was also something that Moroccan men perpetrated on Moroccan women. The only examples of this, however, came during periods of great instability and in the context of military raids. In other words, rape was used as a war tactic. In 1507, when the Moroccan leadership of Safi was in question, the Portuguese, under the command of Diogo de Azambuja, and their then ally, `Ali bin Washman, allowed the Beni Maker tribe to invade the city and terrorize those opposed to Washman. This terror included the sacking of homes and the mass rape of women and girls. In 1515, during the period of extreme instability following the Portuguese defeat at Mamora, chaos and intertribal warfare led to a series of violent acts, including rape.[100] Does this mean rape of Moroccan women by Moroccan men did not happen except during military encounters? Probably it did, as rape is notoriously under-reported, but there is no overt evidence to demonstrate this. Still, Moroccan notions of honor would have precipitated a blood feud should a rape have occurred. This powerful consequence may have been a strong mitigating factor limiting rape to wartime.[101]

---

[99] *CSC*, 44-6; Figanier, 127. Figanier describes the attacks on this woman in a very prim manner: "*Os dois* [Leitão and the woman] *entenderam-se e, uma noite, a moura abria a porta do quarto onde o Capitão já adormecera; o companheiro entrou e matou-o com quarto ou cinco agomiadas, depois do que fugiram ambos pela janela . . . .*" (Figanier, 127). Note how Figanier's description of the events tacitly accuses the woman of an act of treachery.

[100] "Letter from the Inhabitants of Safi to D. Manuel," Safi, 13 August 1507, *SIHMP*, 1:136-138; "La conquête de Safi par les portugais, 1508," *SIHMP*, 157; "Letter from the Inhabitants of Safi to D. Manuel," Safi, 2 July 1509, *SIHMP*, 180, 193; "Proclamation of Nuno Fernandes de Ataíde to the Tribes," n. l., after 19 September 1515, *SIHMP*, 1:759-760.

[101] See Raymond Jamous, *Honneur et baraka: Les structures sociales traditionnelles dans le Rif* (New York: Cambridge University Press, 1981), 65-97 and Pierre Bourdieu, *Outline of a Theory of Practice*, trans. Richard Nice (New York: Cambridge University Press, 1997), 60-61. On a related note, I have been unable to find any accounts of non-slave Portuguese women being raped, either by Portuguese or Moroccan men.

Another violent crime for which there is evidence is murder. With the exception of what seems to be a straight revenge killing of António Leitão de Gamboa, mentioned above, the three murders for which there is evidence appear to have been politically motivated. The first is the murder of Moses Dardeiro, a Jew who worked as an interpreter and negotiator for the Portuguese from 1509 until his murder in December 1512. It is unclear who murdered him. Two parties were accused: Yahya-u-Ta`fuft, the *alcaide dos mouros* of Dukkala, and the leaders of Almedina. If Yahya were guilty, he did it because Dardeiro allegedly was spying on him and reporting that he was carrying out illegal and treasonous activities without the knowledge of the Portuguese. If the leaders of Almedina were guilty, they had killed him to make it look like Yahya was guilty so that they could accuse Yahya and have him and his style of overbearing leadership removed by his Portuguese masters.[102] Yahya-u-Ta`fuft himself was murdered in 1518 as the result of a conspiracy involving several Moroccan tribes. In 1519, an unnamed *alcaide dos mouros* was murdered as an act of political rebellion by the Awlad `Amran tribe. These latter two cases are discussed in chapter six.

Punishments

Criminals, when arrested and convicted, are inevitably punished. When meted out by the Portuguese, these punishments did not differ greatly from that seen in Portugal during the same period. The punishment of criminals normally had a corporal component, primarily whipping, maiming, or execution. The *Ordenações Manuelinas*, a compendium of laws in effect during the reign of D. Manuel and beyond, lists the punishments prescribed for various crimes. For example, anyone found in Lisbon or the royal court after vespers and carrying a loaded crossbow was to be imprisoned, fined 4,000 *reis*, publicly whipped, and then exiled to the island of São Tomé for two years, unless he was of elite status whereupon he would be spared the whip, but exiled for three years. If anyone actually fired a weapon in a royal palace, he would have one hand cut off, unless he was an extremely high-ranking noble (*fidalgo de solar, ou de cota d'armas*) who would be sentenced to overseas exile for four years. Injuring judicial or

---

[102] Tavim, *Os judeus*, 376-378; Racine, "Service and Honor," 77-78.

royal officials and bureaucrats or threatening and injuring witnesses resulted in having a hand cut off and a ten-year exile to Africa. Thieves who stole something worth more than one silver mark were punished by death, while someone who broke into a house but could not be proven to have stolen anything was publicly whipped and exiled for life to São Tomé. Those who stole something valued between 400 *reis* and one mark were to be whipped and have their ears cut off. Anyone from any sector of society found guilty of sodomy could be burnt at the stake. Those guilty of incest with close family members would be burnt, while those convicted of having sex with someone outside the nuclear family were exiled to North Africa for ten years. Finally, any man who raped a woman, so long as she was not a slave or a prostitute, would be executed.[103] These examples give a flavor of the sort of punishments meted out by Portuguese justice, though the letter of the law and its practice could and did diverge.

How were these forms of physical and monetary punishment transferred to the administration of Moroccans? Under traditional Moroccan law, it seems that, except for extremely violent crimes, such as murder and rape, criminals were punished only with fines or, if they did not have enough coin, the seizure of goods.[104] This is borne out by the recommendation of D. Álvaro de Noronha, *capitão* of Azamor, evidently replying to a letter – no longer extant – from King D. Manuel establishing punishments for crimes committed by Muslims while under Portuguese jurisdiction. Noronha said that, according to local custom, people were punished for their crimes by fines or confiscation of goods, and that physical punishment, such as the cutting off of ears or whipping, is more "scandalous" to them than confiscating an offender's entire wealth.[105]

This is a prime example of a Portuguese commander attempting to maintain power over subjected Moroccans by appeasing

---

[103] See volume V, *passim* of the *Ordenações Manuelinas* for numerous examples. Those cited here come from V, VI; V, X, 5-6, 9; V, XII; V, XIII; V, XIIII; V, XXXVIII, 1-2. See also Coates, 26.

[104] See the two *qanūns* of Yahya-u-Ta'fuft issued in 1512, published in both Arabic and French in *SIHMP*, 1:316-329. For a brief analysis and historical background to these ordinances as well as their full texts, see also P. Gros, "Deux kanouns marocains du début du XVIe siècle," *Hespéris* 18 (1934): 64-75.

[105] "Letter from D. Álvaro de Noronha to D. Manuel," Azamor, 12 April 1519 [or 1521], *SIHMP*, 2:238.

some of their cultural sensibilities. Although the religious status of Moroccan Muslims as infidels would have "allowed" Portuguese Christians to treat them with the most outrageous violence possible, the widespread application of this assumption would have caused a state of great instability in Portuguese-controlled Morocco.[106] Success in a frontier zone, where several cultures mix within contested space, requires attempts at understanding and accommodating at least some of the less-dominant culture's needs (see chapter six).

Nevertheless, executions of Moroccans by Portuguese were fully permitted by Portuguese kings, so long as the Moroccans had committed a capital crime. As detailed in chapter eight, D. Nuno Mascarenhas had executed Muslims for robbery and kidnapping.[107] In another instance, Nuno Fernandes de Ataíde caught a Moroccan stealing thirty of the one hundred camel-loads of barley that he was transporting to Safi to pay the tribute for his village. Ataíde says that while he had the right to hang the offender, he let him live in the hope that he would bring the grain to Safi soon. Nothing more is said on the matter, but the threat of execution should the grain not arrive in a timely manner remained.[108]

Finally, Portuguese *capitães* sometimes took it upon themselves to interpret punishments in the most profitable way. In 1525, Gonçalo Mendes Sacoto, the *capitão* of Safi, captured "certain Muslims" who had once been Christian but had apostatized. This vague description is all that is known of these Muslims, who may have been Portuguese *mouriscos* who moved to North Africa or may have been captives who converted to Christianity and later escaped. Mendes decided that, instead of executing these apostates as he legally had the right to do, he would instead sell them as slaves and use the profits from the sale for pious works in the city. He realized 110,000 *reis* from the sale and used it on construction of the cathedral and other "necessities." Garcia de

---

[106] David Nirenberg, *Communities of Violence: Persecution of Minorities in the Middle Ages* (Princeton: Princeton University Press, 1996), 31.

[107] "Letter from D. Nuno Mascarenhas to D. Manuel," Safi, 11 March 1517, *SIHMP*, 2:65.

[108] "Letter from Nuno Fernandes de Ataíde to D. Manuel," Safi, 12 December 1514, *SIHMP*, 1:661.

Melo, the man who replaced Mendes as *capitão* of Safi in 1526, reported on this action of Mendes' and concluded that it "seemed just" to him.[109]

Conflict Resolution

But the Portuguese judiciary was not used exclusively to punish. Inherent in the execution of judicial action is conflict resolution.[110] On a smaller scale, it prevents crime from spiraling into an endless series of vigilante revenge killings; on a larger scale, it can preserve peace and prevent war. Just such a situation occurred in southern Morocco in the mid-1520s.

In late 1524, Sharif Ahmed al-A`raj negotiated a truce with the *capitães* of Safi and Azamor, building on the success of a three-month truce concluded in September 1523.[111] Pero Machado and rabbi Abraham Rute negotiated the 1524 peace. Despite the peace, two servants of the Sharif had been captured by people from Azamor and sent to Portugal as slaves. Meanwhile, some Portuguese from Safi had stolen cattle belonging to the Sharif's allies and sold them to Azamor. Consequently, the 1524 peace was extremely short-lived.

A second peace, negotiated in late 1525 by Ibrahim Benzamiro, had similar problems. According to the Sharif, the people of Azamor had attacked a caravan, capturing the men and taking the goods (mainly beeswax) and all the animals. The *capitão* of Safi attacked another caravan, resulting in the deaths of all the caravan traders. Moreover, he had, in further violation of the truce, enslaved allies of the Sharif and sent them to Portugal. In short, the Sharif said that if D. João III wanted this peace to last, he needed to punish the perpetrators of these crimes and pay restitution for property losses.

Furthermore, the Sharif requested that the king send a judge to Safi to investigate the criminals and dispense royal justice. The Sharif probably had something in mind similar to the Granadan *al-qādi bayna-l-mulūk*, who heard only complaints of Christians against Muslims, and the Castilian *alcaldes entre los cristianos y los moros*, sometimes called *jueces de las querellas*, who heard complaints of Muslims against Christians. These

---

[109] ANTT, Gavetas XX, 4, 24, in *GTT*, 10:391.

[110] Julius R. Ruff, *Violence in Early Modern Europe, 1500-1800* (New York: Cambridge University Press, 2001), 73-74.

[111] *SIHMP*, 2:351n1.

institutions developed along the Castilian-Granadan frontier to prevent trans-frontier reprisals and vendettas.[112]

It does not appear that D. João III dispatched a judge to southern Morocco; furthermore, the lack of evidence for any sort of extended judicial oversight of frontier relations – other than by the *capitães* themselves – indicates that nothing similar to the Castilian-Granadan model was ever established. D. João III did, however, remove Gonçalo Mendes Sacoto as *capitão* of Safi and replaced him with Garcia de Melo. Moreover, he ordered the new *capitão* to compensate the Sharif's allies for their loses. This amounted to approximately 3,000 *reis* as well as the lives of seven men. Because three men had been killed during raids and four others captured and later sold to Castile, it was impossible to return the same seven men. Consequently, Garcia de Melo simply replaced them with seven enslaved Muslims currently residing in Safi. Apparently this was enough to satisfy the Sharif, for he agreed to a revised peace, as negotiated by Ibrahim Benzamiro, in 1526.[113]

Portuguese kings dispensed justice against their representatives in Morocco not only to improve relations with Moroccan leaders but also to address grievances and maintain order among the Portuguese population itself. The first hint that the king had that something was amiss with one of his officials was typically a letter sent from Morocco. Normally, these letters came from high-ranking officials (the *capitão*, *contador*, *feitor*, *almoxarife*, or *adail*), nobles, knights, and sometimes, merchants. Letters might also come from non-Portuguese, typically elite Moroccan allies or Jews serving in important positions such as interpreters. Not all of these complaints were believed, but when they were, the king normally sent a man to investigate the issue, or even

---

[112] José Enrique López de Coca Castañer, "Institutions on the Castilian-Granadan Frontier, 1369-1482," in *MFS*, 145-147 and Angus MacKay, *Spain in the Middle Ages: From Frontier to Empire, 1000-1500* (London: 1977), 198-199.

[113] "Letter from Mawlay Ahmed al-A`raj to D. João III," n. l., 10 December 1525, *SIHMP*, 2:351-353; ANTT, Gavetas XX, 4, 24, in *GTT*, 10:391; "Letter from Mawlay Ahmed al-A`raj to Garcia de Melo," n. l., 10 September 1526, *SIHMP*, 2:357-358. Compare the similarities between the royal response to this incident and to the massacres committed by Luís de Sacoto, discussed chapter seven, and by D. Rodrigo de Castro, discussed below.

called the accused to Portugal to discuss the charges.[114] If the charges were concluded to be true, then the punishment ranged from removal from office to exile.

In one instance, João Lopes de Alvim, *feitor*, and Cristóvão de Almeida, *escrivão de feitoria*, wrote to D. Manuel in December 1507 to complain about the poor way in which Diogo de Azambuja governed the recently-captured city of Safi. They claimed that Azambuja did not administer justice properly and that the city remained depopulated of Moroccans because of his unfair leadership.[115] In this case, the complaint had little effect. The situation in Safi was too volatile for D. Manuel to replace the wily Azambuja, who had established the important Portuguese trading post of São Jorge da Mina in Guinea in 1482. Azambuja remained the *capitão* of Safi until the summer of 1509.[116]

Simão Correia, the *capitão* of Azamor, was accused in 1517 of several irregularities by Duarte Alcoforado, a member of the city's garrison. According to Alcoforado, Correia had pilfered the fortresses' grain supply for himself and his closest associates during a period when grain was scarce and prices were high. On another occasion, the son of a Moroccan sheikh had converted to Christianity and moved to Azamor. Instead of seeing this as a victory against Islam to be celebrated, a greedy and opportunistic Correia allegedly enslaved the man and sold him to Castilians. Alcoforado asked that the king send someone to investigate these crimes. It is unclear if such an investigation was ever conducted, but Correia was replaced as *capitão* within four months.[117]

Vicêncio Ambrum, the *feitor* and *almoxarife* of Santa Cruz, was accused of financial malfeasance of some sort, most likely embezzlement. D. João III requested that an inquiry be made into his account books. The inquiry found that Ambrum had committed a

---

[114] Among those called to Portugal was Yahya-u-Ta`fuft, the *alcaide dos mouros* of Dukkala. For a full account of this episode, see Racine, "Service and Honor," 76-82.

[115] "Letter from João Lopes de Alvim and Cristóvão de Almeida to D. Manuel," Safi, 25 December 1507, *SIHMP*, 1:146.

[116] *SIHMP*, 1:159n4 and Bailey W. Diffie and George D. Winius, *Foundations of the Portuguese Empire, 1415-1580* (Minneapolis: University of Minnesota Press, 1977), 154.

[117] ANTT, CC I, 22, 55, printed in Fagundes, "Documentos," 142-145. Also see the table printed in Fagundes between pages 124 and 125.

crime. He was sentenced in 1531 to four years' exile in sub-Saharan Africa. Later, for reasons unclear, the king pardoned Ambrum. He was then reinstated as *feitor* and *almoxarife* of Santa Cruz in 1534. He continued to serve in these capacities until at least August 1540.[118]

At the end of June 1541, D. Rodrigo de Castro, the *capitão* of Safi, embarked on a raid of a large encampment of Moroccans a few leagues from the city. His purpose was to inflict as much damage on allies of the Sharif as possible in order to avenge what he wrongly believed had been a slaughter of the Portuguese women and children in Santa Cruz when it was captured. To this end, he and his men descended on the encampment and purposefully targeted the women and children there for massacre. He described the scene: "We killed four hundred people, most of them women and children . . . and, *when we tired of killing*, we captured eighty souls." Shortly after this raid, a group of residents of Safi wrote to D. João III and asked him to relieve D. Rodrigo of his office. They were unconcerned with the morality of the massacre. Instead, they charged that the *capitão* had so hastily organized the raid that lack of provisions caused several Portuguese to die from dehydration and the intense heat of Morocco in late June. Although it is difficult to say for certain, it seems that D. João III believed these accusations. At the end of 1541, the king replaced D. Rodrigo with Luís de Loureiro, who served as *capitão* just long enough to complete the abandonment of the city in early 1542.[119]

Conclusion

This chapter has highlighted issues that political and military historians of the Portuguese presence in Morocco have largely ignored. The issues examined herein are the mundane structural elements that make conquests and frontier settlement possible after the initial military

---

[118] ANTT, CC I, 43, 42; CC I, 68, 4; *CJ, Perdões e legitimações*, 9, f. 219v; *CJ*, 19, 223-223v, published in Figanier, 324-325 and 333-335.

[119] "Letter from D. Rodrigo de Castro to D. João III," Safi, 8 July 1541, *SIHMP*, 3:454-463 (emphasis mine); "Letter from Various Residents of Safi to D. João III against D. Rodrigo de Castro," Safi, 9 July 1541, *SIHMP*, 3:464-467; Durval R. Pires de Lima, *História da dominação portuguêsa em Çafim (1506-1542)* (Lisbon: 1930), 101, 103. The massacre is mentioned in Charles R. Boxer, *Women in Iberian Expansion Overseas, 1415-1815: Some Facts, Fancies and Personalities* (New York: Oxford University Press, 1975), 15.

intrusions. The complexity of maintaining a frontier outpost should never be underestimated or reduced to military success or failure.[120]

The Portuguese occupation of southern Morocco was an expensive undertaking. Although itemized budgets in the modern sense did not exist in the early sixteenth century, we can estimate what this expansionist project might have cost the royal treasury. First, purchasing and shipping wheat from Portugal, Andaluzia, the Azores, and elsewhere cost about 7 *reis* per kg (using calculations discussed above). Consequently, importing the not unusual amount of 100,000 kg of wheat per year cost 700,000 *reis*, while in an extraordinary year when 500,000 kg was imported, it cost the royal treasury 3,500,000 *reis*. Annual construction costs, especially in the initial years, probably ran between one and three million *reis*, at least in the large cities of Azamor and Safi.[121] Added to this were *moradia* (living allowance) payments that often attained millions of *reis* per year, as well as salaries for soldiers and royal officials that were between 4 and 6 million *reis* per year.[122] Therefore, in a year when no grain was imported and construction and repair costs were minimal, a large city like Azamor or Safi might expend 5 to 7 million *reis*. In a year when large amounts of grain are imported and construction costs were high, the annual expenditures might rise above 10 million *reis*. If then, we use an average of 7 million *reis* per year for Azamor and Safi and 3.5 million *reis* per year for the smaller cities of Mazagão and Santa Cruz, the total expended from 1508 through 1542 is a staggering 650 million *reis*.

Anecdotal evidence claims that the Moroccan fortresses were always a drain on royal resources. Was this true? For the three years, 1514, 1515, and 1516, the *feitoria* of Azamor collected 151,423 *reis* in duties on merchandise entering or leaving the city, 1,175,700 *reis* in

---

[120] Another factor is the ability of the frontiersmen to reach accommodation with the local inhabitants. See chapters three and (especially) six for more on this issue.

[121] Housing grants in Azamor in 1516 alone cost approximately 1.3 million *reis* (see above). The Portuguese in Safi spent at least 5 million *reis* in a five-year period from 1508-1513 (see above).

[122] An average of 250 people collected *moradia* payments in Azamor, with the payments averaging 8,000 *reis* and 48 *alqueires* (538 kg) of grain per year (Fagundes, 113; ANTT, CC II, 19, 12; CC II, 21, 49; CC II, 23, 45; CC II, 34, 126; CC II, 42, 176; CC II, 70, 134; CC II, 71, 30; CC II, 96, 181; CC II, 108, 71; CC II, 108, 109; NA 137; NA 138; CC II, 236, 83; CC II, 236, 84; CC II, 236, 89; CC II, 236, 112; CC II, 236, 124). Salary calculation's can be found in chapter two.

customs fees, and 265,108 *reis* from the sale of fish. The *feitor* also collected 10.5 million *reis* for the sale of royal merchandise, though how much of this is profit is unclear. These numbers add to 12,092,230 *reis*, or just over 4 million per year on average.[123] In other words, Azamor was operating at a loss of at least 1 million *reis* per year during this period. By 1535, the annual operating deficits were too great for the royal treasury to sustain. In March of that year, D. João III secured a loan for 10,000 *cruzados* (4,000,000 *reis*) from his bankers using gold from São Jorge da Mina as collateral. All of this money was used immediately to pay backlogs on salaries and other expenses in Azamor and Safi.[124]

Nevertheless, the money spent by Portuguese kings in southern Morocco demonstrates that they did as much as possible to ensure the success of their fortresses. As of 1535, D. João III was not ready to abandon these fortresses. Still, only six years later, the inability to fund all necessary expenses eventually led to the capture of one fortress and the abandonment of two others in southern Morocco. As the Sa`adids increased in strength and accumulated more powerful and more accurate weapons, the only way for the Portuguese to maintain their fortresses was to modernize their defenses and maintain larger garrisons. The success of the modernization of Mazagão's walls, enabling the Portuguese to maintain this enclave until 1769, demonstrates that when the crown was willing, it could maintain at least the enclaves, if not the surrounding territory, that it had already taken. In the end, however, it simply was impossible for the Portuguese treasury to fund a widespread colonization project in southern Morocco.

The frontier had pushed back.

---

[123] Anselmo Braamcamp Freire, "Cartas da quitação de D. Manuel," in *Arquivo Histórico Português*, 4:239-240.

[124] John Vogt, *Portuguese Rule on the Gold Coast, 1469-1682* (Athens, GA: University of Georgia, 1979), 92. At least 5,000 *cruzados* were sent to Azamor alone in August 1535 to pay back salaries and other expenses (ANTT, CC I, 55, 129).

Table 4.1: Wheat Imports in kilograms (662 kg = one *moio* of wheat)[125]

YEAR	Azamor	Mazagão	Safi	Santa Cruz
1514			195,290	
1515	143,654[126]			
1516	135,710[127]			140,344
1517	475,316	87,053		
1520	230,376	92,680	334,972	50,974
1521	369,396	141,668		
1522			181,388	219,122
1523			108,567	88,707
1524			54,946	
1525	153,584		133,724	
1530	Unknown Quantity			
1533	350,000[128]			
1535				41,044
1536	516,360			
1538	129,090			
1539	188,670			
1540	Unknown Quantity		52,960	
1541	564,355			

---

[125] Note that other foodstuffs were imported but are not listed here. These include: rye, lentils, and hard tack. Sources for Table 4.1: Fagundes, "Documentos," Tables II and III (between pages 120 and 121); *SIHMP*, 2:176-177, 3:259; ANTT, CC I, 56, 75; CC II, 44, 98; CC II, 50, 1; CC II, 50, 33; CC II, 58, 122; CC II, 63, 21; CC II, 63, 159; CC II, 64, 3; CC II, 66, 70; CC II, 66, 100; CC II, 91, 107; CC II, 91, 122; CC II, 92, 47; CC II, 92, 90; CC II, 92, 119; CC II, 93, 16; CC II, 93, 17; CC II, 93, 32; CC II, 93, 81; CC II, 93, 90; CC II, 93, 98; CC II, 94, 53; CC II, 94, 86; CC II, 98, 41; CC II, 98, 60; CC II, 104, 6; CC II, 104, 24; CC II, 104, 83; CC II, 104, 122; CC II, 105, 16; CC II, 108, 122; CC II, 109, 111; CC II, 110, 68; CC II, 120, 152; CC II, 124, 102; CC II, 125, 84. Note: Based on the fragmentary nature of surviving documentation, this table more than likely does not account for all wheat imports.

[126] 11,234 kg of this amount was surplus wheat sent from Safi (ANTT, CC II, 58, 122).

[127] This entire amount was surplus wheat sent from Safi (ANTT, CC II, 63, 21; II, 63, 159; CC II, 64,3).

[128] This number is based on a guess by Fagundes.

Chapter Five: Trade and Economy

TRADE was a central reason the Portuguese allied with, built, or captured cities in Morocco. There were three main forms of trade that dominated Portuguese commercial interest in southern Morocco. First, the Portuguese often purchased wheat and other grains in the region. In 1438, D. Duarte authorized Portuguese to sell goods to Moroccans so long as they received wheat and other grains in return. In 1455, D. Afonso V authorized a pair of merchants to buy wheat in Safi, Salé, and Al-Anfa.[1] Recall from chapter one that a central reason that the Portuguese attacked Al-Anfa in the late 1460s was that the city had prohibited Portuguese merchants from purchasing grain there. Second, the Portuguese sold manufactured goods (especially cloth) to Moroccans in order to secure gold and silver currency. Finally, the Portuguese purchased Moroccan goods (especially textiles) to use in their trade for slaves in sub-Saharan Africa. As their power expanded in southern Morocco, the Portuguese used monopoly restrictions and violent intimidation to ensure that commercial conditions were as favorable to them as possible.[2]

Southern Morocco had long been known for its abundance of goods. Duarte Pacheco Pereira, in his *Esmeraldo de Situ Orbis* (c. 1506), summarized the Portuguese interest in these areas. The Wadi Sebu River entering the sea at Mamora led to a highly fertile plane where many cattle were raised and extensive crops harvested. Moreover, about one league inland from the mouth of the river there was an island that provided much firewood. The land near Salé was also very fertile, providing "grain, meat, fish, and honey, and many other good things, and many good horses." The Umm al-Rabi` river flowing by Azamor

---

[1] Paulo Drumond Braga, "A expansão no norte de África," in A. H. de Oliveira Marques, ed., *A expansão quatrocentista* (Lisbon: Editorial Estampa, 1998), 309.

[2] For a good brief account of the development of the Portuguese (and Castilian) Atlantic trading systems, see Kenneth Maxwell, "Portugal, Europe, and the Origins of the Atlantic Commercial System, 1415-1520," *Portuguese Studies* 8 (1992): 3-16.

provided "marvelous fishing," yielding large numbers of shad, while Azamor itself and its surrounding lands were described as "well supplied with grain, meat, fish, and many other things." Pereira described the entire Dukkala region as "a land of great fertility for grain and meat." The territory between Azamor and Safi provided wheat and barley, a great abundance of meat and game, and the sea provided fine fishing. Pereira considered Safi one of the best trading locations, with the usual abundance of grain, meat, and fish, but it also provided fine horses, gold brought from Guinea, "hides of all kinds," honey, and beeswax, among other things. Pereira described the recently-completed fortress of Santa Cruz in terms similar to Safi, taking care to emphasize Guinea gold in the region. Massa, fifty kilometers south of Santa Cruz at the mouth of the Wadi Massa, served as an emporium for goods brought to the city by the residents of the High Atlas. These goods included grain, fruit, honey, beeswax, as well as iron, copper, and hides.[3] Oddly, Pereira neglected to mention any textile production, though his contemporary, Valentim Fernandes, highlighted Azamor and Safi as important sources of cloth and clothing. Fernandes also added that in the region around Santa Cruz dyes like indigo and red and black lacar were especially plentiful and that Safi provided a good supply of gum arabic.[4]

In order for the Christian Portuguese to secure these goods, both before and after their conquest activities, they had to trade with Muslims and Jews. Trade between the three religions was certainly nothing new for any of the parties involved. Jews and Muslims living in Portugal until 1497 were involved in various forms of commercial activity from international trade to artisanal activity to agriculture. For example, in the early fifteenth century, Portuguese Muslims comprised more than 30% of producers of raisins and dried figs in the Algarve.[5] The Portuguese also maintained extensive trade links with the kingdom

---

[3] Duarte Pacheco Pereira, *Esmeraldo de Situ Orbis* ed. Damião Peres (Lisbon, 1988), chaps. 15-21. *Esmeraldo* is also available in the English translation of George H. T. Kimble (London: Hakluyt Society, 1937).

[4] Vitorino de Magalhães Godinho, "Ceuta e Marrocos," in Idem, *A economia dos descobrimentos henriquinos* (Lisbon: Livraria Sá da Costa, 1962), 113.

[5] Manuela Santos Silva, "Para o estudo da produção frutícola do concelho de Loulé (Os 'Livros de Repartição da Fruta' do século XV)," in *Actas da III jornadas de história medieval do Algarve e Andaluzia* (Loulé: Câmara Municipal de Loulé, 1989), 258.

of Granada until its final destruction in 1492. Portuguese trade with Morocco was also extensive, with Moroccans often exchanging gold coins for fruit grown in the Portuguese Algarve. In years of poor harvests for Morocco, Portuguese merchants often acted as middlemen, purchasing grain from northern Europe and transporting it to Morocco. Such was the case, in fact, in 1414, one year before the conquest of Ceuta.[6]

If the only trade desired was a transfer of goods between Morocco and Portugal, the extensive Portuguese conquests, especially in southern Morocco, would have been unnecessary. However, the Portuguese were interested in two larger goals: 1) obtaining substantial quantities of goods that could be traded in sub-Saharan Africa for gold and slaves and 2) preventing Castile from expanding into Morocco and the rest of Africa after 1492. The long-term plan was to enrich the Portuguese crown by preventing any maritime competition. The plan worked brilliantly for a time. Fortunately for the Portuguese, the Castilians were distracted by their expansion into the Americas or a large-scale trade war may have developed between the two kingdoms.

In light of these foregoing considerations, this chapter is divided into two parts. Part one discusses the commercial infrastructure inside each of the Portuguese fortresses in southern Morocco and the mechanisms used by the Portuguese to maintain their dominant commercial position along the Moroccan coast. Part two examines in detail some of the commodities traded by and with the Portuguese in Morocco. Where possible, Jewish and Moroccan mercantile activities are discussed, though the primary focus of this chapter is Portuguese commerce.

Infrastructure

The trading infrastructure within the Portuguese fortresses consisted of two main parts: the *feitoria* and the *alfândega*. The *feitoria* oversaw the transfer and sale of all goods between the king and local merchants, whether they were Portuguese (or European), Jewish, or Moroccan. The *feitor* purchased necessary goods from local merchants

---

[6] Magalhães Godinho, "Ceuta e Marrocos," 111. See also, Gomes Eanes de Zurara, *Crónica do Conde D. Pedro de Meneses*, ed. and intro. Maria Teresa Brocardo (Lisbon: Calouste Gulbenkian Foundation, 1997), chap. LXXXI (pp. 524-525).

and then exported them to their destinations beyond Morocco. He also took orders from local merchants and concluded both short- and long-term contracts with those who wished to purchase goods provided by the Portuguese king. Finally, he marketed goods that had not been requested or contracted but simply shipped to Morocco in the hope that they would sell. Each *feitor* and *feitoria* was part of a worldwide network of royal trading houses stretching from northern Europe to Africa, India, and even to China and Japan. Requests for goods needed in one area were fulfilled in another. This network helped make the Portuguese empire successful.[7]

The *alfândega*, or customs house, oversaw the flow of local goods into and out of the fortresses. The man in charge of customs was known as the *almoxarife*. For example, if a Moroccan sold vegetables to residents of a fortress, he was obliged to pay a ten percent duty at the customs office on the value of the goods he was able to sell before he was permitted to leave the city. Similarly, if a Moroccan merchant entered a Portuguese fortress and purchased an item within the fortress, he was required to pay a ten percent exit duty on that item. Jews living in Azamor and Safi, as part of their privileges, were exempted from paying duties on goods entering or leaving by land, but were required to pay on any waterborne traffic.[8] For examples of duties on various goods, see Table 5.1.

Once goods not intended for export had entered the fortresses, they were sold mainly at the central market, or *çoquo* (from the Arabic *sūq*). There are also indications that Portuguese, Jewish, and Moroccan shopkeepers purchased some of these goods for resale in their shops at higher prices.[9] To ensure that goods were traded fairly at the market,

---

[7] Virgínia Rau, "Feitores e feitorias: "Instrumentos" do comércio internacional português no século XVI," in *Estudos sobre história económica e social do antigo regime* (Lisbon: Editorial Presença, 1984), 141-99 and Idem, "Nota sobre os feitores portugueses na Andaluzia no século XV," in *Estudos de história medieval* (Lisboa: Editorial Presença, 1986), 132-137. *Feitores* stationed in areas not controlled by the Portuguese, whether in Europe or elsewhere, often acted as the king's ambassadors as well as a representative of Portuguese commerce in general.

[8] See chapter three.

[9] ANTT, *Livro das Ilhas*, f. 128, published in José Alberto Rodrigues da Silva Tavim, *Os iudeus na expansão portuguesa em Marrocos durante o século XVI: origens e actividades duma comunidade* (Braga: Edições APPACDM Distrital de Braga, 1997), 528. Portuguese artisans (see chapter two) undoubtedly purchased materials at market to convert into finished goods.

the Portuguese appointed an *alcaide do çoquo* to oversee all transactions and address any problems arising within the marketplace.[10] This control extended outside the Portuguese fortresses. When the Shawiyyan tribes came to the northern bank of the Umm al-Rabi` River, within sight of Azamor, to trade their goods with the Portuguese and others, the Portuguese appointed one of their own, João Folgado, as *alcaide* of the "Shawiyyan Market."[11] Furthermore, all merchants who used weights and measures in their business were required to have their measuring devices inspected and licensed to assure fairness. The official in charge of this task was called the *almotacé* (from Arabic *al-muḫtasib*).[12]

While the Portuguese and Jews appear to have received fair and honest treatment at the hands of these and other commercial officials, the same was not always the case with Moroccan Muslims. Azamor during the 1520s seems to have been especially problematic. In 1523, Duarte Lopes, likely one of the interpreters in Azamor, wrote to the king on behalf of Myram, the wife of Ya`qūb al-Gharbiyya, a Portuguese ally. Myram had complained to Lopes that many Muslims reported being charged exploitative and illegal rates by the *porteiros* who collected customs duties from those leaving the city.[13] They were forced to pay four *reis* in duties for each *alqueire* of barley. This was a horrendous tariff, considering barley rarely sold for more than ten *reis/alqueire* and often sold for less than seven. Meanwhile, other Muslim traders reported having large percentages of their goods seized outright upon entering the city.[14] In 1527, António Leite, the *capitão* of Mazagão, reported that Jorge Viegas, the *capitão* of Azamor, was illegally

---

[10] *SIHMP*, 1:523n2; 1:584n1.

[11] ANTT, CC I, 22, 58, published in Maria Augusta Lima Cruz Fagundes, "Documentos Ineditos para a Historia dos Portugueses em Azamor," *Arquivos do Centro Cultural Portugues* 2 (1970): 145-147.

[12] The *almotacés* in mainland Portugal had the power to impose price controls, though there is no evidence anything of this sort occurred in Morocco.

[13] Royal law since at least 1516 had prohibited *porteiros* from collecting any duties or fees from any merchants. A problem similar, but not as extensive, to the one described in the text existed in Safi in 1516 and 1517 ("Alvará of D. Manuel," Lisbon, 2 January 1517, *SIHMP*, 2:55). Clearly enforcement was a problem.

[14] "Letter from Duarte Lopes to D. João III," Azamor, 10 August 1523, *SIHMP*, 2:316-317.

charging Muslims twenty percent customs duties, rather than the normal ten percent, on all merchandise entering the city. There were even reports from Azamor that Viegas seized all of the possessions of some of the merchants, turning them away from the city with nothing.[15] Nevertheless, the king permitted Viegas to remain as *capitão* of Azamor until spring 1529, when Muslim residents of Azamor accused him of extorting money from them. D. João III could not allow resentment to spread within the fortress walls, and he recalled Viegas to Portugal almost immediately.[16]

Contraband

While "contraband" may not fit under any modern definition of infrastructure, political leaders during the early modern period considered preventing their trade laws from being broken as a necessary component of their economic policy. Portuguese kings were no exception. Non-Portuguese were permitted to trade along the Moroccan coast so long as they received a license from the Portuguese king. This was to ensure that Portuguese merchants and Portuguese *feitores* did not face unnecessary competition. While many merchants adhered to these conditions, many did not.

Of greatest concern to the Portuguese was any sale of war materiel to enemy Moroccans, in particular, the Sa`adids, who increasingly challenged the Portuguese as the sixteenth century progressed. Historian Weston Cook, Jr., in fact, states unequivocally that "contraband trade is inextricably linked to the rise of the Sa`adian state."[17] Among those involved in this trade were Castilians, Italians, French, English, Jews and New Christians. This was despite the fact that papal prohibitions against Christians selling arms to Muslims had been in effect for centuries. Moreover, royal law prohibited this trade as well.[18]

---

[15] "Letter from António Leite to D. João III," Mazagão, 5 February 1527, *SIHMP*, 2:391-395.

[16] "Letter from Mestre Rodrigo to D. João III," Azamor, 15 November 1527, *SIHMP*, 2:423 and "Letter from the Inhabitants of Azamor to D. João III," Azamor, spring 1529, *SIHMP*, 2:459-465.

[17] Weston Cook Jr., *The Hundred Years War for Morocco: Gunpowder and the Military Revolution in the Early Modern Muslim World* (San Francisco: Westview Press, 1994), 139.

[18] *SIHMP*, 1:54n2 and ANTT, *Leis*, I, f. 93.

One of the great entrepots for weapons and other contraband items was the cove town of Tarkuku, located about twenty kilometers north of Santa Cruz. Reports of illegal trade in Tarkuku reached the Portuguese king as early as 1511. The town amounted to a free city, avoiding control by either the Portuguese or the Sa'adids until the Sharif brought the city to heel in the 1520s.[19] This state of affairs did not mean that the Portuguese sat by idly while these illegal acts occurred so close to their fortress.

In 1514, Afonso Rodrigues, the *feitor* of Santa Cruz, reported to the king that merchants from Cadiz and Genoa were continuing to trade with Tarkuku. Apparently these non-Portuguese merchants provided better prices or selection, because Rodrigues claimed that most local Moroccan merchants were going to Tarkuku, causing trade in Santa Cruz to plummet. This was worrisome because, unlike the other fortresses where raiding could provide economic stimulus, Santa Cruz had very little opportunity for raiding because "there are not slaves except in time of famine." These slaves were, in fact, normally brought to the city by Moroccan allies who had raided the settlements of non-allied *mouros de guerra*.[20] The solution, argued Rodrigues, was to send a "well-armed" ship to anchor off the coast of Tarkuku and prevent foreigners from landing at the port.[21]

Nothing seems to have been done until three years later in 1517, when the Portuguese launched a punitive attack on Tarkuku. Near the end of the year, a large contingent of Portuguese knights and soldiers along with Moroccan soldiers provided and led by their Moroccan ally, Sheikh Melik bin Daud, departed Santa Cruz during the evening. They marched overnight to Tarkuku. As dawn broke, they dashed from their hiding places and entered the city. They captured many Muslims, both adults and children, enslaving them. The Portuguese also captured a large number of Christian merchants, mostly Genovese and Castilian, whom they took to Santa Cruz where

---

[19] Cook, 171.

[20] "Letter from Afonso Rodrigues to D. Manuel," Santa Cruz, 11 September 1514, *SIHMP*, 1:614. See chapter eight for more on the slave trade.

[21] "Letter from Afonso Rodrigues to D. Manuel," Santa Cruz, 4 June 1514, *SIHMP*, 1:564-565. This raises the issue that Santa Cruz was unlike the other Portuguese fortresses in that it never had a large sphere of influence and seemed unable to compel large numbers of Moroccans to do their bidding, unlike in the Dukkala area.

they were freed and ordered to return to Europe, despite the calls from some Portuguese to sell these merchants at a slave auction as punishment for living in Islamic lands and earning their living from illegal trading with Muslims. They also seized many valuable goods, including grain and livestock.[22] Despite the success of this raid, Tarkuku was again a flourishing city in less than one year. The resurgence was helped by threats issued by the Sharif that any Moroccans who traded with the Portuguese in Santa Cruz faced raids by Sa`adid forces on their lands. The illegal trade in arms continued until the fall of Santa Cruz in 1541.[23]

In the Dukkala region, it was New Christians and Jews most often accused of selling banned items, especially military items, to enemy Moroccans. According to João Afonso, who had been to Marrakech numerous times on diplomatic missions, New Christians living in North Africa had, by the late 1530s, joined some of their Jewish relatives in selling spear points, crossbows, and matchlock rifles to Sharifan forces in Marrakech.[24] What, if anything, came of Afonso's accusations is unknown.

Commodities

This section discusses some, but certainly not all, of the commodities traded in Portuguese-controlled Morocco. The items discussed below are those about which more can be said than simply, "Yes, this item was bought and sold during this period." Attentive readers will note that the trade in slaves is not discussed below, despite its importance to the Portuguese economy. Those interested in a discussion of the slave trade, should consult chapter eight.

---

[22] *CSC*, 34-36; *CDM*, 4:139; "Letter from *qā'id* Melik to D. Manuel," Santa Cruz, 30 July 1517, *SIHMP*, 2:129-130. Sheikh Melik bin Daud was the leader of a tribe, likely Arab, known to the Portuguese as the Izarrar (*CSC*, 29n4).

[23] "Letter from Fernão Taveira to D. Manuel," Santa Cruz, 28 May 1518, *SIHMP*, 2:186; ANTT, CC I, 43, 49. In 1513, the village of Tamrakht, 12km north of Santa Cruz, was also a location where Martin de Haya, a merchant from Cadiz, had established a flourishing trading business (see, "Letter from Afonso Rodrigues to D. Manuel," Santa Cruz, 24 December 1513, *SIHMP*, 1:472).

[24] "Report of João Afonso to the *Mesa da Consciência*," Safi, 25 September 1539, *SIHMP*, 3:222.

Textiles

Textiles were one of the most important and successful trade items in Portuguese Morocco. Moroccans were keen to purchase cloth and finished clothing manufactured in Europe and brought to their markets by the Portuguese. The gold and silver used by Moroccans to purchase these items was then typically used to fund fleets to India where spices and other goods were purchased.[25] The Portuguese meanwhile purchased large amounts of Moroccan clothing that were prized by peoples further south along the African coast. The Portuguese would then trade the Moroccan clothing as well as some European textiles for slaves. The largest Portuguese trading center in sub-Saharan Africa was São Jorge da Mina, established along Africa's Gold Coast in 1482. It is illustrative of the way in which the Portuguese conducted commerce.

The Gold Coast had been frequented by Portuguese traders since the early 1470s, but in order to increase trade volume and to prevent Castilian incursions, King D. João II ordered that a more permanent fortress be built. The construction of the fortress was overseen by none other than Diogo de Azambuja, who would later conquer Safi for King D. Manuel.[26] Among the textiles sold there were *lambens* (mantles) that "consisted of a single piece of cloth sewn along the sides with armholes cut and a poncho-like opening in the center for the wearer's head." These garments came in a variety of styles and colors, with those that were striped with blue, white, red, and green being among the most popular. Particularly prized *lambens* might bring as much in trade as the cost of a male slave in Benin. Also popular were the *aljaravias*, similar to a *burnous* or cloak with half-sleeves and an attached hood. These also came in varied styles depending on the location of manufacture. To give some idea of the profit margins on this trade, raw cloth (*pano*) could be purchased in Morocco normally for

---

[25] Robert Ricard, "Le commerce de Berbérie et l'organisation économique de l'empire portugais aux XVe et XVIe siècles," in *Études sur l'histoire des portugais au Maroc* (Coimbra, 1955), 99-100.

[26] John Vogt, *Portuguese Rule of the Gold Coast, 1469-1682* (Athens, Georgia: University of Georgia Press, 1979), 7-30.

less than sixty *reis* per *vara* and sold in São Jorge da Mina for 240 *reis*, a 400 percent increase.[27]

How were these goods acquired by the Portuguese? Although they were purchased from various regions throughout North Africa, this study focuses on southern Morocco and Dukkala in particular. In that region, the textile trade was controlled mostly by Jews, who signed contracts with the Portuguese to supply them with the required items. For example, Meyer Levi was given a contract to supply *lambens* to the Portuguese in Safi. The exact length of this contract is unclear, but he supplied goods from 1512 until at least 1514. The textiles were manufactured in Marrakech by Moroccan Muslim weavers, and then purchased and transported to Safi by Levi. According to Heitor Gonçalves, Safi's *feitor*, the end products were of very fine quality. Although animosity and outright warfare was the status quo between Portuguese and Marrakechi leadership, commercial advantage helped to dampen the antagonism.

As is common with many trading ventures, Levi encountered problems. In 1514, Heitor Gonçalves requested that Levi manufacture a large number of woolen mantles, known as *haiks* (also called *alquices*), and other clothes for sale at the Portuguese enclave of Arguim (established in 1445 near Cap Blanc on the northwestern coast of modern Mauritania). Levi invested 300 ounces of silver (c. 96,000 *reis*) of his own funds in the production of these goods and advanced the finished products to the *feitoria* in Safi. After two months, Levi had still not been paid and was due to send another 1,000 *haiks* and 200 *lambens* to Safi as part of his normal contract. Levi wrote to D. Manuel pleading his inability to sustain such debts and asked the king to order the *feitor* to make the payment. The payment requested was 2,000 *cruzados* (800,000 *reis*) and an unspecified sum of black lacar and *bordates* (see below), demonstrating that the Portuguese were far in arrears. In addition to collecting the money he was owed, Levi likely planned on reselling the lacar and *bordates* through other Moroccan commercial

---

[27] Vogt, 67-68, 75; ANTT, CC II, 69, 172; CC II, 70, 38. The *lamben* is similar to the modern Moroccan *gandoura* or *hambel*, while the modern version of the *aljaravia* is the *aljalabiya*.

connections.²⁸   Another Jewish supplier of clothing was Yehuda Benzamiro. In late 1514, the *Casa da India* had requested another large delivery of clothing that could be sold in Arguim. The Portuguese in Safi called on both Levi, who had yet to receive payment for the previous order, and Benzamiro to deliver 2,000 *haiks*.²⁹

The clothing trade was not limited to Safi. In 1519, a group of Jews, including one Ya`qūb Tuson, signed a three-year contract with the Portuguese in Azamor to supply 3,000 *alquices* per year.³⁰ Azamor, in fact, was described by a chronicler of the early sixteenth century, Valentim Fernandes, as a fine place to acquire "*alquices* and *aljavarias* and *lambens* which are taken to the blacks."³¹ Santa Cruz seems to have had much less of this activity. The only extant contract where a Jew supplied textiles to the Portuguese in Santa Cruz was for three *haiks* and six pairs of leather boots in 1533.³²

While Jews controlled the majority of this trade, a few Moroccan Muslims contracted directly with the Portuguese. The largest of these contracts was concluded in 1530 in Lisbon by the two commercial agents of Al-`Attar, a Moroccan *qā'id* who controlled Tadla and was allied with the Portuguese from 1523. Al-`Attar received a variety of goods, including black lacar, pepper, cinnamon, nutmeg, cloves, and ginger, valued at 5,508 *cruzados*, or more than 2.2 million *reis*. In exchange, he was to provide beeswax (at 1,300 *reis/arroboa*) equal to 2,254 *cruzados*, and various styles of *haiks* (*abanes* – 250 *reis* each, *meios tascontes* – 720 *reis* each, and *sardões* – 350 *reis* each) for the other 2,254 *cruzados*. These items were to be delivered to the *feitor* in Azamor who was then ordered to send the clothing south to Arguim where it would be traded mainly for slaves. In order to guard the royal

---

²⁸ "Letter from Heitor Gonçalves to D. Manuel," Safi, 18 June 1512, *SIHMP*, 1:333; "Letter from Heitor Gonçalves to D. Manuel," Safi, 15 December 1512, *SIHMP*, 1:367; "Letter from Meyer Levi to D. Manuel," Safi 14 November 1514, *SIHMP*, 1:653-654.

²⁹ "Letter from Nuno Gato to D. Manuel," Safi, 14 November 1514, *SIHMP*, 1:655-657.

³⁰ "Letter from D. Álvaro de Noronha to D. Manuel," Azamor, 18 May 1519, *SIHMP*, 2:242 and ANTT, CdGA, 5.

³¹ Magalhães Godinho, "Ceuta e Marrocos," 113.

³² ANTT, CC II, 186, 24. Juda Budara, the Jew who signed this contract, was actually Abraham Benzamiro's agent in the city of Santa Cruz (ANTT, CC II, 169, 113 and Tavim, *Os judeus*, 547).

monopoly on the spice trade, D. João III required that Al-`Attar sell his spices exclusively within Morocco.[33]

Revenues from the duties on exports of textiles were very lucrative for individual fortresses and, more importantly, the particular *capitão* who sold them to merchants heading to southern Africa. In 1520, officials in Safi petitioned King D. Manuel to make their city the exclusive handler of all trade in *haiks*. The *capitão* of Azamor, D. Álvaro de Noronha, argued that the opposite should be true, for, according to him, *haiks* brought to Azamor were less expensive.[34] The lower price for the textiles was likely due to the fact that they were fabricated in the city of Almedina, fifty kilometers south of Azamor, while Safi received most of its textiles from Marrakech, 150 kilometers inland. What Noronha did not take into account was the difficulty of transporting the textiles from Azamor to the sea, two kilometers distant, as large vessels could not negotiate the Umm al-Rabi` River inland due to shifting and treacherous sandbars. In the end, the king appears to have made no changes, allowing both cities to compete for the textile trade.

The Portuguese were not just exporters of cloth, but importers as well. As in most times and places, an exotic version of an everyday item often fetches a premium. In the case of Moroccan purchasers, cloth made in Europe was such a favored item. Estêvão Vaz reported that, at least prior to 1510, cloth from Southampton, England (known as *amtonas*) was especially popular with purchasers in Safi. Each year, he had been able to sell between ninety and one hundred of these for a total of fifteen to twenty *miticais* (or 6,300-8,400 *reis*) after purchasing them in England for about 3,400 *reis*, "not including freight charges and transportation risks." About 2,000 smaller, lower-quality pieces (what today we might call "seconds") of Southampton cloth were purchased each year for about 330 *reis* each and sold in Safi for between 420 and

---

[33] "Contract with Al-`Attar," Lisbon, 1-2 August 1530, *SIHMP*, 2:544-548 and Tavim, *Os judeus*, 288-289, 317. The two commercial agents were Ya`qūb de Medina, a Jew from Azamor, and Sidi Sa`id, a Moroccan Muslim.

[34] "Letter from D. Álvaro de Noronha to D. Manuel," Azamor, 18 April 1520, *SIHMP*, 2:274.

840 *reis*.[35] Other popular cloth included *gallueus*, made in Galway, Ireland, and *pecetas*, a finely woven English cloth.[36]

According to Heitor Gonçalves, the *feitor* of Safi, *bordates*, a style of cotton fabric originally manufactured in Egypt, had become the central item of commerce in Dukkala by 1512. The *bordates* sold by the Portuguese were manufactured in large part in England, though a smaller percentage came from Portugal itself.[37] In June of that year, Gonçalves told the king to send as many *bordates* as possible because they were the most important item needed "in order to make money quickly."[38] Two years later, Afonso Rodrigues, the *feitor* of Santa Cruz, seconded this assessment, saying that in dealing with both Muslim and Jewish merchants, "if all we have to sell are *bordates*, we run out quickly."[39] Moroccan buyers even had color preferences, noted by the Portuguese in their efforts to tailor their products to the buyer; they preferred dark blues, greens, yellows, and some reds.[40]

While Jews and Muslims had roles in supplying the Portuguese with Moroccan-made textiles, these groups had little influence in the import and sale of goods made in Europe. Consequently, those who did not wish to wait for the next shipment of European cloth and compete to buy it, would conclude contracts with the Portuguese. For example, a group of Muslims and Jews living near Santa Cruz concluded a contract in 1514 with the king for the purchase of 2,000 *bordates* and 100 *quartilhas* (possibly a type of cloth wrapped around the head like a turban). It was, in fact, common for the king, through his representatives in the *feitoria*, to contract directly with Jews and Muslims. This was done partly in defense of the royal right to a monopoly on *bordates* declared in 1512 in view of their popularity and

---

[35] "Letter from Estêvão Vaz to D. Manuel," Lisbon, 27 February 1510, *SIHMP*, 1:224-225.

[36] "Letter from João Lopes de Alvim and Christôvão de Almeida to D. Manuel," Safi, 25 December 1507, *SIHMP*, 1:146-147.

[37] Tavim, *Os judeus*, 308.

[38] "Letter from Heitor Gonçalves to D. Manuel," Safi, 18 June 1512, *SIHMP*, 1:332 and "Letter from Heitor Gonçalves to D. Manuel," Safi, 15 December 1512, *SIHMP*, 1:367-368.

[39] "Letter from Afonso Rodrigues to D. Manuel," Santa Cruz, 4 June 1514, *SIHMP*, 1:563.

[40] "Letter from Estêvão Vaz to D. Manuel," Lisbon, 27 February 1510, *SIHMP*, 1:224.

profitability.[41] The Jewish Benzamiro family was heavily involved in the commerce in *bordates*. In fact by 1524, they maintained an agent in Lisbon who, among other commercial activities, concluded contracts with the king for the purchase of *bordates*. These particular textiles became so popular and valuable, that they were at times used by the Portuguese amongst themselves in place of currency until D. Manuel prohibited this in 1516 in order to ensure that these goods were sold at prices he set.[42]

Precious Metals

The Portuguese trade in precious metals was quite diverse. In Morocco, the main form of metal was coin, usually gold and silver, but also copper. Morocco had an abundance of gold, most of which entered via the caravan routes from Ghana and Mali.[43] A significant portion of the gold acquired by the Portuguese was shipped to Arguim and São Jorge da Mina where it was used to purchase slaves from local African merchants. A large majority of these gold and silver coins were collected as the purchase price for goods sold to Moroccans by the Portuguese. Another source was taxation, mainly in the form of customs duties.

Even before the conquest of southern Moroccan cities, the Portuguese *feitor* in Safi reported that he accumulated large sums of gold as the result of commercial activities. The *feitoria* averaged over 3,400 *dobras* (13,600 *reis*) per month in gold between 1491 and 1500 (see Table 5.2). The *feitoria* of Azamor had a much lower rate, only 89,920 *dobras* from July 1486 until February 1501, or 513 *dobras* (2,052 *reis*) per month.[44] The gold passing through Safi did not stop once the Portuguese controlled the city. By 1526, in fact, Garcia de Melo, the *capitão*, suggested to the king that he establish a royal mint in the city to

---

[41] Tavim, *Os judeus*, 308.

[42] "Letter from D. Nuno Mascarenhas to D. Manuel," Safi, 9 December 1516, *SIHMP*, 2:48-49. The Benzamiro agent was Bras Reinal, a New Christian. See Tavim, *Os judeus*, 311-312.

[43] Vitorino Magalhães Godinho, *Os descobrimentos e a economia mundial*, 4 vols. (Lisbon: Editorial Presença, 1982-85), 1:72-78.

[44] Magalhães Godinho, *Os descobrimentos*, 1:144.

streamline the process of converting Moroccan coinage to Portuguese coinage.[45]

Money changing was also a great source of profit for the Portuguese. This was especially true in the Sus region near Santa Cruz. This area of Morocco was gold rich but silver poor. Consequently, during the initial years of the Portuguese presence in Santa Cruz, when word spread through the region that a ship had landed carrying silver coins, local Moroccans of all sorts flocked to the city to exchange their gold for silver or to purchase goods with gold, receiving silver as change. For example, in December 1513, the *feitor* of Santa Cruz realized a profit of fourteen percent on this exchange, and in September 1514, the *feitor* placed a value of 360 *reis* of silver for every *mitical* of gold, though the gold was actually worth 450 *reis*. Consequently, the *feitor* realized a profit of twenty-five percent.[46] It was no secret to the Moroccans that the Portuguese were interested in precious metals. Sheikh Melik bin Daud, a Portuguese ally in the Sus region, stated in a letter to D. Manuel in 1517 that if he were granted certain additional privileges, it would assist him in defeating the Sa`adids and "opening the road to copper and gold" to enter the area in greater quantities.[47]

Jews also participated in the gold and silver industries, usually after the gold had entered the Portuguese controlled cities. At least one Jewish goldsmith worked in Azamor in 1517. It seems likely that he was not the only one.[48]

Food

The food consumed by the Portuguese cities was acquired in four basic ways: tribute, purchase, seizure, and cultivation. Cultivation, tribute, and seizure are discussed elsewhere (see chapter four). This section is devoted exclusively to trade methods used by the Portuguese

---

[45] "Letter from Garcia de Melo to D João III," Safi, 5 October 1526, *SIHMP*, 2:378. In fact, Garcia de Melo told the king that he would fund a portion of the construction costs of the mint in exchange for a percentage of the profits. There is no record of the mint having ever been built.

[46] *DCC*, 70-71, 118.

[47] "Letter from *qā`id* Malik to D. Manuel," Santa Cruz, 30 July 1517, *SIHMP*, 2:131.

[48] ANTT, CC II, 71, 25.

to acquire food by purchase from Jewish and Moroccan Muslim merchants.

Until 1519, it seems that the Portuguese in Azamor had relied on their own herds and the purchase of meat from Moroccan herders to supply their city. During that year, however, there was a shortage of meat and very few people could afford it. Consequently, the city entered into a contract with Ya'qūb Tuson, the Jewish merchant, to supply the city that year with 8,000 *arrobas* of beef at 80 *reis* per *arroba*.[49] Another way that the Portuguese in Azamor secured meat that year was by providing protection to the Awlad Subeita tribe. The Awlad Subeita moved their tents to a field near the city and had planted their crops there. In exchange for the protection afforded to them and their crops from raids by other Moroccan groups, the Subeita sold some of their livestock to the Portuguese.[50]

Grain and bread were the most important food staples in the Portuguese cities. In fact, even before the Portuguese had established *feitorias* in Azamor and Safi, they were purchasing grain from southern Morocco. Due to the precarious nature of the grain supply in Morocco, as discussed in chapter four, the Portuguese were constantly preoccupied with information regarding planting and harvests. In fact, one of the most important services performed by Moroccan informants was to report on how the crops of the *mouros de pazes* were progressing.[51] This information allowed the Portuguese to predict whether or not tribute quotas would be met and if any additional grain would be available for purchase. When harvests were abundant, Jews and Moroccan Muslims were able to profit by selling grain to the Portuguese (Table 5.3 and 5.4).[52]

Although grain shortage in Portuguese fortresses was almost as common as overabundance (see Table 4.1), there were occasions when the Portuguese actually sold grain to Moroccans. In 1518, for example, the *feitor* of Santa Cruz sold nearly 7900 *alqueires* (58,618 kg) of barley to

---

[49] "Letter from D. Álvaro de Noronha to D. Manuel," Azamor, 18 May 1519, *SIHMP*, 2:240-242 and ANTT, CC I, 24, 81.

[50] "Letter from D. Álvaro de Noronha to D. Manuel," Azamor, 15 December 1519, *SIHMP*, 2:260-263: "*dam-nos muyta lenha e muyta carne.*"

[51] "Letter from António Leite to D. Manuel," Mazagão, 20 October 1517, *SIHMP*, 2:177.

[52] For an overview of Jews in the grain trade, see Tavim, *Os judeus*, 271-283.

local *mouros de pazes* for the rather high price of 35 *reis/alqueire* (4.7 *reis*/kg). This situation seems to have been an attempt to retain the allegiance of the local Moroccans who were facing great shortfalls in their harvests, while at the same time profiting from their misfortune. The barley had, in fact, been imported, likely from Portugal, with the orders of the king that it be sold to the allied Moroccans. Fernão Taveira, the *adail* of Santa Cruz, recommended that the king send a large shipment of wheat so that it, instead of money, could be used to purchase slaves from the local Muslims who would need the wheat to survive.[53]

Many other foods were traded in large quantities, though references to specific trading of these goods is rare. There were large quantities of dates, loquats, figs, and raisins brought from the Moroccan interior to the Portuguese fortresses. Vegetables, including onions, turnips, and cucumbers, arrived in Portuguese cities regularly. These items were traded by Jews and Muslims alike.[54]

Spices and Drugs

In the sixteenth century, these two commodities were often grouped together, one of the reasons being that the majority of them came from the same location: India. The trade in these items was a royal monopoly, in that all spices legally entering Morocco did so through royal channels. Most of these spices were either sold or traded for goods available in Morocco, as with *qā'id* Al-`Attar discussed above. At times, however, spices and drugs were given to Moroccan allies as rewards for their services (see chapter six).

This sector of commerce was ongoing and profitable. In 1516, the *feitor* of Safi requested that the king send him thirty or forty *quintais* of pepper to sell to Moroccans.[55] The *feitoria* of Azamor received at least five *quintais* of pepper and one *quintal* each of cloves and

---

[53] "Letter from Fernão Taveira to D. Manuel," Santa Cruz, 28 May 1518, *SIHMP*, 2:186-187.

[54] Tavim, *Os judeus*, 285-286 and "Letter from Nuno Gato to D. Manuel," Safi, 4 July 1516, *SIHMP*, 2:13.

[55] *GTT*, 4:452-453. One *quintal* is equal to 4 *arrobas* or about 60 kg.

cinnamon to sell in Morocco in 1519.[56] In Safi in 1523, pepper sold for nearly 700 *reis* per *quintal*.[57]

Lacar, used both as a textile dye and a medicinal ingredient, was especially popular. Lacar came from south Asia: Laos, Siam, Pegú, and Martabão. It was desired for purchase both by Moroccans and Jews. The commerce in lacar was on par with the commerce in textiles. In fact, D. Manuel had paid *fronteiros* partly with lacar and *bordates*, possibly to attract them to Morocco with the lure of easy profits from the sale of these goods. The king ended this policy in 1516, likely to increase his own profits as the *fronteiros* could profit greatly from slave trading and the sale of seized grain.[58] Portuguese historian Vitorino Magalhães Godinho believed that during the sixteenth century, all of Morocco absorbed between 300 and 500 *quintais* of lacar per year.[59] This conclusion is borne out by documents relative to southern Morocco. For example, Safi imported 100 *quintais* in 1518, and in 1519, Safi and Azamor together requisitioned 150 *quintais* of lacar.[60] The cost of lacar appears to have been between thirty and forty cruzados (12,000-16,000 *reis*) per *quintal*, the price paid by Jews and Moroccan Muslims who purchased the lacar directly from Portuguese *feitors* in Morocco.[61]

Indigo

Indigo (*anil*), a deep blue vegetable dye used in the textile industry, was one of southern Morocco's greatest exports. In fact, the Dra region (east of the Sus), controlled by the Sharif, was known to Moroccans and Portuguese alike as the "Land of Indigo." It was Jews, as they did with many goods, who purchased and transported indigo

---

[56] ANTT, CC I, 24, 53.

[57] "Letter from D. João III to Gonçalo Mendes Sacoto," n.l., June or July 1523, *SIHMP*, 2:310.

[58] "Letter from D. Nuno Mascarenhas to D. Manuel," Safi, 9 December 1516, *SIHMP*, 2:48-49 and ANTT, CC II, 60, 110.

[59] Magalhães Godinho, *Os descobrimentos*, 3:177.

[60] ANTT, CC I, 22, 43; CC I, 24, 53; CC II, 73, 19.

[61] Tavim, *Os judeus*, 302-305. As with most commerce, the names of prominent Jewish families – Benzamiro, Levi, Rute, Çofem, Adibe – are dominant.

from its Moroccan producers to the Portuguese fortresses.[62] Once inside the Portuguese fortresses, indigo sold for between 1,000 and 4,000 *reis/quintal*. Although much of the indigo purchased by the Portuguese was exported to Portugal and Europe for use in the textile industry, the Portuguese used some of it in Morocco. For example, Rui Dias de Aguiar, the *capitão* of Santa Cruz, purchased four *arrobas* of indigo in 1533 in order to dye flags being manufactured for the city's ramparts.[63]

Beeswax

Moroccan beeswax, especially that found in Dukkala, was of high quality, and was traded around the world. By the middle of the sixteenth-century, it could be purchased on the streets of Mexico City in large quantities.[64] The Portuguese had been importing Moroccan beeswax since the establishment of their *feitoria* in Safi in the 1460s. Taxes on beeswax had generated an average of 200 *miticais* per year while Safi was under Islamic control.[65] There is no reason to believe that this revenue stream did not continue apace. The wax trade continued even after the Portuguese abandoned Safi, as it was an important commodity throughout Iberia under Philip II, following his conquest of Portugal in 1580.[66]

The wholesale trade in beeswax seems to have been controlled entirely by Moroccan Muslims. In fact, Al-`Attar, the Moroccan *qā'id* with whom the Portuguese had many commercial dealings, figured prominently in the trade. Jews living in Portuguese fortresses usually served as middlemen, transporting the wax along caravan routes from the Moroccan hinterland to the Portuguese-controlled coast. Among these Jews were Ya`qūb Adibe and Ya`qūb de Medina.[67]

---

[62] "Letter from Rabbi Abraham Rute," Safi, 12 October 1512, *SIHMP*, 1:357; Tavim, *Os judeus*, 295-297.

[63] ANTT, CC I, 44, 111 and CC II, 186, 124.

[64] Robert Ricard, "Les places portugais du Maroc et le commerce d'Andalousie," in *Études sur l'histoire des Portugais au Maroc* (Coimbra: University of Coimbra, 1955), 154.

[65] *DCC*, 35.

[66] Tavim, *Os judeus*, 293.

[67] ANTT, CC I, 8, 17; CC I, 31, 71; CC II, 166, 100; "Contract with *qā'id* Al-`Attar," Lisbon, 1-2 August 1530, *SIHMP*, 2:544-548; Tavim, *Os judeus*, 293, 546.

Once the wax entered the Portuguese fortresses, however, individual Portuguese were able to profit from it. For example, within four months of the conquest of Azamor, D. Manuel granted Francisco de Almeida, the city's *adail*, two wax-making shops that had once been managed by the Muslim inhabitants of the city.[68] Almeida, therefore, likely controlled Azamor's wax and candle supply.

Animals, Hides, and Leather

The commerce in animals and animal products was ubiquitous. The most important of these animals were camels and horses. Camels were extremely important for caravan merchants who took advantage of their abilities to travel long distances while heavily laden. Meanwhile, horses were used mostly for individual transportation and for war, though a significant number were exported by the Portuguese.

Moroccans had exported horses for centuries, and the Portuguese had long been among their customers.[69] After the Portuguese conquests in southern Morocco, they continued to buy horses from Moroccan sources for use in their raiding activities locally, to export to Portugal, and to transport to Arguim and São Jorge da Mina to trade for slaves and gold. Horses were also required as tribute from some Moroccan tribes and villages and were seized by the Portuguese during raids.[70]

The camel trade within the Portuguese fortresses seems to have been dominated by the Jews. When camels were seized during Portuguese raids, they were used to transport seized goods to the Portuguese city, and then sold to Jews.[71] These Jews then likely used them in their caravans or sold them to other Jews or Moroccan merchants. It also seems that, at times, the Portuguese did not acquire camels at the same time as a large seizure of grain. As a result, they

---

[68] *CM*, 11, f. 2v. The king granted monopolies on other goods as well. Jorge de Melo, the same man who had been granted the license to construct Mazagão in 1505, received a monopoly on the sale of soap in Azamor, which he retained until the city was abandoned in 1541 (*CM*, 15, f. 28; *SIHMP*, 1:106).

[69] Pereira, *Esmeraldo*, 59, 67, 73. See also the fifteenth-century trade agreements between Portugal and Safi and Portugal and Azamor discussed in chapter six.

[70] "Letter from Nuno Fernandes de Ataíde to D. Manuel," Safi, 30 August 1514, *SIHMP*, 1:604; *DIB*, 498.

[71] *GTT*, 5:463-471.

were forced to rent camels to transport their booty. This occurred at least twice. In 1514, the *capitão* of Azamor rented thirty-four camels from a Moroccan Muslim, Sa`īd Adut, for a bargain rate of 4,080 *reis*, while in 1517, the *capitão* of Safi rented seventy-nine camels from "certain Muslims" for 19,200 *reis*.[72]

The hides of animals, both in their natural state and tanned into leather, were another important trade item. The skins involved in this commerce came from camels, cows, sheep, and goats. Leather was needed within the Portuguese fortresses for numerous items: shoes, sacks, saddles, parchment, etc.. Moroccans themselves used hides for similar items as well as in the construction of the tents used by the nomads.

The trade in hides was controlled by Moroccans, who raised and slaughtered the animals. Jews again often acted as middlemen, buying the hides directly from the Moroccans inland or contracting to sell a certain number of hides to the Portuguese. The vast majority of the hides sold to the Portuguese remained in Morocco, for Portugal itself normally had an abundant supply of hides and leather. While hides could be sold for cash, they were often traded for goods that could be sold later. For instance, Jewish merchants living in the Sus region often brought hides and leather to Santa Cruz in order to trade for textiles and clothing that they later sold to Moroccans in the region.[73]

Wood

Wood was essential for construction and repair in cities for two reasons: wood was used for framing and building small structures and wood fueled the *fornos de cal*, ovens that baked stone in order to create the lime needed for mortar used in stone construction. In 1513, the *feitor* of Santa Cruz, Afonso Rodrigues, told the king that if the local Moroccan Muslim allies were not supplying them with wood that they gathered quite a distance away, then work on the fortress would have been impossible. Gathering wood could, in fact, be quite dangerous. During one expedition to gather firewood in the Sus region, a group of Moroccans led by the Portuguese ally, Sheikh Melik bin Daud, were

---

[72] ANTT, CC II, 53, 80; CC II, 54, 120; CC II, 68, 134.

[73] Tavim, *Os judeus*, 294.

attacked by men loyal to the Sa`adids. Half of the thirty men with Melik were either captured or killed.[74]

Wood might also be supplied by contract. In 1514, the Portuguese in Azamor had given a contract to supply firewood for its construction efforts to an unnamed Jew. According to Vasco de Pina, the *vedor das obras* in charge of overseeing all construction, this Jew was involved in profiteering, charging 200,000 *reis* for wood that cost him 70,000 *reis* to procure. Pina concluded, "I am not sure if I will pay him because it seems a bit expensive for the wood" that he brought.[75] Even without a contract, merchants who arrived at Portuguese fortresses with any amount of wood could always sell to the Portuguese.[76] The majority of timber and lumber, however, was imported from Portugal and Madeira.[77]

Paper

Paper is a trade element that is often forgotten, though in a culture as bureaucratic as the Portuguese, it should not be. Additionally, ink and quills were essential for the work of record keeping and correspondence. The majority of writing supplies were shipped to the *almoxarife* of each fortress directly from Portugal. He controlled access to the supplies, which were paid for by other Portuguese officials when they needed them. It seems that the vast majority of these supplies were used by the *contador* and his functionaries who maintained account records for the entire fortress. In fact, of the forty-five extant purchase orders for paper and ink, only one was made by someone other than a member of the *contador's* staff. This one request was made in 1516 by the *escrivão das obras* in Mazagão for one ream (*resma*) of paper.

The use of paper and ink by the *contadors* of each fortress was quite heavy, during many years averaging two reams of paper and 1.5 – 2.5 liters (c. .5 – 1 *canada*) of ink per month. The costs for these goods

---

[74] "Letter from Afonso Rodrigues to D. Manuel," Santa Cruz, 24 December 1513, *SIHMP*, 1:474 and ANTT, Gaveta 15, 19, 19, also cited in *HP*, 3:459.

[75] "Letter from Vasco de Pina to D. Manuel," Azamor, 30 March 1514, *SIHMP*, 1:523-524.

[76] ANTT, CC II, 124, 197.

[77] See, for example, ANTT, CC I, 18, 94; CC II, 15, 88; CC II, 45, 47; CC II, 96, 41.

were minimal. One ream of paper sold for between 250 and 400 *reis*, though averaged 300, while ink sold for as little as 80 *reis/canada* to as much as 150 *reis/canada*. Consequently, the *contador* of each fortress spent between 500 and 700 *reis* in an average month for paper and ink. Although most of these supplies came from Portugal, the *contador* of Santa Cruz had to purchase paper from Yehuda Budara, the local Jewish agent for the Benzamiro family, on at least two occasions in 1525 and 1531.[78]

Conclusion

There is nothing especially startling about Portuguese commercial activities in southern Morocco. Where they felt they had leverage, the Portuguese tried to exploit their power in order to gain extra revenues, such as with the commerce in textiles and with money changing. This extended to royal profits when the king declared a royal monopoly on high-revenue items including spices and *bordates*. Moreover, some Portuguese leaders, disobeying royal proclamations, used their dominant position in order to exploit small-scale Moroccan Muslim merchants for easy gain, by charging them excessive duties or stealing their goods outright.

In the main, the Portuguese appear to have been successful merchants. This success was due to two main things: experience in the region and military power. By the middle of the fifteenth century, after decades of trading with southern Morocco, the Portuguese were able to make commercial alliances with what they learned were the most prosperous cities in the region. Eventually, they conquered these cities as their policy changed from one of *trade and alliance* to one of *conquest and trade*. Moreover, a stable Portuguese currency and their initially overwhelming military might provided stability for portions of Morocco during the politically chaotic years in the late fifteenth and

---

[78] For Budara, see ANTT, CC II, 126, 29 and CC I, 48, 4. For the *escrivão's* request, see ANTT, CC II, 64, 83. ANTT, CC I, 48, 93; CC I, 50, 82; CC I, 51, 13; CC I, 52, 31; CC I, 52, 86; CC I, 52, 93; CC II, 46, 94; CC II, 47, 112; CC II, 48, 14; CC II, 48, 47; CC II, 49, 98; CC II, 50, 208; CC II, 51, 44; CC II, 53, 34; CC II, 55, 85; CC II, 56, 67; CC II, 59, 61; CC II, 60, 164; CC II, 62, 19; CC II, 62, 116; CC II, 63, 77; CC II, 64, 19; CC II, 65, 15; CC II, 65, 107; CC II, 65, 123; CC II, 65, 126; CC II, 67, 30; CC II, 68, 113; CC II, 70, 69; CC II, 72, 64; CC II, 91, 60; CC II, 94, 123; CC II, 97, 98; CC II, 98, 130; CC II, 100, 99; CC II, 101, 44; CC II, 107, 82; CC II, 117, 8; CC II, 119, 106; CC II, 127, 54; CC II, 128, 106

early sixteenth centuries. This stability provided many Moroccan and Jewish merchants with a steady market for their goods.

While the period was one of danger for non-allied villagers and nomads who faced the wrath of Portuguese raiding parties, large-scale merchants willing to cross political frontiers and trade according to Portuguese rules could normally secure satisfactory profits. Still, profits earned in commercial activities should be judged alongside the extractive and exploitative tributes and raiding activity discussed in other chapters. In short, profits accrued to the strong few at the expense of the weak many.

Table 5.1: Ten Percent Customs Duties (in *reis*) on Goods Entering Safi (1512)[79]

ITEM	DUTY	DUTY PER UNIT	PRICE PER UNIT
150 goat skins	210	1.4	14
180 goatskin canteens (*marroquis*)	420	2.3	23
1 *haik* (low quality)	5	5	50
80 *alquices*	500	6.25	62.5
30 cow skins	210	7	70
1 *alcola* of honey	7	7	70
1 *alcola* of butter	7	7	70
1 sheep	10	10	100
1 *haik* (high quality)	10	10	100
3 *tareas* of wool	56	18.7	187
1 cask of fish[80]	26	26	260
8 *arrobas* of beeswax	210	26.25	262.5
1 cask of capers	28	28	280
1 cask of meat	28	28	280
1 ox	40	40	400
1 cow	40	40	400
1 *covado* of lacar[81]	50	50	500
4 *quintais* of gum arabic	420	105	1050
1 *quintal* of indigo	105	105	1050

---

[79] Source for Table 5.1: "Letter from Nuno Gato to D. Manuel," Safi, 29 May 1512, *SIHMP*, 1:312-315.

[80] The Portuguese word that I translate as "cask" is *jarra*. I have been unable to determine the exact size of this object.

[81] Note that this tariff was charged as a measurement, which initially seems strange given that lacar was a resinous substance used in the production of varnishes, red dyes, and medicines. Apparently, lacar was deposited on twigs by the lac insect and then gathered and sold in that manner. Consequently, taxing it by the length of the twigs became common.

Table 5.2: *Dobras* of gold handled by Safi's *feitoria* (1491-1500)[82]

DATE	AMOUNT	MONTHLY AVERAGE
July 1491 – June 1495	206,795	4,308
July 1495 – February 1498	97,378	3,043
March 1498 – September 1500	72,886	2,430
Total	377,059	3,428

Table 5.3: Jewish sales of wheat and barley to the Portuguese

DATE	SELLER NAME	CITY	AMOUNT	SOURCE
1508, Nov 27	Isaac Benzamiro	Safi	392 *alqueires* wheat	CC II, 15, 156 and 157
1509, Jan 1	Isaac Benzamiro	Safi	150 *alqueires* wheat	CC II, 16, 45
1513, Nov 30	Isaac Benzamiro	Safi	138 *moios* and 8 *alqueires* wheat	Tavim, 274
1514, June 6	Çocam	Azamor	2 *covas* [?] barley	CC II, 48, 18
1514, Nov 7	Unknown	Azamor	2 *moios* and 48 *alqueires* barley	CC II, 52, 215
1523, Oct 20	Ya`qūb Adibe	Azamor	57 *alqueires* barley	CC II, 3, 80

---

[82] Source for Table 5.2: Magalhães Godinho, *Os descobrimentos*, 1:144.

Table 5.4: Moroccan Muslim sales of wheat and barley to the Portuguese

DATE	SELLER NAME	CITY	AMOUNT	SOURCE
1514, Nov 7	Al-Mansur	Azamor	4.5 *moios* barley	CC II, 52, 215
1516, Nov 17	`Abda and Ghrabiyya tribes	Safi	339 *moios* wheat	CC II, 67, 42
1517, Apr 1	Salema Musa	Safi	171 *fangas* barley	CC II, 69, 2

Chapter Six: Political Alliances on the Frontier: Forging Trust and Loyalty out of Chaos and Suspicion

THE FRONTIER is a place where war and peace are made and remade; consequently, it is a highly militarized zone. Historian L. P. Harvey, for instance, argues that Islamic Granada, in the final centuries of its existence during which Christian forces inexorably chipped away at its territory, maintained a strong military esprit de corps due to the "continuous *omnipresence of the frontier*."[1] It might, in fact, be argued that should the need for a high state of militarization subside, a frontier no longer exists. Treaties, truces, and the breaking of them are constant features of a frontier zone, marking its instability, its nature as contested space, and the political confusion and ambivalence of the people who dwell in the area. "Mediation, parley, arbitration, and truce were among the mechanisms whereby two warring and militarized societies attempted to contain and curtail their own aggression in partly conquered countries. They are the frontier institutions of a society at war."[2] Such "mechanisms" provide a breathing space or a period of rest before the inevitable recommencement of hostilities.

António Leite, *contador* of Azamor, believed that the Portuguese fortresses in southern Morocco were in a much more violent and militarized atmosphere than those in the north. He had previously served in Tangiers and Arzila for "a long time" before King D. Manuel reassigned him to Azamor in early 1514. In July of that year, Muslims from Shawiyya raided the area, skirmishing with the Portuguese and even capturing five unfortunate Portuguese who were fishing along the banks of the Umm al-Rabi` River. Leite concluded

---

[1] L. P. Harvey, *Islamic Spain, 1250-1500* (Chicago: University of Chicago Press, 1990), 21 (emphasis in original).

[2] Rees Davies, "Frontier Arrangements in Fragmented Societies: Ireland and Wales," in *MFS*, 87.

that, even with all the peace agreements made with the tribes and villages of the region, he had needed to ready for battle more times during the short period that he had resided in Azamor than in all the time he had spent in northern Morocco.[3] Because of this instability, the Portuguese needed as many local political allies as possible to succeed in their goal of conquering and controlling large portions of Morocco. Even with the Portuguese advantage in gunpowder weapons in the fifteenth and early part of the sixteenth century, it would have been impossible for them to accomplish more than the occupation of small coastal enclaves, and even that likely would have proven costly and exceedingly difficult.[4]

In order to gain more power and territory, the Portuguese needed local allies, but making and keeping Moroccan allies was similarly an extremely difficult business. In the period under study, local Moroccan leaders were faced with three choices: 1) alliance with the Portuguese, 2) ties with the Wattasids or Sa`adids (or the Hintati until 1524/5), or 3) they reverted to tribal alliances or supported the autonomous *zāwiyas* of the Sufis.[5] Furthermore, as the balance of power shifted between the "Big Three," small tribal or village groups reconsidered their alliances and switched sides, sometimes more than once. The available documentation allows for a fairly detailed examination of how the Portuguese sought to create and maintain political alliances. The documents also allow us, through a Portuguese filter, to gain some insight as to why persons and groups allied with the Portuguese and with Moroccan powers switched sides at certain moments.

The goal for the Portuguese in Morocco was to create and maintain a power base that could provide for them a defensive buffer, a source of tribute, a region for peaceful commerce, and a supply of

---

[3] "Letter from António Leite to D. Manuel," Azamor, 27 July 1514, *SIHMP*, 1:585.

[4] For a thorough discussion of this military advantage, see Weston Cook, Jr., *The Hundred Years War for Morocco* (San Francisco: Westview Press, 1994).

[5] Dahiru Yahya, *Morocco in the Sixteenth Century: Problems and Patterns in African Foreign Policy* (London: Longman, 1981), 2-3. *Zāwiyas*, also known as ribats, were technically religious hermitages, though most had large landholdings and controlled the labor of hundreds of clients, thus making the leaders of *zāwiyas* more akin to landed nobility. See Vincent J. Cornell, "Socioeconomic Dimensions of Reconquista and Jihad in Morocco: Portuguese Dukkala and the Sa`did Sus, 1450-1557," *International Journal of Middle East Studies* 22 (1990): 384. Also see, "Zāwiya," in *EI(1)*, 1220.

soldiers. The Portuguese program in Morocco was not a traditional colonization and settlement program, such as had occurred in Iberia as Muslim polities were expelled from the region. In those instances, leaders granted charters to towns newly under Christian control and encouraged Christian settlement, even if, in some locations, a large population of Muslims remained.[6] Conquest in Morocco had the goal of suzerainty and alliance, not the wholesale expansion of Christian settlement. The frontier zone, in other words, marked the limit of pacified Moroccan territory.

Alliances before Direct Conquest

Before the Portuguese began direct, landed conquest of southern Morocco, their main goal was to have access to Moroccan trade, especially the grain and textile markets. The Portuguese needed to buy wheat to supplement their own harvests, while they purchased Moroccan textiles to trade for slaves further south along the African coast (see chapter four). The Portuguese typically required the cities or villages with which they traded to enter an agreement allowing access to the Moroccan markets and permitting reciprocal trade between Moroccan and Portuguese merchants. The three largest areas in southern Morocco where the Portuguese carried on trade prior to conquest or the construction of their own fortresses were Safi, Azamor, and Massa (near where the fortress of Santa Cruz would eventually be constructed).

In the mid- to late-fifteenth century, Portuguese ships often stopped in these three areas in order to trade for cloth that they later used to trade for slaves in western Africa.[7] During the latter part of his reign, D. Afonso V (1438-1481) concluded a treaty of protection and trade with Safi, and this accord was confirmed by D. João II (r. 1481-1495) in 1488. We know little of the conditions of this accord, though by at least 1479 a Portuguese *feitoria* was active in the city and a small chapel had been constructed by 1491. The *qā'id* of Safi was to pay tribute of 300 *miticais* per year, either in cash or in kind, and two good

---

[6] See, for example, José Valente, "The New Frontier: The Role of the Knights Templar in the Establishment of Portugal as an Independent Kingdom," in *Mediterranean Studies* 7 (1998): 49-65.

[7] For a detailed discussion of this trade, see John Vogt, *Portuguese Rule on the Gold Coast, 1469-1682* (Athens, GA: University of Georgia Press, 1979).

horses. He was to protect the *feitor* and all Portuguese living in the *feitoria*. In return, the citizens of Safi could sail to Portugal in Portuguese ships and engage in commerce, paying only the duties that Portuguese subjects themselves would pay.[8]

In 1486 D. João II concluded a treaty with Azamor. The city of Azamor, located on the Umm al-Rabi` River, was to pay a tribute of 10,000 shad each year, charge no taxes on royal ships, allow the Portuguese to buy horses, and permit the construction of a *feitoria* and the residence of a *feitor* within the city. Not everyone near Azamor agreed with this treaty, prompting D. João II to send a force of about 1200 men to compel local *dawwārs* to pay tribute. After a brief but bloody fight, in which 900 Muslims were killed and 400 captured, they submitted and paid tribute.[9] Unlike Safi and Massa, Azamor would remain a turbulent ally until the Portuguese conquest of the city in 1513.

In late 1496, three notables from Massa, `Abd al-`Aziz, Hammu bin Barka, and Sidi Yahya, traveled to Portugal in order to enter into an agreement whereby D. Manuel became their suzerain. As with the other cities, this seems to have been an agreement borne of economic concerns. In any event, they agreed to be loyal and perform deeds in the service of the king. As a symbol of this loyalty, they were to give two horses per year to the king and ensure that any goods sold by the king or purchased by the king in Massa would be free of all taxes and duties, though any non-royal Portuguese ships or ships from foreign kingdoms would be required to pay all Massan duties. Furthermore, they were to allow the establishment of a fortified *feitoria* in their town and permit the Portuguese *feitor* and all of his servants to live in Massa. The local inhabitants were to provide a large portion of the labor to help construct the *feitoria* and sell food, at fair prices, to any Portuguese workers sent to complete the project. Until the fortified *feitoria* could be completed, the inhabitants of Massa were required to provide the *feitor* with "a good and secure house" in which to live and store royal merchandise. To control the area's commerce even more,

---

[8] "Letter Patent of D. Manuel," Lisbon, 9 December 1500, *SIHMP*, 1:60-62.

[9] "La conquête de Safi par les portugais, 1508," in *SIHMP*, 1:151-161; "L'Établissement de la suzeraineté portugaise sur Azemmour, 1486," in *SIHMP*, 1:1-3; and António Dias Farinha, *Os Portugueses em Marrocos* (Lisbon: Instituto Camões, 1999), 26-27. For the treaty with Azamor, see *SIHMP*, 1:4-24.

the treaty did not allow the residents of Massa to trade with any Europeans, other than representatives of the Portuguese king, unless they had permission from the *feitor*.

In exchange for all of these concessions, Massa and its people were to receive protection from all Portuguese and servants of Portugal. The king promised that anyone under his authority would treat the inhabitants of Massa well and deal with them fairly in matters of commerce, and he assured the Massans that he would directly inform his admirals and naval captains of this new regulation. The residents of Massa also received the economic benefit of being able to travel to any part of Portugal or its possessions and trade their goods, paying only the taxes and duties that any Portuguese would. If they were taking an ocean-going journey, however, they were to sail in Portuguese ships which were required to transport and feed up to six Massan merchants per voyage without charge.[10]

Portuguese policy towards Morocco began a gradual shift in priorities very early in the sixteenth century, as D. Manuel embarked upon his crusading and messianic program designed to encircle and subjugate all of Islam. He hoped to conquer all of North Africa and the Mamluk Sultanate, including the holy city of Jerusalem. This belief was shared by many among the Portuguese nobility, as can be seen in one stanza of a poem written by Luís Henriques to celebrate the capture of Azamor in 1513:

> *Cresce seu [d'el rei] mando, seus reinos alarga*
> *por seus capitães na gente infiel,*
> *o grão poderio dos Mouros embargo*
> *em grã quantidade por Guerra cruel.*
> *Ó mui sereníssimo Rei Manuel,*
> *a Esfera que trazes sera triunfante,*
> *se com tuas gentes passares avante,*
> *ganhando a Casa que foi d'Israel!*[11]

---

[10] "Letter from D. Manuel to the Inhabitants of Massa," Estremoz, 11 January 1497, *SIHMP*, 1:31-35. See also *HP*, 3:542-544. The friendly relationship with Massa declined following the capture of a Jew by João Lopes de Sequeira in 1510 (see chapter eight for an account of this episode) and was over by 1517 when Pero Leitão, the *capitão* of Santa Cruz, launched a raid against the city.

[11] "De Luis Anriques ao duque de Bragaça, quando tomou Azamor, em que conta como foi," in *Cancioneiro Geral* (Lisbon, 1516), fol. 103v. My prose translation is as

At one point, in 1501, it seemed as though D. Manuel himself would lead an expeditionary force to North Africa. According to Damião de Góis, the king desired to imitate his royal ancestors and "be their companion in the glory" that resulted from the conquest of infidel lands. D. Manuel's beliefs may therefore be seen as a continuation of the Joachimite millenarianism surrounding D. João I's struggles with Castile and his conquest of Ceuta.[12] This messianic viewpoint should not necessarily be considered extraordinary along a Christian-Islamic frontier. For example, Angus MacKay describes the late medieval Castilian-Granada frontier as "an eschatological one." The Spaniards believed that the Antichrist would appear in Seville and subsequently be defeated by a Spanish Messianic king. This battle would purge Islam from Iberia and would allow the Messianic king to then conquer Jerusalem and the remainder of the world for Christ.[13]

D. Manuel had more worldly considerations as well, hoping to establish a series of trading fortresses along the entire length of the African coast and block Castile's access to the African trade.[14] Consequently, the king sought to establish large fortresses that were under direct Portuguese control. Despite increasing the number of weapons and amount of supplies sent to the northern Moroccan fortresses in 1495 and receiving a grant of 50,000 *cruzados* from the Portuguese *cortes* to cover expenses of the North African wars, the king, perhaps still short on funds because of the rapidly increasing

---

follows: "The king's *capitães* increase his power and enlarge his lands among the infidels. The great power of the Muslims weakens, in large part due to bloody war. Oh most serene King Manuel, the Sphere [a symbol of authority] that you bring will be triumphant, if you and your men continue onward, winning the House that was Israel's [i.e., Jerusalem]!"

[12] Luís Filipe F. R. Thomaz, "Factions, Interests, and Messianism: The Politics of Portuguese Expansion in the East, 1500-1521," *The Indian Economic and Social History Review* 28 (1991): 97-109; Sanjay Subrahmanyam, *The Portuguese Empire in Asia, 1500-1700: A Political and Economic History* (New York: Longman, 1993), 45-51; *CDM*, 1:114-115; Margarida Garcez Ventura, "O Algarve nos primórdios da expansão: um sermão milenarista em Lagos (12 de Julho de 1415)," in *Actas das III jornadas de história medieval do Algarve e Andaluzia* (Loulé: Câmara Municipal de Loulé, 1989), 265-272.

[13] Angus MacKay, "Religion, Culture, and Ideology on the Late Medieval Castilian-Granadan Frontier," in *MFS*, 241. Such an interpretation of the Christian-Islamic frontier might help to explain why the Portuguese were able to transform the defeated and foolish king, D. Sebastião, into *O Desejado*.

[14] "Le partage des conquêtes entre L'Espagne et Le Portugal, au Maroc et sur la côte au sud du Maroc," *SIHMP*, 1:203-212.

expenditures in Brazil and India, began this process in southern Morocco by contracting with members of the Portuguese nobility to perform the work.[15] In 1505, the king gave permission to Jorge de Melo to erect a fortress at Mazagão at his own expense, and in the same year, granted a similar privilege to João Lopes de Sequeira to build a fortress in the territory of the Massa allies. This second fortress came to be known as Santa Cruz do Cabo de Gué (modern Agadir).[16] The reasons for choosing these two locations are never made explicit, though may be guessed. Mazagão was located on the ocean only ten kilometers from the mouth of the Umm al-Rabi` River. Its location would therefore give the Portuguese access to trade routes and perhaps act as a stage for a conquest of Azamor and/or a way of siphoning

---

[15] David Lopes, *A Expansão em Marrocos* (Lisbon: Editorial Teorema, 1989), 28. The privatization of colonization and expansion was similar to the captaincy system employed by the Portuguese in the Atlantic islands of Madeira, Azores, and Cape Verdes and later in Brazil after 1533, the greatest difference being that while the grants to Melo and Sequeira were limited in geographical size, grants to Brazilian donatary captains were, theoretically, massive. Donatary captaincies were established to allow Portuguese economic exploitation of Brazil and to prevent other Europeans, particularly the French, from gaining the upper hand in the region. The donatary captains were men with strong connections in the Portuguese court and from a similar social level as Melo, a *fidalgo* and commander of the king's mounted crossbowmen, and Sequeira. The Brazilian captains received most of the revenues that would have gone to the king and were given great powers over appointments, justice, and land grants. In short, just as the medieval practice of grants of lordship was continued in Brazil, so too was it attempted, albeit briefly, in Morocco. See H. B. Johnson, "Portuguese Settlement, 1500-1580," in *Colonial Brazil*, ed. Leslie Bethell (New York: Cambridge University Press, 1987), 13-16; António Vasconcelos de Saldanha, *As capitanias do Brasil: antecedents, desenvolvimento e extinção de um fenómeno atlântico* (Lisbon: CNCDP, 2001); Filipe Nunes de Carvalho, "Da instituição das capitanias-donatarias ao estabelecimento do governo-geral," in *O império luso-brasileiro, 1500-1620*, ed. Harold Johnson and Maria Beatriz Nizza da Silva (Lisbon: Editorial Estampa, 1992), 114-136.

[16] "Letter Patent of D. Manuel," Santarém, 21 May 1505, *SIHMP*, 1:108-113. The letter patent granting Sequeira the right to build seems to have disappeared, but the letter to Melo is extant. We can assume that the letters were quite similar. Melo was given permission to administer and own his fortress forever and to pass it to his heirs, so long as he obeyed certain conditions. In exchange for building and maintaining the fortress at his own cost, Melo received a ten percent duty on all grain and merchandise that passed through the city, though any other taxes could only be created with the approval of the king. Should Melo make subject and collect tribute from any Muslims living within six leagues of the fortress, he could retain all of that tribute for himself. Melo was also given the power of a *capitão*, to appoint people to offices and oversee justice within the fortress. The king, nevertheless, reserved the right to take the fortress from Melo or his heirs, provided a fair price was paid for the fortress and the yearly income it generated. If, however, Melo voluntarily wanted to give up ownership of the fortress, the king would simply pay him double what he had already spent on its construction and maintenance.

away economic power. Santa Cruz's location provided a Portuguese claim to the region that was of increasing interest to Castilians and would create a city that having access to the trade that normally flowed up the Wadi Sus River to Tarudante, about 100 kilomaters to the east. Only Santa Cruz was built; Mazagão did not get beyond planning stages at that time. Although Sequeira's construction of Santa Cruz was opposed by members of the nearby Hesqima tribe, the support he received from the Massa allowed construction to proceed quickly.[17] It might be said that without the alliance of the Massa, this fortress may still have been built, but would have been much more costly as the number of soldiers needed to protect the workers would have been extensive.

Between 1472 and 1542, the Portuguese made four attempts to build fortresses on vacant land in Morocco without the use of local allies. All of these attempts failed quickly. The first was in 1489 at Graciosa, fifteen kilometers up the Wadi Lukkus. Muhammad al-Sheikh, the Wattasid sultan, seeing the obvious threat that this new fortress would pose to his control of the region, surrounded the construction zone and periodically bombarded the workers. Within a few months, D. João II recognized the impossibility of completing the fortress under these conditions and concluded a peace so that the Portuguese could retreat without being harmed.[18] The second example was the Castelo Real at Mogador (modern Essaouria; al-Sawira). In 1506, D. Manuel ordered Diogo de Azambuja to construct the fortress. The fortress was built despite what chronicler Duarte Pacheco Pereira described as constant attacks from the local Berber and Arab inhabitants. This animosity undoubtedly contributed greatly to the rapid demise of the fortress in 1510.[19] Thirdly, in 1515 the Portuguese attempted to build a fortress at São João da Mamora at the mouth of the Wadi Sebu. Although construction of a rudimentary fortress was completed in early August, Portuguese success was short-lived. The

---

[17] Pierre de Cenival, "Introduction," in *CSC*, 15 and Farinha, *Portugueses em Marrocos*, 29.

[18] Farinha, *Portugueses em Marrocos*, 27-8; Cook, 117-118; Lopes, *A expansão*, 27.

[19] "Mogador," *SIHMP*, 1:120-127, Duarte Pacheco Pereira, *Esmeraldo de Situ Orbis* 3rd. ed., introduction and notes by Damião Peres (Lisbon: Academia Portuguesa da História, 1988), 69, and Martin Malcolm Elbl, "Portuguese Fortifications in Morocco: A Concise Overview," *Portuguese Studies Review* (2000): 90.

Wattasid sultan mercilessly attacked, forcing the Portuguese to abandon the location after the loss of 4,000 Portuguese lives and substantial sums of money.[20] The final attempt was in Aguz from 1521 to 1525. During these four years, the fortress faced constant attack by forces loyal to the Sharif. With no local allies to act as a buffer, D. João III decided to abandon the fortress in 1525.[21]

The lessons of Graciosa, Mogador, Mamora, and Aguz serve to highlight the point that prior to the conquests of existing cities, when the Portuguese concluded a treaty, they were able to have stable and pragmatic trading relations if not always amicable ones. These four attempts were moves of force that were unable to succeed without a buffer of allied Moroccans. Even Mogador would have cost many lives and much treasure to hold, though the argument can be made that with the success of the Portuguese in Dukkala, the hostile groups living near Mogador might have, eventually, been brought to heel.

Thus, in southern Morocco, before the period of direct conquest began around 1508, Portuguese alliances were very general, concentrating primarily on reciprocal trade agreements and some amount of military protection for Moroccans, both from the predations of Europeans, including Portuguese, and from other Moroccans. Although many of these elements would remain after 1508, the dominant position of the Portuguese would soon make the creation and maintenance of these alliances based not on reciprocity but on submission.

Negotiation, Hostages, and the Creation of "Trust"

There is little doubt that the influence of historical Christian-Islamic relations in medieval Portugal and Iberia weighed heavily on the Portuguese mentality. The frontier in medieval Iberia represented not only a political and military boundary but also the frontier of the ideology of the Reconquest. As a result, all frontiers with Islam were –

---

[20] "L'Expédition de la Mamora (juin-août 1515)," in *SIHMP*, 1:695-702. See Cook, 148-149, for details of the fighting at Mamora.

[21] This Aguz fortress should not be confused with a fortress of the same name erected three kilometers up the Tensift River by Diogo da Azambuja in 1507 and then abandoned later in the year. The new Aguz fortress was located on the coast at the mouth of the Tensift. See "Letter Patent of D. Manuel," Sintra, 25 August 1508, *SIHMP*, 1:171-172 and 171n1 and "Letter from D. João III to Gonçalo Mendes Sacoto," n. l., Summer 1523, *SIHMP*, 2:309-310.

in some manner – considered impermanent, a temporary barrier preventing the triumph of Christian righteousness.[22]

For the Portuguese, then, one of the most troublesome issues with alliance formation was to establish a mechanism whereby they could trust people whom many of them deemed naturally treacherous because they were Muslims.[23] Consequently, the establishment of trust was not the creation of a mutual respect between two equals built up over time and through the successful completion of acts of loyalty, but rather the creation of a system whereby the Portuguese believed they had created a situation in which an ally had no choice *except* to obey them. Such a situation was created in many ways, but the most prevalent was through the use of hostages. The mechanisms whereby alliances were created and maintained have been ignored almost entirely by historians of Portuguese Morocco. When allies are discussed, it is simply to state how and when they served the Portuguese, normally in strictly military terms. In effect, modern historians have simply parroted what Portuguese chroniclers had already argued, only usually with the increase of detail that results from archival research.

The desires of sixteenth-century Portuguese to create an artificial trust combined, paradoxically, with a belief in their own dominance. Despite the overwhelming numerical superiority of Moroccans to Portuguese, the Portuguese operated with the mentality of a dominant group. Indeed, when it came to access to tools of war, especially crossbows, guns, and artillery, there was no question that the Portuguese were much more powerful despite their small numbers. In frontier regions where force typically determines control, perceived dominance gives the group believing itself to be dominant an important psychological edge.

This feeling of domination caused the Portuguese to act in some ways as if they were administering a *mouraria* filled with a *mudéjar* (subject Muslims living in a Christian polity) population, rather than attempting to unify and control diverse and antagonisitic groups within an expansive region. Within the kingdom of Portugal, Muslims had

---

[22] Manuel González Jiménez, "Frontier and Settlement in the Kingdom of Castile (1085-1350)," in *MFS*, 49-50.

[23] See, for example, "Letter from Nuno Fernandes de Ataíde to D. Manuel," Safi, 12 September 1514, *SIHMP*, 1:634-635, and "Letter from António Leite to D. Manuel," Mazagão, 22 July 1518, *SIHMP*, 2:203.

lived, until their expulsion in 1497, in corporate municipal bodies known as *mourarias*, governed by a *comuna*. *Mouraria* (or *aljama*) refers to the physical space in which the Muslims were allowed to live, and the *comuna* refers to all of the administrative, legal, and religious structures that allowed Muslims, by royal writ, to have their own identity within a Christian kingdom, despite being subject to the general laws of the realm.[24] The king of Portugal granted each *comuna* a *foral* (pl. *forais*) memorialzing its rights and duties. In general, the Muslims were allowed to follow the religious precepts of Islam as well as Islamic law, so long as they did not run counter to royal law, which forbade proselytizing among Christians. For instance, the head-tax on the individuals in the *mouraria* was called the *alfitra*. This was based on the Islamic *al-fiṭr*, which began as a donation to the poor made at the end of Ramadan but was converted during the thirteenth century into an obligatory capitation tax by the Marinids and continued by the Christian kings. Furthermore, there was a ten percent tribute tax known as the *azaqui* placed on all fruits, livestock, merchandise, precious metals, and moveable goods. At first glance this might seem like the Christian tithe, but it was actually based on the Qur'ānic *al-zakāh*, requiring a ten percent tax on all goods and property, the proceeds of which were used for the betterment of the community. In effect, the Christian kings collected their tithe without offending religious sensibilities.[25] The *forais* restricted Christians and Jews from entering a *mouraria* and harming the Muslims, and decreed that the *comunas* could elect their own *alcaide* (from *al-qā'id*) who would administer the area.[26]

The most important position within the *comuna* was the *alcaide*. Before the reconquest, when the Muslims had been ruled by an Islamic king, the king appointed the *alcaide* who decided questions of marriage, divorce, probate, and litigation over property. He was also responsible for the protection of orphans and minors. Moreover, if needed he could direct the Friday prayers and act as the treasurer of the

---

[24] Maria Filomena Lopes de Barros, *A comuna muçulmana de Lisboa (séculos XIV e XV)* (Lisbon: Hugin, 1998), 20 and A. H. de Oliveira Marques, *Portugal na crise dos séculos XIV e XV* (Lisbon: Editorial Presença, 1986), 33.

[25] Barros, *A comuna muçulmana*, 63-64.

[26] Barros, *A comuna muçulmana*, 13.

community. After the Portuguese took over, the *alcaide* was elected by the *comuna*, unlike in Castile and Navarre. By the fourteenth and fifteenth centuries, however, this election had to be ratified by the Portuguese king. The elected term varied from one to six years, depending on the terms of the *foral*, and an *alcaide* could be reelected.[27]

The Portuguese in Morocco transferred many of these practices directly and others in spirit. The *alcaide* became the royally-appointed *alcaide dos mouros* who was in charge of overseeing large regions, often with diverse groups of people who had historic animosities with each other. This made his job extremely complex, difficult, and dangerous. The *alcaide dos mouros* ensured that Islamic law and Moroccan custom were followed as closely as possible, except where Portuguese law specifically overrode it.[28] Moroccan Muslims were also required to pay a tribute (in effect, a head tax) to their Portuguese suzerains, normally in the form of grain. The size of this tribute varied depending on the treaty negotiated with the Portuguese.

Other laws that existed within Portugal were unnecessary in Morocco. For instance, Portuguese *mudéjars*, who often had a similar physiognomy to Christian Portuguese, were required to wear special clothing to identify them so that Christian subjects might be "protected" from them. Consequently, they were required to wear traditional Islamic clothing with a white, yellow, or red moon sewn to it.[29] In Morocco, all wore traditional Islamic clothing and, with very few Moroccans able to speak Portuguese, there was no common tongue to blur ethnic distinctions.

With a dominant mindset and clear military domination, at least until the 1520s, the Portuguese were able to enter many alliance negotiations with the smaller Moroccan political entities on extremely

---

[27] Barros, *A comuna muçulmana*, 31-33.

[28] See "Letter Patent from D. Manuel," n. l., July 1516, *SIHMP*, 2:6-9 and "Plan of the Accord with the Shawiyya," Azamor, end of 1522, *SIHMP*, 2:303-307, for samples of privileges granted to *alcaides dos mouros*. At least two *alcaides* were murdered by fellow Morrocans: Yahya-u-Ta`fuft in 1518 ("Letter from D. Nuno Mascarenhas to D. Manuel," Safi 11 March 1518, *SIHMP*, 2:178-182) and an unnamed *alcaide* who had only held his post for a brief period in 1519 ("Letter from Álvaro do Cadaval to D. Manuel," Azamor, early 1519, *SIHMP*, 2:219-220).

[29] Oliveira Marques, *Portugal na crise*, 398.

favorable terms.[30] This is not to say that alliance negotiations were nothing more than a session in which the Portuguese dictated terms, but that they had the upper hand. This was especially true of the Dukkala region after the conquests of Safi (1508) and Azamor (1513) as the Portuguese quickly carved out a large sphere of influence. The Portuguese called the Moroccan Muslims who had allied with them the *mouros de pazes* (lit. "Muslims of Peaces"), or "allied Muslims," while those who had not submitted to Portuguese domination were known as *mouros de guerra* (lit. "Muslims of War").

As the region of Portuguese control expanded, each newly allied group (tribe, village, city) negotiated a peace treaty and tribute agreement with the Portuguese. The most common circumstance that brought Moroccan leaders to the negotiating table with the Portuguese was a recent display of Portuguese military prowess, such as the conquest of a city, the defeat of a large army sent by one of the more powerful Moroccan leaders, or a punishing raiding campaign. For example, in December 1510, a massive Moroccan force besieged the city of Safi. The force was comprised of members of nearly every tribal confederation and town for hundreds of kilometers and, by what seem exaggerated Portuguese accounts, consisted of 600,000 people with 200,000 of them combatants. Nevertheless, with superior weapons and reinforcements from Madeira, the Portuguese were able to break the siege after a week of fighting, with very few losses.[31] This spectacular defeat put those who had participated in the battle to flight or brought them to the negotiating table. Negotiations typically included the Portuguese *capitão, contador*, interpreters, scribes, the *alcaide dos mouros*, and the leaders of the group seeking alliance.[32] Other than those

---

[30] Even during this dominant era, there were brief periods when Portuguese prestige was threatened and negotiations were made much more difficult. These events presaged increasing Portuguese problems in Morocco after the mid-1520s.

[31] "Letter from Nuno Gato to D. Manuel," 3 January 1511, *SIHMP*, 1:271-280. See chapter seven for a detailed discussion of this siege.

[32] In fact, although the *capitão* had the power to conclude treaties himself, he normally refused to conclude treaties until the *alcaide dos mouros* could be present, as it was the *alcaide's* prerogative to participate in the negotiations and the *alcaide* who would have to enforce any treaty. See, for example, "Letter from Simão Correia to D. Manuel," Azamor, 3 October 1516, *SIHMP*, 2:34-36 and "Letter from D. Nuno Mascarenhas to D. Manuel," Safi, 29 July 1518, *SIHMP*, 2:207-212.

present at the talks, we do not know much about how these particular negotiations proceeded, but we do know their results.

According to a tribute book that has been transcribed and published by Moroccan historian Ahmed Boucharb, the towns, villages, and nomadic *dawwārs* were typically required to pay annual tributes (known as *parias*) in the form of grain, normally wheat but sometimes barley or a combination of the two. Tribute might also consist of other goods, such as animals or honey. The size of the tribute varied by the size of the group that had entered into the agreement. Small villages and nomads paid less, while city residents paid more. For instance, the village of Oeres, in which there were sixty dwellings, was obliged to pay 300 *alqueires* of wheat and 200 of barley per year. This works out to five *alqueires* of wheat and three and one-third *alqueires* of barley per dwelling. The Beni Maker, a large Berber tribe living in the vicinity of Safi, was obliged to pay eight *alqueires* of wheat or sixteen *alqueires* of barley per dwelling per year. These amounts were, in fact, the median size of tribute. By contrast, residents of the cities of Almedina and Tazarote were to pay one camel load of wheat per dwelling per year. According to calculations at the time, one camel could carry twenty-five *alqueires*. Additionally, Tazarote was to give the *capitão* of Safi a falcon and a horse.

Furthermore, most, though not all, groups that concluded a treaty in 1511 and 1512 were required to submit hostages to the Portuguese to ensure that the agreements would be honored and the payments would be made. Hostages were effectively human collateral. Typically, the larger the overall tribute amount was, the greater number of hostages required by the Portuguese. Based on the names listed in the tribute book published by Boucharb, every one of these hostages was the son of a leader who had entered the treaty. The hostages ranged in age from thirteen to twenty-eight years old, with ages under eighteen being the most common.[33]

---

[33] "Letter of Nuno Gato to D. Manuel," Safi, 4-5 December 1510, *SIHMP*, 1:259-261; "Livro dos tributos reais com os Mouros e Alarves da cidade de Almydina, com toda a Duquela e terra de Shyadma com seus castelos, Contribuyam aos reys deste reyno; os quaes comecaram a pagar nos annos de 1510 e 1512," ANTT, NA 869, published in *DIB*, 493-519. A reference to this tribute book is made in "Letter from Nuno Gato to D. Manuel," Safi, 12 May 1512, *SIHMP*, 1:303.

It was hostages, in fact, that the Portuguese utilized in order to create a situation that allowed them to deal as confidently as possible with Moroccan Muslims. They were the most important mechanism for the creation of trust. The exchange of hostages to solidify agreements was common along the frontier between Islam and Christianity in medieval Iberia and among Moroccans as well.[34] Consequently, it was not an innovation on the part of the Portuguese to do this, though it did become, except in rare cases, the sine qua non for any agreement, especially in the initial stages. Hostages are also the tool of choice for a militarily dominant group that faces the uncertainty of predicting the behavior of a less powerful group retaining a large degree of freedom of action.[35]

Numerous examples might be cited, but three serve to make the point. First, one of the few examples of a Portuguese who willingly submitted to being held hostage in Morocco was D. Fernando, the Infante Santo, or "Holy Prince," who was held in Tangiers from 1437 until his death in 1443, as a guarantee that the Portuguese would return Ceuta to Moroccan control. The Moroccan forces that had utterly destroyed the Portuguese army at Tangiers could dictate terms for the evacuation of that army, and the most important condition was their desire to hold a high-ranking hostage to guarantee compliance. The army was evacuated, but Ceuta was never returned to the Moroccans and the royal hostage, D. Fernando, died in captivity.[36] In 1471, the Portuguese conquered Arzila, capturing the son of the man who would soon be the Wattasid sultan, Muhammad al-Sheikh. The Portuguese

---

[34] For Iberia, see R. I. Burns, *Islam Under the Crusaders: Colonial Survival in the Thirteenth-Century Kingdom of Valencia* (Princeton: Princeton University Press, 1973), 168; Idem, "How to End a Crusade: Techniques for Making Peace in the Thirteenth-Century Kingdom of Valencia," in Idem, *Moors and Crusaders in Mediterranean Spain* (London: Variorum, 1978), IV:3-4; José Enrique López de Coca Castañer, "Institutions on the Castilian-Granadan Frontier, 1369-1482," in *MFS*, 133. For examples of hostage exchanges between Moroccans, see, "Letter from D. Nuno Mascarenhas to D. Manuel," Safi, 11 March 1518, *SIHMP*, 2:179-180 and "Letter from Inácio Nunes Gato to D. João III," Safi, 30 May 1541, *SIHMP*, 3:409.

[35] Robin Frame, "Military Service in the Lordship of Ireland, 1290-1360: Institutions and Society on the Anglo-Gaelic Frontier," in *MFS*, 101.

[36] Peter Russell, *Prince Henry "The Navigator": A Life* (New Haven: Yale University Press, 2001), 167-194; D. Fr. João Álvarez, *Chronica do Infante Santo D. Fernando* ed. Mendes dos Remedios (Coimbra, 1911); Paulo Drumond Braga, "O Mito do 'Infante Santo'," in *Ler História* 25 (1994): 3-10.

took the young boy to Lisbon where they held him until a peace agreement could be reached with his father and it was clear that his father would honor the agreement. The boy was later returned to his father and inherited the throne in 1504. Finally, when the Portuguese were establishing their *feitoria* in Massa in 1497, they might be seen as the dominant group in that the leaders of Massa had called on the Portuguese to be their protectors in exchange for economic access. The king of Portugal, fearful that his *feitoria* might come under attack before its defensive walls could be completed, required that the leaders of Massa send fifteen of their sons as hostages to Portugal to remain there until all work was satisfactorily completed.[37]

For the Portuguese hostage-holder, hostages created the artificial trust required for one simple reason: hostages were the children and wives of hostage-givers. Few men would deliberately violate a trust if it cost them their family. Nevertheless, there are at least a few cases of valueless Moroccan leaders giving low-status hostages to the Portuguese in an effort to gain more political latitude. They paid commoners from their tribe or village to place their children with the Portuguese instead. In 1514, an outraged Rui Barreto, *capitão* of Azamor, disclosed that a number of the hostages given to guarantee various peace treaties were the sons of commoners, rather than leaders. He reported that the parents of the boys had been compensated by their leaders with cows and sheep.[38] For Barreto, this was clearly an indication of bad faith, if not potential treachery. More generally, this indicates that hostage exchange was not a fool-proof mechanism for the establishment of trust, but it was the best available.

Protocol of hostage exchange required that, while those submitting the hostages had to comply with conditions necessary to ensure their eventual return, those holding the hostages had to treat them humanely and provide their room and board. From the sparse evidence available, it seems that Moroccan hostages in Portuguese hands were treated well, with their food and shelter provided at royal expense. Because the number of these hostages could be quite large, the expense were often considerable. On 4 January 1509, the *capitão* of

---

[37] "Letter from D. Manuel to the Inhabitants of Massa," Estremoz, 11 January 1497, *SIHMP*, 1:35.

[38] "Letter from Rui Barreto to D. Manuel," Azamor, 21 February 1514, *SIHMP*, 1:494.

Safi ordered that Isaac bin Zamiro be paid 12,750 *reis* for 150 *alqueires* of wheat to be used to feed an unknown number of Moroccan hostages held in Safi.[39] In June 1512, there were fifty-three hostages being held in Safi, though this was likely an exceptionally large number since treaty negotiations were still in progress after the rupture caused by the 1510 siege.[40] In December 1512, the number had decreased to thirty-three and cost the Portuguese 6,000 *reis* per month to feed and house them.[41] In 1521, the *feitor* of Azamor spent 80,000 *reis*, providing food for 44 Muslim hostages over ten months.[42]

Expenses could mount when particularly important hostages arrived with servants. For instance, in 1521, a group of Moroccan women and their retainers arrived in Azamor as hostages. For their maintenance, the *capitão* ordered that six oxen and twenty-eight goats be purchased for a cost of 5,200 *reis* and given to them.[43] Hostages, it seems, were housed with residents who could afford to maintain them during their stay. These residents would later be reimbursed for their expenditures by the royal treasury. For instance, João Mendes, the *contador* of Azamor in 1522, was paid 3750 *reis* per month every month for the five hostages who were living at his house.[44] An order of 27 July 1523, required Benito Maça, the *feitor* of Azamor, to house "some Muslim women, their children and slave, and to care for [*sustentar*] them for as long as they stay there."[45] While it might be expected that these female hostages would face the problem of unwanted advances from their male hosts, there is no evidence of this happening. It also seems that, at least in Safi, the Portuguese appointed someone full-time to

---

[39] ANTT CC II, 16, 45.

[40] "Letter from Heitor Gonçalves to D. Manuel," Safi, 18 June 1512, *SIHMP*, 1:332.

[41] "Letter from Heitor Gonçalves to D. Manuel," Safi, 15 December 1512, *SIHMP*, 1:367. This came to 182 *reis* per person per month. This was roughly equivalent to the monthly salary of a mounted page and nearly one hundred *reis* more than that of a *degredado* serving in the infantry (See Table 2.3).

[42] ANTT, CC II, 100, 103.

[43] ANTT CC II, 98, 33.

[44] ANTT CC II, 105, 84 and 96.

[45] ANTT, CC II, 109, 45. Although hostages were almost always kept at the homes of Portuguese, there are at least two references to Sheikh Melik bin Daud, a Moroccan ally of the Portuguese near Santa Cruz, holding hostages in 1517 and 1518 (ANTT, CC II, 72, 150 and CC II, 74, 90).

supervise and act as liaison for the hostages. In 1512, that man was João Cotrim, who apparently spoke both Arabic and Berber fluently.[46]

Despite the necessity of treating hostages well in order to ensure stability in political relations with the Moroccans, suspicions often crept into the relationships between the two sides. In one instance, many of the Moroccan leaders who had given their wives and children as hostages to D. Álvaro de Noronha, the *capitão* of Azamor, believed that he had sent some of them to Castile to be sold into slavery. To put a stop to these rumors, all the affected leaders were brought to the city of Azamor in February 1519 and shown their families. Martim Vaz, temporary *contador* of Azamor, then recorded their affidavits that they had seen their family members and that the *capitão* had done nothing improper.[47]

Hostages were held for varying periods. For example, in 1519, D. Nuno Mascarenhas, the *capitão* of Safi, heard a rumor that a large force, led by the Hintati amirs and consisting of several large tribal groups, would soon attack Safi. He quickly began negotiations with the Gharbiyya and `Abda tribes in order to end their intertribal squabbles so that they could form a united force with the Portuguese against the upcoming attack. The parties concluded a treaty, and the leaders of each group sent hostages to Safi as a guarantee. Soon thereafter, the enemy coalition disintegrated as its members began to fight amongst themselves. Consequently, there was no need for Mascarenhas's defensive alliance, and he quickly returned the hostages.[48]

Hostages were a particularly devious political tool, causing great anguish to the giver of the hostages, leading, normally, to his compliance. In December 1513, a sheikh of the Hesqima tribe, Mimūn, appeared before the new *capitão* of Santa Cruz, Francisco de Castro, and told him that the former *capitão*, João Lopes de Sequeira, had taken two of his children to Portugal because he owed him fifty ounces of silver. By this date, these hostages had been held for nearly

---

[46] "Letter from Heitor Gonçalves to D. Manuel," Safi, 15 December 1512, *SIHMP*, 1:369. Gonçalves says of Cotrim that "*sabe muyto bem as lynguas d'esta terra.*"

[47] ANTT CC I, 24, 31; Maria Augusta Lima Cruz Fagundes, "Documentos Ineditos para a Historia dos Portugueses em Azamor," *Arquivos do Centro Cultural Portugues* 2 (1970), 151-152.

[48] "Letter from D. Nuno Mascarenhas to D. Manuel," Safi, 10 February 1519, *SIHMP*, 2:227-229.

one year. An anguished Mimūn asked that D. Manuel return the children to Santa Cruz and put them in Castro's custody so that he could at least visit them while he gathered the money to pay his debt. Afonso Rodrigues, the *feitor* of Santa Cruz, advised the king to do this, as Mimūn seemed like a good person deserving of this courtesy.[49]

These examples do not mean that Moroccan leaders simply submitted to all terms offered by the Portuguese and then handed over their loved ones. On the contrary, negotiation was a contingent process that was not governed strictly by which group in the discussions could be considered the dominant one. Moroccan leaders, of course, made their own demands and suggestions, and the context of recent events could have a profound effect on the success or failure of negotiations. A recent Portuguese military success or defeat could result in many new allies or in old allies abandoning them. Finally, negotiation was not just face-to-face talks, but also the symbolic acts of the two sides outside the confines of direct discussions that aided in the establishment of trust and alliance.

The demands of Moroccan leaders were, at times, problematic for the Portuguese. Appeals for the return of captives who had been seized during warfare and made slaves were, in fact, a common request of Moroccan leaders who were in negotiations with the Portuguese. The kings of Portugal normally supported such exchanges in the interests of promoting peace and stability, but some Portuguese, living in Morocco and seeking personal gain, were not interested in diplomacy. For example, when Nuno Fernandes de Ataíde, the *capitão* of Safi, was negotiating a treaty with the city of Almedina in 1512, he requested that the king pay indemnities to the owners of captives from Almedina before he would release them. Not surprisingly, he owned a number of these captives.[50]

One Moroccan requested, somewhat impractically, that the negotiations and the alliance that resulted from them between his people and the Portuguese be kept as secret as possible due to his fear of reprisals. During the conquest of Azamor in 1513, all the Muslim residents of the city fled. Shortly thereafter, many of them wished to

---

[49] "Letter from Afonso Rodrigues to D. Manuel," Santa Cruz, 24 December 1513, *SIHMP*, 1:476.

[50] ANTT, CC I, 11, 83, also cited in *SIHMP*, 1:309n2.

return to their homes, entering into negotiations with their new Portuguese lords. One of these groups was the Shawiyyans who had been living in Azamor. Lud, the Shawiyyan representative sent as an ambassador to Portugal in order to conclude an agreement with D. Manuel, asked that the king allow the residents of Azamor to return to live in the city.[51] If they were not allowed to live within the city, then they should be allowed to live on a nearby cape on the river because "they are fishermen" and because they knew how to make *cal* (baked lime used in mortar) for the city, which was very important at the moment. Lud ended the letter asking the king to keep his travels to Portugal as secret as possible because if the Wattasid sultan discovered them, he would capture him and have him burnt.[52]

Just as fear in a chaotic context affected Lud's requests, instability also promoted changes in the alliance structure. Many Moroccan leaders, especially of smaller groups, tried to predict the changing winds and join with the groups they thought would afford them the most protection at that moment. It was much like an exercise in reading constantly shifting tea leafs. Despite occasional calls for holy war (*jihād*) against the Portuguese issued by the Hintati, the Wattasids, and especially the Sa`adids and the rural *zāwiyas*, more practical and worldly concerns drove the decision-making of most Moroccans.[53] As Robert I. Burns argues, "The movements of any actor in the frontier drama . . . must be assessed against the international pressures, limitations, and options affecting him."[54] In other words, actors are only as loyal as their options. The Portuguese knew this and worked diligently to create a situation that limited the scope of a Moroccan leader's actions to the greatest extent possible.

---

[51] It was not uncommon for Moroccan leaders to visit the Portuguese court in order to confirm an alliance, though typically all the negotiations were concluded in Morocco. For some examples, see "Letter from D. Manuel to the Inhabitants of Massa," Estremoz, 11 January 1497, *SIHMP*, 1:31-35; "Letter from Nuno Gato to D. Manuel," Safi, 12 May 1512, *SIHMP*, 1:302; ANTT, CC I, 15, 122; CC I, 17, 63; CC I, 17, 57.

[52] "Letter from Lud to D. Manuel," n. l., c. 5 December 1513, *SIHMP*, 1:457-458.

[53] It should also be kept in mind that while the Wattasids and the Sa`adids were calling on all zealous Muslims to expel the Portuguese infidels, they were engaged in war with each other for control of the rest of Morocco.

[54] Robert I. Burns, "The Significance of the Frontier in the Middle Ages," in *MFS*, 320.

There are numerous examples of the Portuguese gaining new allies shortly after a great victory. The political climate in Dukkala after the Portuguese victory against a besieging army in December 1510 has already been mentioned. But such influences could be felt on a smaller scale as well. In February 1514, the Portuguese launched devastating raids against the Sharquiyyan villages of Benacafiz and Tafuf (60-70 kilometers upriver from Azamor), resulting in the death and capture of hundreds of Moroccans. Shortly thereafter, leaders from the nearby towns of Tejeste and Seita as well as other leaders in the area made their intentions known to travel to Azamor and begin peace negotiations.[55]

Conversely, a loss of Portuguese military prestige could lead to the evaporation of allies. A particularly startling example of this can be seen in the Dukkala region surrounding Safi from 1515 to 1518. Since the breaking of the 1510 siege of Safi, the Portuguese had been a nearly unstoppable force in southern Morocco. D. Manuel therefore saw the time as propitious to construct a new fortress, that of São João da Mamora at the mouth of the Wadi Sebu. As mentioned earlier, the Wattasid sultan forced the Portuguese from their location in August 1515, after killing 4,000 of them. This was the first chink in the armor of the Portuguese, though with Nuno Fernandes de Ataíde in command in Safi, things remained in Portuguese control, a brief period of unrest notwithstanding.

In May 1516, however, Ataíde was killed during a raid. Because Yahya-u-Ta`fuft, the powerful *alcaide dos mouros* of Dukkala, had been recalled to Lisbon in August 1514 due to false accusations of disloyalty, no one was able to calm the fear of Portugal's allies or to restrain their desire to break their alliances. Among others, the Arabs of `Abda and Seja had allied with the Sharif, while those of Gharbiyya had allied with the Hintati ruler in Marrakech. Fortunately for the Portuguese, Yahya-u-Ta`fuft returned to Safi on 21 July 1516, and by the middle of August, he had successfully renegotiated alliances with most of the breakaway leaders.[56] This renewed Portuguese prominence

---

[55] "Letter from João de Meneses to D. Manuel," Azamor, c. 15 February 1514, *SIHMP*, 1:482-484; "Letter from João de Meneses to D. Manuel," Azamor, 18 February 1514, *SIHMP*, 1:485-488; *CDM*, 3:190-192.

[56] "Mort de Nuno Fernandes de Ataíde," *SIHMP*, 2:1-5; *CDM*, 4:14-19; "Letter from Yahya-u-Ta`fuft to D. Manuel," Safi, 9 August 1516, *SIHMP*, 2:24-26; Matthew T.

lasted about eighteen months. In February 1518, Yahya-u-Ta`fuft was assassinated by Ghanem and Ishshu, two brothers from the `Abda tribe, with the complicity of many other tribal groups in the area. Although allies did not break away as catastrophically as they had in 1516, this marked the beginning of the gradual and ineluctable contraction of Portuguese influence and power in southern Morocco.[57]

Finally, negotiation cannot be understood without reference to the symbolic value of Portuguese actions. An important reason for this was the language barrier, for where differing languages impede communication, "politics must of necessity be practiced through symbols, myths, and rituals."[58] Although interpreters were available during face-to-face negotiations, the daily interactions with Portuguese and Moroccans needed to have some sort of symbolic currency to convince the non-elite Moroccans of Portuguese goodwill. As regards negotiation and alliance, this meant that the Portuguese needed to appear, at least on occasion, to make an effort to understand the sentiments and practices of Moroccans. The Portuguese needed to make gestures towards peace and alliance, and not just towards war and conquest, in order to make alliance-building possible.

After a battle in 1525 in which Sa`īd-u-Mubarek, the cousin and brother-in-law of the Sharif, was killed, António Leitão de Gamboa, the *capitão* of Santa Cruz, ordered that his body be buried, as he had never noted a custom among the Muslims to ransom corpses, as the Portuguese did, and confirmed this suspicion by questioning the *mouros de pazes* who were with him. In this case, however, the Sharif sent two men to request that the body be returned to him. Leitão thought it would be best to do this, disinterred the body, and even ordered it dressed in a silk *marlota* (cloak) that he owned. In explaining

---

Racine, "Service and Honor in Sixteenth-Century Portuguese North Africa: Yahya-u-Ta`fuft and Portuguese Noble Culture," *Sixteenth Century Journal* 32 (2001): 76-80, 83.

[57] "Letter from Yahya-u-Ta`fuft to D. Manuel," Safi, 28 March 1517, *SIHMP*, 2:69; "Letter from Mascarenhas to D. Manuel," Safi, 11 March 1518, *SIHMP*, 2:178-82; "Letter from Mascarenhas to D. Manuel," Safi, 29 July 1518, *SIHMP*, 2:204-13; "Letter from Mascarenhas to D. Manuel," Safi, 3 September 1518, *SIHMP*, 2:214-18; *CDM*, 4:171-173, which incorrectly gives the date of Yahya's death as 1521; *HP*, 3:497-98; Durval R. Pires de Lima, *História da dominação portuguêsa em Çafim (1506-1542)* (Lisbon, 1930), 43, 79; Racine, "Service and Honor," 88.

[58] William Palmer, "That 'Insolent Liberty': Honor, Rites of Power, and Persuasion in Sixteenth-Century Ireland," *Renaissance Quarterly* 46 (1993): 310.

his charitable and tender action to D. João III, he said that "this may seem strange to Your Highness, but to those who know this land, I believe that in this I did you a great service."[59] Clearly, Leitão hoped that this would lead to better relations with the Sharif. In the end, it may have helped accomplish this goal as a two-year peace agreement was concluded with the Sharif later that year.[60]

General pardons and releases were also an important symbolic element of Portuguese generosity in power. After the disastrous defeat at Mamora in August 1515, a brief period of rebelliousness and lawlessness erupted in Dukkala as rumors began to circulate that the Portuguese would soon be expelled from Morocco and the Sharif's military would fill the vacuum.[61] This lasted less than a month, and by September 1515, order and peace were being reestablished in the region. In order to solidify this restored stability and to prevent recrimination, Ataíde took the unusual step of pardoning everyone, "Arab and Berber," for any crimes he might have committed during this period. Ataíde included even the crimes of murder and rape. Furthermore, he promised that once an ally returned to peace, he would not be made to pay any sort of financial penalty, only the tributes that had been previously agreed to before his rebellion.[62] Although we can only guess at the feelings of those whose family members had been raped or murdered, this ploy seems to have reestablished peace, as Ataíde was, by December 1515, engaging in distant expeditions beyond Tednest, over 100 kilometers to the south.[63]

Symbolic actions were also calculated to instill obedience in Moroccans. When Moroccan leaders traveled to Portugal in order to meet with the king and conclude peace agreements, it appears as though they were required to swear an oath of loyalty.[64] This oath was

---

[59] "Letter from António Leitão de Gamboa to D. João III," Santa Cruz, 16 January 1525, *SIHMP*, 2:336, 340.

[60] For other events leading up to this peace, see chapter four.

[61] "Letter from Álvaro do Tojal to D. Manuel," Safi, 21 August 1515, *SIHMP*, 1:742.

[62] "Proclamation of Nuno Fernandes de Ataíde to the Tribes," n. l., after 19 September 1515, *SIHMP*, 1:759-760.

[63] "Letter of Nuno Fernandes de Ataíde to D. Manuel," Safi, 15 December 1515, *SIHMP*, 1:764-767 and *SIHMP*, 1:759n1.

[64] Oaths of loyalty were, in fact, commonly recited when Portuguese were appointed to positions. See *Ordenações Manuelinas*, I, I, 2-6; I, II, 2; I, XXIX, 2 and 5; I, LV, 4, for

filled with Islamic religious resonance and chivalric overtones, though, according to L. P. Harvey, the oath was clearly written by someone who, trying to impress Muslims with symbols of their religion, did not understand Islam very well.[65] All key Moroccan allies were given symbols of their alliance, which reminded them of their oaths. These devices typically included royal banners or flags (*bandeiras*), drums (*atambores*), well-made tents (*tendas*), and valuable gifts of clothing. As explained in a treaty agreement of 1522, these objects were "the principal sign" that a person was allied with the Portuguese and had "royal protection."[66]

Nuno Fernandes de Ataíde alluded to another motive of sending Moroccan leaders to Portugal: to instill awe in them. In a letter to the king that accompanied a group of new allies to Portugal, Ataíde wrote, "I remind Your Highness that you ought to order that Sintra, which is so different from Dukkala and their *dawwārs*, be shown to [these] Muslims. I won't speak of things in Lisbon, because they will see them, and I believe that nothing will impress them more than the Mint."[67] Sintra, a verdant and breezy village that housed a royal palace, is located about thirty kilometers north-west of Lisbon. In addition to the difference in climate from hot, dry Dukkala, a ruined medieval castle, once controlled by Islamic forces, sits atop a seemingly

---

examples of oaths sworn by newly appointed *regedores, desembargadores, corregedores, ouvidores, juizes de fora, chanceler mor, governador da justicia na casa do civil*, and *alcaides mores*.

[65] L. P. Harvey, "*Aljamia Portuguesa* Revisited," in *Portuguese Studies* 2 (1986): 1-14. The text of the oath is in Harvey and David Lopes, *Textos em Aljamía Portuguesa* (Lisbon, 1897), 50-51:

> Juro por Deus, por Deus, por Deus, criador do ceo e da terra, e por suas circumstancias visiveis e invisiveis, e polo meu profeta Mufumade Almostafa, que pregou e firmou e mostrou a fé que nós outros mouros e salamões queremos, e polo alcorão, e o qual está escrito em arabigo, a fé que nós outros temos, e polo salseiro de Davi, e polos evangelhos de Jesu Cristo, e polos cento e vinte e quarto profetas de Deus, de que Adão foi o primeiro, e pola alma do menino meu padre, e pola vida de meus filhos, e pola minha cabeça, e pola espada que cinjo, eu pormeto de fazer tal cousa.

[66] For some examples, see "Letter from Yahya bin Belsbā` to D. Manuel," n. l., end of May 1517, *SIHMP*, 2:91-92; "Letter from `Abd al-Rahman bin Haddu to D. Manuel," n. l., after January 1521, *SIHMP*, 2:287; "Peace Agreement with the Shawiyya," Azamor, end of 1522, *SIHMP*, 2:306. For more information on gifts given to Moroccan allies of the Portuguese, see below.

[67] "Letter from Nuno Fernandes de Ataíde to D. Manuel," Safi, 13 May 1512, *SIHMP*, 1:307.

unattainable precipice. Showing the Royal Mint to the Moroccan dignitaries was clearly calculated to demonstrate the vast wealth, at least relative to these tribal leaders, of the Portuguese, hinting at the benefits that might accrue as the result of loyal service.

Mistrust

Nevertheless, loyalty and trust were commodities often in short supply in Portuguese-occupied Morocco. Constant shifting of alliances as well as a Portuguese belief in the intrinsic perfidy of Muslims did much to undermine any trust that could be formed between the two groups. Some, though not all, of the Portuguese in Morocco believed that one's religion determined the worth of one's word. When Nuno Fernandes de Ataíde confronted D. Rodrigo de Noronha, a friend of Yahya-u-Ta`fuft, with strenuous accusations of Yahya's disloyalty, Noronha defended his friend saying that the charges were false. Ataíde could not believe that Noronha would defend Yahya because Ataíde was a Christian while Yahya was a Muslim. Ataíde concluded that because he was Christian and Yahya a Muslim that Noronha should believe his co-religionist.[68] Moreover, although it is difficult to find extensive evidence of it in these sources, it is clear that many Moroccans had similar opinions about the motivations underpinning Christian behavior.

The underlying belief that religion created honesty and trust would prove disastrous in May 1533 for the *capitão* of Santa Cruz, Simão Gonçalves da Costa. One of the *capitão's* most trusted servants was Diogo, a Moroccan who had converted to Christianity "many years" earlier. Diogo had keys to everything in the fortress, including the aptly named *porta da treição*.[69] As the *capitão* ordered everyone in the city to take a daily rest (*sesta*) between noon and one o'clock, Diogo chose this time to commit his treason: opening the *porta da treição* to several thousand of the Sharif's troops, who had somehow managed to

---

[68] "Letter from Nuno Fernandes de Ataíde to D. Manuel," Safi, 12 September 1514, *SIHMP*, 1:634-635.

[69] The "treason door" existed so that during a siege, troops could directly enter or exit a fortress in a hidden location rather than through the main gate. The *porta da treição* in Santa Cruz granted access both to the land and the beach. Diogo had a key to this gate, which was in the fortresses' cellar, "*porque trazia galinhas na cava e ia-lhe dar de comer*" (*CSC*, 56).

approach undetected to within a few hundred meters of the fortress. Fortunately for the Portuguese, an old woman was sitting on a veranda and saw the enemy sneaking into the fortress. She alerted the city with screams of "Treason!" The *capitão*, who slept through the screams, was caught and killed by the infiltrators. Nevertheless, the Portuguese were able to fairly quickly clear the city of enemy troops, forcing some to jump to their deaths from high fortress walls. A siege of several days followed, at the end of which only forty men in the fortress were capable of fighting. Yet, the Sharif and his troops finally withdrew and Santa Cruz was saved.[70]

The Portuguese were not alone in the belief that religion affected one's trustworthiness. In a few places, we can see that Moroccans felt that Christianity was reason for concern.[71] In June 1517, when Yahya-u-Ta`fuft was at the nadir of his popularity in Safi and Dukkala, he was taunted, by both Portuguese and Moroccans, as he walked through the streets. The Moroccans said that he "was a Christian," implying that by his loyalty to Portugal he had been stained by the "Portuguese" religion. In fact, Yahya said that the attacks against his character were worse from his co-religionists than from Christians, some of whom had questioned his loyalty since his appointment as *alcaide dos mouros* in 1511.[72] This simmering animosity represents an undercurrent of dislike for the Christian Portuguese overlords that was normally hidden.

The Portuguese themselves believed that there was a generalized religious animosity against Christians pervading Islamic Morocco. In 1519, D. Manuel, perhaps reacting to the murder of Yahya-u-Ta`fuft during the previous year and the resultant disorder in Dukkala, suggested that a Christian should be named the new *alcaide* of al-Khemis, the suburb just outside the southern gate of Safi. D. Nuno Mascarenhas argued that this would be very disruptive, requiring many

---

[70] *CSC*, 56-76. Diogo apparently had other Moroccan residents of Santa Cruz assisting him. Following the Portuguese victory, the goods of all the "*mouros de treição*" were confiscated and redistributed to residents of Santa Cruz. For example, one Pero Ribeiro received a horse (ANTT CC I, 51, 80).

[71] In fact, Islamic legal doctrine of the period posited that normal relations between the two religious groups was a state of war (Castañer, 130).

[72] "Letter from Yahya-u-Ta`fuft to D. Nuno," Safi, after 24 June 1517, *SIHMP*, 2:107-108 and Racine, "Service and Honor," 85.

Political Alliances

new laws and customs, and would likely put the residents of al-Khemis to flight. In short, the plan to Christianize leadership of any Moroccan Muslims would be a "great disservice" to the king.[73]

In addition to a general distrust of Muslims, the Portuguese had a difficult time adapting to the internal rivalries and animosities within Morocco. How the Portuguese conceived "Moroccans" as opposed to "Muslims" reveals another level of uncertainty and confusion that could lead to a lack of trust. Some Portuguese would maintain the fiction that the Islamic identity of Moroccans overrode all other considerations. Heitor Gonçalves, the *feitor* of Safi, reported to the king that many nomadic Arab tribes, as well as the `Abda and the Gharbiyya confederations, had all paid their tribute on time due to the influence of Yahya-u-Ta`fuft, whom they greatly respected "because he is a Muslim as they are."[74] Two years later, in 1514, another Portuguese reported to the king that due to the fact that Yahya was a Berber, many times the Arabs did not want to obey him. In this case, ethnicity seemed a more effective explanation for the behavior of Moroccans than religion.[75] Beyond this were various political bickerings between Arab tribal groups or Berber tribal groups, where economics or politics were the likely explanations. It was a confusing situation that could easily give rise to distrust and suspicion.

Another problem for the Portuguese was what they saw as the Moroccan exploitation of alliance for their own benefit. Taking titles beyond what the Portuguese deemed appropriate was one concern. `Abd al-Rahman, the *qā'id* of Safi before the Portuguese conquest, took to calling himself the "Lord of Safi" (*senhor de Safi*). D. Manuel quickly reprimanded him for this, commenting that only he, as king and suzerain, was permitted to employ that title.[76] In 1512, Yahya-u-Ta`fuft was accused of ordering Moroccans in his *alcaidaria* to address him as "king." Although he may not have used the Portuguese "*rei*," he did

---

[73] "Letter from D. Nuno Mascarenhas to D. Manuel," Safi, early 1519, *SIHMP*, 2:223-224. For more on al-Khemis, see *SIHMP*, 1:273n1.

[74] "Letter from Heitor Gonçalves to D. Manuel," Safi, 15 December 1512, *SIHMP*, 1:368.

[75] "Letter from Estêvão Rodrigues Berrio to D. Manuel," Tavira, 19 May 1514, *SIHMP*, 1:555-556.

[76] "Instructions of D. Manuel for `Ali bin Washman," n. l., 15 June 1500, *SIHMP*, 1:55-56.

want to be addressed by the roughly equivalent Arabic titles of "amir" and "sultan." The fear among some Portuguese was that Yahya might be plotting to expel the Portuguese from Safi and establish his own principality.[77]

During the autumn of 1519, members of the Awlad Subeita moved their tents and came to live near the walls of Azamor. They did this so that they could have Portuguese protection while they grew their grain crops during the rainy season. The Portuguese welcomed them, offering them protection and benefiting from the firewood and meat that the Awlad Subeita provided for them. After the growing season was over, the tribe's cattle were fat and they were flush with grain, but refused to store any of it in Azamor. This angered the *capitão* of Azamor, D. Álvaro de Noronha, who felt that the Awlad Subeita had taken advantage of the Portuguese for their own benefit and were ungrateful for the protection they had received. Noronha asked the king to order that they leave the grain in Azamor.[78] The Moroccans in this case wanted to retain freedom of action that they would lose if the Portuguese kept all of their grain, not to mention the fear that the Portuguese might refuse to distribute it to them should the city of Azamor experience one of its recurring grain shortages.

According to at least one Portuguese official, many Moroccans were even able to exploit their brief rebellions for personal financial gain. António Leite suggested in 1518 that the Portuguese policy of welcoming back lapsed allies with no punishment and, in fact, giving them gifts to welcome their return, was fatally flawed. He listed a series of treasons committed by various "Muslims" and argued that they would never learn to behave unless they were punished for their wrongs. For Leite, the Portuguese were reinforcing negative behavior,

---

[77] "*Qanūn* of Yahya-u-Ta`fuft," n. l., 16-25 June 1512, *SIHMP*, 1:316-325; "*Qanūn* of Yahya-u-Ta`fuft," n. l., June 1512, *SIHMP*, 1:326-329; "Letter from Nuno Fernandes de Ataíde to D. Manuel," Safi, 19 August 1512, *SIHMP*, 1:337-353; "Deposition against Yahya-u-Ta`fuft," n. l., early 1513, SIHMP, 1:378-80; "Deposition against Yahya-u-Ta`fuft," n. l., after 28 January 1513, *SIHMP*, 1:381-384; Racine, "Service and Honor," 76-78.

[78] "Letter from D. Álvaro de Noronha to D. Manuel," Azamor, 15 December 1519, *SIHMP*, 2:260-263; "Letter from D. Álvaro de Noronha to D. Manuel," Azamor, 18 April 1520, *SIHMP*, 2:273-275.

and the Moroccans were happily committing increasingly grievous treasons in order to become increasingly wealthy.[79]

D. Nuno Mascarenhas echoed these sentiments later that same year. He described a recent peace agreement reached with the `Abda tribes as "one that we hold as genuine, because it is won by the lance and not by bribes (*peitas*)." Nevertheless, Mascarenhas was still cynical about the long-term stability of this peace. According to him, raiding by Mawlay al-Naser, the brother of the Wattasid sultan, in Dukkala during June 1518 had forced the `Abda to conclude a peace because they feared that "thousands" of their children would die of starvation without a treaty and thus alliance was a way to get food from the Portuguese king. Moreover, it seems that for protection, most of them came to live near Safi, where they could receive military protection as well as plant crops.[80]

One of the ways that the Portuguese attempted to combat their uncertainty about the political behavior of Moroccans was with information and reconnaissance. Although much of this information came from *alcaides dos mouros*, assorted Moroccan allies, and Jews, when none of these other sources of information was available or trustworthy, the Portuguese would risk a great number of their own men if they felt an urgent need for information. In July 1518, fearing the "malice and falsities" that the Gharbiyya had engaged in recently by stalling peace negotiations, D. Nuno Mascarenhas concluded that the only way to discover truly what was happening in the region was to send a group of Portuguese to reconnoiter. His concern is evident as he sent 300 cavalry to the area, ordering them to depart Safi at two o'clock in the morning so that they could cover the twenty-five to thirty kilometers distance before first light. Early the next day, they encountered a large group of Moroccan soldiers and attacked. They killed fifteen or twenty of them and captured 160 as well as some livestock. The expedition uncovered little other information, but did compel the leaders of the Gharbiyya to return to the negotiating table.[81]

---

[79] "Letter from António Leite to D. Manuel," Mazagão, 22 July 1518, *SIHMP*, 2:203: "*bem lhes pode parecer que cada vez que maoyrres trayções ffyzerem serão mylhor peytados.*"

[80] "Letter from D. Nuno Mascarenhas to D. Manuel," Safi, 3 September 1518, *SIHMP*, 2:216-217.

[81] "Letter from D. Nuno Mascarenhas to D. Manuel," 29 July 1518, *SIHMP*, 2:209-211.

Another way of gathering information outside of normal channels was through the use of spies. Although the identities of these spies are never revealed in letters, it seems most likely that they were Moroccan Muslims because they could move throughout Morocco without arousing suspicions. Also unclear is whether these spies worked for the Portuguese simply for monetary gain, or if the Portuguese held family members of the spies hostage.[82]

Benefits of Alliance

Given the contingent and often frightening nature of Portuguese-Moroccan alliance, the benefits of those pacts were nonetheless seen as important and valuable enough to endure their many problems. The benefits for both groups can be classed, for the most part, into two main categories: economic and military.

The economic benefits for Moroccans existed on two levels: personal benefits for the elites and more generalized benefits for their tribes and villages. When a Moroccan leader concluded an alliance with the Portuguese or performed an act that the Portuguese felt was particularly helpful to them, the Portuguese rewarded that leader with some form of wealth. The *alcaide dos mouros* of a region was typically given a valuable yearly stipend (*tença*) as well as one-fifth of all booty seized as the result of military activity. For example, from 1511, Yahya-u-Ta`fuft received a yearly stipend valued at 16,000 *reis*. After January 1517, this stipend was increased to the extraordinary sum of 96,000 *reis* per year. Such payments were, however, questioned. D. Nuno Mascarenhas argued later that year that it would be better to dispense with Yahya's services and use his *tença* to fund an increase in the Portuguese military forces in Morocco.[83]

Gifts such as money, trade goods, and clothing were typical of rewards given to servants of the Portuguese. Diogo de Azambuja, the

---

[82] "Letter from D. Nuno Mascarenhas to D. Manuel," 11 March 1518, *SIHMP*, 2:180. It is likely that they were paid, as that had been Portuguese practice in the past ("Letter from Nuno Gato to D. Manuel," Safi, 3 January 1511, *SIHMP*, 1:279).

[83] ANTT, N. A. 597, f. 122r; "*Nos praz que elle aja pera sy o quinto do despojo das cavalgadas que se fezerem, com he comtyudo na carta [de] detrymenaçam que temos dada, de como se ham de repartyr as cavalgadas amtre os Cristãos e os Mouros*," in "Letter Patent from D. Manuel," n. l., July 1516, *SIHMP*, 2:7; ANTT, Cartas Missivas, I, 49 (published in David Lopes, *Textos em Aljamía Portuguesa* (Lisbon, 1897), 118-119); "Letter from D. Nuno Mascarenhas to D. Manuel," Safi, 29 July 1517, *SIHMP*, 2:125.

first *capitão* of Safi, gave 3,600 *reis* and some silver marks to a group of "Muslims from `Abda" for information they had provided to him.[84] Valuable trade goods might also be given as rewards. One `Abd al-Rahman from Sūr al-Qdim was given half an *arratel* of Indian cloves for an unspecified service he had performed for the Portuguese. Mimūn, a resident and later *alcaide* of Almedina, was given five *covados* of cloth from Antwerp that was in the stocks of the *feitoria* at Safi as a reward for the information (*muitos avisos*) that he had given the Portuguese. Sidi Ya'qūb, the *qā'id* of Tamrakht, was given half an *arroba* of olive oil, worth about 150 *reis*, for his constant and willing service to the Portuguese. Still others were given figs and bread.[85]

Moroccan-style clothing, however, seems to have been the reward of choice. Its use was constant. On 12 March 1509, Diogo de Azambuja granted three men from Almedina, `Ali Muhammad, Muça, and `Isa, each one barrette and one cotton hat (*touca de bordate*), as well as four *dobras*, for providing him with important news.[86] Yahya bin Belsbā`, a sheikh of the Awlad Sa`īd, a Shawiyyan tribe, agreed to become a servant of the Portuguese and work to bring all of Shawiyya into the Portuguese fold. He agreed to this on condition that the Portuguese provide him with money (100 *wakiyyas*) and clothes (two scarlet *marlotas* and two velvet *marlotas*). These very fine gifts would show him to be an honored servant of the Portuguese and increase his own wealth substantially. The gifts were to be delivered by Yūsuf Adibe, the *rabi mor* of Azamor.[87] D. Álvaro de Noronha suggested that D. Manuel give nice clothing to some unidentified Muslims who had captured important leaders who served Mawlay al-Naser, the Wattasid

---

[84] ANTT, CC II, 16, 61.

[85] "Order of Pedro de Azevedo," Safi, 6 December 1509, *SIHMP*, 1:221-222 and "Payment Order from Luís de Loureiro," Santa Cruz, 30 May 1537, *SIHMP*, 3:103; ANTT, CC II, 108, 1. The cloth is called *pano de Condado* and has raised questions as to exactly which "county" in the Low Countries it came from. Based on the overwhelming production of this cloth in Antwerp, Flanders, it should be considered that the country referred to is Flanders (*SIHMP*, 1:221n4).

[86] ANTT, CC II, 16, 131.

[87] "Letter from Yahya bin Belsbā` to D. Manuel," n. l., end of May 1517, *SIHMP*, 2:91-92. A quality *marlota* could be worth as much as 1,000 *reis* (ANTT, CC II, 62, 135). Unlike the Portuguese who only gave gifts to Moroccan leaders, King James I (1213-1276) of Aragon routinely disbursed gifts to the entire populace of Islamic cities once they surrendered to his forces. See Burns, "How to End a Crusade," 10-11, 13.

viceroy. Noronha argued that this was important because one year before, the Wattasid sultan himself had given about 700 items of clothing to Shawiyyan leaders, who were still at odds with the Portuguese.[88] Noronha believed that if the Portuguese king was seen by the Moroccans as generous with clothing, then he might be able to sway the Shawiyyans to his side. Clothing was also generally bestowed upon all Moroccans who visited Lisbon, normally to conclude peace agreements with the king.[89] In fact, the giving of clothes (*dar vestiaria*) was one of the most common gifts that Portuguese kings bestowed upon Portuguese nobility.[90] Consequently, the cross-cultural respect for gifts of clothing allowed for a common symbolic language among the two groups and helped bridge the gap of mistrust.[91]

A small number of elite Moroccans also benefited from preferential treatment regarding taxes. The Catholic Church wanted the Muslims of Dukkala to pay the tithe, as the rest of the king's subjects did.[92] The Bishop of Safi, D. João Sutil, first tried to impose this in 1516, but Yahya-u-Ta`fuft persuaded him that with so many Muslims in rebellion against the Portuguese, the time was not propitious for imposing a tax. D. Manuel agreed and granted the

---

[88] "Letter from D. Álvaro de Noronha to D. Manuel," Azamor, 29 June 1518, *SIHMP*, 2:193.

[89] ANTT, CC I, 15, 122; CC I, 17, 63; CC I, 17, 57; "Alvará of D. Manuel," Lisbon, 28 August-9 September 1514, SIHMP, 1:609; "Alvará of D. Manuel," Lisbon, 4-14 November 1514, *SIHMP*, 1:651-652.

[90] Diogo Ramada Curto, "A cultura política," in *História de Portugal*, ed., José Mattoso (Lisbon: Editorial Estampa, 1997), 3:127. See also, Julian Pitt-Rivers, "Honor," in *International Encyclopedia of the Social Sciences* (New York: The Macmillan Company, 1968), 6:507 and João Cordeiro Pereira, "A estructura social e o seu devir," in *Portugal: Do renascimento à crise dinástica*, ed., João José Alves Dias (Lisbon: Editorial Presença, 1998), 281-3.

[91] This practice was not limited to only North Africa. Two examples from the *Documentos sobre os portugueses em Moçambique e na Africa Central, 1497-1840; Documents on the Portuguese in Mozambique and Central Africa 1497-1840*. 8 vols. (Lisbon: National Archives of Rhodesia and Nyasaland and CEHU, 1962-75) demonstrate this point. In Mozambique in 1506, the captain of Sofala gave four *covados* of *Condado* cloth to a Muslim "because he does service for the King our Lord [D. Manuel]" (1:719). Nor was the practice limited to Muslims. In the same year, the *capitão* of Sofala gave "six *covados* of coloured *Condado* cloth and nine yards of white Brittany *lenço*" and one *barrete baixo* to "Pero[,] a Negro turned Christian[,] because he knew the Kaffir tongue and spoke Arabic well and was in the service of the King our Lord" (1:383).

[92] Compare with Muslims living in Portugal who were required to pay the *azaqui* (mentioned above).

Muslims a moratorium on payments for two years. Two years stretched to three by the time of the Bishop's visit to Dukkala in 1519, but he brought with him a command of D. Manuel that the Muslims begin paying the tithe. When D. Nuno Mascarenhas attempted to execute this order, many Muslims arrived with papers they had received from the king in the past that exempted them from taxes.[93] The Bishop argued that this was not a tax, but a duty to the church, and so royal law had no bearing on its collection. The Muslims then argued that they be exempted for one more year before they had to begin paying. Then, to keep the most important leaders from becoming angry, the latter were permanently exempted from the tithe; this included Sa`īd, Yahya's nephew and successor as *alcaide dos mouros* of Dukkala, and four or five others. The Bishop did not like this because it cut into his revenue, but he respected the opinion of Mascarenhas about what would work best in the king's service in Dukkala. The Bishop asked the king to put this state of affairs in writing so that no more people could be exempted from the tithe.[94]

As elites often do, they received the greatest personal benefits. But alliance with the Portuguese also had economic benefits for the mass of Moroccans. This is not to say that they would not have been able to have a healthy and prosperous economy if they were not under the control of the Portuguese, just that benefits did accrue to them. It was in the best interests of the Portuguese to fund a portion of the military and defensive expenditures of their allies, both to keep them happy and to ensure that they would be prepared to fight when the Portuguese called on them. For example, after the city of Almedina

---

[93] I have been unable to locate any of these exemption documents or any other references to these documents. Nevertheless, the existence of these exemptions shows that negotiations extended beyond defining group tribute obligations. Tribal and village leaders clearly were able to extract more privileges from the Portuguese than just the promise not to attack their people. (Compare these exemptions with the various exemptions given to Muslims living in the Lisbon *mouraria* in the fourteenth and fifteenth centuries. See Barros, *A comuna muçulmana*, 73-81, 174-175.)

[94] "Letter from the Bishop of Safi to D. Manuel," Santa Clara de Lisboa, 6 March 1520, *SIHMP*, 2:270-271. The king's willingness to forego collection of the tithe indicates that the majority of royal revenue from Morocco came from the sale of trade goods and the collection of trade duties. This was not the case in medieval times. See R. I. Burns, "A Medieval Income Tax: The Tithe in the Thirteenth-Century Kingdom of Valencia," in Idem, *Moors and Crusaders in Mediterranean Spain* (London: Variorum, 1978), X:438-452.

was sacked by the members of the Gharbiyya confederation during the chaos of August 1515, Nuno Fernandes de Ataíde funded the repair of the city's gates, including providing nails and wood.⁹⁵ The *capitão* of Santa Cruz gave iron to nearby allies so that they would be able to shoe their horses and thus fight more effectively.⁹⁶

Allies could also be reimbursed for losses incurred during military operations on behalf of the Portuguese, though such payment often had to be requested and was slow in coming. Malik bin Daūd, the *qā'id* of Izzara near Santa Cruz, was allied with the Portuguese and had served valiantly in several raids. During one of these, against a caravan en route to Massa, the horses of three of his relatives were killed. Malik asked D. Manuel to replace these horses because his men had proven themselves in the service of Portugal but did not have the means to buy new ones.⁹⁷ One Muslim leader, Sidi Haddū, planned to travel personally to Lisbon to ask the king to pay him and his people some money for the great services they had done for the Portuguese. The leader felt he had been short-changed.⁹⁸ Such losses during military excursions extended to the loss of a leader's own people to captivity by forces loyal to the Wattasid sultan or the Sharif. Consequently, the Portuguese often funded the ransoms of these captured allies.⁹⁹

The most important economic benefit, however, was access to markets. When the Portuguese conquered Safi and Azamor, they gained control of the two great coastal emporia in the Dukkala region. People who had lived in those cities or traded with those cities needed that trade to prosper, and in some cases survive. Moroccans often specifically requested a place to sell their goods in or near Portuguese-controlled cities as a condition of peace agreement.¹⁰⁰ These economic benefits, of course, came with a price. For instance, the Awlad 'Amran, allied with the Portuguese in mid-1512, were required to

---

⁹⁵ ANTT, CC II, 59, 70 and CC II, 59, 161.

⁹⁶ ANTT, CC II, 123, 194, also cited in *SIHMP*, 2:338n3.

⁹⁷ "Letter from the *qā'id* Malik to D. Manuel," Santa Cruz, 30 July 1517, *SIHMP*, 2:131.

⁹⁸ "Letter from D. Álvaro de Noronha to D. Manuel," Azamor, 29 June 1518, *SIHMP*, 2:193.

⁹⁹ ANTT CC II, 69, 134 and CC II, 105, 117. See chapter eight for more on captivity.

¹⁰⁰ "Peace Agreement with the Shawiyya," Azamor, end of 1522, *SIHMP*, 2:306.

obtain permission from the Portuguese in order to travel to Marrakech and sell their merchandise as they had always done in the past.[101]

The military benefits of an alliance with the Portuguese were significant. Due to the chaotic situation in southern Morocco, caused both by the collapse of centralized power in Morocco and by the Portuguese invasion, alliance with the Portuguese could provide protection. Sheikh Sa`īd Bogozmão was the leader of a group of allies who lived near Santa Cruz. Because of the great loyalty that he had shown the Portuguese, Sa`adid forces had mercilessly attacked his people. Nevertheless, he told his children that when he died, especially if it were while serving the Portuguese, that they should remain servants of Portugal for "dying in the service of one's lord is not a bad thing." Sheikh Sa`īd asked the king to send to him and his people some Portuguese cavalrymen and riflemen so that they could go and drive the Sa`adids away from Santa Cruz.[102]

Sheikh Sa`īd's request was not unusual, for the Portuguese made it a point to punish those who attacked their allies, both to maintain Portuguese prestige and to inform the non-allied Moroccans of the force they would have on their side if they did become allies. For example, after the assassination of Yahya-u-Ta`fuft, D. Nuno Mascarenhas sent a Portuguese force to capture his killer and destroy anyone who had assisted him. In 1519, D. Álvaro de Noronha raided into Sharquiyya territory in response to an attack on a caravan of their Awlad Subeita allies. Noronha's forces killed a large number of people and captured seventy others, as well as the leader of the attackers, Al-Naser bin Duma, *qā'id* of the Awlad Ya'qub. Al-Nasr was eventually ransomed for 100,000 *reis*.[103] This action resulted in a three-fold positive result for the Portuguese and their allies: protection for the Awlad Subeita, maintenance of Portuguese prestige, and an economic benefit for the captor(s) of Al-Naser.

The previous example shows that benefits for the Portuguese of having Moroccan allies were largely economic and military. One of

---

[101] "Letter from Nuno Fernandes de Ataíde to D. Manuel," Safi, August 1512, *SIHMP*, 1:255.

[102] "Letter from Sheikh Sa`īd to D. Manuel," n. l., after May 1517, *SIHMP*, 2:93-94.

[103] "Letter from D. Álvaro de Noronha to D. Manuel," Azamor, 15 December 1519, *SIHMP*, 2:261-262.

the most important goals of the Portuguese was the steady and rapid increase in the population of Moroccans under their suzerainty. This provided a great amount of prestige for them and, more importantly, created a buffer zone to hold more powerful enemies at bay. Al-Nasr bin Yūsuf al-Hintati, the king of Marrakech, until the Sa`adid conquest of the city in 1524/5, seems to have recognized this early on. After failing in a direct attack on the Portuguese in Safi in 1510, Al-Hintati launched an attack in 1512 on the Portuguese allies of `Abda and Gharbiyya, with the belief that if these two confederations fell, then Safi would fall. He was easily defeated by forces under the command of Yahya-u-Ta`fuft.[104] As already discussed, one of the ways to ensure growth of this buffer zone was by demonstrating their military prowess, through raids and through defense and protection of current allies. But, to say that the Portuguese could do this on their own would be a lie. They needed particularly strong and effective Moroccan *alcaides*.

A good *alcaide* was able to anticipate trouble for the Portuguese before it happened and stop it, maintaining regional stability. The example of Yahya-u-Ta`fuft has already been mentioned.[105] In 1518, Mawlay `Abd al-Rahman bin Haddu, a sheikh in the Sharquiyya federation, renounced his animosity towards the Portuguese and became their ally. Furthermore, he was appointed the *alcaide dos mouros* over the entire region of Sharquiyya. To confirm this agreement, he traveled to Portugal to speak with D. Manuel. While there, he mentioned that Portugal's other allies, the `Abda and Gharbiyya confederations, were historical enemies of the Sharquiyya Arabs. Because this could lead to suspicion among allies, `Abd al-Rahman suggested that a contingent of thirty to forty cavalrymen from each group be allowed to ride with his men as they passed through the region enforcing laws, thus preventing any detrimental rumors from

---

[104] "Letter from Rabbi Ibrahim bin Zamiro," Safi, 12 October 1512, *SIHMP*, 1:356-361.

[105] For a full account of Yahya's service to the Portuguese, see David Lopes, "Os Portugueses em Marrocos no Tempo de D. Manuel," in *HP*, 3:453-544; David Lopes, *Textos em Aljamia Portuguesa*, 2nd ed. (Lisbon: Imprensa Nacional, 1940), 107-210; Racine, "Service and Honor," 67-90.

being initiated. The king thought this a fine idea, and it was soon implemented.[106]

The protection of good allies was exhibited in another way: the flow of information. In March 1514, ʿIsa, a Moroccan who could speak either Spanish or Portuguese, came from his home of Bu al-Aʿūan, about 60 kilometers east of Azamor, offering his services to Rui Barreto, the *capitão* of Azamor, in order "to show himself a great servant" of the king. No reason is given for this, though it may have been to prevent a raid on his village, like those on nearby Benacafiz and Tafuf a few weeks earlier. In any case, Barreto ignored warnings from Muslims in Azamor not to trust him and ordered ʿIsa to acquire information about the movements of the Wattasid sultan and his army. ʿIsa returned home and quickly sent a messenger to Azamor with news.[107] D. Álvaro de Noronha reported in 1518 that he had been corresponding "almost every day" with various sheikhs in Sharquiyya who supplied him with valuable information that, in fact, comprised the bulk of the news Noronha sent to the king. Noronha added that one of the leaders among the Shawiyyans was his "friend" and had provided him with important information regarding Wattasid troop movements in the area.[108]

Finally, it was the Moroccans who supplied the bulk of foot-soldiers for the Portuguese. When Yahya-u-Taʿfuft traveled throughout Dukkala fighting enemies of the Portuguese, he often had a force of several thousand, though only a few hundred at most, sometimes not even one hundred, were Portuguese. It appears that finding Moroccans to serve as soldiers was fairly simple. D. João de Meneses, in preparation for a series of raids near Azamor in 1514, announced his plans to the Arab tribesmen encamped near Azamor and Mazagão. In anticipation of their share of booty, so many of them left the area that the work on the defenses of both cities – the reason

---

[106] "Letter from D. Manuel to D. Nuno Mascarenhas," Évora, 8 October 1520, *SIHMP*, 2:278-279 and "Letter from ʿAbd al-Rahman bin Haddu to D. Manuel," n. l., after January 1521, *SIHMP*, 2:287.

[107] "Letter from Rui Barreto to D. Manuel," Azamor, 14 March 1514, *SIHMP*, 1:507.

[108] "Letter from D. Álvaro de Noronha to D. Manuel," Azamor, 28 June 1518, *SIHMP*, 2:191, 193.

the tribes had been there in the first place – could not continue.[109] A few months after this raid, members of the Awlad Dūib, under the leadership of Muhammad Benelim Chaberim, were placed in charge of protecting workers, both Moroccan and Portuguese, building the fortress at Mazagão.[110]

The economic benefits of having Moroccan allies were also important for the Portuguese.[111] First and foremost, members of the allied groups paid tribute in the form of grain to the Portuguese. Although payment could be sporadic, especially in years with a poor harvest or with excessive military activity, it provided an important source of food for the Portuguese. The most important economic benefit for the Portuguese was access to Moroccan markets.

In a sense, the Portuguese were trying – through their attempts to control tribal groups and therefore access to trade networks – to do what leaders in North Africa had done for centuries. Historian Yves Lacoste, seconded by Abun-Naser, argues that the North African state of the Middle Ages "was essentially a political and commercial centre of gravity which exercised around it more or less effective control over a more or less significant number of tribes, each of which remained, nevertheless, relatively autonomous."[112] Indeed, the ability of tribes to relocate themselves outside of the Portuguese sphere of influence within a few days was always a great concern to the Portuguese, as can be seen very clearly in the relations between the Arabic-speaking Awlad `Amran tribe and the Portuguese.

---

[109] "Letter from Vasco da Pina to D. Manuel," Azamor, 30 March 1514, *SIHMP*, 1:524 and "Letter from Francisco and Diogo Arruda to D. Manuel," Azamor, 31 March 1514, *SIHMP*, 1:528. Although Moroccan Muslims and Portuguese Christians fought side-by-side in nearly every battle and skirmish, there were still animosities among the troops. Cristóvão Correia and an unnamed Muslim got into a fight over Correia's claim that the Moroccan had stolen some items from him. Ataíde described what was stolen as trivial (*hũas cabeçadas*) ("Letter from Nuno Fernandes de Ataíde to D. Manuel," Safi, 12 September 1514, *SIHMP*, 1:635).

[110] "Letter from António Leite to D. Manuel," Azamor, 27 July 1514, *SIHMP*, 1:578n1.

[111] For a detailed discussion of this topic, see chapter five.

[112] Yves Lacoste, "General Characteristics and Fundamental Structures of Mediaeval North African Society," in *Economy and Society* 3 (1974):4, cited in Jamil M. Abun-Nasr, *A History of the Maghrib in the Islamic Period* (New York: Cambridge University Press, 1987), 19.

Negotiation and Alliance: A Case Study of the Awlad `Amran

Although a case study might be done on any number of the tribes or villages with which the Portuguese had relations, the Awlad `Amran is a tribal group that is particularly representative of the conclusions in this chapter. The Awlad `Amran were really two tribes, the Awlad `Amran lithali, located near Safi, and the Awlad `Amran discani, located near Azamor. These two large groupings contained numerous sub-groups that could and did make decisions to act on their own. Moreover, the two Awlad `Amran tribes were also members of a six-tribe confederacy of Arabs known as the Sharquiyya. The other four tribes were the Awlad Ya`qub, the Awlad Subeita, the Awlad Bu `Aziz, and the Awlad Frej.[113] Most of the Sharquiyya Arabs originally had been members of the Banu Hilal tribe living in eastern Algeria and Tunisia. In the late twelfth and early thirteenth centuries, the Masmuda Berber Almohads had them settle in Dukkala in order to pressure the local Sanhaja Berber pastoralists who disagreed with the Almohad regime. At a later date, the Almohads moved more Arab tribes to the Dukkala region; these later arrivals came to be known as the Gharbiyya.[114]

The first mention of the Awlad `Amran in Portuguese sources comes as part of the larger Sharquiyya confederacy in 1502. The confedration had apparently concluded an agreement allowing the Portuguese access to the area that became known as Mazagão in order to trade with the local Moroccans and to buy grain from them. This follows the standard pre-conquest pattern of initial relations between the Portuguese and a Moroccan group centering on economic advantages for all sides. In December of that year the Sharquiyya complained to D. Manuel that the chief Portuguese negotiator, Rui Gil Magro, had acted in such an offensive manner towards them that many of the Muslims wanted to kill him. To make matters worse, they claimed that he was no longer "on good terms either with the

---

[113] *SIHMP*, 1:85n2; 277n4. I will try to maintain uniformity in description when possible. Often, however, sources are unclear as to exactly which subsection of the Awlad `Amran is being discussed or if all portions of the tribe are being discussed simultaneously.

[114] Cornell, "Socioeconomic Dimensions," 382. In the *Livro dos tributos* published in *DIB*, 510, the Awlad Yusuf are described as "Sharquiyya, nomadic Arabs of Dukkala" (*xerquja, alarves de duquella*). I have been unable to discover if they are a subgroup of one of the six tribes mentioned in the text, or if they are, in fact, a seventh tribe.

Christians, the Muslims, or the Jews." Consequently, they asked that D. Manuel send a new representative, even suggesting the names of a few people with whom they had dealt before.[115]

After this there is a silence of seven years, until the Awlad ʿAmran are mentioned as having been invited, by a Moroccan ally of the Portuguese, to come to Safi to negotiate a treaty.[116] If they ever did negotiate, it did not result in any lasting agreement as the Sharquiyya confederacy joined in the December 1510 siege of Safi. In fact, the Awlad ʿAmran arrived "early," before the other Sharquiyya tribes.[117] The devastating defeat of this siege by the Portuguese led many groups to reconsider the viability of maintaining their posture of animosity towards the invaders, and the Awlad ʿAmran were no exception. By May 1512, representatives from both subsections of the Awlad ʿAmran – Dia for the lithali and the unnamed nephew of ʿOmar bin Mira for the discani – had traveled to Lisbon, along with other Moroccan leaders, in order to finalize treaty agreements made earlier in the year.[118]

In January 1512, the Awlad ʿAmran lithali had concluded an agreement whereby they gave tribute to Safi each year in the amount of 1,000 camel-loads of wheat, 400 camel-loads of barley, and four horses that met the *capitão's* approval. Additionally, they made payments of sheep and butter. There does not seem to be an extant copy of the tribute agreement with the Awlad ʿAmran discani, but in addition to what was likely a large amount of wheat and barley, they were to pay three horses each year, as well as sheep and butter.[119] According to Ataíde, one of the most influential persons in helping to conclude this

---

[115] "Letter from Bu Sbaʿ and Salem to D. Manuel," Mazagão, 2 December 1502, *SIHMP*, 1:74-76 and "Letter from the notables of Sharquiyya to D. Manuel," n. l., c. December 1502, *SIHMP*, 1:83-86. It is unclear how this situation resolved itself, though prior to the 1510 siege of Safi, the Portuguese were on good terms with at least one of the sheikhs who signed the 1502 letter ("Letter from ʿAli bin Saʿid to D. Manuel," Azamor, 3-12 November 1510, *SIHMP*, 1:249-254).

[116] "Order of Pedro de Azevedo," Safi, 6 December 1509, *SIHMP*, 1:221.

[117] "Letter from Nuno Gato to D. Manuel," Safi, 4-5 December 1510, *SIHMP*, 1:260.

[118] "Letter from Nuno Gato to D. Manuel," Safi, 12 May 1512, *SIHMP*, 1:302.

[119] *DIB*, 515 and "Letter from Nuno Fernandes de Ataíde to D. Manuel," Safi, 19 August 1512, *SIHMP*, 1:340.

negotiation was Moses Dardeiro, a Jew who had served as an interpreter and negotiator for the Portuguese since 1509.[120]

As a condition for the peace treaty of 1512 between the Awlad `Amran discani and the Portuguese, Nuno Fernandes de Ataíde, *capitão* of Safi, and Ibrahim Benzamiro, the influential Jewish merchant, were ordered by King D. Manuel to return four Muslim slaves to the Awlad `Amran as a goodwill gesture. These slaves had earlier been seized from `Omar bin Mira, a notable of the Awlad `Amran discani. These slaves were a young woman with a son that still nursed, a boy about fifteen or sixteen, and an old woman. Based on the descriptions of these captives, it is possible that they were related to `Omar in some way, especially the young woman who may have been his wife, sister, or daughter. The first three slaves belonged to Ataíde and the last one to Benzamiro. A point of contention was that the two owners of the slaves felt wronged by having to part with their property, and so Ataíde ordered Nuno Gato, the *contador* of Safi, to pay them the value of the slaves. Gato, also *alfaqueque mor* (official in charge of ransoming Portuguese captives), refused to use royal funds set aside for ransoming Portuguese captives to reimburse these men for their losses unless the king so ordered it.[121] It seems that the king agreed to disburse the funds, for the Awlad `Amran discani became allies with the Portuguese shortly thereafter. As in many other situations, the greed of those living in Portuguese fortresses threatened to interfere with the larger political concerns of the Portuguese kings to maintain peace and stability in North Africa.

Just as it seemed that the Awlad `Amran were going to be allied with the Portuguese, Nuno Fernandes de Ataíde decided to do something that he hoped would strengthen Portuguese influence over the inhabitants of Dukkala: He kidnapped a top leader among the Awlad `Amran, Lahsen bin Zaur. Ataíde reasoned that the only way to gain greater control over Dukkala was to fragment the Moroccan leadership as much as possible. He believed that the Awlad `Amran

---

[120] "Letter from Nuno Fernandes de Ataíde to D. Manuel," Safi, 13 May 1512, *SIHMP*, 1:305-306; José Alberto Rodrigues da Silva Tavim, *Os judeus na expansão portuguesa em Marrocos durante o século XVI: origens e actividades duma comunidade* (Braga: Edições APPACDM Distrital de Braga, 1997), 376.

[121] "Letter from Nuno Gato to D. Manuel," Safi, 14 May 1512, *SIHMP*, 1:309-310 and "Letter from Nuno Gato to D. Manuel," Safi, 13 May 1512, in *DCC*, 44-45.

had too much influence over regional politics and especially over the Gharbiyya tribes. Consequently, by kidnapping the leader of the Awlad `Amran, the Gharbiyya leaders would be more disposed to negotiate on their own. Ataíde then requested that D. Manuel send a letter ordering Lahsen come to Lisbon, which Ataíde felt would calm Lahsen about the scandalous way he had been treated and would quell rumors about his treatment. Miraculously, Ataíde's action did not cause the Awlad `Amran to go into open rebellion, as they began paying their tributes by June 1512.[122] Lahsen was freed by August 1512.[123]

Also in August 1512, Dia, along with fifteen or twenty notables of the Awlad `Amran lithali only, came to Safi in order to inform Ataíde that they were loyal to Portugal and that they did not plan to join the Hintati ruler of Marrakech in his recent declaration of a holy war against the Portuguese. Nevertheless, they did ask for permission to travel to Marrakech in order to sell some of their merchandise there, as they had always done; nothing indicates that this permission was refused. During their visit to Safi, the allies brought 100 camels laden with wheat and apparently claimed that they would be able to pay all of their tribute within one month. Ataíde reported to D. Manuel that clearly whatever gifts and reward (*mercê*) the king had given those of the Awlad `Amran who had traveled to Portugal earlier in the year must have been effective. Like most Portuguese, Ataíde believed that gift giving was an essential component of alliance; consequently, he suggested that when other Moroccan leaders came to Portugal, they should be dealt with similarly.[124]

But faith in one's allies was difficult for the Portuguese to maintain. One Lahsen Amejjot wrote to Ataíde in October 1512 to inform him that the leaders of the Awlad `Amran, Awlad Subeita, Awlad Ya`qūb, and the city of Almedina were plotting some sort of treasonous activities.[125] Lahsen's accusations initially appeared to be

---

[122] "Letter from Heitor Gonçalves to D. Manuel," Safi, 18 June 1512, *SIHMP*, 1:332.

[123] "Letter from Nuno Fernandes de Ataíde to D. Manuel," Safi, August 1512, *SIHMP*, 1:355.

[124] "Letter from Nuno Fernandes de Ataíde to D. Manuel," Safi, August 1512, *SIHMP*, 1:355 and "Letter from Rabbi Abraham Rute," Safi, 12 October 1512, *SIHMP*, 1:357.

[125] "Letter from Lahsen Amejjot to Nuno Fernandes de Ataíde," n. l., c. 12 October 1512, *SIHMP*, 1:362-365.

correct in the case of the Awlad ʿAmran, as they were soon putting distance between themselves and their Portuguese allies. Heitor Gonçalves, *feitor* of Safi, informed the king on 15 December 1512 that the Awlad ʿAmran had moved a great distance from Safi (*estam arredados d'esta terra*), and it appeared that they would plant their crops far from the city as well. Gonçalves took all this to be a "bad sign."[126]

Nevertheless, in October 1513, the Awlad ʿAmran had not broken with the Portuguese, despite the failure of many of them to make their tribute payments of sheep and butter as they had agreed to do. By this time, in fact, all of the members of the Awlad ʿAmran that the Portuguese had captured and sent to Portugal as slaves during the period before the conclusion of the 1512 peace had returned to Morocco. They were, in fact, in Safi, being held hostage to ensure that the Moroccan side of the bargain was met. Although Ataíde feared that they were not going to pay the agreed tribute, he believed that many among the Awlad ʿAmran truly wanted to pay the tribute and were not just trying to perpetrate a fraud. Among these were Dia, whom Ataíde described as a "very good servant" of Portugal. Consequently, Ataíde would wait until the spring harvest to make his decision as to whether or not he should return the slaves to Portugal.[127]

The Awlad ʿAmran remained allies in February 1514, as the Portuguese rested with a group of Awlad ʿAmran *dawwārs* while returning from a raiding expedition against the villages of Benacafiz and Tafuf. The previous night, the Portuguese had slept unmolested in Mers al-Sultan, in the territory of the Awlad Zid, a subgroup of the Sharquiyya Awlad Frej.[128] Nevertheless, discontent was growing within certain portions of the Awlad ʿAmran.

In March 1514, the Wattasid sultan and a large force of soldiers had traveled to Salé, located along the coast about 160 kilometers northwest of Mazagão and about 15 kilometers south of Mamora. There he ordered his brother, Mawlay al-Naser, viceroy of Meknès, to persuade allies of the Portuguese in Dukkala to switch sides and to

---

[126] "Letter from Heitor Gonçalves to D. Manuel," Safi, 15 December 1512, *SIHMP*, 1:368.

[127] "Letter from Nuno Fernandes de Ataíde to D. Manuel," Safi, 29 October 1513, *SIHMP*, 1:446-447.

[128] *CDM*, 3:192 and "Letter from João de Meneses to D. Manuel," Azamor, c. 15 February 1514, *SIHMP*, 1:482-484, 482n2.

equip (*aparelhar*) those allies with whatever was necessary to have them join the sultan's forces. According to Rui Barreto, the *capitão* of Azamor, among those with whom Al-Naser negotiated were Muhammad bin Muhammed and Al-Kurimat, notables of the Awlad `Amran discani.[129] In fact, according to Amaco, the sheikh of Al-Khemis, a suburb of Safi located outside the city's southern gate, it was Muhammad, "above all others," who was responsible for the sultan coming to Salé in the first place. By April 1514, Muhammad had broken from his alliance with the Portuguese and joined the Wattasid sultan in what the Portuguese feared would be an assault on the recently-conquered city of Azamor. Although the Awlad `Amran had broken with the Portuguese, many of the tribes in the Sharquiyya confederation remained loyal. In fact, the Awlad Frej and Awlad Ya`qub were relocating towards the city of Almedina in order to help quell an uprising there against Portuguese authority.[130]

Wattasid designs to besiege Azamor were temporarily disrupted on 16 April 1514, when a Portuguese forces led by D. João de Meneses and Nuno Fernandes de Ataíde and consisting of 1,000 Portuguese lancers, 1,000 Moroccan lancers, and 1,000 unidentified foot-soldiers attacked Mawlay al-Naser's force about eight leagues from Azamor. Although al-Naser commanded, according to the Portuguese, 4,000 lancers, 900 matchlockmen (*espingardeiros*), and 10,000 foot-soldiers, the Portuguese handily defeated him, killing more than 4,000 of al-Naser's men, including al-Kurimat, while only losing thirty-two of their own cavalry (no losses are given for non-mounted combatants). Al-Naser's remaining force fled in disorder.[131]

Meanwhile, the Wattasid sultan began his siege, arriving in sight of Azamor on 17 April, the Saturday before Easter, 1514, and taking seven days to arrange his growing supply of allied troops.

---

[129] The sources seem to indicate that these two men led a small, dissident faction of the Awlad `Amran, but by the end of the Wattasid campaign the entire Awlad `Amran tribe was in rebellion.

[130] "Letter from Rui Barreto to D. Manuel," Azamor, 14 March 1514, *SIHMP*, 1:504-511; "Letter from Rui Barreto to D. Manuel," Azamor, 1 April 1514, *SIHMP*, 1:534-539; "Letter from Estêvão Rodrigues Berrio to D. Manuel," Tavira, 19 May 1514, *SIHMP*, 1:554.

[131] "Letter from D. João de Meneses to D. Manuel," Azamor, c. 16 April 1514, *SIHMP*, 1:540-541; "Letter from Estêvão Rodrigues Berrio to D. Manuel," Tavira, 19 May 1514, *SIHMP*, 1:554; *CDM*, 3:195-199.

Apparently this was part of a larger plan to besiege both Safi and Azamor and drive all the *mouros de pazes* into rebellion. Before the siege of Azamor began, the Wattasid sultan sent his brother, who had regrouped from his recent defeat, to conquer Almedina. He accomplished this easily, executing most of the city's leaders, though Mimūn, the Portuguese-appointed *alcaide*, was able to escape to Safi with his wives, children, and servants. Mawlay al-Naser next marched his force toward Safi to besiege it. There, however, he was met by the Moroccan force of Yahya-u-Ta`fuft and a small contingent of Portuguese knights. During two major battles, separated by perhaps a week, Yahya utterly defeated al-Naser's forces, capturing over 1,000 men and 800 horses, along with other booty. The Wattasid plans of forcing the Portuguese from Dukkala had failed.[132]

After this defeat, the rebellious Awlad `Amran quickly tried to make amends with the Portuguese. They had apparently been persuaded by the superior Wattasid numbers to break from their alliance with the Portuguese, but now it was clear to them that they had miscalculated. According to Estêvão Rodrigues Berrio, the son of al-Kurimat became "the head (*cabeceiro*) of the Awlad `Amran" as the result of his father's death in battle. The unnamed son, learning that his wife, his brothers, and all his servants (*toda sua casa*) had been captured and brought to Azamor, traveled to the city and submitted to the Portuguese. In effect, these war captives became hostages, compelling this unnamed leader to act the way he did. D. João de Meneses told him that he would accept his loyalty again if he would prove it by capturing al-Naser. The new leader of the Awlad `Amran then gathered "his people and those of Dukkala" (i.e, both groups of Awlad `Amran) and attacked al-Naser's force, capturing 1,500 horses and a "great number" of men and women in addition to booty. Al-Naser himself escaped, seeking refuge in the territory controlled by the Hesqura tribe east of Dukkala. In order to solidify this revived alliance, it appears that Muhammad bin Muhammad and four other notables of the Awlad `Amran, along with three slaves and an interpreter, traveled to Portugal in September 1514, in order to meet with D. Manuel. The

---

[132] *CDM*, 3:199-202; "Letter from João de Meneses to D. Manuel," Azamor, 6 May 1514, *SIHMP*, 1:546; "Letter from António Correia to D. Manuel," Tavira, 10 May 1514, *SIHMP*, 1:549-551.

meeting went well, as all the Moroccans, including the slaves, were given gifts of new clothing.[133]

The renewed alliance appeared to be stronger than ever, as certain members of the Awlad `Amran and Sharquiyya Arabs were, by the summer of 1514, providing information to Portuguese in Safi.[134] Nevertheless, by December of that same year, a small faction of Awlad `Amran, under the leadership of Rahho bin Shahmut, had relocated to the protective orbit of Marrakech.[135] The majority of the Awlad `Amran, however, was not in any sort of rebellion, for in April 1515, Portuguese forces, returning from a failed (and rather foolhardy) attempt to capture Marrakech, stopped to eat dinner at Tazarot, a town in Awlad `Amran lands. While there, the Awlad `Amran treated them to a great banquet of "cows, sheep, hens, bread, and fruit."[136]

As discussed elsewhere, the disastrous Portuguese defeat at the hands of the Wattasid sultan at Mamora in August 1515, drove many *mouros de pazes* into open rebellion against the Portuguese, accomplishing the failed Wattasid goal of one year earlier. Rebellion in this case does not necessarily mean any direct attacks against the Portuguese, but rather the refusal to aid the Portuguese, either with men or goods. In addition to bombarding the Portuguese at Mamora, the sultan sent his forces into the countryside to pillage the allies of the Portuguese. As a result, the `Abda and Gharbiyya confederations fled south to Tensift and the protection of the Sharif. This was especially alarming to the Portuguese who had considered the `Abda among the "most loyal" of all the allied Moroccans. Most of the Awlad `Amran appear to have remained until August in their traditional lands or lands of other Sharquiyya tribes. By late August, however, the Shaquiyya

---

[133] "Letter from Estêvão Rodrigues Berrio to D. Manuel," Tavira, 19 May 1514, *SIHMP*, 1:554. "*Mafamede Mafamed Xeque principall*" is mentioned in *SIHMP*, 1:610n2 and *DCC*, 124-125.

[134] "Statement of Rabbi Abraham Rute," Safi, 11 September 1514, *SIHMP*, 1:628-629. The information given regarded alleged traitorous acts performed by Yahya-u-Ta`fuft. Among those giving information was Rahho bin Shahmut, a notable of the Awlad `Amran, who later killed Nuno Fernandes de Ataíde in battle in May 1516 and whose daughter, Zahra, would marry Mawlay `Abd al-Qader, the son of Mawlay Muhammad al-Sheikh, the Sa`did ruler (*SIHMP*, 1:628n2).

[135] "Letter from Nuno Fernandes de Ataíde to D. Manuel," Safi, 12 December 1514, *SIHMP*, 1:663 and "L'Expédition de la Mamora (juin-août, 1515)," *SIHMP*, 1:701.

[136] *CDM*, 3:271 and "Expédition contre Marrakech, 23 avril 1515," *SIHMP*, 1:692.

confederation had relocated to Uarar, a large seasonal lake about seventy kilometers east of Safi, with the Awlad ʿAmran located still "a bit further away" (*hum pouco mays arredado*). Chaos reigned in Dukkala as old scores were settled and looting and thievery became the norm. Nevertheless, Nuno Fernandes de Ataíde, sensing that without allies the Portuguese would have a difficult time in Dukkala, hoped to negotiate with representatives of Sharquiyya soon. By September, the Awlad ʿAmran, now located near Marrakech, had made known to the Portuguese their great desire to negotiate and return to their lands. It seems clear that the Awlad ʿAmran were willing to ally with whoever seemed to promise them the most benefits so long as they could remain on some portion of their tribal lands. By the end of September 1515, Ataíde had forgiven all the rebellious tribes for their rebellions and the crimes they committed during them. A tenuous alliance had returned.[137]

The Awlad ʿAmran, as alluded to previously, were not a monolithic group. The small faction under Rahho bin Shahmut, whom Damião de Góis called one of the "bravest knights" among the Awlad ʿAmran, that had moved to territory near Marrakech after their alliance with the Wattasid sultan in 1514, remained in rebellion. In May 1516, after having restored order to Dukkala, Ataíde responded to a complaint from the Awlad Mutʿ that they had been harassed by Rahho's group; consequently, Ataíde organized a large punitive force. Although this group of Awlad ʿAmran were defeated, Rahho and twenty-four horsemen were able to regroup and follow Ataíde's men, who had taken many captives – including Rahho's wife – and much booty. In a desperate attack, Rahho succeeded in tossing a spear through Ataíde's neck, killing him. In response, the Moroccans who had been with Ataíde, the ʿAbda and Gharbiyya, turned on the Portuguese, killing or capturing them. Believing that the Portuguese in Safi, with Ataíde dead and Yahya in Portugal, were helpless, the people

---

[137] "Letter from Álvaro do Tojal to D. Manuel," Safi, 21 August 1515, *SIHMP*, 1:740-744; "Letter from Nuno Fernandes de Ataíde to D. Manuel," Safi, 27 August 1515, *SIHMP*, 1:753; "Letter from Nuno Fernandes de Ataíde to D. Manuel," Safi, 19 September 1515, *SIHMP*, 1:756; "Proclamation of Nuno Fernandes de Ataíde to the Tribes," after 19 September 1515, *SIHMP*, 1:759-760; "L'Expédition de la Mamora (juin-août, 1515)," *SIHMP*, 1:701.

of Dukkala, including the Awlad `Amran, returned to a state of rebellion.[138]

This episode clearly reveals the instability and lack of trust inherent in the alliances between the Portuguese and their Moroccan counterparts. The Moroccans seemed to be motivated mainly by the desire for security and order. The death of Ataíde instantaneously transformed allied soldiers from the `Abda and Gharbiyya tribes into enemies. This episode also demonstrates the grave need of the Portuguese for allies within Morocco as they employed troops from two tribes that less than one year ago had sought to break away from the Portuguese, if only for a period of two to three months.

It was important for the Portuguese that they reassert power in Dukkala as quickly as possible. To this end, D. Manuel appointed D. Nuno Mascarenhas, then in Arzila, the new *capitão* of Safi. He also ensured the quick return of Yahya-u-Tafuft to Safi from Portugal; he arrived on 21 July 1516. By 9 August, Yahya had concluded peace agreements with the 'Abda, Gharbiyya, and Seja groups. The Awlad `Amran were conspicuously absent, though Yahya had written to them asking if they wanted to return to Safi and negotiate a settlement.[139] Simão Correia, the new *capitão* of Azamor, had also written to the Awlad `Amran. He received a response in late August.

The leaders of the Awlad `Amran, three of whom are named – `Omar bin Mira, Ahmed al-Wafi, and Al-Naser bin Zeghmim – wrote that they were happy at the arrival of Correia and Mascarenhas and that they wished to come and discuss a peace in Azamor. They only wanted one thing as a show of good faith: the release of their children who were being held hostage.[140] They had apparently concluded, after observing all the Dukkalan tribes returning to alliance with the Portuguese, that Portuguese control of the region would last for some years longer. This letter, along with the gift of a falcon, was delivered to Simão Correia by a messenger from the Awlad `Amran. Correia,

---

[138] "Mort de Nuno Fernandes de Ataíde (mai 1516)," *SIHMP*, 2:1-5 and *CDM*, 4:14-18: "*hum dos mais esforçados cavalleiros da Cabilda de Vleidambram*".

[139] "Letter from Yahya-u-Ta`fuft to D. Manuel," Safi, 9 August 1516, *SIHMP*, 2:24-26 and *CDM*, 4:7, 18-19.

[140] "Letter from the Awlad `Amran to Simão Correia," n. l., after 29 August 1516, *SIHMP*, 2:30-33.

Political Alliances

upon reading the letter, decided to release four of the hostages that he was holding. He brought them before the messenger and dramatically removed their shackles and brought them new clothing to wear. He then sent the five men on their way with a safe conduct so that all of the Awlad `Amran might come to Azamor for negotiations.[141]

It is unclear whether or not negotiations ever took place. If they did, only a portion of the Awlad `Amran returned as allies. In March 1517, Yahya-u-Ta`fuft and his troops skirmished with and defeated a Hintati force led by both Al-Naser bin Yūsuf and his cousin, Mawlay Muhammad (known to the Portuguese as the "Lord of the Mountains"). Yahya reported that among the enemy were "many from the Awlad `Amran." Although most of the men among the Awlad `Amran escaped this battle, Yahya's men captured many women and children who had been abandoned. Although these women were richly dressed and some of the men with Yahya appear to have wanted to rape them and steal their jewelry, Yahya, hoping to bring the Awlad `Amran to the negotiating table, ordered that the women and children be allowed to return to their husbands. As a servant of the Portuguese, Yahya understood the important symbolic value of a goodwill release of captives. As a result, many *faqīrs* came to Yahya to ask for negotiations on behalf of the Hintati, but apparently not the Awlad `Amran.[142]

On 5 September 1517, a group of messengers representing both branches (lithali and discani) of the Awlad `Amran as well as the Awlad Ya`qub, arrived in Azamor. They told Simão Correia that their tribes would return in peace to Dukkala on the condition that they did not have to associate either with Yahya-u-Ta`fuft or the Gharbiyya Arabs, as they were their "enemies." Correia, not wishing to undermine Yahya's authority completely, reached a compromise with the Awlad `Amran, offering to appoint an *alcaide dos mouros* who would administer their lands himself, though would still owe obedience to Yahya. The

---

[141] "Letter from Simão Correia to D. Manuel," Azamor, 3 October 1516, *SIHMP*, 2:34-36. (Also with the Awlad `Amran were other some subgroups of the Awlad Ya`qub.) Correia furthermore stated that he had written to Yahya-u-Ta`fuft in order to inform him that, as *alcaide dos mouros* of Dukkala, he would not conclude any agreement with the Awlad `Amran unless Yahya were present as well.

[142] "Letter from Yahya-u-Ta`fuft to D. Manuel," Safi, 28 March 1517, *SIHMP*, 2:67-69 and "Letter from Yahya-u-Ta`fuft to D. Manuel," Azamor, 27 April 1517, *SIHMP*, 2:76-78.

Awlad ʿAmran were amenable to this idea, and Correia appointed Saʿid Mimūn (probably the sheikh of Almedina) as the *alcaide*. Correia then wrote to Yahya, asking him to approve the idea, and wrote to the king, asking him to tell Yahya to approve the idea.[143]

Either the Awlad ʿAmran were a fragmented bunch, or they had not decided to negotiate, because on 9 September 1517, a group of forty of their cavalry attempted to steal some cattle that were grazing near Safi's walls. Mascarenhas and several others succeeded in chasing them away and saving the cattle. Mascarenhas speculated that these men "may have been some thieves that, in all times of war and peace, practice their trade."[144] In other words, he thought this raid might simply be the act of a few criminals rather than one of political rebellion. On the same day, D. Rodrigo de Noronha reported to the king that there was news that the Awlad ʿAmran lithali, who had been living near Marrakech, were returning to their lands in Dukkala in order to plant crops for the year.[145] This would seem to indicate that they were planning on concluding a peace with the Portuguese. But they were planning something far different.

They became involved in the murder of Yahya-u-Taʿfuft. Although it appears that members of the ʿAbda were the prime movers behind the assassination plot, members of the Awlad ʿAmran participated, capturing ten Portuguese who were with Yahya and selling them into slavery in Marrakech. The motivation behind the participation of the Awlad ʿAmran was both to ingratiate themselves with the Hintati (or thank them for providing a safe refuge for the past few years) and to take revenge on someone whom they believed had been instrumental in reducing their once formidable power in Dukkala: Yahya-u-Taʿfuft.[146] Despite this treasonous action, the Portuguese were unable or unwilling to attack the Awlad ʿAmran, as they and other

---

[143] "Letter from Simão Correia to D. Manuel," Azamor, 5 September 1517, *SIHMP*, 2:164-167.

[144] "Letter from D. Nuno Mascarenhas to D. Manuel," Safi, 9 September 1517, *SIHMP*, 2:169: "*Estes podyham ser alguns ladrhões que em todo tempo de gera ou de paz usão de seu hofycyho.*"

[145] "Letter from D. Rodrigo de Noronha to D. Manuel," Safi, 9 September 1517, *SIHMP*, 2:172-173.

[146] "Letter from D. Nuno Mascarenhas to D. Manuel" Safi, 11 March 1518, *SIHMP*, 2:178-182.

Political Alliances

Sharquiyya Arabs remained in the far-eastern portion of the Dukkala region. Instead, the Portuguese focused their martial vengeance on the central perpetrators of this treason, the `Abda.

In June 1518, Mawlay al-Naser, the Wattasid viceroy of Meknès, raided eastern Dukkala, attacking and defeating, during a period of a few days, the Awlad `Amran lithali, Awlad `Amran discani, Awlad Subeita, and Awlad Ya`qub, with the last three groups receiving the most damage. As these tribes fled their lands, they were joined by the `Abda, who feared an attack by al-Naser. These five tribes then invaded and conquered the lands of the Awlad Mut`, located between Shyadma and Marrakech. The Gharbiyya, who had invaded eastern Dukkala with al-Naser, took much booty and began to return to their homeland, but then reconsidered as al-Naser resolved to follow the routed tribes in order to destroy them. The Gharbiyya, after its leaders submitted their children as hostages to al-Naser to ensure that they would not flee during battle, maintained their allegiance with al-Naser.[147]

Now unable to seek refuge near Marrakech with the Hintati, who were beholden to the Wattasids, the Awlad `Amran had two choices: try to survive alone or return to an alliance with the Portuguese. In July 1518, four leaders of the Awlad `Amran arrived in Safi, offering to open peace negotiations and give as many of their wives and children as hostages as necessary. Negotiations progressed well, reaching the stage where one of the leaders of the Awlad `Amran promised to stay in Safi until the needed hostages arrived. Instead, much to Mascarenhas's surprise, the hostage fled a few days later. Nevertheless, "in a short space," tribal representatives returned with another proposal. They said that they felt Mascarenhas might not trust them, that he felt that they were just using negotiations to buy time in order to attack the Gharbiyya and seize some of their grain (*pãys*). They then added that all they wanted was peace and that if Mascarenhas gave them a safe conduct, then they would return quickly with all of the agreed to hostages. Moreover, they said that if anyone among their tribe took even "one ear of wheat" from another tribe before the peace

---

[147] "Letter from D. Nuno Mascarenhas to D. Manuel," Safi, 30 June 1518, *SIHMP*, 2:197-199. An incomplete account of al-Naser's initial incursion into Dukkala is given in "Letter from D. Álvaro de Noronha to D. Manuel," Azamor, 28 June 1518, *SIHMP*, 2:188-191.

negotiations were complete, then Mascarenhas could conclude that they were traitors. Mascarenhas, although extremely suspicious, agreed to the safe conduct, but warned them that if they tried any treachery, then he would attack them, making it a point to seize as many captives as possible. After they departed, Mascarenhas then sent his brother, D. Pedro Mascarenhas, with three hundred lancers to find and observe what a small group of Awlad 'Amran, camped five or six leagues from Safi, were doing. D. Pedro discovered a group of Awlad 'Amran, guarded by men armed with crossbows, harvesting grain growing on Gharbiyya land. D. Pedro's men then attacked, killing fifteen or twenty and capturing 160. D. Nuno had been right to be suspicious.

  The evening of the attack, two riders from the Awlad 'Amran arrived in Safi, saying that they had all been tricked by one among them, Dia, who had wanted the peace to fail for some reason. Despite the treachery, Mascarenhas felt that this was still the best chance for peace in Dukkala in recent times, and he was determined to not lose it. He sent Rabbi Abraham Rute, the *rabi mor* of the Jews of Safi, with the two men to renegotiate the peace, keeping the same two conditions previously mentioned. As a gesture of good faith, Mascarenhas sent the tribe a camel and returned two esteemed captives who appear to have been captured during earlier military actions: the niece of a sheikh named Luar and a male slave of Rahho bin Shahmut, both dressed in new clothing. So desirous of peace was Mascarenhas, that he empowered Rute to free more captives if necessary and give to five or six of the most important leaders twenty ounces of silver each. Rute arrived in Tazarot where the leaders of the Awlad 'Amran were located and, after a brief period of negotiations, the peace seemed to be ready for conclusion. However, Sidi Haddu arrived from Azamor saying that he had been made the *alcaide dos mouros* over all the Sharquiyya tribes and that no peace could be concluded except in Azamor and in his presence. Moreover, he said that he did not want any hostages and that he would give each of the notables of the Awlad 'Amran fifty ounces of silver and a *marlota*. The leaders of the Awlad 'Amran told Rute that although they could not conclude the peace at the moment, it was actually for the best. Now, not allied with Christians and with the Wattasid force disbanded, they could return to Marrakech and retrieve grain and wealth they had stored there. After this, they promised to return and conclude a peace with the Portuguese. Rute departed for Safi.[148]

By September 1518, Mascarenhas believed that he had concluded a lasting peace agreement with the `Abda. There had, however, been no word from the Awlad `Amran, and Mascarenhas now called their earlier promise to return and conclude a peace an *engano* (trick).[149] The Awlad `Amran appear to have maintained communication with the Portuguese, though the parties made little progress. At the beginning of 1519, D. Álvaro de Noronha, the *capitão* of Azamor, appointed a new *alcaide dos mouros* of Sharquiyya who appears to have been a relative of Yahya-u-Ta`fuft. The new *alcaide* then traveled with a group of representatives of the Awlad `Amran to their encampment. There, for an unknown reason, he was killed.[150] Noronha sent thirteen Portuguese cavalrymen to punish the murderers. Instead, nine of the Portuguese were captured and sold into slavery, while the remaining four were able to escape and return to Azamor despite being seriously wounded.[151]

From the end of December 1518 until the middle of February 1519, D. Nuno Mascarenhas said that Dukkala had been the scene of numerous battles with *mouros de guerra*. A force headed by Muhammad al-Hintati, his two brothers, and a son of the king of Marrakech – called the "Four Kings" by local inhabitants – organized a large coalition of Moroccans, including the Awlad `Amran. The goal of this coalition was to attack and destroy all the Moroccans who had allied with the Portuguese and seize their grain for food. Mascarenhas resolved to do all that he could to protect his allies, even those with questionable loyalty, because he knew that if the invasion succeeded, then Safi "and all the land would be totally lost and without hope of ever having peace with any *alarves*, which would be extremely inconvenient for [His]

---

[148] "Letter from D. Nuno Mascarenhas to D. Manuel," Safi, 29 July 1518, *SIHMP*, 2:207-212. Sidi Haddu was one of the leaders of the Awlad Bu Zid (*SIHMP*, 2:193n4).

[149] "Letter from D. Nuno Mascarenhas to D. Manuel," Safi, 3 September 1518, *SIHMP*, 2:215-216.

[150] If this new *alcaide* was indeed one of Yahya's relatives, then perhaps he was killed simply as a continuance of the Awlad `Amran's vengeance upon Yahya that they now extended to his family, or at least those who could influence them politically.

[151] "Letter from Álvaro do Cadaval to D. Manuel," Azamor, early 1519, *SIHMP*, 2:219-220.

Highnesses' service and the retention of the land." It would appear that the Awlad `Amran had determined that the Portuguese were already in decline and that it was better for them to ally with the Hintati. Fortunately for the Portuguese, the Hintati forces began fighting amongst themselves before they could do any serious damage to Dukkala.[152]

The Awlad `Amran were still in rebellion in December 1519, as were the Sharquiyyan Awlad Ya`qub. The Awlad Subeita, however, had moved near to Azamor and had planted their crops there. This indicates a peace agreement had been reached with this member of the Sharquiyya confederation.[153] The Awlad `Amran then disappear from the documentary record, implying that they rarely, if ever, had dealings with the Portuguese after this period, save for one final reference. The Sharif, preparing for his final push into Dukkala in 1541, suspected that the Awlad `Amran, among others in Dukkala, might join the Portuguese against him if Portuguese reinforcements arrived. To prevent this, he had the children of all the leaders arrested and held hostage.[154] So, even until the evacuation of the Portuguese in 1541, it seems that the Awlad `Amran, while they may never have again openly allied with the Portuguese after 1517/8, kept the option available should it seem a better form of protection.

Conclusion

The relationship between the Portuguese and their Moroccan subjects, former subjects, and potential subjects was an extremely complex one. No one on either side was governed exclusively by slogans, political agendas, or religious ideology, though these all had influence. For some Moroccans, the arrival of the Portuguese was a blessing, for others it was a curse. The frontier in sixteenth-century Morocco was not simply a religious or political one; it was also a frontier of economic opportunity and daily stability.

---

[152] "Letter from D. Nuno Mascarenhas to D. Manuel," Safi, 10 February 1519, *SIHMP*, 2:227-229: *"e toda a tera fyquava de todo perdyda e sem esperança de se poder aver mays paz de nenhum Alarve, ho que era tam gramde ymqovynyente pera ho servyço de Su'alteza e sostymento da tera".*

[153] "Letter from D. Álvaro de Noronha to D. Manuel," Azamor, 15 December 1519, *SIHMP*, 2:260-263.

[154] "Letter from Inácio Nunes Gato to D. João III," Safi, 30 May 1541, *SIHMP*, 3:409.

Weston Cook, Jr. argues "Portugal became an adept manipulator of locality politics, perpetuating the debilitations of internecine war." Cook attributes this manipulation to the violence of Portuguese raids that "perpetuated conflicts since Moroccan disorder was essential to hold down the cost of Portuguese order."[155] While the actions of the Portuguese may have indeed contributed to conflict between Moroccan groups – over resources, for instance – it is not possible to consider the actions of the Portuguese as somehow part of a larger, well-considered, and "adept" plan designed to make the Portuguese goal of extensive suzerainty more easily obtainable. In fact, because it was the goal of the Portuguese monarchs to establish suzerainty over as much of Morocco and in as short a time as possible, any actions taken by the Portuguese in Morocco that detracted from local stability were counter to espoused royal policies.

The interpretation offered by Vincent Cornell is more in keeping with the evidence presented in this chapter. Cornell argues that the Portuguese recognized that most of Morocco was controlled either by elite secular rulers (the *qā'ids*, for instance) who, as a class, were known as *a`yān*, or by heads of religious orders (*shuyūkh* or *murābiṭūn*) who controlled *zāwiyas* in remote areas. Rightly assuming they could never ally with religious zealots, the Portuguese concentrated on the *a`yān*. The Portuguese were able to build networks of clientage using the *a`yān* that enabled them exert their influence over large territories. It was this technique, rather than perpetuating local conflicts, that yielded the best results for the Portuguese. In return for their allegiance, the Moroccan elites received economic and status rewards as well as military protection for their people. The elites did not, however, receive "membership in the Portuguese aristocracy" as Cornell supposes.[156]

Finally, it is clear that the events in this region are similar to what has occurred in the contested spaces along differing frontier regions in other times. Rees Davies, describing the medieval frontiers created by the English invasions of Ireland and Wales, could be speaking about the sixteenth-century frontier in Morocco created by

---

[155] Cook, 111, 118.

[156] Cornell, "Socioeconomic Dimensions," 384. Cornell adds that the religious leadership in Morocco (i.e., *zāwiyas*) was much more amenable to aiding the Sa`adids rather than the Portuguese.

the invading Portuguese: "Countries in which the units of political power and governance are multiple and which lack a central, stable, unchallenged supervisory source of jurisdiction and power have their own internal complex frontiers and have to devise their own working solutions for dealing with the problems raised by such frontiers."[157] The constant negotiations between the Portuguese and Moroccans show this, as local Moroccan leaders considered with which more powerful group they should ally. Within a brief period of time, one tribal group could be in territory clearly controlled by the Wattasids, Hintati, or Sa`adids and then suddenly in territory clearly controlled by the Portuguese. Negotiation, flight, and the reading of the symbolic currency in the actions of the Portuguese and other powerful entities were some of the ways that Moroccan leaders sought to address the complexity and uncertainty of their situations.

In his analysis of the Castilian-Granadan frontier, José Enrique López de Coca Castañer addresses another issue important in the understanding of Portuguese-Moroccan relations. Castañer argues that conflicts along a frontier were often motivated by local and personal issues, "with the result that there [is] a local search for stability and local arrangements [evolve] as one of the principal mechanisms which [respond] to the destabilizing effects of these conflicts."[158] In most senses, this assertion applies more to the Portuguese than the Moroccans, for the Portuguese living in Morocco had to determine ways to win and, more importantly, maintain the confidence of Moroccan leadership so that they could conduct trade and receive tribute. The Portuguese had to learn quickly that gifts of clothing were symbolically significant to Moroccans and that when releasing elite captives as a goodwill gesture, it was important to clothe them in expensive attire. D. Nuno Mascarenhas had to have the wisdom to refuse his king's suggestion that a Christian be appointed as the *alcaide* of al-Khemis near Safi because he knew that it would cause great instability. Overwhelming force and violence may have allowed the Portuguese a foothold in Morocco, but the development of local understandings was necessary if they wished to remain there.

---

[157] Davies, "Frontier Arrangements," 80.

[158] Castañer, "Institutions," 147.

Chapter Seven: Military Violence in Portuguese Southern Morocco: Preparation, Action, and Response

AS SEEN in the previous chapter, violence was one of many tools used by the Portuguese in order to gain and maintain alliances with Moroccan groups. Violence, in fact, was one of the most widespread phenomena in southern Morocco during first half of the sixteenth century. The political chaos and economic uncertainty characteristic of Moroccan life during these years combined with the colonial ambitions of the Portuguese to contribute to this climate. Violence was not used simply as a tool for political ends; it could occur at any moment. Perhaps nothing exemplifies this more than what appears to have been a horrible misunderstanding just outside the gates of Safi in April 1537.

After weeks of negotiations, the *capitão* of Safi, D. Rodrigo de Castro, had concluded a peace agreement with Sharif Ahmed al-A`raj, the Sa`adid ruler of Marrakech. The Sharif had sent his agent, Qassim, to Safi in order to conclude the peace. Together, Qassim and D. Rodrigo walked along Safi's walls proclaiming that a three-year peace had been concluded. In their joy, many Portuguese, despite the warnings of the city's *adail* (chief military official), rode outside the city walls in order to celebrate and entertain themselves by playing games. At this moment, while the riders were off guard, Bu Dbira, a Moroccan leader loyal to the Sharif and ignorant of the new peace, attacked the Portuguese, killing five, wounding three, and capturing many. After they got over the shock of the event, D. Rodrigo sent his chief negotiator, João Perez, along with Qassim to visit Bu Dbira and explain the situation. Bu Dbira soon returned his captives and, due to the unfortunate circumstances, the Portuguese made no effort to punish him. In short, five men died violently in the midst of celebrating a peace as the result of bad timing.[1]

---

[1] "Account of the Proclamation of the Peace of Safi," Safi, 25 April 1537, *SIHMP*, 3:96-102.

Military violence (i.e., violence perpetrated by organized groups of men, sometimes, but not always, in the name of a political leader or a political goal) was the most prevalent form of violence and is most widely discussed in the available sources. Frontiers in general are associated with war and fragmentation of society, and the Portuguese-Moroccan frontier was no exception.[2] Military violence affected everyone. The Portuguese had to build highly-fortified cities in order to withstand periodic sieges by Wattasid and Sa`adid forces. Moroccan villagers and nomads had to worry about attacks by both Portuguese and Moroccan militias, as well as tribal rivals.

I prefer the use of the term "military violence" to "political violence" for the simple fact that all the violent acts discussed in this section were perpetrated by organized groups of armed men though not necessarily under a direct order from a ruler for a political goal. In fact, some of the military violence perpetrated by the Portuguese in Morocco was decidedly contrary to the policies and regulations implemented by their king. Nevertheless, it is true that politics and violence were so intertwined that it is difficult to separate them. Such a division is made here simply for analytical ease and not some ill-conceived notion that politics somehow only encompasses negotiations and treaties rather than bloodletting.

Military violence can be further dissected into three stages. Firstly, there is the preparation for and anticipation of an act of military violence. In this case, the specific activity of readying a city to defend against a siege is most important. The act of military violence itself is the second stage. This chapter will discuss two major types of military violence: siege warfare and raiding activity. The final stage is the aftermath of military violence. Clearly, one of these consequences is the destruction or seizure of goods, discussed both below and in chapter four. Another important consequence of military violence was the capture of combatants and non-combatants. This is a complex phenomenon and will be discussed in chapter eight.

Military encounters were moments of especial desire for many Portuguese. Nuno Gato, for instance, described the *enemy* force that

---

[2] For examples from Europe and the Americas, see the essays in *MFS* and Donna J. Guy and Thomas E. Sheridan, eds., *Contested Ground: Comparative Frontiers on the Northern and Southern Edges of the Spanish Empire* (Tucson: University of Arizona Press, 1998).

besieged Safi in 1510 as "the most beautiful sight in the world."³ António Leitão de Gamboa, the *capitão* of Santa Cruz, described a skirmish with Sa'adid forces in which a few dozen men on each side were killed and wounded by saying that "it was a beautiful (*fremosa*) thing to see such heated battle (*pelleja tam quente*)."⁴ Julius R. Ruff describes the effect that violence had on early modern Europeans: "It at once shocked and repelled people by its brutality. But it also fascinated many because it so contradicted religious precepts and social norms."⁵ While the Portuguese were Europeans, they were neither in Europe nor committing violence against other Europeans, especially not European Christians. After all, killing infidels in the name of Christ had been explicitly licit since 1095, when Urban II declared the First Crusade. Christian knighthood had become a holy vocation; violence, a way to achieve salvation.⁶ By the sixteenth century, the holy aspects of violence were secondary in the minds of the Portuguese in North Africa, while martial glory, honor, and spectacle were of prime concern.⁷

It would, however, be a mistake to characterize all Portuguese as enamored with battle and martial violence. For instance, shortly before the siege of Safi in 1510, a group of about one hundred Moroccans on horseback approached Safi after dark and stole some cows and a few donkeys. The *capitão* of Safi, Nuno Fernandes de Ataíde, along with about fifty cavalrymen pursued the thieves. When they caught up with them, there was an extended standoff that frightened a few Portuguese to the extent that they fled. Of these, two were chased down by the Moroccans and killed, including Afonso Vaz, whom Ataíde described in a letter to the king as a good and valiant man, despite his apparent cowardice. Ataíde continued, recommending to the king that he provide some sort of pension for Vaz's wife and

---

³ "Letter from Nuno Gato to D. Manuel," Safi, 3 January 1511, *SIHMP*, 1:275. For more on this siege, see below.

⁴ "Letter from António Leitão de Gamboa to D. João III," Santa Cruz, 16 January 1525, *SIHMP*, 2:339.

⁵ *Violence in Early Modern Europe, 1500-1800* (New York: Cambridge University Press, 2001), 28.

⁶ C. Warren Hollister, *Medieval Europe: A Short History* 8th ed. (San Francisco: McGraw Hill, 1998), 196-198.

⁷ Racine, "Service and Honor," 74-76.

children because "he died in your service." A few more skirmishes followed, resulting in many injuries on both sides, but the Moroccans escaped with the livestock and the Portuguese, after getting lost for a brief time, returned to Safi around midnight. This description of battle is remarkable for its understanding and forgiveness of the fear felt by the Portuguese as they confronted an enemy force twice as large as their own at night. It also describes how violent even a small skirmish like this could be. Among the injured were Pedro Lourenço de Melo, pierced by lances three different times; Espinosa, shot by an arrow; and two horses, one of which died.[8]

Defensive Construction

From their experience in northern Morocco, the Portuguese had learned that it was essential for their survival that they build strong fortifications.[9] Such construction was expensive, requiring a large labor force as well as skilled architects to direct it. Moreover, the Portuguese were not defending small castles, but rather huge urban areas. For example, the walled portion of Safi was approximately two kilometers wide and had seventy-four towers for defense, and in some parts, the wall was wide enough to ride a horse.[10] Much of this defensive wall was in place before the Portuguese conquered the city, but they needed to strengthen and maintain it. Immediately following the Portuguese takeover of Safi, for example, Diogo de Azambuja wrote to D. Manuel saying that he needed to strengthen the city's towers and build a new cistern. To this end, he asked that the king send construction supplies as soon as possible.[11] Additionally, in all of their fortresses in southern

---

[8] "Letter from Nuno Fernandes de Ataíde to D. Manuel," Safi, 5 December 1510, *SIHMP*, 1:265-268.

[9] For an extensive discussion of the architecture of Portuguese fortifications throughout Morocco, see Martin M. Elbl, "Portuguese Urban Fortifications in Morocco: Borrowing, Adaptation, and Innovation along a Military Frontier," in *City Walls: The Urban Enceinte in Global Perspective*, ed. James D. Tracy (New York: Cambridge University Press, 2000), 349-385. This work also contains some fine photographs of the remains of Portuguese fortifications at Safi, Azamor, and Ceuta.

[10] *SIHMP*, 1:275n.2 and n.3 and "Letter from Nuno Fernandes de Ataíde to D. Manuel," Safi, 4 January 1511, *SIHMP*, 1:293.

[11] "Letter from Diogo de Azambuja to D. Manuel," Safi, 13 December 1507, *SIHMP*, 1:141.

Morocco, the Portuguese built a small, central keep (*torre de menagem*) in order to house top officials and the *feitoria*.

In addition to building walls and castles, smaller structures were needed to ensure the proper functioning of the Portuguese military machine. For example, Henrique de Parada, the *vedor das obras* of Safi, was ordered to build a storehouse for the city's gunpowder.[12] Workers in Azamor built a munitions storehouse (*casa de artelharia*) within a few months of the Portuguese conquest.[13] A more mundane, though equally important building was the *palheiro*, where hay and barley was stored for Portuguese war horses.[14]

Portuguese construction techniques were similar to those native to Morocco, making extensive use of brick or stone and mortar. One of the most difficult to obtain and expensive items necessary for this construction process was *cal*: lime used in mortar and created by baking stones in ovens. According to Francisco and Diogo de Arruda, the architect brothers who had been sent to Azamor to guide the construction of its defenses, the *cal* manufactured from Moroccan stone was fine for repairs and minor construction, but was almost useless for large-scale building because it could not withstand great weight or meet defensive requirements. They reported to the king that the Moroccan inhabitants of Azamor had covered the city walls with plaster to protect the *cal*, but as soon as the plaster cracked, water washed it away "as if it were clay." Consequently, they requested that the king send 2,000 *moios* of *cal* from Portugal so that, at the very least, they could cement all of the foundations with it.[15]

The manufacture of *cal* was a labor- and resource-intensive process. First, large ovens, called *fornos d'enpreitada* or *fornadas de cal*, were required in order to cook the rocks until they became ash. Often, the Portuguese had to build their own ovens, such as in Mazagão,

---

[12] ANTT, CC II, 60, 19.

[13] "Letter from Rui Barreto to D. Manuel," Azamor, 21 February 1514, *SIHMP*, 1:499; "Letter from Nuno Gato to D. Manuel," Azamor, 5 December 1513, *SIHMP*, 1:455; "Letter from Francisco and Diogo de Arruda to D. Manuel," Azamor, 31 March 1514, *SIHMP*, 1:525-529.

[14] ANTT, CC II, 126, 14. This mentions repairs performed on the *palheiro* of Azamor in 1525.

[15] "Letter from Francisco and Diogo de Arruda to D. Manuel," Azamor, 31 March 1514, *SIHMP*, 1:526-527. See also, *HP*, 3:531.

where they had eight working ovens by July 1514, and Santa Cruz, but they were also able to use extant ovens, such as those in Azamor and Safi. The baking process required an extremely hot and long-burning fire that consumed large quantities of firewood. This was often a problem, as wood was in short supply. The Portuguese in Santa Cruz, in fact, were dependent on purchasing firewood from Moroccans who gathered it at some distance from the Portuguese fortress.[16] The Portuguese in Azamor, meanwhile, received wood from tribal allies and Jewish contractors.[17]

Construction of fortifications and buildings within the cities was an extremely contingent process. It could be halted for any number of reasons, including lack of tools and materials, lack of workers, or even bickering among those in charge of directing the process. Diogo de Azambuja, in charge of construction and repair in both Safi and Mogador (Castelo Real) in 1507, created a laundry list of items he needed to complete his tasks: *cal*, excavation engineers (*cavouqueiros*), blacksmiths, forges, iron, steel, picks, wedges for breaking stone (*cunhas marras*), and mattocks (*enxadas alferces*).[18] Supply problems were not always this extensive. Nuno Gato, the *contador* of Safi, complained that the excavations to ready the ground for construction at Mazagão went slowly because there were no baskets (*cestos* and *alcofas*) to use for the removal of earth; instead, the dirt was carried out awkwardly on stretchers (*padiolas*).[19] The Arruda brothers asked the king to send more wood from Madeira to Mazagão, as they had already used up the previous supply on the construction of Azamor's keep (*torre de menagem*). Additionally they requested brick, tools, and more masons

---

[16] "Letter from Nuno Gato to D. Manuel," Azamor, 5 December 1513, *SIHMP*, 1:456; "Letter from Afonso Rodrigues to D. Manuel," Santa Cruz, 24 December 1513, *SIHMP*, 1:474; "Letter from António Leite to D. Manuel," Azamor, 27 July 1514, *SIHMP*, 1:577.

[17] "Letter from D. Álvaro de Noronha to D. Manuel," Azamor, 15 December 1519, *SIHMP*, 2:260-263 and "Letter from Vasco de Pina to D. Manuel," Azamor, 30 March 1514, *SIHMP*, 1:523-524. These episodes are discussed in detail in chapter five.

[18] "Letter from Diogo de Azambuja to D. Manuel," Safi, 13 December 1507, *SIHMP*, 1:142-143.

[19] "Letter from Nuno Gato to D. Manuel," Azamor, 31 March 1514, *SIHMP*, 1:532.

and laborers be sent to Mazagão so that construction might proceed quickly.[20]

Labor for these construction projects could also be problematic. The Portuguese seem to have supplied the majority of the skilled labor, such as masons and excavators, as well as some of the unskilled labor. Moroccans, in many cases, provided the majority of the unskilled labor, hauling rocks, *cal*, and other goods from place to place, though there were some Moroccans who worked as masons. Without Moroccan labor it was often impossible to continue construction. D. João de Meneses, in preparation for a series of raids near Azamor in 1514, announced his plans to the allied Arab tribesmen who were encamped near Azamor and Mazagão. The members of these tribes, who had been earning wages as construction labor, joined Meneses's army in anticipation of their share of booty, abandoning their jobs. Consequently, the construction of these two cities could continue only at a greatly reduced rate.[21] When the fortress of Mazagão was modernized in 1542, the labor was exclusively Portuguese, due to the expanded power of the Sharif and consequent lack of Moroccan allies who could be used as labor. There were at least 400 men employed in this task: fifty masons, fifty excavators, and 300 laborers.[22]

Construction tasks were sometimes delayed due to bickering or to a change in priorities. The most important priority was defense. Although the Portuguese wanted to have churches and monasteries in their fortresses, these were often built slowly, as discussed in chapter four. A fine example of changing priorities occurred in Safi in 1516, after Nuno Fernandes de Ataíde's death and the subsequent chaos in the region. Despite the fact that there was a need to build a structure to house the *Casa dos Contos* (Treasury House), as its current location was in a ruined building, construction energies turned toward strengthening the city's defenses in anticipation of possible Moroccan

---

[20] "Letter from Francisco and Diogo de Arruda," Azamor, 31 March 1514, *SIHMP*, 1:527-528.

[21] "Letter from Vasco da Pina to D. Manuel," Azamor, 30 March 1514, *SIHMP*, 1:524 and "Letter from Francisco and Diogo Arruda to D. Manuel," Azamor, 31 March 1514, *SIHMP*, 1:528. Moroccans as laborers are discussed in greater detail in chapter three.

[22] "Letter from Luís de Loureiro to D. João III," Mazagão, 15 December 1542, *SIHMP*, 4: 114.

attacks.²³ The worst sort of change in priorities was a *capitão* who did not care about defenses at all. Mestre Rodrigo, the New Christian physician of Azamor from 1521 until at least 1528, claimed that *capitão* Jorge Viegas cared only about "seeking and finding ways of acquiring and maintaining wealth" rather than defending the city and focused on conducting raids more than any previous *capitães*.²⁴

Another source of delay was a lack of money. Money for construction normally had to be found in the overall operating budget of each fortress, from which salaries, pensions, and stipends, among other things, were paid. For example, in Safi in 1510, 800,000 *reis* were quickly spent on *moradias* (living allowances) and on buying essential supplies with the result that Nuno Gato, the city's *contador*, was able to say legitimately that the city was low on funds needed for construction and repairs.²⁵ In 1512, Gato again declared that there was no money to pay wages and wrote to the king in desperation, "I would pray your Highness to send [the money] as soon as possible, because these men have incurred such debts in the taverns, and I such shame for being the one to cover for them, that I no longer dare to go by the market."²⁶ In fact, work on strengthening the defenses of Azamor was delayed because workers allegedly spent more time complaining about late pay than working.²⁷

The problems were not just in the initial years. In 1536, Manuel de Sande, the *capitão* of Mazagão, reported to the king that he had borrowed money from Jews in Azamor in order to buy sixty *moios* of *cal* to complete work on a plumbing system designed to carry water from the city's cistern to fountains.²⁸ Luís de Loureiro informed the king in December 1542 that there had been no money to pay any of the construction workers in Mazagão for the past three months.

---

²³ "Letter from Nuno Gato to D. Manuel," Safi, 4 July 1516, *SIHMP*, 2:14-15.

²⁴ "Letter from Mestre Rodrigo to D. João III," Azamor, 15 November 1527, *SIHMP*, 2:418-424 and "Letter from Mestre Rodrigo to D. João III," Azamor, 12 January 1528, *SIHMP*, 2:425-428.

²⁵ "Letter of Nuno Gato to D. Manuel," Safi, 4-5 December 1510, *SIHMP*, 1:261-262.

²⁶ "Letter from Nuno Gato to D. Manuel," Safi, 12 May 1512, *SIHMP*, 1:301-302.

²⁷ "Letter from Vasco de Pina to D. Manuel," Azamor, 30 March 1514, *SIHMP*, 1:523.

²⁸ "Letter from Manuel de Sande to D. João III," Mazagão, 21 September 1536, *SIHMP*, 3:63.

Additionally, food supplies were running low and workers were beginning to show a lack of interest in completing their tasks. He asked the king to send both money and food as soon as possible.[29]

Siege Warfare

All of this defensive construction had a single goal: to protect the Portuguese against direct attacks and, especially, sieges. Other than the two-day siege of Azamor in 1513 by Portuguese forces, all other sieges in Morocco during this period were conducted by Moroccan forces against the Portuguese. The simple explanation for this is that only the Moroccans could assemble the number of troops necessary to attempt a siege. If the Portuguese could have mounted their own siege force, they would surely have attempted the capture of Marrakech, as it was long a dream both of the *fronteiros* and their king.[30]

The Portuguese typically had at least several days, if not weeks, warning before a besieging force arrived to encircle one of their fortresses. As indicated in the previous chapter, their Moroccan allies often provided them with information that indicated the coming siege. But the Portuguese also constructed an elaborate system of surveillance around their fortresses in order to prevent any sneak attacks should their normal channels of information fail them. The defenses were designed both to observe the arrival of a besieging force and – more commonly – to prevent the activities of small-scale Moroccan raiding parties.

The first line of defense was the *atalaias*, small towers built on the summits of hills near each fortress. The men who stood watch in these towers were also known as *atalaias* (from the Arabic *al-tal`a*, meaning hill). There were several lookout posts around each city; for instance, Safi had ten *atalaias* in 1511. If they saw something suspicious that warranted an alert, they replaced the "all-is-well" flag on their poles with the "alert" flag. This was known as *dar rebate*, or "to give warning."

---

[29] "Letter from Luís de Loureiro to D. João III," Mazagão, 15 December 1542, *SIHMP*, 4:117.

[30] Matthew T. Racine, "Service and Honor in Sixteenth-Century Portuguese North Africa: Yahya-u-Ta`fuft and Portuguese Noble Culture," *Sixteenth Century Journal* 32 (2001): 81-82. The conquest of Fez in the north of Morocco was another long-term goal of the Portuguese kings. See Marcel Bataillon, "La rêve de la conquête de Fès et le sentiment imperial portugais au XVIe siècle," in Idem, *Études sur le Portugal au temps de l'humanisme* (Coimbra, 1952), 101-107 and *HP*, 3:511 and n.4.

When this flag was raised, a watchman in a high tower in the city, known as the *rebate*, rang a bell (a process known as *tocar a rebate* or *dar o repique*) to alert everyone of the danger.[31] Another component of this defensive system were the *atalhadores* (lit. those who impede or prevent) who routinely scouted the countryside searching for any untoward activity by Moroccans and for locations that could be used to ambush Portuguese troops. The *escuta* also served to gather reconnaissance, though typically he was sent out only before a Portuguese raid, not as a matter of routine.[32]

Once the besieging force had arrived, the fortresses themselves needed to be able to withstand them. This was much easier during the early years of Portuguese occupation, for the Moroccan forces did not yet possess good artillery.[33] After the 1541 siege of Santa Cruz, in which Sa`adid forces occupied a nearby hill and mercilessly shelled Portuguese fortifications until they were shattered and could be easily overrun, it was clear to the Portuguese that they needed to rethink their defensive constructions. The castle of Mazagão, the only city that the Portuguese retained in southern Morocco after 1542, was completely rebuilt between 1541 and 1542 by João de Castilho and João Ribeiro, working with fellow architects Benetto da Ravenna and Francisco de Holanda. João de Castilho, in fact, said that the resultant fortress was "as beautiful as any in Spain." The original castle, built between 1515 and 1517, has been called by one historian, "a quaint throwback" that would have been unable to withstand new artillery. Proving its worth, the new castle withstood a devastating siege in 1562.[34]

---

[31] António Dias Farinha, *Os Portugueses em Marrocos* (Lisbon: Instituto Camões, 1999), 49 and ANTT, NA 597, f. 116v-119r. For examples of this process, see "Letter from Nuno Fernandes de Ataíde to D. Manuel," Safi, 4 January 1511, *SIHMP*, 1:285 and "Letter from João de Meneses to D. Manuel," Azamor, 5 December 1513, *SIHMP*, 1:450.

[32] David Lopes, *A expansão em Marrocos* (Lisbon: Teorema, 1989), 43.

[33] Weston Cook Jr., *The Hundred Years War for Morocco: Gunpowder and the Military Revolution in the Early Modern Muslim World* (San Francisco: Westview Press, 1994), *passim*.

[34] "Les travaux de Mazagan en 1541," *SIHMP*, 4:9-12; "Letter from João de Castilho to D. João III," Mazagão, 6 January 1542, *SIHMP*, 4:13; "Letter from Luís de Loureiro," Mazagão, 6 February 1542, *SIHMP*, 4:32; Farinha, *Os Portugueses*, 44-45; Elbl, "Portuguese Urban Fortifications," 376, 381. An eyewitness account of the 1562 siege is recorded in Agostinho de Gavy de Mendonça, *História do cerco de Mazagão* (Lisbon: 1890) and is available in English translation in John R. C. Martyn, ed. and trans., *The*

The walls of each fortress were the strongest and most important line of defense for the Portuguese. Where possible, the Portuguese had strengthened existing walls as well as constructed a series of defenses outside of the walls. The walls surrounding Azamor and Safi were quite extensive. In fact, the existing wall around Azamor was so long that the Portuguese felt it difficult to defend. Consequently, they constructed a redoubt (*atalho*) that connected the existing wall to the edge of the river, shortening the length of wall that needed to be defended and preventing the possibility of the entire city being surrounded by land-based troops.[35] Yet another *atalho* was constructed in Azamor beginning in 1517. The order from the king outlining the construction contained the exact location for the new construction, the dimensions for its parts, and the materials to be used. Furthermore, D. Manuel required that all expenses be catalogued in a single book so as not to promote waste and that two men would each hold one key to the chest in which the money was stored which required both keys to open it. This would, the king believed, prevent corruption.[36]

All Portuguese fortifications in southern Morocco were constructed along the seacoast or a riverbank so that goods could be easily unloaded from ships. During a siege, this was especially important as soldiers, weapons, and food would need to be delivered to the city by ship. In order to prevent enemy forces from hindering this process, the Portuguese built several *couraças*. These were low walls that were normally perpendicular to the fortress wall and were designed to stop or slow an attacker enough that he could be killed before reaching moored boats.[37] *Couraças* definitely existed in Mazagão and Safi, and may have existed in Azamor and Santa Cruz. Portuguese fortresses were also typically surrounded by a moat that, especially when filled

---

Siege of Mazagão: A Perilous Moment in the Defence of Christendom against Islam (New York: Peter Lang, 1994).

[35] "Letter from João de Meneses to D. Manuel," Azamor, 1-9 December 1514, *SIHMP*, 1:463 and n. 2.

[36] Maria Augusta Lima Cruz Fagundes, "Documentos inéditos para a história dos portugueses em Azamor," *Arquivos do Centro Cultural Portugues* 2 (1970): 148-149.

[37] Elbl, "Portuguese Urban Fortifications," 364-367. The Portuguese appointed an official, the *couraceiro*, to maintain the *couraça* (ANTT, CJ, Doações, 48, f. 57v, published in Sousa Viterbo, *A armaria em Portugal* (Lisbon: Acadmenia Real das Ciêcias, 1908).

with water, produced a difficult barrier for an attacking force. Moreover, in front of the main landward gate (the *porta do campo*) there normally existed a series of defensive works, such as a ravelin (a triangular outwork), and a series of trenches (*valos*) and fences or palisades (*tranqueiras*).[38] Finally, within the fortress itself was a central keep that was highly fortified and acted as the main area of refuge during any intense bombardments.[39]

To withstand a siege, stout defenses were not enough; there also needed to be enough artillery and manpower to defend the fortress. Artillery was especially important, as it gave the Portuguese a decisive edge over Moroccan armies until the 1530s. For example, Rui Barreto, the *capitão* of Azamor, told the king in February 1514 that he was returning only three of the six large cannons (*bombardas grossas*) that had been brought to Azamor in 1513 in order to assist in the conquest of the city. He argued that although the walls of the city seemed strong, maintaining the three *bombardas* would create an almost impregnable barrier.[40]

The Portuguese deemed artillery to be essential to their safety in Morocco. The *feitor* and the *escrivão de feitoria* of Santa Cruz complained in 1514 to the king about the lack of artillery in the fortress. They said that three *bombardas* and one *berço* (mid-sized cannon) that had been shipped to the fortress had arrived broken and needed to be replaced. Moreover, a ship that had been transporting more artillery to Santa Cruz had been captured by French privateers. Finally, another group of ships that had been transporting, among other things, artillery, had foundered on a nearby reef.[41]

For purposes of defensive combat, the walls of Portuguese fortresses were divided into small areas, typically delineated by a tower or the edge of a structure. These divisions were called *estancias*. One commander was given charge of each *estancia* along with a portion of

---

[38] Farinha, *Os Portugueses*, 45-48. The *couraça* of Safi was designed and its construction supervised by Lourenço Argueiro ("Letter from D. Rodrigo de Castro to D. João III," Safi, 24 June 1540, *SIHMP*, 3:250).

[39] Lopes, *A expansão*, 44.

[40] "Letter from Rui Barreto to D. Manuel," Azamor, 21 February 1514, *SIHMP*, 1:496-497.

[41] "Letter from Afonso Rodrigues and Francisco Fernandes to D. Manuel," Santa Cruz, 11 September 1514, *SIHMP*, 1:617-618.

the soldiers in the fortress and was charged with defending that section of wall from enemy attack. Depending on the difficulty of defending each section, it might be as short as sixty *braças* or as long as 240 *braças* (one *braça* = c. 2.2 meters). For example, Safi's walls were divided into fourteen *estancias*, a number that apparently stayed constant, at least in 1510 and 1515. The defenders slept in their *estancias*, both during sieges and when the arrival of an attacking force was predicted. During the summer of 1515, all the soldiers of Safi had slept in their *estancias* for thirty days in anticipation of the arrival of a Wattasid force.[42]

When an enemy force arrived to begin its siege, Portuguese soldiers along with any of their allies who might be in the city, defended its walls from enemy attempts to breach them. If the situation were particularly grave, people who normally would not fight, such as Jews and women, would also mount the walls.[43] The infantrymen lined the walls and stood by to defend the city should the walls be assaulted or breeched. Crossbowmen and matchlockmen also stood on the walls to shoot any of the enemy who approached within their range. These two groups of men, along with the *gente do campo* (i.e., *atalaias, atalhadores, escutas,* and *almocadéns* (guides who served with raiding parties)) were commanded by their own captain, known as the *anadel*.[44] Although the cavalry played a more important role in raiding, it did at times engage smaller groups of the enemy that had approached the city. Finally, men in charge of the artillery (*bombardeiros*) were of central importance during a siege, as it was often the superior firepower of the Portuguese that held off an enemy force, either until reinforcements could arrive or the enemy simply gave up and retreated. The *bombardeiros* were commanded by the *condestável dos bombardeiros*. The total number of soldiers in each fortress ranged from about 350 to several thousand, but averaged around 600 (see Table 7.1).

---

[42] "Letter from Nuno Gato to D. Manuel," Safi, 3 January 1511, *SIHMP*, 1:273-275 and "Letter from Nuno Fernandes de Ataíde to D. Manuel," Safi, 4 August 1515, *SIHMP*, 1:722. The Wattasid force never arrived.

[43] Jews were typically a small percentage of the armed men. In Azamor in 1517, a year in which the Portuguese portion of the garrison was at a low ebb, Jews comprised about 100 out of the 800 soldiers, or about 12.5 percent, present in the city ("Letter from Simão Correia to D. Manuel," Azamor, 20 May 1517, *SIHMP*, 2:86).

[44] Lopes, *A expansão*, 41. Each of the *anadeis* was beholden to the *adail* and the *capitão*, the two senior military leaders in each fortress.

Although the role of Portuguese women in sieges is rarely mentioned in documentation, surviving evidence from chronicles indicates that they were often crucial to success. If the situation in a siege were not particularly desperate, women typically were involved in ensuring that a steady supply of gunpowder and shot reached the men in their *estancias*. They also prepared food and tended to the wounded.[45] In extreme situations, they would dress as soldiers and walk along the walls of a fortress to confuse the enemy as to the number of fighting men in a fortress. There are even rare accounts of women engaging in combat and killing Moroccans.[46]

During a brief siege of Santa Cruz in 1533, Sa'adid forces succeeded in blowing a hole in the city's wall with their cannons. The night after this event, all the Portuguese in the city, including women and girls, helped repair the breach. In fact, one woman, six or seven months pregnant, carried stones to the work site that were so large that two men had to lift them onto her back. With her help and that of every other non-injured person in the fortress, the Portuguese succeeded in repairing the hole. In fact, the chronicler claims that when Sharif Muhammad al-Sheikh awoke the next day and saw the miraculous repair work, he felt that the Portuguese had used some magical evil. Thus, to keep away the evil, he said, "*Adhubillahi min al-Shaytān al-rajīm*": God keep the cursed Satan away! The chronicler adds that the spectacle of the wife of the *escrivão da feitoria* wearing a flowing white dress and walking the walls of the castle made it seem as though she were a witch who rebuilt the wall. Although according to the chronicler there remained within the fortress only forty men capable of fighting and although we cannot know if the fear of witchcraft actually affected the Moroccans, the Sharif and his men lifted the siege and retreated. The Portuguese took the added precaution of having women, wearing helmets and carrying lances, walk the walls of the

---

[45] Ana Maria S. A. Rodrigues and Maria de Fátima Moura Ferreira, "Mulheres portuguesas em Marrocos: imagens do quotidiano feminino nos séculos XV e XVI," in *O rosto feminino da expansão portuguesa* (Lisbon: Comissão para a Igualdade e para os Direitos das Mulheres, 1995), 1:425.

[46] *AA*, 1: 11, 13 and Gomes Eanes de Zurara, *Crónica do Conde D. Pedro de Menezes*, (Oporto, 1988), 233, 241-242. Although no accounts exist of Portuguese women killing Muslims in southern Morocco, given the carnage of the 1541 siege of Santa Cruz, it is likely that, at least in that instance, such events occurred (see below).

fortress so that it would appear as though the garrison were still at fighting strength.⁴⁷

Provisions were also made so that were a fortress wall breached, the "honorable women" and their children would receive protection. In Safi, the market area was to serve this purpose during an expected 1515 siege. While in Azamor in May 1517, an area inside the *feitoria* was prepared for these people.⁴⁸ One wonders what the less "honorable" women and children were supposed to do. During the final day of intense fighting before Santa Cruz fell to the Sharif in March 1541, large numbers of civilian men joined women and children in hiding under the fortress' *cal* ovens.⁴⁹

Two well-documented sieges show all the important components of siege warfare. Moreover, because they come at both chronological extremes of this study (1510 and 1541), they demonstrate the differences in the success and failure of Portuguese and Moroccan tactics and military technology. The sieges are the December 1510 siege of Safi that was successfully repelled, and the September 1540-March 1541 siege of Santa Cruz that resulted in the capture of the fortress and many of its inhabitants by Sa`adid forces.

The 1510 Siege of Safi⁵⁰

The siege of Safi in December 1510 was, in many ways, the result of generalized anti-Portuguese sentiment and the decision of important Moroccan political leaders not to allow the Portuguese to maintain more than a small trading presence in Morocco. A small, fortified *feitoria* in Safi was one thing, but control of the entire city and all of the wealth channeled through it was another. With a massive Muslim force led by Al-Naser bin Yūsuf al-Hintati and his cousin, Muhammad al-Hintati, and which included the Sharquiyya and Ghrabiyya Arabs, the Shyadma Berbers, as well as smaller Berber and Arab tribes, the Portuguese were rightly concerned about this force.

---

⁴⁷ *CSC*, 68-78.

⁴⁸ "Letter from Nuno Fernandes de Ataíde to D. Manuel," Safi, 4 August 1515, *SIHMP*, 1:723 and "Letter from Simão Correia to D. Manuel," Azamor, 20 May 1517, *SIHMP*, 2:87.

⁴⁹ *CSC*, 120-122.

⁵⁰ For a brief discussion of the siege, see Durval R. Pires de Lima, *História da dominação portuguêsa em Çafim (1506-1542)* (Lisbon, 1930), 36-42 and *HP*, 3:480-481.

Nuno Gato described the assembled Muslims as allegedly attaining 600,000 souls, with 200,000 of them being combatants. In the style of the times, these numbers were likely exaggerations, but clearly the Moroccan force was huge. The Portuguese fortress, by contrast, only had 900 fighting men. Despite this numeric imbalance, Gato described the astonishing sight of so many people covering every speck of land thus: "It seemed to me that it was the most beautiful sight in the world."[51] It may have been a dazzling sight, but it was also an ominous one as the besiegers played drums constantly and communicated during the night with signal fires.[52]

Although the Portuguese had knowledge of forces marching towards Safi by late November 1510, the Moroccan forces did not begin arriving until 13 December, completely surrounding the city, "from sea to sea," by the 23rd. In a fine mark of bravado, Nuno Gato, the *contador* of Safi, commented on the numbers of enemy troops that were predicted to arrive: "The more that come, the more that will die." Nevertheless, he reported in the same letter, "we look all the time towards Cape Canaveal [modern Cape Safi, located five kilometers north of Safi] to see if the aid is coming." In preparation for the arrival of the besieging force, the Portuguese, in addition to requesting reinforcements, went to work patching, if not rebuilding, the weak spots in the city's walls. Despite nearly three years of Portuguese occupation of Safi, the walls were still in bad condition, owing to the lack of financial resources. Additionally, dilapidated houses were demolished to provide rocks to drop on assaulting troops, and firing slits were cut into all of the city's towers. The *capitão*, Nuno Fernandes de Ataíde, wrote to the king telling him that, as of 5 December, there were only 900 "fighting men" in Safi, emphasizing the dire need of reinforcements to fight the impending siege.[53]

---

[51] "Letter from Nuno Gato to D. Manuel," Safi, 3 January 1511, *SIHMP*, 1:275, 277-278; "Letter from Nuno Fernandes de Ataíde to D. Manuel," Safi, 4 January 1511, *SIHMP*, 1:285; Pires de Lima, 36. Gato named as many of these groups as possible: Awlad `Amran (lithali and discani), Awlad Ya'qub, Awlad Bu Aziz, Awlad Subeita, Gharbiyya, Selalim, Seja, the Berbers between Azamor and Almedina, and the Shyadma Berbers.

[52] "Letter from Nuno Fernandes de Ataíde to D. Manuel," Safi, 4 January 1511, *SIHMP*, 1:291, 292.

[53] "Letter from Nuno Fernandes de Ataíde to D. Manuel," Safi, 5 December 1510, *SIHMP*, 1:265-266; "Letter from Nuno Gato to D. Manuel," Safi, 4-5 December 1510,

The Moroccans constructed siege towers (*bastilhões*), palisades (*tranqueiras*), and bastions (*baluartes*) and set "some artillery" in place. Nuno Fernandes de Ataíde had, by way of Christian merchants in Azamor and the Portuguese at Santa Cruz, sent word to Madeira for reinforcements. These reinforcements were approved and paid for by D. Isabel de Noronha, the wife of the governor of Madeira, Simão Gonçalves da Câmara, because her husband was in Portugal at the time. It was, in fact, quite common for Gonçalves (and his wife) to send a relief force whenever called upon by Portuguese in North Africa. Damião de Góis reported that during his tenure as governor of Madeira, Gonçalves had sent troops at least once to every Portuguese stronghold in Morocco.[54]

While awaiting the arrival of reinforcements, Nuno Fernandes de Ataíde organized the defense of the city. First, he ensured that artillery was in the proper position. According to Ataíde, the Portuguese had twelve pieces of artillery, ten large *bombardas* and two smaller *tiros de fogo*. These were positioned along the top of the wall to create the most effective field of fire.[55] On the 22nd of December, Ataíde and a number of horsemen rode out to one of the *atalaias* near the city in order to observe the Moroccan troops. Although the Moroccans saw the Portuguese, they did not attempt to attack them en masse, though there were some skirmishes. When Ataíde had completed his reconnaissance, he returned to the city and checked on his men. They had been positioned in their *estancias*, eating and sleeping there, since the night of the 13th, and would remain there until the siege was lifted. Among these was D. Rodrigo de Noronha, whose *estancia* encompassed twelve towers and 204 *braças* of wall, and who had

---

SIHMP, 1:259-264; "Letter from Nuno Gato to D. Manuel," Safi, 3 January 1511, *SIHMP*, 1:272; "Letter from Nuno Fernandes de Ataíde to D. Manuel," Safi, 4 January 1511, *SIHMP*, 1:289-290.

[54] "Letter from Nuno Gato to D. Manuel," Safi, 4-5 December 1510, *SIHMP*, 1:259-264; "Letter from Nuno Fernandes de Ataíde to D. Manuel," Safi, 5 December 1510, *SIHMP*, 1:265-266; "Letter from Nuno Fernandes de Ataíde to D. Manuel," Safi, 4 January 1511, *SIHMP*, 1:284-285; Pires de Lima, 41; *CDM*, 3:50-51. It was apparently fairly common for the wives of *capitães* to take over official functions in their husbands' absence. See, for example, Paulo Drumond Braga, "D. Maria de Eça, capitoa de Ceuta nos meados do século XVI," in *O rosto feminino da expansão portuguesa* (Lisbon: Comissão para a Igualdade e para os Direitos das Mulheres, 1994), 1:433-437.

[55] "Letter from Nuno Fernandes de Ataíde to D. Manuel," Safi, 4 January 1511, *SIHMP*, 1:287-289.

command of the city's Jews. The Jews were, in turn, led by Isaac and Ismail Benzamiro.[56] As already mentioned, Jews taking up arms in the service of the Portuguese was quite rare, and shows the seriousness of the siege. There are, in fact, no known examples of Jews going on raids with the Portuguese, so their participation in military violence was strictly defensive in nature.[57]

In addition to the need to provide weapons and ammunition to the soldiers, preparations were needed to ensure that the soldiers were fed. Because they were in a combat situation, it was the responsibility of the royal treasury to pay for the men's meals. This, reported the *contador*, had been expensive. During the seventeen days that the Portuguese manned their *estancias*, Ataíde continuously circulated a pack animal (*azêmola*) loaded with hard tack through the troop positions so that the men could take what they needed. He also provided each *estancia* with jugs of wine, "to aid the men's work," and with figs. The *contador* supported this distribution because it was very cold at night, and the food and wine helped the soldiers stay up on the walls and maintain their vigilance, instead of returning to the ground where it was warmer.

Once the Moroccans had their troops in position, they launched a series of assaults against Safi, attempting to climb or breach the walls. Ataíde created a rapid response force that would go to the area of Safi's defenses that was most vulnerable at any given moment in order to push the attackers away. This force was led by Ataíde himself, Lopo Barriga, the *adail* of Safi, and Nuno Gato, the *contador*. The rest of the group was composed of nobles and knights, who were good warriors and whom Ataíde trusted.

The Portuguese had another weapon: spies among the Moroccans. Nuno Gato mentioned vaguely that "some ounces" of silver had been disbursed to several Moroccans for providing information (*avisos*) to the Portuguese during the siege. There is, however, only one specific example of the effectiveness of these spies.

---

[56] "Letter from Nuno Gato to D. Manuel," Safi, 3 January 1511, *SIHMP*, 1:273-275 and "Letter from Nuno Fernandes de Ataíde to D. Manuel," Safi, 4 January 1511, *SIHMP*, 1:285-286.

[57] José Alberto Rodrigues da Silva Tavim, *Os judeus na expansão portuguesa em Marrocos durante o século XVI: origens e actividades duma comunidade* (Braga: Edições APPACDM Distrital de Braga, 1997), 394-396. See chapter three for more details.

On 22 December, Ataíde learned from one of his spies that the Moroccans intended to attack Safi that night, using the darkness to their advantage. Ataíde quickly ordered that each *estancia* be well supplied with powder pots (*panelas de polvora*), pitch, tar, boiling oil, and a store of cedar torches (*fachas de cedro*) with which to illuminate the walls. The Moroccans approached the city walls but, seeing the Portuguese so well prepared, retreated and did not attack that evening.[58]

The Portuguese would, however, use these weapons to great effect on 27 December, the date on which the Mashanzaya Berber tribe, considered by Moroccans to be elite warriors, arrived near Safi. According to the Portuguese, they seemed to be noble men dressed in scarlet and wearing beautifully-crafted breastplates and helmets, while some had shields detailed with gold. In their company were matchlockmen, crossbowmen, and artillerymen, who were reportedly very skilled at aiming their cannon. These warriors were all commanded by a cloaked (*acubertado*) figure on horseback. These men soon attacked the city walls with ladders, axes (*alferçes*), picks (*picões*), and other objects to help breach the walls. The Portuguese quickly responded to this danger with gunfire, crossbow fire (*setadas*), powder pots (*panelas de polvora*), tar, pitch, and boiling oil. They succeeded in repelling the attack, leaving the bodies of 400 of the attackers dead at the base of the wall.[59]

No more spies were forthcoming, apparently, so Ataíde decided to sneak out of Safi and capture one of the enemy in order to learn their plans. He and eight others rode out of the city and, in attempting to capture someone, ended up killing two Moroccans. This was seen by a large group of the enemy nearby, who charged after the Portuguese, but they were able to return safely to Safi.[60]

---

[58] "Letter from Nuno Gato to D. Manuel," Safi, 3 January 1511, *SIHMP*, 1:277-279 and *CDM*, 3:53. Dropping objects on attackers was a common defensive practice. The residents of Azamor, while defending their city from the attacking Portuguese in 1508 and 1513, dropped beehives – in addition to rocks, burning objects, and flaming arrows – from their walls ("Account of the Attack of Azamor," n. l., 10-12 August 1508, *SIHMP*, 1:166 and "Letter from Jorge Pires to Fernando de Castro," Azamor, 4 September 1513, *SIHMP*, 1:407).

[59] *CDM*, 3:53-54; "Letter from Nuno Gato to D. Manuel," Safi, 3 January 1511, *SIHMP*, 1:276; *SIHMP*, 1:70n1.

[60] *CDM*, 3:54.

On 30 December, the Moroccans made their last attempt to take the city. Ataíde seems to have known it would be coming, as he noted the night before that the Moroccans had been furiously communicating with each other by means of drums and signal fires. They mounted a great assault on the city, at one point standing near the wall of the city taunting the Portuguese to shoot them. The Portuguese responded as they had before, raining down gunfire and burning objects onto the attackers. The fire was so heavy that, according to Góis, it "blotted out the sun." Ataíde rode to each *estancia*, leaving reserve troops at the weakest points. According to Nuno Gato, his presence inspired the troops, giving them renewed vigor for the battle. After more than 600 of the attackers died without summiting the walls of the city, they retreated. The next day, they ended their seventeen-day siege. As they retreated in disorder, Ataíde and a group of 400 Portuguese horsemen, pursued whomever they could, killing some and capturing many.[61]

The Portuguese may or may not have been able to break the siege without the help of reinforcements from Madeira and Cadiz, Spain, who began arriving on 28 December. Once all the relief forces had arrived, the number of fighting men in Safi had grown from 900 to 2,000.[62] Moroccan forces began to retreat on 31 December. Ataíde does speculate, however, that because the Moroccans had seen reinforcements arriving by ship, it disheartened them and, in combination with their defeat on 30 December, they decided to withdraw. This shows that without the advance warning that the Portuguese had of the coming siege, reinforcements would never have arrived in time to assist them. Even with advanced warning, the first reinforcements took nearly one month to arrive. In fact, two groups of reinforcements arrived on 31 December, after the Moroccans had begun their retreat.[63]

---

[61] "Letter from Nuno Fernandes de Ataíde to D. Manuel," Safi, 4 January 1511, *SIHMP*, 1:292-295; *CDM*, 3:54-55: "*de maneira que encobrião ho sol*"; "Letter from Nuno Gato to D. Manuel," Safi, 3 January 1511, *SIHMP*, 1:279.

[62] Pires de Lima, 41.

[63] "Letter of Nuno Gato to D. Manuel," Safi, 4-5 December 1510, *SIHMP*, 1:259-264; "Letter from Nuno Fernandes de Ataíde to D. Manuel," Safi, 4 January 1511, *SIHMP*, 1:284-296; "Letter from Nuno Gato to D. Manuel," Safi, 3 January 1511, *SIHMP*, 1:271-280. This last letter also contains a list of those in charge of defending certain

With or without reinforcements, however, the Moroccans had little chance against the Portuguese in 1510. For one thing, the Portuguese had superior artillery; in fact, the Moroccans had few pieces of artillery, and certainly none that could pound a walled city into submission. Furthermore, Safi's easy access to the sea and a protected anchorage for ships meant that so long as supplies and men could be sent from abroad, the city could hold out indefinitely. In scarcely thirty years, the balance would tip almost completely in favor of the Moroccans.

The 1540-1541 Siege of Santa Cruz[64]

A siege that was much more successful for Moroccan forces was that conducted by Sharif Muhammad al-Sheikh against the Portuguese stronghold of Santa Cruz from September 1540 until March 1541. This siege had better leadership, more artillery, and the benefit of thirty years of experience fighting the Portuguese. When the fortress fell to the Sharif's forces, Santa Cruz had about 1,400 people living in it.[65] Unlike the siege of Safi in 1510, very little correspondence survives to describe the event. Fortunately, we have the *Chronicle of Santa Cruz do Cabo de Gué*, written between 1560 and 1570 by an anonymous knight who was an eyewitness to the events and appears to have served in Santa Cruz from 1525 onward.[66]

After 1530, with the Sharif having consolidated his power in the Sus region of Morocco, Santa Cruz remained a thorn in his side. Consequently, he attempted to blockade or besiege it often after that year. The two largest attempts being the siege of May 1533, in which an ill-equipped army foundered against Portuguese fortifications and artillery, and the successful siege of September 1540-March 1541. The conquest of Santa Cruz began a domino effect that led to the decision

---

portions of Safi during the siege, and it gives the attack/siege positions of many of the tribes participating in the action.

[64] This siege is also discussed in Joaquim Figanier, *História de Santa Cruz do Cabo de Gué (Agadir) 1505-1541* (Lisboa: Agência Geral das Colónias, 1945), 192-214.

[65] "Letter from D. João III to the Count of Castanheira," Almeirim, 23 February 1541, *SIHMP*, 3:309. This population was likely 95% or more European Christian, with the remainder possibly Jews and Moroccan Muslims. Santa Cruz never had a very large non-Christian population, unlike Safi and Azamor.

[66] Pierre de Cenival, "Introduction," *CSC*, 7-10.

to abandon Safi and Azamor and concentrate Portuguese forces in southern Morocco in the single fortress of Mazagão.[67]

The siege of 1540-1541 came at the end of a four and one-half years' truce between the Portuguese and Muhammad al-Sheikh that had been concluded on 28 March 1536, with Luís de Loureiro, then *capitão* of Santa Cruz. During this respite, the Sharif built up his arsenal of cannons, matchlock rifles, and other military equipment. Moreover, he began construction on a fortress atop a nearby hill, known to the Portuguese as the Pico. It seemed clear to the Portuguese that the Sharif planned to bombard their city from this location once the truce expired. Loureiro sent a messenger to the Sharif telling him that if he did not halt construction, then the Portuguese would break the truce and attack. The Sharif disregarded the warning and completed construction, though he did remove cannons from the small fortress until the expiration of the truce in September 1540. Their bluff called, the Portuguese could do little but watch impotently from Santa Cruz. They did, however, attempt to strengthen their defenses by building a tall, lengthy earthen wall in front of the fortress with several large cannon on top of it.

In 1538, Loureiro wrote to King D. João III and asked that he be removed from his command because he missed his wife and children. In addition to being a family man, Loureiro may have seen the handwriting on the wall and sought to be relieved of his command before Santa Cruz came under attack by the strengthening forces of the Sharif. The king granted his request and replaced him with D. Guterres de Monroi, who had been interim governor of Santa Cruz for a brief period in 1534; he would be its last.[68]

The siege itself began on 26 September 1540. Between 50,000 and 70,000 Sa`adid troops, many of whom were armed with matchlock rifles or on horseback, had surrounded Santa Cruz while their compatriots bombarded the city from the Pico using large artillery pieces known as *maimonas*.[69] The Portuguese were able to return fire

---

[67] Cenival, "Introduction," *CSC*, 17-19. For more on the abandonment decision, see the concluding chapter of this study.

[68] *CSC*, 84-86 and 84n1.

[69] These cannons were so large that it was impossible for a man to wrap his arms around a ball that was shot from them. See Figanier, 194.

quite successfully and kill many soldiers and destroy some of the smaller artillery near the fortress walls. Nevertheless, according to the chronicler, the Portuguese were at a great disadvantage because their gunpowder was limited due to the infrequent arrival of supply ships, whereas the Sharif seemed to have an unlimited supply. The Sharif, in fact, purchased most of his military supplies from the Genoese and Castilian merchants, who continuously violated Portuguese claims of control of the area's trade as well as the papal prohibition on the sale of war materiel to Muslims.[70]

The military commander for the Sharif was named Mūmin bin Yahya bin al-`Ilj. As his name (bin al-`Ilj) indicates, he was the son of a Christian who had become a Muslim.[71] According to the story, his father was a Genoese merchant who impregnated the daughter of the *qā'id* of Teceut (Tiut). The father discovered this liaison and gave the merchant an ultimatum: either convert to Islam and marry his daughter or be executed. They were married. By some means, their son, Mūmin, became a great commander under the Sharif. During the siege of Santa Cruz, he commanded the entire military, and even the Sharif's three sons, Muhammad al-Harran, `Abd al-Qadir, and `Abd al-Rahman, answered to him.[72]

When the Sharif's forces began arriving near Santa Cruz in September 1540, D. Guterres de Monroi sent requests for assistance

---

[70] *CSC*, 86-90; Figanier, 193; Jamil M. Abun-Nasr, *A History of the Maghrib in the Islamic Period* (New York: Cambridge University Press, 1987), 210. For more on trade disputes between the Portuguese and other Europeans, see chapter five.

[71] `Ilj (Port. *elche*) is Arabic for infidel, but in these particular cases it referred to Christians who had converted to Islam. The Portuguese version of the word translates best as "renegade," implying that a person who converted betrayed not only his soul, but also his people. Often, these renegades converted for reasons of commercial gain, serving as military advisors for Islamic leaders. For more information, see Isabel M. R. Mendes Drumond Braga, *Entre a Cristandade e o Islão: cativos e renegados nas franjas de duas sociedades em confronto* (Ceuta: Instituto de Estudios Ceutíes, 1998), 75-141; Miguel Angel de Bunes Ibarra, "Reflexiones sobre la conversión al Islam de los renegados en los siglos XVI y XVII," in *Hispania Sacra* 42 (1990): 181-190; Sanjay Subrahmanyam, *The Portuguese Empire in Asia, 1500-1700: A Political and Economic History* (New York: Longman, 1993), 249-256; Timothy J. Coates, *Convicts and Orphans: Forced and State-Sponsored Colonizers in the Portuguese Empire, 1550-1755* (Stanford: Stanford University Press, 2001), 86-93.

[72] *CSC*, 90-92; Diego de Torres, *Relación del origen y suceso de los xarifes y del estado de los reinos de Marruecos, Fez, y Tarudante*, trans. ed. and intro. Mercedes García-Arenal (Madrid: Siglo Veintiuno de España, 1980), 110; "Letter from António Leitão de Gamboa to D. João III," Santa Cruz, 16 January 1525, *SIHMP*, 2:337.

and reinforcements; however, answers to these calls were slow in coming. By this time, sieges had been become common, and the Portuguese king complacent. None of the previous sieges had been successful, so why should this siege be any different?[73] At the beginning of December 1540, Manuel da Câmara, the governor of Madeira, arrived with twenty-two knights and seventy-five to eighty men who were either artisans, who helped strengthen the city's defenses, or soldiers. D. João III believed that this number of men was twice the necessary amount, despite the fact that the king had earlier written to Monroi informing him that he was sending 200 men.[74]

By the end of December, more than 200 Portuguese had been killed or wounded by Moroccan artillery. Monroi, concluding that he could not count on his king, sent to the Canaries for reinforcements and supplies. He also sent a ship to Safi, requesting gunpowder and "anything else they could spare." Only a single ship answered the call, arriving "with good men but few." After the besieging force increased the intensity of assaults on the city in mid-February, Monroi decided to try one last time to get reinforcements from Portugal. He ordered two older and respected men, an "honored knight" who had at one time been an *almocadém*, and Francisco da Costa, the city's *ouvidor*, to travel to Lisbon. Monroi hoped that their reputations might cause the king to reconsider the seriousness of the situation and send reinforcements and supplies.[75] Unknown to Monroi was that the king had finally already decided to send a supply ship to Santa Cruz. The ship left Lisbon sometime after 23 February carrying enough wheat, wine, olive oil, meat, and vegetables to feed the city's residents for three months. Also on the ship were one hundred matchlockmen, supplies of gunpowder and munitions, and feed for the fortresses' sixty horses.[76] The effort

---

[73] Portuguese overconfidence was so great that D. João III signed an order naming D. Afonso de Monroi, D. Guterres' son, the *capitão* of Santa Cruz should his father die during the siege. The order was issued in Lisbon on 18 March 1541, seven days *after* the city had fallen. In short, the chain of command was of greater concern to the king than what seemed like an impossibility: the loss of Santa Cruz to the Moroccans. See ANTT, CC I, 69, 69 (published in Figanier, 343).

[74] *AJ*, 2:172 and Figanier, 196.

[75] *CSC*, 92-96, 98.

[76] "Letter from D. João III to Count of Castanheira," 23 February 1541, Almeirim. *SIHMP*, 3:309-310.

was too little too late, and could not have arrived at Santa Cruz until after the city fell to the Sharif. By the final days of the siege, the chronicler reported that "women and children" were dying of hunger.[77]

By February 1541, the besieging force had grown from its original 50,000 to 70,000 to around 122,000 composed of 20,000 cavalry, 40,000 matchlockmen (*espingardeiros*), 12,000 crossbowmen, and 50,000 tribesmen who were most likely in the role of infantry soldiers. In addition to Moroccans, there were Turks and Jalofs in the Sharif's army.[78] Monroi recounted that by January 1541, nine massive *maimonas* were in place on the Pico, raining destruction on Santa Cruz. Like the other Portuguese strongholds, Santa Cruz had been built using techniques to withstand fifteenth-century artillery, not the more powerful guns employed by the Sharif's army.[79] This bombardment had required frequent and repeated repairs to the city's walls. Moreover, the number of light artillery and matchlock rifles at the Sharif's disposal was so vast that "one could not believe how many there were."[80]

Besides worrying about dwindling supplies, a massive enemy force, and weakened defenses, the Portuguese had to contend with destructive accidents. In one incident, while grinding the coarse grains of gunpowder that served for cannons into the fine grains needed for matchlock rifles, a spark was emitted by the grinding action of the

---

[77] *CSC*, 106. This might suggest that supplies of food were rationed to favor male soldiers who needed their strength in order to fight. A brief account of Monroi's attempts to secure aid can be found in "Letter from D. Guterres de Monroi to D. João III," Tarudante, 2 April 1541, *SIHMP*, 3:365-374. (Note that this letter was written shortly after Monroi had been captured. As with the anonymous chronicler of Santa Cruz, this letter attempts to demonstrate that Monroi did as much as possible to save Santa Cruz with the resources he had. It acts as both a bureaucratic report and an attempt to restore honor to his name.)

[78] *CSC*, 96, 110. The chronicler describes the Jalofs as "fighting not like men, but devils." He provides proof of this assertion by describing a Jalof who, having been run through the chest by a lance, pulled himself, by means of the lance, toward his Christian attacker, intending to continue the fight. Before he could do this, however, someone else stabbed the Jalof with a sword and he died.

[79] See Cook, 194-200 and Elbl, "Portuguese Urban Fortifications," *passim*. More generally, see Geoffrey Parker, *The Military Revolution: Military Innovation and the Rise of the West, 1500-1800*, 2nd. ed (New York: Cambridge University Press, 1996), esp. chapter 1.

[80] "Letter from D. Guterres de Monroi to D. João III," Tarudante, 2 April 1541, *SIHMP*, 3:369.

mortar and pestle, causing a flash fire that resulted in the burning of three men. Another gunpowder fire occurred in the São Simão bulwark, burning an artilleryman and a boy. On 11 March, one day before the city fell, an entire barrel of gunpowder exploded, lifting thirty-three men into the air, killing most of them and leaving the few survivors badly burned. One of those killed was Rodrigo de Carvajal, the husband of D. Mécia de Monroi, the *capitão's* daughter. Manuel da Câmara survived the blast but was horribly burned and his kneecap was shattered. The chronicler describes this incident with the characteristic cynicism that marks his account of the siege: "Everything was against us, even the gunpowder."[81] The day the fortress fell, the Portuguese had created a booby trap for the invaders. They placed four barrels of gunpowder in a room, intending to detonate them should the Moroccans capture it. Due to a foolish mistake, the powder was ignited, causing a flash, rather than an explosion, that burned about a dozen Portuguese.[82]

The volatility of gunpowder had caused problems in Santa Cruz before. During the 1533 siege of Santa Cruz, the wives of the *almoxarife* and the *alcaide mor* were dispensing gunpowder from the storehouse. At one point, "an old man, who had been in the fortress many years," entered the room with a lit match (*morrão*), causing many barrels of gunpowder to explode. Everyone in the room was blown into the air. The body of Goterres de Senabria, a Castilian who had been living in Santa Cruz, landed on the roof of the keep. Meanwhile, soldiers standing on the wall of the castle were pummeled from the sky by body parts. The wife of the *almoxarife* "was burnt to a crisp" (*fez-se carvão*), while the wife of the *alcaide mor* had been blown out a window and landed on the beach, completely naked except for a pair of red boots and without a bruise or burn on her. Nevertheless, she was dead.[83] While siege-related accidents were costly and terrible, the true horror was the massive army besieging the fortress.

The assault that would lead to the capture of Santa Cruz began on 16 February 1541. By the afternoon of Friday, 11 March, after

---

[81] *CSC*, 98, 100. Guterres puts the number of dead at thirty-nine ("Letter from D. Guterres de Monroi to D. João III," Tarudante, 2 April 1541, *SIHMP*, 3:370).

[82] *CSC*, 116.

[83] *CSC*, 68-72.

twenty-two days of continuous fighting, the Sharif's troops had breached the wall of the fortress. The Portuguese fought valiantly, sometimes gaining the upper hand and pushing the forces back. Every sort of combat possible occurred: hand-to-hand with swords, barrages – typically from Sa`adid forces – from matchlock rifles, and artillery bombardment.[84] Occupying the defensive position, the Portuguese were nevertheless able to kill their enemy in much greater numbers than they themselves were being killed. In fact, both D. Guterres de Monroi and the chronicler reported that blood from dead Moroccans formed a small stream that flowed into the ocean and turned the sea red near the fortress.[85]

The Portuguese initially succeeded in repelling the 11 March breach. Sa`adid forces were, according to the Portuguese chronicler, greatly disheartened and contemplated a withdrawal. At this moment, the Sharif's son, Muhammad al-Harran, stepped in to rally the troops. He yelled, "I swear to God and by God and I swear again that I will have sinned if I leave here without having captured this fortress!" He then began walking towards a ladder that would take him onto a roof that was still in possession of the Portuguese. At this point, one of his knights grabbed him by the arm and took his place on the ladder. Upon reaching the top of the ladder, a Portuguese cleaved his head open with a hatchet and his lifeless body fell back down the ladder. This act of sacrificial bravery rallied all the Moroccan troops that had been hiding in order to avoid Portuguese artillery and gunshot to come out into the open. According to the chronicler, it was an astonishing number, whose swords and spears reflected the light of the sun.[86]

As the rejuvenated Moroccan forces began to push into Santa Cruz again, many in the fortress, sure that it would be taken, were unable to bear the thought of being captured and jumped into the sea, swimming towards two ships waiting off the coast. These ships had earlier bombarded the Pico, but had exhausted their supply of gunpowder, and so anchored offshore. Both Monroi and the chronicler, in fact, blame the ships for the loss of the fortress, arguing

---

[84] *CSC*, 102-122.

[85] *CSC*, 106-108 and "Letter from D. Guterres de Monroi to D. João III," Tarudante, 2 April 1541, *SIHMP*, 3:370.

[86] *CSC*, 110-112.

that if they had not been there, then no one would have left the fortress and it could have been defended. The chronicler added that many of those who abandoned the fortress died in the rough seas; seas so rough that it seemed "even the sea was against us." Moreover, the Sa'adid troops launched two *zabras* (small galley-like ships) into the sea in order to kill as many Portuguese as possible. They only bothered to take one person captive, a Portuguese noble who wore a gold chain around his neck. They thought this man would bring a valuable ransom.[87]

The sight of so many Portuguese abandoning the fortress further rallied the Moroccans who charged the fortress in even greater numbers. By this time, only two hundred Portuguese soldiers remained able to fight. They put up a fierce resistance, killing over three thousand Moroccans from their entrenched positions before surrendering.[88] As the situation became more desperate, and more and more Moroccans were able to penetrate the fortress, it gradually became clear to the remaining defenders that they were going to lose. At one point, Monroi and about forty knights who were with him noticed a large group of Moroccans near the church. In response to the *capitão's* desire to attack these invaders, the knights with him responded, "Since we are going to die, let's die fighting like knights." To which the *capitão* gave the Santiago – "Santiago and death to the Moors!" – and they charged. This group of Moroccans fled before them.[89]

Those who were not soldiers met the violence in their own way. Some were among those who went over the city walls and attempted to swim to safety. One woman walked through the streets of Santa Cruz, holding a cross aloft and exhorting her fellow Christians

---

[87] "Letter from D. Guterres de Monroi to D. João III," Tarudante, 2 April 1541, *SIHMP*, 3:371 and *CSC*, 112-114. The chronicler says of the ships, "*Já que não prestarão pera nos fazerem bem, prestarão pera nos fazerem mal.*" Guterres went a bit further asking the king to hunt down and punish any men who abandoned the fortress and swam to the safety of the ships: "*E hos homens que se lamçarão ao mar merecem muy bem castiguados, e mamda-los buscar pelo rreyno e a ylha da Madeira, primcypalmente os que tinhão estamçyas de que me tinhão dado sua menajem.*" For a similar request, see "Letter from Henrique Vieira to D. João III," Tarudante, 20 April 1541, *SIHMP*, 3:398.

[88] *CSC*, 114-116 and "Letter from D. Guterres de Monroi to D. João III," Tarudante, 2 April 1541, *SIHMP*, 3:372.

[89] *CSC*, 116-118.

to keep fighting and give their lives for their faith.[90] A cobbler, Manuel Fernandes, fearing the life awaiting his children should they be captured, killed his son and one of his daughters and was about to kill his other daughter when some Sa`adid soldiers killed him.[91] The chaos and fear felt by the Portuguese might be compared with that shown by the Moroccans fleeing Azamor when it was captured by the Portuguese in 1513. Luís Henriques, a Portuguese poet, described it as follows:

> *Os mouros de dentro, que viram crescer*
> *Seu mal e seu dano, sem bem esperar,*
> *Com grande temor de vidas perder*
> *Leixaram cidade por vidas salvar.*
> *Fugindo sem tento, com tal pressa dar,*
> *Qu'ò sair da porta muitos se matavam,*
> *Os pais pelos filhos se não esperavam,*
> *Mulher por marido podia aguardar.*[92]

Indeed, the military violence and its effects had come full circle in southern Morocco. The Portuguese were now the ones in fear for their lives and experiencing the anxiety of not seeing their spouses or children again.

By the morning of 12 March, the Portuguese had surrendered to the Sharif's army. About 1,000 Portuguese and 7,800 Moroccans had died during the siege. The Portuguese men, women, and children who had hidden under the *cal* ovens emerged and were taken captive, forming part of the approximately 600 who were enslaved.[93] One of these people was Manuel Rodrigues, the *escrivão de feitoria*. As he stood

---

[90] Figanier, 213.

[91] "Report of D. Rodrigo de Castro," n. l., after 12 March 1541, *SIHMP*, 3:343.

[92] "De Luis Anriques ao duque de Bragaça, quando tomou Azamor, em que conta como foi," in Garcia de Resende, *Cancioneiro Geral* (Lisbon, 1516), fol. 105r. My prose translation of this stanza is as follows: "The Muslims inside, who saw their evil and sins increase, abandoned the city, without delay, in order to save themselves, fearing for their lives. They fled carelessly and in such a hurry that many died while passing through the city gate; parents not waiting for their children, wives waiting in vain for their husbands."

[93] Figanier, 214. Note that with the small number of reinforcements that arrived in Santa Cruz, the population had grown to about 1,600 from the 1,400 previously mentioned.

amongst his captors, he noticed one of them whom he knew and called a friend, Barque Malik. He spoke with him, hoping to be freed, and showed him a sack of money that he had secreted before the fighting. Malik and some associates soon bashed Rodrigues' head, killing him and taking his money.[94]

According to the chronicler, it was the fault of D. João III that Santa Cruz fell. If he had only sent reinforcements and supplies, the valiant effort of the Portuguese who were already there would have been sufficient to defeat the Sharif.[95] As mentioned above, D. João III had, by mid-February, finally realized the seriousness of the situation in Santa Cruz. In fact, in response to rumors that the Sharif was sending another force to besiege Mazagão, the king quickly readied a relief force. Among other things, he had all large ships – both Portuguese and foreign – that were moored in the harbors of Lisbon, Setúbal, Sesimbra, and Alcácer do Sal seized. They were then to be evaluated for their sturdiness and, if suitable, mounted with cannons and used in the relief force.[96] None of this mattered, of course, to the Portuguese who had been captured with the fall of Santa Cruz.

Unlike the siege of 1510, the Portuguese may not have been able to hold out even if several hundred or even several thousand reinforcements had arrived. The problem of relating the seriousness of the siege to the king points out the weakness of not having a viceroy in command of the entire Moroccan area, or at least the southern area, with another viceroy serving in the north. Such a chain of command may have allowed the king to trust the judgment of a single appointed leader and react more quickly. Moreover, the defensive walls of Santa Cruz were not strong enough to withstand the modern artillery that the Sharif had been able to acquire over the past decades. So long as the Moroccans could ensure a steady supply of gunpowder and shot, they had the upper hand.

---

[94] *CSC*, 120-124.

[95] *CSC*, 100.

[96] "Letter from D. João III to the Count of Castanheira," 7 March 1541, Almeirim, *SIHMP*, 3:311-312. The predicted siege never materialized, and the relief armada was never sent. Figanier called D. João III's attitude toward the siege of Santa Cruz "*frouxa*".

Raids and Skirmishes

While sieges and siege warfare may have been the most dramatic and costly form of military violence, the most common form was raiding. The Portuguese word describing a group of soldiers who attacked Muslims by surprise is *almogaveria*. This word, in turn, was also used to describe the raid itself (also used were *entrada* and *rebato*), not just the participants. In southern Morocco, it was not just Portuguese who participated in these raids, but Moroccan allies as well. It is clear that for many on the frontier, the economy of greed outweighed the dogma of religion. These raids typically had political and economic goals: to supply captives to work as slaves or to be sold into slavery elsewhere for a profit, to intimidate a group or region into submitting to Portuguese suzerainty, to punish the transgression of an allied group, and to supply food for the Portuguese by stealing it.[97]

One of the most important members of the raiding party was the *almocadém*. This man typically spoke Arabic and sometimes Berber and spent considerable time riding through the countryside with a small group of horsemen in order to discover the safest and most efficient routes for the Portuguese to conduct their troop movements. In fact, vague evidence indicates that some of these military guides appear to have been Moroccan Muslims who had converted to Christianity and shown a desire to serve the Portuguese.[98]

As a rule, Portuguese-led raids were swift and brutal. A typical force would consist of a few hundred cavalrymen and an equal or larger number of foot soldiers. The total number in a force might range from 500 to upwards of 3-4,000. The soldiers carried the weapons of the day: crossbows, matchlock rifles, lances, and swords. To increase the potency of a raiding force, they often brought small artillery pieces with

---

[97] Paulo Drumond Braga, "A expansão no norte de África," in *A expansão quatrocentista*, ed. A. H. de Oliveira Marques (Lisbon: Editorial Estampa, 1998), 312-313, 320, 322-324. Raiding is a typical symptom of a frontier region. See, for example, Robin Frame, "Military Service in the Lordship of Ireland, 1290-1360: Institutions and Society on the Anglo-Gaelic Frontier," *MFS*, 101-126 and the discussion of *bandeirante* raids in John Hemming, "Indians and the Frontier," in *Colonial Brazil*, ed. Leslie Bethell (New York: Cambridge University Press, 1987), 145-189.

[98] Lopes, *A expansão*, 43.

them, pulled by horses. Artillery was especially helpful against smaller towns and villages with wooden or earthen walls.[99]

Raids often occurred at great distances from Portuguese fortresses in an effort to extend the Portuguese sphere of influence and to seek out villages that had yet to be plundered. For example, in February 1514, the Portuguese launched devastating raids against the Sharquiyyan villages of Benacafiz and Tafuf (60-70 kilometers east of Azamor). The Portuguese force, led by D. João de Meneses and Rui Barreto, consisted of 900 (or 1,200, according to Góis) mounted lancers and 1000 infantry with crossbows and matchlock rifles. The majority of the cavalry in this force was Portuguese, while Arab tribes provided a significant portion of the infantry. They first reached the town of Benacafiz, which was defended by three palisades (*cercas*) and 400 fighting men. The town was allied with the Wattasids and even flew many of the Wattasid flags on top of the "*forteleza da villa*." While the men of the town tried to hold off the attackers, the women and children fled to the city's gate along the Umm al-Rabi` River and tried to swim across the river to safety. While many were able to save themselves, a large number of women and children drowned. D. João de Meneses commented, likely from a combination of economic and humanitarian motives: "It was pitiful to see women and children dying." The village defenders could only hold out for a brief period against the overwhelming military strength of the Portuguese. Once all the goods and captives had been gathered from the town, the Portuguese put it to the torch.

In the meanwhile, a smaller contingent of Portuguese went to the neighboring village of Tafuf. Disheartened by the defeat of Benacafiz, the residents of Tafuf abandoned the town before the Portuguese arrived. Nevertheless, many had yet to jump into the river, and so had to fight off the Portuguese before they could swim to safety. In the end, only three or four people from Tafuf were killed, while most escaped by swimming, though some were captured. Thus, in the space of three hours of battle, the Portuguese *almogaveria* conquered two villages, killed ninety-four people, captured 180-190, and took much booty, including wheat, barley, chickens, and other foodstuffs.

---

[99] "Letter from Nuno Fernandes de Ataíde to D. Manuel," Safi, 29 October 1513, *SIHMP*, 1:447.

When D. Bernardo Manuel, who had led the attack on Tafuf, rejoined with the other Portuguese forces, D. João de Meneses embraced him and kissed him joyously for all that they had accomplished that day.[100]

While most raids had destruction, intimidation, and the seizure of people and goods as their goals, some raids had reconnaissance as an additional goal. Probably the best example of this is the series of raids against Marrakech in 1514 and 1515. In October 1514, Diogo Lopes, the *almocadém* of Safi, raided into territory near Marrakech, and some of his Muslim allies succeeded in banging on the gates of the city before they were driven off by Marrakechi forces. On 22 January 1515, Nuno Fernandes de Ataíde led a group of 300 Portuguese and 300 Moroccans against villages near Marrakech. No force was sent to counter the Portuguese raiding party, and the gates of Marrakech were closed for defense. Some of the Portuguese rode to one of the gates and, using chalk and charcoal, wrote their names and the names of "their ladies" (*suas damas*) on the gate itself. The lack of response from the Hintati ruler to these two raids indicated to the Portuguese that the forces within Marrakech were weak and that it might be possible to capture the city. Consequently, in April 1515, Ataíde, in conjunction with the new *capitão* of Azamor, D. Pedro de Sousa, gathered 550 Portuguese and 2500 allied Moroccans for another expedition against Marrakech. On 23 April, the Portuguese-led forces fought a four-hour battle outside the gates of the city until they were compelled to retreat.[101]

It must be noted that Moroccans conducted their own raids, both against fellow Moroccans and against Portuguese. However, in southern Morocco at least, these raids were typically on a much smaller scale than those launched by the Portuguese. In 1521, a leader of the Gharbiyya named Ya`qūb, an on again off again ally of the Portuguese, had made a series of raids near Mazagão. He and his men had on several occasions approached within sight of the castle wall in order to

---

[100] "Letter from João de Meneses to D. Manuel," Azamor, c. 15 February 1514, *SIHMP*, 1:482-484; "Letter from Vasco da Pina to D. Manuel," Azamor, 30 March 1514, *SIHMP*, 1:524; "Letter from Francisco and Diogo Arruda to D. Manuel," Azamor, 31 March 1514, *SIHMP*, 1:528; *CDM*, 3:48, 190-192. D. Bernardo Manuel was the *camareiro mor* of the king and had participated in the conquest of Azamor (*SIHMP*, 1:492n2, 537n1).

[101] "Account of an Expedition to the Gates of Marrakech," Safi, 22 January 1515, *SIHMP*, 1:676; "Expédition contre Marrakech, 23 avril 1515," *SIHMP*, 1:687-692; *HP*, 3:499-504; Lopes, *A expansão*, 31-33.

steal Portuguese livestock. Moreover, during these raids, Ya`qūb and his men had killed many Portuguese and their Moroccan allies and even had briefly besieged Mazagão.[102]

Conclusion

Life on the Portuguese-Moroccan frontier was violent and bloody, especially during the ubiquitous military encounters. The anonymous chronicler of Santa Cruz mentions a particularly grizzly incident during the brief siege of 1533. As a group of Moroccans retreated from the walls of the fortress after a failed assault, one of them was hit by a shot from a small cannon (*falcão*), severing his head from his body. Decapitation notwithstanding, the body ran three or four more paces before it fell to the ground. This performance was greeted by hoots and cheers from the Portuguese who observed it.[103]

Despite the Portuguese glee at the theatrical death of one of their enemy, violence does not seem to have been taken to the extreme lengths along the Portuguese-Moroccan frontier that it was along the Castilian-Granadan frontier. Angus MacKay states that "it was common practice . . . [for Castilian frontiersmen] to return from their forays with the severed heads or the sliced-off ears of their defeated Moorish opponents." One particularly harsh example of this practice occurred in 1487, when Rodrigo Ponce de León had defeated and killed 320 Granadans and then executed eighty more who had been captured. He then returned home in triumph with an even 400 heads mounted on lances.[104]

---

[102] "Letter from António Leite to D. Manuel," Mazagão, 12 November 1521, *SIHMP*, 2:291-293. Leite blamed the poor state of Mazagão's walls (a result of alleged mismanagement of supply shipments from Azamor under *capitão* D. Álvaro de Noronha) for permitting such a small group of men to besiege the city. For more on Ya`qūb, see *SIHMP*, 2:291n1.

[103] *CSC*, 66.

[104] Angus MacKay, "Religion, Culture, and Ideology on the Late Medieval Castilian-Granadan Frontier," in *MFS*, 228-229. Compare this to the similarly ruthless military tactics used by King James I during his conquest of Valencia in the thirteenth century. R. I. Burns, *Islam Under the Crusaders: Colonial Survival in the Thirteenth-Century Kingdom of Valencia* (Princeton: Princeton University Press, 1973), 158-159.

There is absolutely no evidence that either the Portuguese or the Moroccans ever carried out such gruesome symbolic mutilations.[105] It makes sense that they would not. Because the Castilians felt that all of Iberia should be free from Islamic political control, they were motivated to achieve a higher level of ferocity in their militaristic dealings with Muslims. The Portuguese in Morocco, on the other hand, while perfectly willing to kill and capture, were obliged in their current circumstances to live with Moroccan Muslims if they wanted to survive in Morocco.[106] As mentioned in chapter four, physical punishments for most crimes were culturally reprehensible to Moroccans, and so it may be that such a notion also restrained the Portuguese. Moreover, as the Portuguese often conducted their raids with the aid of Moroccan soldiers or had their raids conducted for them exclusively by Moroccans, this would also temper any misguided zeal that might otherwise lead to mutilation of corpses.

While mutilations were not recorded, massacres were. The rarity of these acts and the circumstances surrounding them make them the exception that proves the rule. Luís Sacoto, the *capitão* of Santa Cruz, suffered a defeat during a raid at the hands of one Ambre [Ibrahīm?] Mansūr and his men. Sacoto, vowing to avenge the deaths of more than fifty Portuguese knights, requested and received assistance from the Canary Islands of nearly one thousand men. Sacoto then led the force to hunt down Mansūr. He was not able to find Mansūr, but he and his men massacred a Moroccan village, engaging in horrendous acts of violence. A group of the Canary Islanders allegedly cut a baby in half in front of his mother. When word of this massacre reached King D. João III, he ordered that Sacoto be arrested and returned to Portugal for punishment. The king would not stand for massacres that would make his position in Santa Cruz less favorable to the local people.[107] The other massacre, already discussed in chapter four, resulted from miscommunication. D. Rodrigo de Castro, the

---

[105] Perhaps the closest event to a mutilation was when the Sharif ordered the heads of all non-elite Portuguese female captives, regardless of age, to be shaved after they had marched from Santa Cruz to Tarudante (*CSC*, 124: It was a "*couza bem piadoza de ver ir as donas velhas honradas com suas quabeças brancas a defora e as moças com seus louros cabelos dependurados, chorando e gridando, semelhando outra Hierusalem.*").

[106] See chapter six for more on this.

[107] *CSC*, 50-54.

capitão of Safi, mistakenly believed that Moroccan forces had slaughtered Portuguese women and children following their conquest of Santa Cruz. In revenge for what he believed had been a massacre, he perpetrated one of his own.[108]

One theme that runs through nearly all episodes of military violence in Portuguese Morocco is their relationship to economics. Preparing to defend against a violent act or recovering from a violent act required monetary expenditure, while those committing violent acts, especially raids, often gained great wealth. For example, one of the major concerns in the construction of Portuguese fortresses was whether or not there would be enough money to pay for the needed labor and materials. Portuguese raiding activity, part of Portuguese policy to expand the Portuguese zone of influence through violence, had as one of its paramount results the enrichment of those who captured people and goods. Meanwhile, those who were captured or had goods seized by force became impoverished. In effect, military violence acted as a conduit in the zero-sum game of resource control.[109]

Military violence also acted, for the Portuguese, as an ennobling agent. Valiant and successful application of military force could enable one to gain an elevated status within society and gain greater privileges in addition to wealth. D. Jaime, the fourth Duke of Bragança, was *persona non grata* in the Portuguese court after he murdered his wife and her alleged lover. By successfully leading the invasion and conquest of Azamor in 1513, he was able to restore his status and reputation. For other Portuguese, employment of violent methods allowed them to elevate their status. For example, D. Manuel elevated Pero Fernandes de Alvelos to the rank of knight (*cavaleiro*) for his valiant participation in a raid near Santa Cruz during which "twenty-nine people were captured, many Muslims died, and many horses,

---

[108] "Letter from D. Rodrigo de Castro to D. João III," Safi, 8 July 1541, *SIHMP*, 3:454-463; "Letter from Various Residents of Safi to D. João III against D. Rodrigo de Castro," Safi, 9 July 1541, *SIHMP*, 3:464-467; Pires de Lima, 101, 103. The massacre is mentioned breifly in Charles R. Boxer, *Women in Iberian Expansion Overseas, 1415-1815: Some Facts, Fancies and Personalities* (New York: Oxford University Press, 1975), 15.

[109] In an entirely different context, David Nirenberg reaches a similar conclusion that "violence and fiscality [march] hand in hand" (David Nirenberg, *Communities of Violence: Persecution of Minorities in the Middle Ages* (Princeton: Princeton University Press, 1996), 89). See the concluding chapter in this study for more on the role of plunder on the Portuguese-Moroccan frontier.

much wheat and other good things were seized."[110] For others, an increase in status might not be forthcoming, but valiant acts could lead to increased living allowances (*moradias*) or a one-time "bonus" payment.[111] The sources are littered with affidavits from Portuguese *capitães* and other high-ranking officials requesting that certain individuals be rewarded for their martial services.[112]

Violence, however, should not be considered merely the act of drawing blood, inflicting physical pain, or taking life and livelihood. It is also the creation or extension of the act of mental anguish, the fear that one's life or goods could be taken at any moment or that one's family might be kidnapped and made slaves.[113] Although it is often difficult to discern such mental states from documentary evidence, it should not be forgotten. Some cowered before the prospect of violence; others remained steadfast in its face. Afonso Vaz fled from a group of Moroccan thieves in the dark and was pursued by them and killed. During the 1533 breach of Santa Cruz's walls, the mistress of the murdered *capitão* refused to reveal the location of the keys to the *cabeceira* (strongbox) even under threat of bodily harm from a group of Moroccans. She survived unmolested.[114]

In Portuguese-controlled North Africa during the sixteenth century, military violence was a component of other issues, including control, power, and greed. Based on contemporaneous notions of violence, the Portuguese cannot be considered extreme, nor can the military uses of violence even be considered as alien to the Moroccan conception for the "appropriate" uses of military violence. Moreover, Portuguese Morocco was a frontier region, and as such it was a region

---

[110] "Alvará from D. Manuel," Lisbon, 15 July 1521, *SIHMP*, 2:289-290.

[111] ANTT, CC I, 22, 50.

[112] For just a few examples, see chapter two; ANTT, CC I, 7, 32; CC I, 7, 37; CC I, 18, 87; CC I, 39, 37; "Letter from D. Manuel to Yahya-u-Ta`fuft," Lisbon, 25 August 1514, *SIHMP*, 1:601-602; "Letter from Luís de Loureiro to D. João III," Mazagão, 4 September 1541, *SIHMP*, 3:519; "Letter from Luís de Loureiro to D. João III," Mazagão, 15 December 1542, *SIHMP*, 4:119; Figanier, 361-363.

[113] See, for example, Ahmed Boucharb, "Les conséquences socio-culturelles de la conquête ibérique du littoral marocain," in *Relaciones de la península ibérica con el magreb (siglos xiii-xvi): actas del coloquio*, ed. Mercedes García-Arenal and María J. Viguera (Madrid: Instituto Hispano-Árabe de Cultura, 1988), 487-521.

[114] *CSC*, 62-64. The chronicler attributes both her courage and her survival to the miraculous intervention of the Holy Spirit.

where "no one [had] an enduring monopoly on violence."[115] In short, in southern Morocco in the first half of the sixteenth century, those who could employ violence for gain did, and those who could not had little choice but to hide or submit.

---

[115] Silvio R. D. Baretta and John Markoff, "Civilization and Barbarism: Cattle Frontiers in Latin America," *Comparative Studies in Society and History* 20 (1978): 590.

Table 7.1: Population of Soldiers in Southern Moroccan Fortresses[116]

YEAR	AZAMOR	MAZAGÃO	SAFI	SANTA CRUZ
1507			50[117]	
1510			900-2000[118]	
1511			524	
1513	15,000[119]		c. 800	720
1514	c. 4,000			
1517	800			
1521	599			
1522	621			
1525	640			
1527				330
1530	618			
1537-38	448 [?]			
1541	700-2500[120]			500-600

---

[116] Soldiers include the *gente da ordenança* and the *fronteiros*. Sources for Table 1: ANTT, NA, 597; Pires de Lima, 26, 36, 41; Fagundes, "Documentos," 106, 113; *CSC*, 24-26, 144; "Letter from Nuno Fernandes de Ataíde to D. Manuel," Safi, 13 May 1513, *SIHMP*, 1:387; "Letter from Rui Barreto to D. Manuel," Azamor, 1 April 1514; "Letter from Simão Correia to D. Manuel," Azamor, 20 May 1517, *SIHMP*, 2:86; "Letter from Jorge Viegas to D. João III," Azamor, 18 September 1525, *SIHMP*, 2:347; "Letter from Luís Sacoto to D. João III," Santa Cruz, 14 March 1527, *SIHMP*, 2:396-397; "Letter from D. Pedro de Mascarenhas to D. João III," Azamor, 9 June 1530, *SIHMP*, 2:528; "Letter from D. João III to the Count of Castanheira," Almeirim, 23 February 1541, *SIHMP*, 3:309; "Letter from D. João III to Fernão Peres," Lisbon, 13 April 1541, *SIHMP*, 3:387-388; "Letter from Luís de Loureiro to D. João III," Mazagão, 15 December 1542, *SIHMP*, 4:114-115.

[117] Safi was seized from the Moroccans in mid-1508, following the arrival of four ships containing an unknown number of Portuguese soldiers. See Pires de Lima, 28.

[118] There were 900 soldiers in Safi before the siege of 1510, and approximately 2,000 once reinforcements arrived.

[119] Note that this elevated number was the force sent to capture the city and quickly was reduced.

[120] 700 was the number before c. 1800 reinforcements sent to guard against a possible siege of Azamor by the Sa`adids following the conquest of Santa Cruz.

Chapter Eight: Captivity and the Captured: Slavery and Sequestration along the Portuguese-Moroccan Frontier

THE MILITARY violence discussed in the previous chapter resulted in the deaths of many, and the capture of many others. For much of recorded history, captivity has been the result of armed encounters between antagonistic groups. The struggles between Christian and Islamic polities have been no different. Although religious difference served as justification for capturing infidels, it was normally military strength and weakness that facilitated it. Frontiers being locations where groups of differing potency meet, captivity (including slavery) is nearly ubiquitous in these regions.[1]

Due to the close relationship of military violence and captivity, it is no surprise that captivity had both economic and political consequences. First, captives were normally a source of economic gain to their captors.[2] Typically, a small number of captives would be of high status and thus would command a high ransom. The remainder of the less valuable captives could be sold as slaves or retained by the original captor as labor. Captivity also had political implications. The release of captives might be used as a goodwill gesture during a period

---

[1] The *bandeirante* raids during Brazil's colonial period are a good example of this. See John Hemming, "Indians and the Frontier," in *Colonial Brazil*, ed. Leslie Bethell (New York: Cambridge University Press, 1991), 145-189.

[2] It should be noted that captivity for the purpose of economic gain was not something practiced only between differing religious groups. It was, for example, practiced by Europeans during the medieval period, with especially notable success by both the French and the English during the Hundred Years' War. See Philippe Contamine, *La vie quotidienne pendant la guerre de cent ans: France et Angleterre (XIVème siècle)* (Paris: Hachette, 1976), 250ff; Maria Ângela Beirante, "O resgate de cativos nos reinos de Portugal e Algarve (séc. XII-XV)," in *Actas das III jornadas de história medieval do Algarve e Andaluzia* (Loulé: Câmara Municipal de Loulé, 1989), 273; Isabel M. R. Mendes Drumond Braga, *Entre a Cristandade e o Islão: cativos e renegados nas franjas de duas sociedades em confronto* (Ceuta: Instituto de Estudios Ceuties, 1998), 19. Also see *DCC*, 130, for an example of the Portuguese paying a ransom to the Azeneges of the Guinea region in order to free a group of Portuguese sailors.

of negotiations, while the continued seizure of captives could be used to terrorize a group until it bowed to the will of a stronger group.

For those who were captured, however, these abstract reasons were of little concern. After all at its point of execution, captivity – the forcible kidnap and sequestering of individual human beings – was an incredibly violent and terrifying endeavor. Captives, especially those with little hope of being ransomed, had to face the prospect of never seeing their homes and families again. All lower-status captives faced years of strenuous labor and mistreatment. Moroccan and Portuguese parents faced the prospects of being separated forever from their children, fearing that they might be forced to change their religion. All female and even some male captives faced the prospect of becoming objects of sexual desire.

While most captives were seized in the aftermath of military activities, they were also taken while tending flocks, fetching water from wells, or fishing from the banks of rivers. The large number of people held in captivity/slavery at any time required the articulation of a system to exchange money between two inimical groups in order to free captives. The key figure in this system as it existed in sixteenth-century Morocco was the *alfaqueque* (discussed below), who worked both for political leaders as well as for religious organizations in order to negotiate the release of captives.

The story of captivity in sixteenth-century Morocco must be reconstructed from scattered sources. There are no detailed accounts of any single person's experience in captivity during this period, only vignettes that seem as much mythical as historical. It is, in fact, this fragmented historical record that requires a focus more on the economic, political, and legal aspects of captivity instead of the personal experiences of captives.

Historical Background

Portuguese Christians and Muslims, both Moroccan and non-Moroccan, had long experience with each other in the sphere of captivity.[3] Members of each side of the politico-religious divide had been capturing and enslaving members of the other side for many

---

[3] Islam has addressed this problem from its origins. The *Qur'ān* itself lists one of the duties of a righteous man as the giving away of wealth for the "redemption of captives" (2:177).

centuries before the Portuguese conquered Ceuta in 1415. During the two centuries when Portugal expanded from the Condado Portucalense to its modern borders in 1249, captivity and ransom were common activities along the frontiers between the Christian and Islamic kingdoms.

In 1198, the Trinitarian Order was founded in France with the specific purpose of redeeming captives. Corporate bodies created with the express purpose of ransoming captives were a symptom of the Crusading Era. Before this time, captives were taken, but ransom arrangements were normally made by individuals.[4] Shortly after its founding, the Trinitarian Order sought to locate chapters strategically along the Atlantic and Mediterranean. In 1207, the Trinitarians entered Portugal, establishing their first monasteries in Santarém and Lisbon, as the majority of the Alentejo and Algarve was still under Islamic control. Despite the existence of similar orders, such as the Order of Our Lady of Grace (the Mercedarians), outside of Portugal, the Trinitarians were the only religious order in Portugal granted the right to engage in the redemption of captives.[5]

After 1249, Moroccan raids along the Algarve coastline, as well as the ever-pervasive sea piracy, took Portuguese men into the hands of Muslims. Similarly, Portuguese corsairs, typically commissioned by the king of Portugal, captured Muslims and their ships. The commonality of this sort of activity is reflected by Portuguese regulations governing the division of captured booty between the king, the admiral, and the sailors. These types of activities expanded greatly after 1415.[6]

Until 1461, the Trinitarians in Portugal had exclusive control of the ransom of Christian captives. During that year, however, D. Afonso V (r. 1438-1481) created the *Tribunal dos Cativos*, which became the exclusive overseer of the ransom of Portuguese captives,

---

[4] Juan Devessa, "Los orígenes de la orden de Nuestra Señora de la Merced," in *Las dos ordenes redentoras en la iglesia*, ed. Juan Manuel Ruiz and Luis Vázquez (Madrid, 1989), 38-39.

[5] Beirante, 274 and Ignacio Vizcargüenaga, "Los orígenes de la orden Trinitaria," in *Las dos ordenes redentoras en la iglesia*, ed. Juan Manuel Ruiz and Luis Vázquez (Madrid, 1989), 9-35.

[6] Paulo Drumond Braga, "A expansão no norte de África," in *A expansão quatrocentista*, ed. A. H. de Oliveira Marques (Lisbon: Editorial Estampa, 1998), 337; Braga, *Entre a Cristandade*, 21-23; Bailey W. Diffie and George D. Winius, *Foundations of the Portuguese Empire, 1415-1580* (Minneapolis: University of Minnesota Press, 1977), 47.

transferring that responsibility to the royal government. Trinitarians attempted to regain control of this activity, but the crown retained the monopoly until a power-sharing agreement was reached with the Trinitarians in 1561. In that agreement, the Order regained control of ransoming captives but the crown retained the right to inspect the process of raising money for ransom to ensure against irregularities and theft.[7] Therefore, in the period covered by this study, it was the Portuguese kings who were ultimately responsible for the ransom of Portuguese captives.

Money for the ransom of Christian captives was obtained in a variety of ways. Wealthy captives might simply send word – typically through the intermediary figure of the *alfaqueque* – to their families of their predicament and then wait for a brief period while the necessary money was sent. For example, the money might be gathered in Portugal, then sent via ship to one of the Portuguese fortresses, and thence taken by the *alfaqueque* to the location where the captive was held. The captive would then, normally, be freed.[8] Elite captives who did not have enough money of their own were sometimes ransomed by the king himself who considered the particular captive too valuable – either a symbolic, status-based valuation, or a fear that certain military secrets might be revealed – to remain in captivity for any extended period of time.

Less fortunate captives would have to wait while the bureaucratic mechanisms for securing their ransom were put into effect. Whether ransoming of captives was controlled by the Trinitarian Order or the royal *Tribunal dos Cativos*, the money that these groups used was acquired through bequests and alms. One method for raising funds was for preachers to go through the cities and countryside preaching of the predicament of the captives and soliciting donations

---

[7] Braga, *Entre a Cristandade*, 145-168; Idem, "Mulheres cativas e mulheres de cativos em Marrocos no século XVII," in *O rosto feminino da expansão portuguesa* (Lisbon: Comissão para a Igualdade e para os Direitos das Mulheres, 1994), 1:439; Idem, "Contribuição Monetária das Comarcas Portuguesas para a Obra da Redenção de Cativos (1523-1539)," in *Brigantia* 14 (1994): 26-29, which contains a discussion of accounting and anti-theft procedures; Beirante, 277-278.

[8] Captives might also work to free themselves and close family members. See the cases of António da Costa and Manuel da Câmara discussed below.

for their redemption.⁹ After 1461, Trinitarian preachers were replaced by their lay equivalents: the royally-appointed *mamposteiros*, officials who were required to ask for alms in churches, monasteries, at pilgrimage sites and in as many locations as possible during Sundays and feast days. They also collected portions of the wine and olive oil harvests each year and then sold them three months later, so as to obtain a good price. As payment for their services, they received a percentage of what they collected, which varied from ten to twenty percent, depending on what was collected, goods or currency.¹⁰ The papacy often assisted the *mamposteiros'* efforts by giving a spiritual reward to those who donated substantial sums with regularity. For example, Pope Pius II issued his bull *Quemadmodum magnis* on 1 February 1462, in which he granted a plenary indulgence, releasing one from all sin upon death, to anyone who donated at least ten *reis* every year.¹¹

Before the Portuguese invasion of Ceuta in 1415 and the slow increase of Moroccan territory under Portuguese control, North African Muslim men were captured primarily during raids and piracy. Their numbers were large enough and the status of some high enough that in 1371, Adela, the *alcaide* and *alfaqueque* of the *mouraria* of Lisbon, was allowed to travel to North Africa to gather funds for the ransom of many Muslims being held captive in Portugal.¹² This is the only reference to an individual *mudéjar* (a Muslim living under Christian rule) *alfaqueque* in Portugal, but the Muslim *comunas* in various Portuguese cities occupied themselves with purchasing the freedom of their coreligionists until they disappeared from Portugal in 1496/7, either because they were expelled or, more frequently, forced to convert to Christianity.

---

⁹ According to Braga, "Contribuição Monetária," 34, residents of particular areas within Portugal typically donated substantially larger sums when members of their own communities were in captivity. It might be safe to speculate that when preachers were aware of a local captive, they emphasized his or her plight while soliciting donations.

¹⁰ Braga, *Entre a Cristandade*, 170-180.

¹¹ Braga, *Entre a Cristandade*, 164.

¹² Maria Filomena Lopes de Barros, *A comuna muçulmana de Lisboa, sécs. XIV e XV* (Lisbon: Hugin, 1998), 99. Islamic communities in Christian-administered Valencia often ransomed fellow Muslims from captivity as well. Mark Meyerson, *The Muslims of Valencia in the Age of Fernando and Isabel: Between Coexistence and Crusade* (Berkeley: University of California, 1991), 83.

The kings of Portugal often allowed individual captives to purchase their own freedom, since that way they would remain in Portugal and practice the valuable skilled services that Muslims had monopolized in urban areas. Moreover, the kings allowed this privilege especially to the skilled lower-status Muslims who had little chance of being ransomed from abroad. Those that could be ransomed from abroad would bring a windfall to their owners. Muslim captives in Portugal might also work to earn their freedom. For instance, in 1471, Muhammad Abelhos was allowed to travel to North Africa in order to work for his relatives and friends so that he might secure his own release and that of his wife and children who remained in Portugal as surety. Finally, if a large number of Moroccans was captured in a single act, Moroccan political leaders had no choice but to respond. In 1472, after the conquest of Alcácer-Ceguer one year earlier, the former head of that city and new Wattasid sultan, Muhammad al-Sheikh, sent his *alfaqueque* to Portugal to negotiate the ransom of many of the people captured when that city fell.[13]

Along the North African frontier between the Portuguese and Moroccans, however, it seems that the mechanisms for redemption were less specialized. Although Morocco was the location of nearly all the Portuguese captives in the fifteenth and sixteenth centuries, *mamposteiros* and their underlings did not exist within North Africa (though of course they still solicited funds throughout Portugal). Furthermore, it appears that money collected for Portuguese captives was either for the less fortunate or for women and children. In other words, many Portuguese captives could not depend strictly on governmental aid to free them. Several examples of this are discussed below, but one given here will illustrate the point. A group of Portuguese captives, originally from Azamor and held for between one and eight years, was freed not by funds from the *Tribunal dos Cativos* but by donations from the residents (*moradores*) of Azamor.[14]

---

[13] Barros, *A comuna muçulmana*, 99-103.

[14] "Letter from Lançarote de Freitas to D. João III," Azamor, 27 June 1526, *SIHMP*, 2:354-355. One wonders if this was due to a lack of donations collected in Portugal, too much competition for those funds, or some kind of redirection of ransom funds to other royal endeavors.

The *Alfaqueque:* Central Figure of Captivity

The *alfaqueque* is a figure with a long history in Portugal, Spain, and Morocco. He was given permission to travel into enemy territory and negotiate the conditions and the cost of the release of one or more captives.[15] Consequently, *alfaqueques* were required to speak the language of the other side and be someone deemed trustworthy. For example, Castilian *alfaqueques* during the fourteenth and fifteenth centuries were usually merchants who often traveled to Granada on business, and so could use their reputations and local knowledge to be effective negotiators. All Castilian *alfaqueques* were expected to behave properly while in Islamic territory, respecting the local customs and norms, with an important condition of their safe conduct being the refraining from saying anything contrary to Islam.[16]

In Portuguese Morocco, each fortress had an *alfaqueque mor* (chief *alfaqueque*), who coordinated the deployment of *alfaqueques* sent to negotiate captive releases and controlled access to ransom and redemption funds, which he tracked in a *livro de alfaquecaria*. The *alfaqueque mor* was paid an annual salary (*tença*) and received a payment for each captive who was freed by the *alfaqueques* working under him.[17] For example, Nuno Gato, who spoke Arabic and who served as Safi's *contador* from 1510 until his death in 1521, was also the city's *alfaqueque mor*. As *contador*, he received 12,000 *reis* per year to which was added another 2,000 *reis* as chief *alfaqueque*.[18] After the conquest of Azamor, Nuno Gato was sent there to oversee the establishment of the royal trade and financial systems. He asked the king to grant him the office

---

[15] Charles J. Bishko, "The Spanish and Portuguese Reconquest, 1095-1492," in *A History of the Crusades*, ed. Harry W. Hazard (Madison: University of Wisconsin Press, 1975), 396-456 and James Brodman, *Ransoming Captives in Crusader Spain: The Order of Merced on the Christian-Islamic Frontier* (Philadelphia: University of Pennsylvania Press, 1986), 7-10.

[16] José Enrique López de Coca Castañer, "Institutions on the Castilian-Granadan Frontier, 1369-1482," in *MFS*, 135-141; Beirante, 274; Angus MacKay, *Spain in the Middle Ages: From Frontier to Empire, 1000-1500* (London: 1977), 198-200, 202.

[17] Braga, *Entre a Cristandade*, 182-183. Unfortunately, no *livros de alfaquecaria* appear to have survived from southern Morocco.

[18] "Letter from Nuno Gato to D. Manuel," Safi, 14 May 1512, *SIHMP*, 1:309-310 and ANTT, NA 597, f. 120. Although it might make sense that the *contador*, as overseer of royal finances, would also be in charge of ransoms and ransom money, the position of *alfaqueque* was not the exclusive territory of *contadores*. In Santa Cruz, one João da Costa was both *adail* and *alfaqueque* from 1516 until his death in 1518 (*SIHMP*, 2:185n1).

of *alfaqueque mor* in Azamor as well.[19] It is unclear if he ever held this office, though by late 1516, João Fernandes was the *alfaqueque mor* of Azamor.[20]

For Portuguese Christians held captive in North Africa, the *alfaqueque* who actually traveled into Muslim territory to negotiate their release was typically a Jew. This is despite the obvious mistrust that the Portugese had of Jews within Portugal, leading to their expulsion, along with the remaining Portuguese Muslims, in 1497. In fact, at least until the 1450s, the Portuguese allowed only Christians to be *alfaqueques*.[21] Jews, especially those recently expelled from Spain and Portugal, were a group that was able to move through North African society with ease, while still retaining much knowledge of European customs and desires. Jews were more likely to speak the relevant languages and in their role as merchants often had established contacts in Moroccan villages and cities. For the Portuguese, once the Jews were safely in North Africa, they were no longer a threat, but an asset.

Furthermore, D. Manuel had barred any New Christians from traveling to any lands under the control of the Wattasids, for fear that Moroccan Jews might encourage them to apostatize. The penalty was to lose all goods and wealth and be exiled to the island of São Tomé.[22] This law effectively prevented New Christians from holding the office of *alfaqueque*. Consequently, it makes sense that the people sent to ransom Portuguese were either Jews or Old Christians, for the Portuguese would not trust a Muslim *alfaqueque* to act in the best interests of Christian captives. When it was a Muslim captive held by

---

[19] "Letter from Nuno Gato to D. Manuel," Azamor, 18 December 1513, *SIHMP*, 1:469. The lack of references to the structure of captive redemption in contemporary sources and the almost non-existent use of "proper" terminology creates the impression that captive redemption was likely a rather ad hoc process. Beirante, 273, suggests that because ransom "is the business of the conquered," it was somehow shameful and inglorious to discuss it, rendering it virtually ignored by Portuguese royal and military sources.

[20] ANTT, CC I, 22, 58, published in Maria Augusta Lima Cruz Fagundes, "Documentos inéditos para a história dos portugueses em Azamor," *Arquivos do Centro Cultural Portugues* 2 (1970): 145-147.

[21] Beirante, 278. The exact date of the entry of Jews into the role of *alfaqueques* assigned to redeem Portuguese Christians is unclear, though I suspect it was post-1497.

[22] José Alberto Rodrigues da Silva Tavim, *Os judeus na expansão portuguesa em Marrocos durante o século XVI: origens e actividades duma comunidade* (Braga: Edições APPACDM Distrital de Braga, 1997), 333.

the Portuguese who was to be ransomed, it was always a North African Muslim *alfaqueque* who was sent to negotiate. Moreover, when Moroccans allied with Portugal were captured by Wattasid or Sa`adid forces, their relatives used their own *alfaqueques* to negotiate for their release. In fact, the Portuguese often gave valuable cloth to these allied Moroccan *alfaqueques* to use as payment for ransoms.[23]

The *alfaqueque* was also both a diplomatic symbol and a diplomat. Just as he was to act in good faith and respect the rules of the governor of the territory that he had entered, so too was that governor to treat him with respect and hospitality. One of the rare mentions of an enemy Moroccan Muslim *alfaqueque* is to one from Tadla who had traveled to Azamor, in order to redeem captives being held there by the Portuguese. On at least two separate occasions, this man stayed in Azamor to conduct negotiations, once for seventeen days and once for eighteen days. During one visit, Ya`qūb Daroque, a Jewish merchant of Azamor, was given the task of stabling the *alfaqueque's* horses; during another, the task of feeding the *alfaqueque* and his assistant as well as stabling their horses and mules. Daroque's expenditures were always quickly reimbursed by the royal treasury. After the *alfaqueque's* first visit in 1536, Daroque was reimbursed 390 *reis* for the cost of barley to feed the horses in the stable and for providing grain for the return trip to Tadla. The second visit in 1537 was more costly, as Daroque provided food for the horses and the men. As a result, he was paid 1,800 *reis* and given twenty-eight *alqueires* of barley.[24]

To mistreat a Moroccan *alfaqueque* would have been to invite similar treatment on an *alfaqueque* representing the Portuguese. Moreover, in the 1530s, as Sa`adid power was coming to parity if not eclipsing that of the Portuguese, mistreating anyone allied with him

---

[23] ANTT, CC II, 69, 134 and CC II, 105, 117. Although I have found evidence of the Portuguese giving only cloth to these *alfaqueques*, it seems likely that they may also have given them money and other goods.

[24] "Order of Payment from D. Álvaro de Abranches," Azamor, 3 July 1536, *SIHMP*, 3:41 and "Order of Payment from António Leite," Azamor, 26 November 1537, *SIHMP*, 133-134. Ya`qub Daroque was apparently a very wealthy merchant as, during the late 1530s, he was reimbursed by the Portuguese for thousands of *reis* per year of expenditures, in cash and kind, realized while hosting various Moroccan diplomats and leaders. In addition to the documents already mentioned, see "Order of Payment from António Leite," Azamor, 20 December 1537, 3:135-136; "Order of Payment from António Leite," Azamor, 4 August 1539, 3:207-208; Tavim, *Os judeus*, 275-276.

would have been a foolish decision. In 1537, for example, Sharif Ahmed al-A`raj concluded a three-year peace with D. Rodrigo de Castro, the *capitão* of Safi. The Sharif dispatched his chief *alfaqueque*, Qassim, to Safi in order to sign the peace agreement and ensure that it was properly proclaimed among the Portuguese and their allies. While there he was served fresh fruits and tasty jams and was treated with great respect. Qassim later traveled to Azamor and Mazagão to ensure the proclamation of the peace there, as the peace applied to the entire Dukkala region.[25]

Another Moroccan *alfaqueque* was from the Wattasid city of Salé. The Portuguese concluded a peace agreement with the Wattasids from 1538 until 1543. It was during this period of alliance that an *alfaqueque* from Salé appears in Portuguese sources. He is never named and is only seen transporting a group of Moroccans who were escaping from Sa`adid territory. In August 1541, a group of eleven Moroccan men arrived in Mazagão. They said that they were fleeing from Giane, a *qā'id* who served the Sharif. Furthermore, they needed to wait for their wives and children because they had left at separate times so as not to arouse suspicion. Luís de Loureiro, the *capitão* of Mazagão, allowed them to stay in the fortress until their families arrived. By early September, some of the wives and children had arrived, but others had been captured by Giane. The Moroccans decided to leave for the Wattasid capital of Fez, sailing on a boat with the *alfaqueque* from Salé.[26]

Capture and Treatment of Captives

To be taken captive was a great fear for many, especially commoners. Elites would normally be treated well, at least in the initial years of their captivity, in the hope that a large ransom would eventually be paid for them. Common-status men and women alike could only look forward to a life of enslavement, while women fully expected and faced sexual exploitation. The fear of capture is reflected in responses to impending capture. Recall, for instance, two episodes

---

[25] "Account of the Proclamation of the Peace of Safi," Safi, 25 April 1537, *SIHMP*, 3:96-102 and "D. Rodrigo de Castro's Report to D. João III on the Peace with the Sharif," Safi, 4 June 1537, *SIHMP*, 3:104-108.

[26] "Letter from Luís de Loureiro to D. João III," Mazagão, 28 August 1541, *SIHMP*, 3:508 and "Letter from Luís de Loureiro to D. João III," Mazagão, 4 September 1541, *SIHMP*, 3:518-519.

mentioned in the previous chapter. First, the drowning deaths of women and children fleeing the Portuguese raiders at Benacafiz. Second, the Portuguese cobbler, Manuel Fernandes, who murdered two of his own children and tried to murder a third for fear of what might befall them once captured by Sa`adid troops who had conquered Santa Cruz in 1541. The fear of captivity knew no political or religious boundaries.

Anyone could be a captive in North Africa: Portuguese, Moroccan, or Jew. Nevertheless, because of the large number of Portuguese raids, Portuguese military superiority until the 1530s, and their zeal for the wealth that could be generated by captives, Moroccan Muslims formed the majority of captives. (In fact, it seems that women and children may have composed a small majority of these captives, as men were often killed during fighting or were able to flee on horseback. The opposite is true of the Portuguese where women and children were never put in a position where they could be captured except following the conquest of a Portuguese city.) As a result of these raids and battles with Muslims, Portuguese Christian men were the second largest group of captives.

On the other hand, Jews, especially Jewish men, were valuable middlemen who could travel easily between both cultures and were useful to both cultures, and therefore avoided captivity almost entirely. Moroccan Jews did not threaten the political power of either group for control of territory and neither group seemed to be able to do without them. The only instance of a Jewish captive that I have encountered is one mentioned in a letter from the Muslim residents of Massa, near Santa Cruz, who reported that one of the Jews living in their village had, on business, visited an area controlled by the Beni Tamer, a Berber tribe. While there, he was seized by servants of João Lopes de Sequeira, the *capitão* of Santa Cruz, who killed a Muslim associate of the Jew and brought the Jew to Santa Cruz. The *qā'id* of Massa, `Abd al-Aziz, and several of his men went to Santa Cruz to free the Jew. There they met with refusal from the *capitão*, who was apparently taking advice from an unspecified member of the influential Jewish family, the Benzamiro. In a letter to King D. Manuel, `Abd al-Aziz hoped that God would "curse" this Benzamiro, and he warned the king to "beware" of him. Although impossible to prove, this may have been a case of intimidation between two Jewish families to secure a larger portion of commerce and Portuguese protection in southern Morocco. The situation was eventually resolved when the captured Jew's family ransomed him for thirty *miticais* and two large "Jewish books" (Talmud?).[27]

The overwhelming majority of Moroccan Muslim captives were acquired by the Portuguese as the result of raiding and warfare against the *mouros de guerra* (Muslims who did not recognize Portuguese suzerainty) in the Moroccan hinterland. For large organized raids, the typical number of captives ranged from sixty or seventy to upwards of five hundred in a single engagement.[28] This massive disruption of population and extraction of wealth from Morocco must have had devastating consequences on family structures, agriculture, and trade.[29] Although forbidden by royal proclamation, Portuguese and Jews were known to purchase enslaved Moroccans from other Moroccans. In other words, the trade in captives benefited members of all religious groups.[30]

When Muslims were captured by the Portuguese, they were immediately shackled in irons and taken to a Portuguese-controlled city where they were auctioned to the highest bidder. One-fifth of the proceeds was given to the *capitão*, one-fifth was collected for the royal treasury, while another fifth was given to the *alcaide dos mouros*, should he happen to have been involved in the raid. The remaining two-fifths (or three-fifths in the absence of an *alcaide dos mouros*) were given to the individual who had captured the Moroccan in the first place. While extremely valuable captives might sell for over 100,000 reis, most sold

---

[27] "Letter from the Inhabitants of Massa to D. Manuel," Massa, 6 July 1510, *SIHMP*, 1:244-246.

[28] "Letter from Rabbi Ibrahim bin Zamiro," Safi, 12 October 1512, *SIHMP*, 1:359-360; "Letter from Nuno Fernandes de Ataíde to D. Manuel," Safi, c. 15 February 1514, *SIHMP*, 1:480-481; "Letter from João de Meneses to D. Manuel," Azamor, c. 15 February 1514, *SIHMP*, 1:482-484; "Letter from D. Nuno Mascarenhas to D. Manuel," Safi, 29 July 1518, 2:210, to cite just a few examples.

[29] Slave-raiding in the northern portion of Portuguese-controlled Morocco may have been less successful. In 1470, for instance, Portuguese in Ceuta actually *purchased* Granadan Muslims from Castilian merchants (Castañer, "Institutions," 148).

[30] See Isabel M. R. Mendes Drumond Braga, *Mouriscos e cristãos no Portugal quinhentista: duas culturas e duas concepções religiosas em choque* (Lisbon: Hugin, 1999), 52, for several examples of this.

for much less.³¹ Unfortunately, with the exception of the high-status and highly valuable captives, the prices paid for captives at auction are unclear. There are, however, some records that reveal the prices for slaves sold between private parties. For these sales, typical prices seem to have been between 6,000 and 16,000 *reis*, with 2,600 being the low-end price and 20,000 the high (see Tables 8.1 and 8.2). One would therefore assume that the prices of captives at auction would be somewhat lower.

If a Muslim captive did not serve as a slave in North Africa, he or she was normally shipped to Portugal, Madeira, the Canaries, or Spain and then sold. Jews were especially active in the purchase of slaves at auction and in their transport to Iberia. Because many captives knew a trade or had skills, they were often sought above the normally unskilled black Africans who were just beginning to arrive in Portugal in numbers.³² Moreover, it became a status symbol to have a Muslim slave as a *criado de estrebaria* (stable hand) or a household servant. In the agricultural regions of Portugal, such as the Algarve, they served as farm hands or boatmen, who freighted goods by river.³³

Not surprisingly, Portuguese land owners who served in Morocco as *fronteiros* also found their time well spent in acquiring laborers. Manuel da Câmara, a royal relative and governor of São Miguel in the Azores, arrived in Santa Cruz in December 1540, in order to help defend the fortress against the Sharif's siege. During the months that he was there, he purchased at least two slaves whom he sent back to the Azores.³⁴ Some of these Muslims exported from Morocco eventually converted to Christianity. Portuguese Inquisition

---

[31] "Payment Order from D. Garcia de Noronha," Safi, 2 January 1535, *SIHMP*, 3:16 and "Letter from Álvaro do Cadaval to D. Manuel," Azamor, 10 May 1517, *SIHMP*, 2:79-81. One Shawiyyan *faqīr* sold for 154,000 *reis*; see below for details.

[32] According to A. C. de C. M. Saunders, *A Social History of Black Slaves and Freedmen in Portugal, 1441-1555* (New York: Cambridge University Press, 1982), 23, black African slaves arrived in Lisbon between the years of 1490 and 1530 at the rate of 300-2,000 per year.

[33] Tavim, *Os judeus*, 330.

[34] *CSC*, 92-96.

records reveal at least fifteen Muslims who converted after serving as slaves in Portugal.[35]

Portuguese captured by Moroccan forces faced a similar future. Following their capture, they were normally taken to a city. Arriving at the city, they were greeted by a jubilant crowd of people who would line the streets and peer out from windows, shouting at the Christian captives and playing musical instruments in celebration.[36] There is no outright evidence of such celebrations directed explicitly at the arrival of Moroccan captives to a Portuguese city, though such occurrences were likely. The return of Portuguese raiders was often greeted by revelry, and these men typically returned with numerous captives.[37]

The disorientation inherent in becoming a captive was likely exacerbated by these exuberant greetings. Furthermore, captives could be faced with a symbolic baptism into their new life without freedom. When Santa Cruz fell to Sharifan forces in 1541, the captives were tied together with rope around their necks and marched for eight days to the city of Tarudante where they were to be sold. Before they entered the city, all the female captives were shorn of their hair, causing them to weep inconsolably while the men watched impotently.[38]

Many Portuguese children who were captured and not quickly ransomed became Muslims. This was normally a forced conversion, though adolescents may have had some choice in the matter. For example, eighteen Portuguese boys between the ages of seven and twelve captured during the fall of Santa Cruz were forcibly converted to Islam in order to serve as playmates for the Sharif's son. Apparently, they never returned to Portugal. In another case, Francisco Lopes was captured near Ceuta around 1562 when he was seven or eight years old. He later converted to Islam, remaining an observant Muslim until he was ransomed twenty-six years later, at which time he faced a hearing for apostasy before the Portuguese Inquisition. Maria Fernandes and her husband, Pedro Barbudo, were captured in Santa Cruz in 1541. It

---

[35] Braga, *Mouriscos*, 50-53. Some of them converted almost immediately after their arrival in Portugal, others only after many years of servitude.

[36] D. Fr. Joao Álvarez, *Chronica do Infante Santo D. Fernando* ed. Mendes dos Remedios (Coimbra, 1911), 47 and *AA*, 1:44.

[37] "Letter from D. Nuno Mascarenhas to D. Manuel," Safi, 3 April 1517, *SIHMP*, 2:73-75.

[38] *CSC*, 124.

is unknown what became of Barbudo, but after two years Maria was forced to convert to Islam and become the concubine of Muhammad al-Harran, the son of Sharif Muhammad al-Sheikh. She was finally ransomed in 1554 by Padre João Nunes, and then brought before the Inquisition in Lisbon. Both Lopes and Fernandes were treated leniently and only required to seek instruction in the Christian faith from a priest. This sympathetic treatment was typical of Portuguese who converted to Islam under duress.[39]

Captives on both sides of the religious divided were treated similarly. The high-status captives, known to the Portuguese as *cativos de conta*, were treated much better than their lower-status counterparts mainly because a large ransom payment was likely forthcoming.[40] They were generally not subjected to harsh living conditions and were spared performing dangerous tasks. Historian Isabel Drumond Braga argues that for elite Portuguese, captivity was viewed mostly as "an expense, a fright, and, of course, an inconvenience."[41] This may have been the general case, but some elite captives died in captivity, despite numerous attempts to ransom them. *Cativos de conta* are discussed in great detail in the section on ransom (below).

Low-status captives were generally forced to wear shackles, kept in poorly ventilated and insalubrious prisons or dungeons, given minimal food and clothing, and required to perform various services

---

[39] *SIHMP*, 5:122 and n2; Braga, *Entre a Cristandade*, 47, 132; Idem, "Mulheres cativas," 1:440-443. Some Portuguese converts who later were ransomed and returned to Christianity were required to explain to the Portuguese Inquisition what they had learned about Islam. These explanations often show confusion about the basic fundamentals of Islam as well as the Arabic language (Braga, *Entre a Cristandade*, 108-117). Even Portuguese renegades who apostatized of their own volition were often treated leniently. For example, one Alexandre Gonçalves had become a Muslim in the past and manufactured crossbows for the Sa`adids, but now wanted to become a Christian again. António Leitão de Gamboa, the *capitão* of Santa Cruz, permitted this so long as Gonçalves arranged an ambush for some of his former Muslim associates. This came to pass, and in an updated version of the prodigal son tale, Gamboa asked the king to reward Gonçalves for returning to serve the Portuguese ("Letter from António Leitão de Gamboa to D. João III," Santa Cruz, 16 January 1525, *SIHMP*, 2:337-341).

[40] "Report of D. Rodrigo de Castro," n. l., after 12 March 1541, SIHMP, 3:342; Ana Roque, "Considerações sobre a mulher no contexto da expansão portuguesa no norte de África (as praças do sul de Marrocos)," in *O rosto feminino da expansão portuguesa* (Lisbon: Comissão para a Igualdade e para os Direitos das Mulheres, 1994), 1:461.

[41] Braga, *Entre a Cristandade*, 56.

and labor, often menial and dangerous.⁴² As might be expected, slaves were subject to physical punishments, both as behavioral correctives and to motivate them to perform their tasks more efficiently. Bento do Souto reported that he was whipped, punched in the stomach, and kicked throughout his captivity in Morocco. Portuguese captives reported that they were often insulted by their owners who called them "Jewish dogs" repeatedly. Portuguese were known to call their Moroccan slaves "dogs" as well.⁴³

Portuguese captives with medical or building skills were put to work in their area of expertise. Those with military skills of importance to the Moroccans were often required to serve in the military or assist in the manufacture or repair of weaponry. In fact, Moroccans were normally reluctant to ransom Portuguese who were top military officials or who were skilled in defensive warfare, such as *atalaias*, *atalhadores*, *escutas*, and *almocadéns*. For their part, Portuguese officials were most anxious to ransom these individuals and return them to their tasks protecting Portuguese fortresses and attacking *mouros de guerra*.⁴⁴ There is no evidence that Portuguese ever employed Moroccan Muslim captives in military capacities.

Captives who could provide little more than a strong back might be put to work in mines, breaking rocks for construction, building walls or other structures, hauling goods from place to place, or cleaning stables. Others served as cooks, maids, waterbearers, and grooms. Agricultural tasks seem to have occupied a majority of the Portuguese held by Moroccans. One Portuguese captured near the end of the sixteenth century reported that his normal tasks involved grinding wheat, carding wool, and working in vineyards and gardens.⁴⁵ Moroccan slaves held by Portuguese in Morocco also typically served as menial labor and domestic help.

One of the threats faced by captives was rape. While normally it was women who were raped, there is one example of a Portuguese man, Simão Gonçalves, from Ceuta, who claimed that he and other Portuguese men were sodomized by Moroccan men in the public baths

---

⁴² Braga, *Entre a Cristandade*, 52, 54-73.

⁴³ Braga, *Entre a Cristandade*, 55.

⁴⁴ Braga, *Entre a Cristandade*, 41-42 and *GTT*, 5:143.

⁴⁵ Braga, *Entra a Cristandade*, 57-59.

of Fez. It is unknown if this practice was common or if it existed in other Moroccan cities. There is no evidence of any Portuguese men raping Moroccan men.[46]

More typical examples of the sexual exploitation of captives were female Moroccan Muslims who had been captured by the Portuguese. In fact, chronicler Bernardo Rodrigues mentions that the preferred age for female slaves was between ten and twenty-five years old. In 1513, Nuno Gato, the *contador* of Safi, came across a large group of women in or near the city of Almedina. For some unexplained reason, there were no men to protect them, and Gato's force captured them easily. He said that among the women captured were some "very beautiful girls."[47]

The documents and chronicles say nothing, however, about any children born of unions between slaves and their owners or what became of them. When such a child was born in Portuguese society, he remained a slave unless he or his mother was specifically emancipated by his owner.[48] Although direct evidence of sexual use and exploitation of Muslim women is rare, D. João de Meneses, the *capitão* of Arzila from 1475 to 1496, present in Arzila again from 1502 to 1505, and then *capitão do campo*[49] of Azamor from 1513 until his death in 1514, wrote a poem to one of his female slaves. Nowhere in the poem is it explicitly stated that she was a Moroccan Muslim, but this is the most logical conclusion given his extended residence in North Africa. In an explicit

---

[46] Braga, *Entre a Cristandade*, 58.

[47] "Letter from Nuno Gato to D. Manuel," Azamor, 5 December 1513, *SIHMP*, 1:454: "*moças muyto formosas.*" He later took the women to Safi where he sold them for a tidy profit for himself and the crown. The extraordinary circumstance of so many women being left unprotected does not make any sense. Even if these women were just slaves or concubines, they would have had some economic value that would have made it profitable to protect them from seizure by the Portuguese. Compare to the manner in which the villagers of Benacafiz protected their wives and daughters from the raiding party led by D. João de Meneses (see chapter seven).

[48] Ana Maria S. A. Rodrigues and Maria de Fátima Moura Ferreira, "Mulheres portuguesas em Marrocos: imagens do quotidiano feminino nos séculos XV e XVI," in *O rosto feminino da expansão portuguesa* (Lisbon: Comissão para a Igualdade e para os Direitos das Mulheres, 1995), 422.

[49] "Governor of the Countryside." See chapter two for a discussion of this term.

account of his love for his slave, Meneses, says, "Cativo sou de cativa,/ servo d'ũa servidor,/ senhora de seu senhor."[50]

It seems that the use of female captives for sexual purposes was something that Portuguese men were much more willing to do than Muslim men, though it did occur on both sides of the religious divide.[51] Portuguese women and girls who were captured by Moroccan Muslims were at times made into concubines. Muslim men were, in fact, allowed to own even Muslim women as slaves, with Islamic jurisprudence apparently recognizing that their primary function would be sexual. Furthermore, any children born to concubines were legally considered free. Other Portuguese women, after becoming Muslims, would often be married to renegade Christians (*elches*), European men who had converted to Islam and now served a Moroccan lord.[52]

Escape, Release, or Ransom: An End to Captivity

For a captive/slave, there were three ways to regain freedom: escape, good-will release, or ransom. Escape, while it may have been more common than the documents show, is rarely mentioned. In 1513, two captured Muslim men escaped from Safi by stealing two of the three horses used for transporting artillery.[53] A rather startling case occurred in 1533. A Muslim slave of Sharif Muhammad al-Sheikh escaped and made his way to Santa Cruz. There, he sought refuge in the city's church and converted to Christianity in order to ensure his freedom. The Sharif, very angry with this slave, sent word to D. João III requesting that he order the Portuguese in Santa Cruz to return the slave to him. Unfortunately, nothing more is known about this case.[54]

---

[50] Garcia de Resende, "Vilancete de D. João [de Meneses] a ũa escrava sua," in *Cancioneiro Geral* (Lisbon, 1516), f. 18. "I am a captive of the captured; I serve a servant, the mistress of her master." Compare to the Zaragosa case mentioned by David Nirenberg, *Communities of Violence: Persecution of Minorities in the Middle Ages* (Princeton: Princeton University Press, 1996), 184.

[51] Ana Roque, "Considerações," 461.

[52] *SIHMP*, 5:122; *Dictionary of the Middle Ages* (New York: Charles Scribner's Sons, 1983), 3:527-529; "Umm al-Walad," in *EI(2)*, 857-859; Braga, *Entre a Cristandade*, 58-59, 107.

[53] "Letter from Nuno Fernandes de Ataíde to D. Manuel," Safi, 29 October 1513, *SIHMP*, 1:447.

[54] ANTT, CC I, 51, 88.

Not all those who escaped were able to return to their homes. In 1513, a Muslim man who had been a slave of Sebastião Lopes, the *almoxarife* of Safi, was apprehended near Azamor after successfully escaping from Safi. The slave was returned to his owner, despite his claims he had become a Christian. His claims were doubted because he had been called by his Arabic name by the Muslims with whom he was discovered.[55] In another case, three Moroccan women had escaped from Azamor. They were tracked down by a group of Moroccan men, who found one dead but returned the other two to the Portuguese. For this, they were paid twenty *cruzados* (8,000 *reis*). The two women were then sold to new owners in Portugal.[56]

Escape was also an option for captured Portuguese, especially non-elite men who had little in the way of monetary resources or court influence. If women and children were captured along with the men, as with the fall of Santa Cruz in 1541, then royal and religious resources were mobilized to ransom as many people as possible.[57] One Portuguese escapee was Mestre João, a *bombardeiro* (artilleryman), who had been captured near Arzila in northern Morocco in 1508, when he was twenty-five years old. He was taken to Fez where he remained in captivity until 1536, when he and sixty-six other Christians escaped and made their way to Portuguese territory. Manuel de Sande, the *capitão* of Mazagão, who fed and housed these former captives while they awaited transport to Portugal, described them as completely destitute as a result of their captivity.[58] While often an individual tragedy, captivity could be extremely valuable for Portuguese leaders. Antão do Rego had been held captive for eight years when he escaped in 1526 and made his way to Azamor. Lançarote de Freitas, the *feitor* of Azamor, noted that Rego's command of Arabic had enabled him to gain extensive

---

[55] "Letter from João de Meneses to D. Manuel," Azamor, 1-9 December 1513, *SIHMP*, 1:466. (Converted Muslims took on a Christian – i.e., a Portuguese – name at their baptism.)

[56] ANTT, CC II, 107, 80.

[57] *CSC*, 142-146. These ransoms are discussed in detail below.

[58] *SIHMP*, 5:122; "Letter from Jacob Rute to his Brother," Fez, August 1536, *SIHMP*, 3:48; "Order from Manuel de Sande," Mazagão, 25 August 1536; "Letter from Manuel de Sande to João III," Mazagão, 21 September 1536, *SIHMP*, 3:60.

knowledge of Wattasid politics during his captivity. Consequently, he was sent to Portugal to brief the king.[59]

A second way for a captive to regain freedom was through the surprisingly common activity of good-will release. This appears to apply almost exclusively to Moroccans held by Portuguese as the only example of a Portuguese released as a good-will gesture by a Moroccan is D. Guterres de Monroi, and his release was under extraordinary circumstances (see below). Several examples of good-will releases were mentioned in chapter six. Among these was the return of four slaves to `Omar bin Mira, a leader of the Awlad `Amran, as one of the conditions of a peace treaty. Yet another example was Yahya-u-Ta`fuft's release of captured women and children after a 1517 battle with the Hintati. These releases had a clear linkage with subsequent peace negotiations. Examples can be multiplied.

For instance, on 4 November 1522, Gonçalo Mendes Sacoto, *capitão* of Azamor, led a raid against an unnamed group of Shawiyyan Muslims. In the battle, many of the Shawiyyan leaders were killed and a great number of people were captured. Among the captives were the wives of the five surviving sheikhs of this group. The sheikhs traveled to Azamor less than ten days after the battle and begged that their wives be returned to them, offering to exchange their sons as hostages as a guarantee that they would remain at peace. Sacoto had the women seized from among the captives as the royal fifth, and then wrote to D. João III asking him if the women should be returned to their husbands or if they should be put up for auction. He added that he preferred the first option because it should ensure a more peaceful region. The king apparently agreed with him, for a peace treaty was concluded with the Shawiyyans at the end of 1522.

As a condition of this peace, `Ali Mumen, the head of the Shawiyyan coalition, was appointed *alcaide dos mouros* over the entire territory of Shawiyya with all the civil and criminal jurisdictional powers that came with the title. `Ali was given the power to negotiate peace treaties, and even take hostages, who would then be forwarded to Azamor and held by its *capitão*. As another gesture of good faith for the peace process, all of the Shawiyyan slaves who had been recently

---

[59] "Letter from Lançarote de Freitas to D. João III," Azamor, 27 June 1526, *SIHMP*, 2:354-355.

captured and purchased, were returned to `Ali, and Sacoto guaranteed that the king would pay the former owners for their expenses of purchase and maintenance of these slaves.[60]

The final way of securing freedom was through the payment of a ransom. Ransoming captives, both Portuguese and Moroccan, could be a lucrative business. When it was known that a particular Moroccan captive – typically a religious leader or a political leader or one of his family members – was a *cativo de conta*, his price at auction would be very high, for the person who purchased him could then sell him back to his people for a great profit. In 1517, for example, a Shawiyyan *faqīr* had been captured.[61] He was auctioned to a consortium of buyers that included two Portuguese and four Jews. The price of this Muslim holy man at auction was 154,000 *reis*, which included ten *cruzados* worth of goods (*alças*). The *faqīr* was then ransomed to his people for five thousand ounces of silver, at a value of 1,600,000 *reis*, and ten *tareas* of wool.[62] The consortium of owners thus made a total profit of over 1.5 million *reis*.

However, the person with the majority stake in the captive, Álvaro do Cadaval, the *almoxarife* of Azamor, was having a problem with the *capitão* of Azamor, Simão Correia. The *capitão*, who had been paid a fifth of the value of the auction price, which was his prerogative in earning one-fifth of all profits of raiding and warlike activity, now demanded a fifth of the ransom price, which was illegal, according to Cadaval. Cadaval wrote to the king protesting Correia's demand, and said that if the king should find the *capitão* in the right, then he would gladly cut off the Muslim's head, which seemed to be about one-fifth of his body, and give it to the *capitão* "*com muy boa vomtade.*" If the letter of the law was not enough to make his case, Cadaval asked the king to consider his son, who had been studying at Salamanca for four years,

---

[60] "Letter from Gonçalo Mendes Sacoto to D. João III," Azamor, 13 November 1522, *SIHMP*, 2:301 and "Peace Treaty with the Shawiyya," n. l., end of 1522, *SIHMP*, 2:303-307.

[61] A *faqīr* is a Muslim holy man whose life is characterized by total rejection of private property and a resignation to the will of God. See *EI(2)*, pp. 757-758.

[62] A *tarea* refers to the amount of work that could be accomplished in a particular amount of time. Thus, without knowing exactly how much wool could be worked during what period of time, it is impossible to quantify the value of wool when a shifting and contingent unit of measurement is used.

and his unmarried daughter. The expense of maintaining his children was great, and he wanted to make some profit on this captive to ease the burden. If the king were kind enough to grant his permission to allow the ransom to continue, then Cadaval would be able to accomplish this.[63]

Moroccans likewise took advantage of the wealth that could be generated by ransoming *cativos de conta*. In late 1521 or early 1522, D. Nuno Mascarenhas, then *capitão* of Safi, led a raiding party that was defeated and captured by Sa`adid forces near Marrakech.[64] The ransom for Mascarenhas was 22,000 *cruzados*. He was quickly able to pay half the price, but then had to deliver two of his sons, one twelve and the other (D. João) nine, who were living in Safi, as hostages to guarantee the remainder of his ransom price.[65] After two and one-half months, Mascarenhas returned with the money and freed his sons. According to D. João, however, the Sharif poisoned them just before they were released. His older brother died in Aguz, while he survived.[66]

Cristóvão Freire, captured along with his brother-in-law, D. Nuno Mascarenhas, was held captive with five other *cativos de conta*: Lopo Barriga (*adail* of Safi from 1508 to 1516), Manuel da Silveira, Lopo de Melo, Luis Gonçalves (*feitor* and *adail* of Safi from 1519 to 1522), and Diogo Lopes (*almocadém* of Safi from 1511 (?) to the 1520s).[67] These six men wrote a letter to D. João III, sometime after

---

[63] "Letter from Álvaro do Cadaval to D. Manuel," Azamor, 10 May 1517, *SIHMP*, 2:79-81. The episode is mentioned briefly in Tavim, *Os judeus*, 332. It is, unfortunately, unknown how this situation resolved itself.

[64] Although Sharifan forces did not seize Marrakech until 1524, by the middle of 1521, the Hintati ruler of Marrakech had become a puppet of the Sa`dids.

[65] The fact that Mascarenhas could raise 11,000 *cruzados* (over 4 million *reis*) from his sources in Morocco, shows the tremendous wealth to be made in Morocco by Portuguese elites.

[66] "Letter of D. João Mascarenhas," n. l., 1540, *SIHMP*, 2:297. The story of poisoning does not make any sense due to the fact that the captors received what they wanted, and the ill-will generated by such an act would have been tremendous. Furthermore, the story of poisoning cannot be confirmed in any other source. Because D. João Mascarenhas wrote this account as part of a letter requesting a larger pension, he may have included the poisoning story to gain more sympathy and therefore more money. In all likelihood, his brother died from either illness or the stress of captivity.

[67] *SIHMP*, 1:267n1, 2:244n2 and ANTT, NA 597, f. 123v. Lopo de Melo is never identified with a title, but appears to have been in Safi in 1509, and perhaps since 1507, and may have remained there permanently or periodically until his capture in 1522

10 September 1523, complaining of the way in which rabbi Abraham Rute (head rabbi of Safi), serving as *alfaqueque*, was sabotaging their chances for freedom.[68] They claimed that Rute, after negotiating a three-month duty-free trade agreement between himself and the Sharif, advised the captors of the Portuguese to watch them closely because they might flee. As a result, they were all put in leg irons. Later, Rute told the Sharif that Freire had access to large sums of money and could pay a sizeable ransom. When negotiations started and Freire pleaded poverty, the Sharif laughed at him (*ryo-se de mim*). Thus, Freire concluded that Rute had betrayed him. The men claimed that Rute was attempting to drive *up* the price that it would cost them for their freedom. Rute allegedly gave a list of all Freire's relatives and of their possessions to the Sharif. He told the Sharif that Manuel da Silveira's father was so rich he could pay 20,000 *cruzados* "without feeling it," and that the father of Lopo de Melo had 300,000 *reis* in rent income each year.

Shortly thereafter, Ismail Benzamiro arrived with a previously agreed ransom amount. The Sharif now refused to accept the payment and wanted to raise the price. The Sharif said that he would free Freire if he added at least 1,000 lance poles (*astes de lamça*) to the previous price, but Freire refused and was put in a tent with an iron collar on his neck and his hands and feet bound, with three black slaves who poked him if he fell asleep. Learning of these charges, D. João III forbid Rute to have anything to do with the negotiations, which were taken over by the Benzamiro family. Rute was, however, allowed to maintain his position as head rabbi of Safi.[69]

Of these six *cativos de conta*, we know most about the experience of Lopo Barriga, some of which may be fabricated or imagined.

("Letter from the Inhabitants of Safi to D. Manuel," Safi, 2 July 1509, *SIHMP*, 1:201). Manuel da Silveria is discussed below.

[68] Why would Rute want to do this? The answer is unclear, though perhaps he sensed waning Portuguese power in Morocco and was engaged in creating an alliance with those he thought would replace the Portuguese as dominant in the region. This compares to Rute's agreement to assist Diogo de Azambuja in sowing discord between Yahya-u-Ta`fuft and `Ali bin Washman that eventually enabled the Portuguese to easily seize the city of Safi in 1508 (*CDM*, 2:59-60). Rute seems to have always wanted to ingratiate himself to whichever side seemed strongest.

[69] "Letter to João III from Six Portuguese Captives," n. l., after 10 September 1523, *SIHMP*, 2:323-328 and Tavim, *Os judeus*, 334-336.

Barriga, the *adail* of Safi, was a *fidalgo* who served in North Africa from 1508 until the late 1520s. In May 1516, he participated in a raid against a North African village. While returning to Safi with the spoils, the Portuguese were attacked by a group of Moroccans and routed. Barriga was made a prisoner of the Sharif. We have two contemporaneous mentions of Barriga's captivity. The first is a letter from September 1517, when he is mentioned as a possible candidate to exchange for an important Muslim taken prisoner during a skirmish.[70] The second is the letter from 1523 mentioned above.

Barriga's captivity is also discussed in the *Diálogo de vária história*, written by the Portuguese, Pedro de Mariz, in 1594. Mariz tells of the extraordinary behavior of Barriga during his captivity. While in his cell, a Muslim insulted Barriga, saying, "You are the Christian about whom are told such valorous deeds in arms? I hoped that you should be free so I could pull out your whiskers." The Muslim then extended a hand and seized Barriga's beard. But Barriga would not stand for it and killed him with a ready-to-hand stick. As punishment, the Sharif ordered 2,000 lashes to be given to Barriga. During this punishment, that would likely have killed any normal man, Barriga showed no emotion. His shredded shirt was later allegedly sent to D. João III. Mariz claims that upon his release, which he erroneously dates as 1524, Barriga wanted to get back into combat with Muslims and that only a few days after regaining his freedom, he was killed. Mariz, however, is incorrect. Ibrahim Benzamiro was only able to secure Barriga's release in 1527. Barriga lived until the end of 1533, dying in Portugal under unknown circumstances.[71]

Even *cativos de conta*, however, could not always expect to be freed. Of the six men who wrote the letter to D. João III in 1523, we know with certainty that Lopo Barriga, Diogo Lopes, and Luis Gonçalves were released. Diogo Lopes was freed sometime before July 1527 and remained *almocadém* of Safi through at least 1528.[72] Luis

---

[70] "Letter from D. Nuno Mascarenhas to D. Manuel," Safi, 9 September 1517, *SIHMP*, 2:169 and "Letter from D. Rodrigo de Noronha to D. Manuel," Safi, 9 September 1517, *SIHMP*, 2:172.

[71] Mariz, 742-3; Tavim, *Os judeus*, 336; "Letter from Garcia de Mello to D. João III," Safi, 5 October 1526, *SIHMP*, 2:372n1.

[72] "Letter from Garcia de Melo to D. João III," Safi, 9 July 1527, *SIHMP*, 2:407-411 and ANTT, CC I, 39, 37.

Gonçalves, captured with D. Nuno Mascarenhas, gained his freedom in an unknown way, though he was presumably ransomed. This occurred sometime before 18 March 1525, the date on a quittance letter that he wrote summarizing his tenure as *feitor* of Safi.[73]

Of the remaining three, we know the fate only of only one: Manuel da Silveira, who had been captured at the same time as D. Nuno Mascarenhas. Despite a direct appeal in 1529 to D. João III to set him free, it was only in 1539 that a price of 12,500 ounces of silver and two Moroccan captives was finally agreed to for his ransom. D. Rodrigo de Castro, the *capitão* of Safi, asked D. João III to send the ransom as quickly as possible. It never arrived. Silveira eventually died in captivity in Marrakech in 1545, more than twenty-three years after being captured.[74] Lopo de Melo and Cristóvão Freire, due to their access to wealth, likely were freed, though there is no record of this. As seen from these examples, the length of time one could remain in captivity could vary from a few days or months to many years.[75]

Another group of Portuguese *cativos de conta* included D. Mécia de Monroi, her father, D. Guterres, the *capitão* of Santa Cruz, and her brother, D. Jerónimo, all captured at the fall of Santa Cruz in 1541. According to the anonymous Portuguese chronicler of Santa Cruz, D. Mécia was very beautiful and quickly became the object of Sharif Muhammad al-Sheikh's affections. However, he wanted her to convert to Islam before he would marry her. She refused, even under threats, such as that of rape by two of the Sharif's slaves. Finally, she told the Sharif that she would marry him if he brought his own brother, Sharif Ahmed al-A`raj, to her in chains. She did not know that the Sharif was already at odds with his brother, and they were soon engaged in war. He captured his brother, and she upheld her promise to convert and marry him. She later gave birth to a daughter who died eight days later, followed by D. Mécia herself eight days after this. According to the

---

[73] *SIHMP*, 244n2.

[74] *SIHMP*, 2:327n1 (the date of 25 June 1529 is really 1539); ANTT, CC I, 44, 14; CC I, 64, 174.

[75] For a self-appraisal of the hopelessness of captivity, see "Letter from Three Captives to D. João III," Marrakech, 1 July 1544, *SIHMP*, 4:142-143. In her study of Inquisitorial records of Portuguese who had been held captive in North Africa during the years 1554-1697, Braga discovered one man who had been held captive for fifty-five years. The average time in captivity was eleven years (*Entre a Cristandade*, 92-94).

chronicler, many people suspected that the Sharif's other wives, jealous of his attentiveness to D. Mécia, had poisoned or bewitched both her and her daughter.[76] Her brother, D. Jerónimo, soon died of grief.

The Sharif eventually freed D. Guterres without accepting any ransom for him because of the bond between them that marriage had formed. In fact, the Sharif gave him the option of becoming one of his deputies. To sweeten the offer, the Sharif promised to allow D. Guterres to build a chapel in which he could worship freely. It was an offer that D. Guterres, pleading old age and the desire to be surrounded by Christians, refused. The Sharif truly loved D. Guterres as a father and freed him with the two black slaves, one male and one female, that D. Guterres had owned at the time of his capture, as well as gifts of three other slaves, two boys and one adult male. The Sharif also returned to him the 12,000 *cruzados* that had already been sent in partial payment of his ransom and gave him a beautiful horse and a pack animal laden with unspecified objects of wealth. D. Guterres was then escorted by two of the Sharif's men to Portuguese-controlled Mazagão in July 1544.[77]

The case of Manuel da Câmara, governor of São Miguel in the Azores, underscores both the greed and negotiating strategies operative in ransom negotiations. As with the case of Cristóvão Freire, Câmara's ransom price gradually increased as his captor learned more about his wealth. Manuel da Câmara had been captured in the fall of Santa Cruz. Shortly thereafter, "a *mourisca* of his," who was presumably a servant and may have been captured in Morocco at some earlier time, arranged with the Sharif to give Câmara his freedom for 12,000 *cruzados* and the return of two Moroccan Muslims he had recently purchased and sent to São Miguel. Upon the arrival of the two Muslims from the Azores, they were taken before the Sharif where they asked him Câmara's ransom price. They informed the Sharif that Câmara was exceedingly wealthy and that 20,000 *cruzados* was a better price.

---

[76] *CSC*, 126-40.

[77] *CSC*, 150-4. For a similar account of these events, see Diego de Torres, *Relación del origen y suceso de los xarifes y del estado de los reinos de Marruecos, Fez, y Tarudante*, ed. and intro. Mercedes García-Arenal (Madrid: Siglo Veintiuno de España, 1980), 112-116, 133. Torres says nothing about rape threats, though he does claim that D. Mécia spent a good deal of time in solitary confinement.

Learning of the new price, Manuel da Câmara was able to secure a loan from free Christian merchants in Tarudante, where he was being held, and buy his freedom at 20,000. He then quickly made for the sea coast, where his brother was waiting off shore in a ship. His haste was warranted, as the Sharif had reconsidered the price yet again and sent a group of soldiers to seize Câmara and hold him for a higher price. Câmara had already boarded the ship and, despite the Moroccan soldiers who sailed a small boat out to sea and attempted with honeyed tongues to persuade Câmara to return with them, he sailed safely to the Azores. Câmara had been held for nearly two years.[78]

We know very little of the individual stories of the approximately six hundred Portuguese "men, women, youths, and children of all sorts" who were captured following the fall of Santa Cruz in 1541.[79] One of the few stories is of the family of Bento da Costa, *escrivão da feitoria* and *alcaide mor* of Santa Cruz from at least 1533. For an unknown reason, but perhaps to secure supplies for his beleaguered city, he had been away from Santa Cruz when it fell. Already a widower, he learned that his two daughters, one son, his mother-in-law, and his sister-in-law and her four children had been taken captive. Fortunately, a generous Castilian merchant, Fernando Gomez, on business in Tarudante, had paid to have all of them freed. The merchant was not entirely charitable, however. He allowed Costa's son, his mother-in-law, his sister-in-law and her two sons and one of her daughters to return to Portugal. To ensure that he would be repaid for his generosity, he kept Costa's two daughters and one of his nieces. Costa, financially ruined due to the capture of all his wealth by the Sharif's men, begged the king to help him. If the king were unwilling or unable to assist him, he feared that the Castilian would soon be destitute financially and would leave Tarudante, abandoning the girls who would then likely become concubines and Muslims. Costa reminded D. João III that his service to the king had cost him his

---

[78] "Letter from Sebastião Gonçalves to D. João III," Tarudante, 9 March 1543; Joaquim Figanier, *História de Santa Cruz do Cabo de Gué (Agadir) 1505-1541* (Lisboa: Agência Geral das Colónias, 1945), 358-359; *CSC*, 140-144.

[79] *CSC*, 144.

youth, his wife, one of his sons, and all of his wealth, and he asked the king to help him retain his "daughters, niece, and [his] honor."[80]

A similar situation befell Henrique Vieira whose wife and children and all his wealth were captured with the fall of Santa Cruz, ironically while he was in Tarudante attempting to negotiate a peace with Sa`adid diplomats. He was, however, able to ransom his family by mid-April 1541 for the sum of 1,070 ounces of silver, or about 342,400 *reis*.[81]

Most Portuguese captives seized in Morocco did not have the status that permitted direct appeals to the king. In 1541, however, such appeals were unnecessary. Because the fall of Santa Cruz and the capture of its residents was so catastrophic for Portugal, the king set about trying to ransom as many of the commoners as possible, both to spare them the rigors of captivity and out of the common belief that they might convert to Islam in order to receive kinder treatment.[82] Given the magnitude of the task, not only was the *Tribunal dos Cativos* active in the ransom process, but so too were Portuguese *misericórdias* (lay brotherhoods), especially that of Lisbon. After all, one of the seven duties spelled out in the *Compromisso da Misericórdia de Lisboa* of 1516 was the ransom of captives. Although *misericórdias* were not part of the official apparatus of captive redemption in Portugal, it is clear that they nevertheless assisted with the ransoms of Portuguese captives in North Africa throughout the sixteenth century.[83]

---

[80] "Letter from Bento da Costa to D. João III," Larache, 6 June 1542, *SIHMP*, 4:46-48. It is unclear what action the king took.

[81] "Letter from Henrique Vieira to D. João III," Tarudante, 20 April 1541, *SIHMP*, 3:397.

[82] Torres, 114.

[83] For more on *misericórdias*, see André Ferrand de Almeida, "As Misericórdias," in *História de Portugal* ed. José Mattoso (Lisbon: Editorial Estampa, 1997), 3:169-176; Isabel dos Guimarães Sá, *Quando o rico se faz pobre: Misericórdias, caridade e poder no império português, 1500-1800* (Lisbon: CNCDP, 1997); Idem, "Shaping Social Space in the Centre and Periphery of Portuguese Empire: The Example of the Misericórdias from the Sixteenth to the Eighteenth Century," *Portuguese Studies* 13 (1997): 210-221. Despite the fact that the establishment of a *misericórdia* became common in all Portuguese imperial settlements from Brazil to Asia, there is very little evidence of their functioning in the southern Moroccan fortresses. This is doubly odd as there were well-established *misericórdias* in Ceuta, Alcácer Ceguer, Arzila, and Tangiers by the early sixteenth century. There was a branch in Santa Cruz from at least 1517, as a record of the importation of incense for the *misericórdia's* church attests. As of 1518, Nuno Martins served as *mordomo da bolsa* (treasurer) of the Santa Cruz *misericórdia*. By 1524, residents in

In the case of the fall of Santa Cruz, D. João III acted quickly to free Portuguese captives. The king, in his capacity as the head of the *Tribunal dos Cativos*, sent a Franciscan monk, Frei António, to Tarudante with the express mission of freeing as many of the children and women that he could.[84] This mission was sent sometime in the first half of 1542, and presumably was delayed even this long as reconnaissance and then funds were gathered to free the large number of captives. Frei António freed a substantial number of captives, though eighteen Portuguese boys between the ages of seven and twelve had been forcibly converted to Islam by the Sharif so that they might be playmates, and later advisors, to his five-year old son, Mawlay `Abd al-Mumin.

In 1543 or 1544, the king approved the mission of Bastião Álvares, a brother of the *misericórdia* of Lisbon, to Tarudante. Álvares was able to free more women and girls, as well as some men. Yet another mission was sent in late 1545, headed by Pero Fernandes, also a brother of the *misericórdia*. He brought with him a group of knights, perhaps to protect the captives he freed, perhaps hoping that military intimidation would free captives more quickly. Fernandes appears to have lingered in Morocco for nearly a year, negotiating with the Sharif and writing letters to the Lisbon *misericórdia* begging them for more and more money so that he might free as many Portuguese as possible (See Table 8.3).[85]

It is unclear what role the *Tribunal dos Cativos* played during the Álvares and Fernandes missions. Did it provide ransom money,

---

Azamor had begun construction on a *Casa da Misericórdia*, and the residents of Safi seem to have had a rudimentary *misericórdia* in place by 1529. With only a total of five documents referring to the brotherhoods in the southern Moroccan fortresses, little can be said about their function in the cities, other than to speculate that they attempted to function like the *misericórdias* in other Portuguese locations. The lack of documentation may have been due to a lack of local support or the loss of most relevant documentation in the capture or abandonment of the fortresses. See, ANTT, CC I, 4, 29; CC I, 20, 75; CC I, 22, 74; CC I, 26, 20; CC I, 30, 94; CC II, 74, 145; CC II, 75, 176; *CJ* 41, f. 91v; Sá, *Quando o rico se faz pobre*, 267-268.

[84] *CSC*, 144-146 and "Letter from Sebastião Álvares to D. João III," Tarundante, 5 January 1542, *SIHMP*, 4:6-8. Diego de Torres described Frei António's mission: "*El fraile rescató muchas mugeres y niños que es la gente que más riesgo corre de tornarse Moros*" (114).

[85] "Letter from Pero Fernandes to D. João III," Mazagão, 7 October 1545, *SIHMP*, 4:178-181 and "Letter from António Veloso to D. João III," n. l., 28 July 1546, *SIHMP*, 4:193-194.

logistical support, or was it simply unable to perform the task of ransoming captives as well as the *misericórdias*? By mid-1546, war between the Sa`adids and the Wattasids resumed, and no more Portuguese could be freed, though it seems that most of those captured during the fall of Santa Cruz were already back in Portugal.

Captivity, Greed, and the Law

As was common for both Europeans and Moroccans of this era, the spoils of victory in war legally included the taking of captives for the purpose of enslaving them. The kings of Portugal, however, wanted to limit any illicit taking of captives (i.e., outside the act of legitimate warfare) as it could lead to recrimination and regional instability. For the most part, this involved the promulgation of laws to prevent the Portuguese from illegally enslaving Muslims from members of allied Moroccan groups and from purchasing Muslim slaves from dubious sources. The desire for wealth guided the lives of many Portuguese in Morocco, perhaps even more so than their oft-stated desire to serve their king well.[86] Consequently, many Portuguese interpreted the laws governing the capture and enslavement of Muslims rather loosely, which is not surprising considering the profit possibilities of the slave trade.

The king had regulations in place that should have prevented any abuses, but greed – on all three sides of the religious troika – often trumped law. In one case, Nuno Fernandes de Ataíde was reprimanded for allowing Moroccans to sell fellow Moroccans in Safi. Ataíde argued that since these Muslims were obviously slaves, that it did not go against the regulations set up by D. Manuel that prohibited the sale of Muslims. In fact, it was a great service to the king. Ataíde's "common sense" argument did not persuade the king, however, who believed that Ataíde's actions would promote fighting amongst Moroccan groups and lead to instability.[87]

In January 1517, D. Manuel issued an *alvará* (royal order) regarding Muslim captives. First, no allied Muslim could be captured and enslaved simply because he had committed a crime (*malefício*). In

---

[86] See the discussion of the plunder along the Portuguese-Moroccan frontier in the concluding chapter of this study.

[87] "Letter from Nuno Fernandes de Ataíde to D. Manuel," Safi, 17 March 1511, *SIHMP*, 1:299.

other words, Muslim criminals were to be punished as prescribed by law. If they committed the crime under Portuguese jurisdiction (e.g., within a fortress), then they were subject to Portuguese law. If they committed the crime outside of the fortress and therefore under the jurisdiction of an *alcaide dos mouros*, then they were to be punished under Islamic law. Second, no Christian could purchase a Muslim from another Muslim even if the seller assured the buyer that he had been enslaved properly. This second measure was aimed at preventing any exacerbation of tribal warfare and thus preserving stability both within and near the border of the Portuguese zone of influence. According to D. Nuno Mascarenhas, the *capitão* of Safi, these policies had already been in effect for many months before the issuance of the *alvará*, because of an earlier *alvará* brought by Yahya-u-Ta`fuft, the *alcaide dos mouros*, in July 1516. In fact, when Pero Leitão, the messenger who brought the January 1517 *alvará*, arrived in Safi, he found four Muslims who had been hanged: two for robbery and two for kidnapping a group of *mouros de pazes* and attempting to sell them in Safi.[88] Mascarenhas wanted to make it clear to the king that justice against illegal slave-trading activity was swift and sure.

Despite the king's wishes and Mascarenhas's assurances, the law was not always followed. During times of peace, many Portuguese *fronteiros* turned to kidnapping to replace the wealth they had previously earned from the sale of war captives. They typically employed the ruse of claiming that Moroccan Muslim merchants who came to Portuguese cities to sell their goods were from a group of *mouros de guerra*, and thus eligible to be captured. In 1517, during a period of relative peace, Yahya-u-Ta`fuft accused many of the king's top officials in Safi, including Nuno Gato, the *contador*, and Heitor Gonçalves, the *feitor*, of engaging in this practice. Although he had worked diligently to re-establish peace in the Dukkala region in service to D. Manuel, Yahya knew that this was not what the *fronteiros* wanted: "The *capitão* and the knights who are here do not want peace, but rather war. They believe this because they do not have any gain (*proveito*) from peace or from the service that I render because they have nothing to seize and divide.

---

[88] "Letter from D. Nuno Mascarenhas to D. Manuel," Safi, 11 March 1517, *SIHMP*, 2:65.

And because of this, they all want to do very bad things to me."[89] In short, the Portuguese leadership in Safi preferred plunder to colonial development. Peace and stability are necessary components to true colonial development not just the maintenance of military enclaves. But we are forced to ask along with historian David Lopes, "How could there have been peace when the State [generally] made itself the protector of slave traders?"[90]

The *alvará* of January 1517 either did not apply to the fortress of Santa Cruz or was never proclaimed there. In May 1517, one Sheikh Sa`īd claimed to have sold countless slaves to the Portuguese in Santa Cruz, and in 1518, Fernão Taveira, the *adail* of Santa Cruz, claimed that the royal fifth taken from these sales generated the most income of all royal enterprises.[91] The location of Santa Cruz away from large population centers and on the periphery of the Sa`adid zone of authority in the Sus may have allowed for Santa Cruz to be exempted from this new law. Because the Portuguese had so few allies in the area and with the Sharif nearby and increasingly powerful, their chances of gaining more allies in the region were slim. Consequently, the proxy slave-raids carried out by Moroccan allies do not seem to have been questioned. In Dukkala, where it was much easier for the Portuguese to gain allies, different rules of conduct helped local relations.

Greed could also create political problems and personal animosity among the Portuguese leadership. In 1519, a group of "thieves" (*ladrões*), who may have been Portuguese, Moroccan, Jewish, or a combination, from Azamor captured a Gharbiyyan Muslim and then sold him to a Jew in Azamor. When the relatives of the enslaved Muslim informed the *capitão* of Safi, D. Nuno Mascarenhas, of this, he gave them a letter demanding that the captive be freed. Mascarenhas claimed that although the messenger who delivered the letter to the Jewish buyer in Azamor actually saw the Muslim in question shackled in leg irons, D. Álvaro de Noronha, the *capitão* of Azamor, falsely reported that the Muslim was no longer in the city. Worse yet, the Jew

---

[89] "Letter from Yahya-u-Ta`fuft to D. Manuel," Safi, after 24 June 1517, *SIHMP*, 2:100-105. Illegal kidnapping and enslavement of Muslims was also common in medieval Valencia (Nirenberg, 34).

[90] *HP*, 3:460.

[91] "Letter from Sheikh Sa`īd to D. Manuel," n. l., c. May 1517, *SIHMP*, 2:94 and "Letter from Fernão Taveira to D. Manuel," Santa Cruz, 28 May 1518, *SIHMP*, 2:185-186.

who had purchased the slave was named Yahuda, who had earlier fled from Safi leaving many unpaid debts. In the end, Noronha would not turn over the slave, and Mascarenhas was forced to write the king to ask him to resolve this matter that had caused "much scandal and instability among the Arabs." Shortly thereafter, a letter arrived from Almedina reporting that some "thieves" from Azamor – likely the same group – had captured a Muslim from just outside their city gates and asking Mascarenhas to write to Noronha to rectify the situation.[92] In response, Mascarenhas wrote directly to the king, commenting sarcastically that since his letters seem to have little effect, he would defer from fulfillment of the Almedinan request until he had a reply from the king on the first matter.[93]

In February 1527, António Leite, the *capitão* of Mazagão, reported that Jorge Viegas, the *capitão* of Azamor, had blockaded Mazagão so that Leite could not stop him from attacking and enslaving the Muslims and *mouriscos* who lived in the area. Leite opined that Viegas "seemed to be following in the footsteps of D. Álvaro de Noronha." Perhaps it was the case that a culture of the pursuit of wealth at all costs had taken root in Azamor. The illegal enslavement of allied Moroccan Muslims was bad enough, but the capture of Christian *mouriscos* (likely former Portuguese Muslims) was a sin. This greed extended to Gonçalo Mendes Sacoto, the *capitão* of Safi, who attempted to enslave Muslim merchants and their families who had traveled to Safi from Mazagão. Leite protested this action in a letter to the king leading to freedom for all of the captives in Safi except for a female Muslim that Sacoto kept for himself. Leite closed his letter with a plea that the king send an investigator (*corregedor*) to verify these accusations, free those held illegally in Azamor, and punish Viegas.[94]

---

[92] Mascarenhas and Noronha clearly had intense disagreements. Moreover, they were each perceived differently by Moroccans who saw Mascarenhas as someone with whom they could work, while they viewed Noronha as a man driven by greed. Could such a situation have been helped with the appointment of a Portuguese viceroy to oversee all of Morocco? In the fifteenth century, D. Henrique (Henry "the Navigator") had tried to implement a viceroyalty of Morocco, which he desired for himself. His idea was never approved. (P. E. Russell, *Prince Henry the Navigator: The Rise and Fall of a Culture Hero* (New York: Clarendon Press, 1984), 16.)

[93] "Letter from D. Nuno Mascarenhas to D. Manuel," Safi, 10 February 1519, *SIHMP*, 2:230-233. *Ladrões* is Mascarenhas' term.

[94] "Letter from António Leite to D. João III," Mazagão, 5 February 1527, *SIHMP*, 2:391-395. Mestre Rodrigo, the New Christian physician of Azamor, also claimed that

Conclusion

Captivity served two major ends. First, Moroccans and Portuguese both profited economically from the ransom of *cativos de conta* and from the cheap labor provided by enslaved captives. At least until 1541, however, it was the Portuguese who realized the greatest economic gain from this process. The profits generated provided revenue for the crown via the royal fifth and personal wealth for Portuguese willing to serve in Morocco. Second, captivity was used as a tool of terror to break the will of Moroccans to resist the Portuguese. Hundreds and probably thousands of Moroccans were enslaved each year during the initial stages of the Portuguese presence in southern Morocco. This must have had an intense psychological impact on them. The Portuguese would not feel anything similar until the fall of Santa Cruz in 1541.

This chapter has presented a rather general and somewhat abstract account of captivity. At its heart, however, captivity was about the lives of individuals. The anguish of D. Nuno Mascarenhas, Bento da Costa, and Sheikh Mimūn (see chapter six) when their children were held captive was repeated time and again on all sides of the religious divide. Individuals faced the prospect of captivity in divergent ways. Manuel Fernandes, the cobbler from Santa Cruz, murdered his children rather than have them face captivity and possible perdition should they convert to Islam. The Muslim residents of Azamor, Benacafiz, and Tafuf fled from their homes in terror with the coming of the Portuguese, many dying rather than face captivity. The Portuguese themselves had a saying to express their own fear of captivity: "*Quem o seu inimigo poupa, nas suas mãos morra.*"[95]

Moreover, the fear of captivity affected everyone at all times, with the possible exception of Portuguese who were safe behind the walls of their fortresses. Once one ventured beyond the protection of

---

Viegas exploited Moroccans in order to increase his wealth. See "Letter from Mestre Rodrigo to D. João III," Azamor, 15 November 1527, *SIHMP*, 2:418-424 and "Letter from Mestre Rodrigo to D. João III," Azamor, 12 January 1528, *SIHMP*, 2:425-428. This is yet another situation where there is no documentation to illuminate what happened next. Viegas remained *capitão* of Azamor until the spring of 1529, when he was replaced by António Leite.

[95] "He who is spared by his enemy will die by his hand." This expression is mentioned in "Letter from António Leite to D. João III," Mazagão, 22 January 1528, *SIHMP*, 2:430.

the walls, captivity could come without warning. For example, in 1514, a group of five Portuguese fishermen were standing on the banks of the Umm al-Rabi` River within sight of Azamor's walls. Nevertheless, a group of Shawiyyan horsemen appeared without warning and captured them.[96] Moroccans engaging in normal daily tasks were also subject to such seizures. In 1541, shortly before the Portuguese abandoned all of their southern fortresses except Mazagão, three Moroccan women and four Moroccan men were pulling water from a well near Almedina when about twenty Portuguese cavalrymen quickly approached and captured them. One man and one woman (husband and wife?) refused to walk to their captivity in Safi; the Portuguese killed them. The other five were taken to Safi and sold as slaves.[97]

Given these chaotic circumstances, it seems almost naïve that Portuguese kings and a few of their representatives in Morocco would attempt to limit the activity of captive-taking and the resultant slave trade. After all, the system that drove the most highly skilled Portuguese nobles and knights to serve on the Moroccan frontier was based on violence and greed.[98] These two elements are unified perfectly in captivity.

---

[96] "Letter from António Leite to D. Manuel," Azamor, 27 July 1514, *SIHMP*, 1:585. One of these men was likely Pero Eanes (Braga, *Entre a Cristandade*, 32).

[97] "Letter from Lopo Barriga to D. João III," Safi, 29 June 1541, *SIHMP*, 3:450-451.

[98] Malwyn Newitt, "Plunder and the Rewards of Office in the Portuguese Empire," in *The Military Revolution and the State, 1500-1800*, ed. Michael Duffy (Exeter: University of Exeter, 1980), 10-28. This issue is explored in greater detail in the concluding chapter of this study.

Table 8.1: Prices for common[99] male Muslim slaves, private-party sales

NAME	YEAR	SOURCE	PRICE IN REIS
Unknown	1537	SIHMP, 3:74	6,400
Almansur	1537	SIHMP, 3:74	9,200
Abderahman	1537	SIHMP, 3:74	12,400
Ares [?]	1537	SIHMP, 3:74	16,000
Ali	1537	SIHMP, 3:74	16,073
Isma`il	1537	SIHMP, 3:74	19,200
Abdallah	1537	SIHMP, 3:74	20,000
Unknown	1537	SIHMP, 3:74	20,000

Table 8.2: Prices for common female Muslim slaves, private-party sales

NAME	YEAR	SOURCE	PRICE IN REIS
Unknown	1523	ANTT, CC I, 29, 59	2,600
Unknown	1524	ANTT, CC I, 31, 12	4,000
Fatima	1537	SIHMP, 3:74	10,900
Almansura	1537	SIHMP, 3:74	14,200

---

[99] By "common," I mean slaves who were not tribal or village leaders or of high status who would fetch extremely high prices in anticipation of a high ransom.

Table 8.3: Ransom prices for Portuguese captured in Santa Cruz[100]

NAME OR DESCRIPTION	RANSOM AMOUNT (IN SILVER ONÇAS)
Mestre Francisco Fernandes, surgeon	1,000
Álvaro Fernandes, surgeon	1,000
Artisans, tailors, cobblers, and commoners (*gente comuna*)	350-400 each
Two black women (*negras*), each with one child	300 each (i.e., price for one woman and her child)
Wives of artisans	c. 600 each
Wife of a street peddler of clothes (*paneiro*) from Lisbon	800

---

[100] Source for Table 2.3: "Letter from António Veloso to D. João III," n. l., 28 July 1546, *SIHMP*, 4:193-194. As can be seen from the table, exact numbers of people ransomed are unfortunately not available.

Conclusion: Lessons from the Frontier

THE CHARACTERISTICS of the Portuguese-Moroccan frontier were similar to those found in other frontier regions throughout history. The composition and character of the population within the Portuguese fortresses was affected by its location along a militarized and contested space. These cities, with their religiously- and ethnically-mixed populations represented the cultural interaction and partial permeability common to frontier environments. Like the antagonistic parties on both sides of the Christian-Islamic Iberian frontier in earlier centuries, the Portuguese and the Moroccans developed mechanisms to negotiate treaties and to reclaim captives. Furthermore, despite periodic violence and chaos, trade flourished in the region, with members of all cultural and religious groups prospering to a greater or lesser extent.

The Portuguese conquest of Moroccan territory created multiple frontiers, where people and ideas battled for allegiance. The most obvious frontiers were religious and political. A Christian colonizing force had established a strong presence in Islamic lands. The Portuguese themselves had viewed their conquests in Morocco since 1415 as a species of crusade. Still, the antagonism between Islam and Christianity and its effects on daily life should not be overestimated. While it was true that the Sa`adid, Hintati, and Wattasid leadership, at one time or another, called for a jihad of all right-thinking Muslims against the Christian Portuguese invaders, not one of these groups forewent attacks on fellow Muslims for political ends. Moreover, the Portuguese freely allied with Moroccan Muslims and (often) vice versa. Many Portuguese Christians used the word "friend" (*amigo*) when describing certain Muslim leaders with whom they had developed useful and trusting relationships. The Portuguese, forced to accommodate difference more readily than they would in their Iberian homeland, treated Jews, Muslims, and Christian converts with more respect in Morocco than they did in Portugal.

Nevertheless, religious difference was a source of mistrust on both sides of the religious frontier and should not be discounted. Members of neither religion held ecumenical worldviews. Moroccans were willing to pay huge sums to ransom religious leaders (*faqīrs*) held in captivity by the Portuguese.[1] Meanwhile, the Portuguese saw the hand of God in their success. During the conquest of Azamor in 1513, the Portuguese noted a shooting star above the city and reported a lightening bolt striking and damaging a bastion, demonstrating God's favor for their task. Once they conquered the city, they discovered ancient church bells that had been taken by the Muslim conquerors of Visogothic Spain. Now these Christian artifacts were recovered, justifying Portuguese intervention in Morocco.[2]

The political frontier might better be called a political nebula. In other words, the unstructured, uncontrolled, constantly contested space between the big four – the Portuguese, the Wattasids, the Sa`adids, and the Hintati (until 1524/5) – was never consistently demarcated. Rather it was filled with numerous tribes, villages, and small urban communities that shifted alliances as they calculated which of these politically powerful groups would have the least detrimental influence on them at any moment. The Portuguese recognized the importance of securing the loyalty of the smaller local tribes and towns, for without their support, the Portuguese would have been unable to accomplish much other than launch occasional raids into the countryside. With local allies, however, the Portuguese were able to control and influence an increasingly large territory, enhancing their trading opportunities and creating a buffer zone against the more powerful and more antagonistic Moroccan leaders. As their supply of allies dwindled during the 1520s, the Portuguese had an increasingly difficult time maintaining their thrust into the Moroccan hinterland.

Another frontier was that of economic opportunity, for Portuguese, Jews, and Moroccans. The frontier of economic opportunity had two aspects: trade and plunder. For the Portuguese, the trading frontier was especially important for the wider imperial

---

[1] "Letter from Álvaro do Cadaval to D. Manuel," Azamor, 10 May 1517, *SIHMP*, 2:79-81. See chapter eight for a detailed account of this episode.

[2] "Letter from the Duke of Bragança to D. Manuel," Azamor, c. 6 September 1513, *SIHMP*, 1:423, 429 and "Letter from Rui Barreto to D. Manuel," Azamor, 21 February 1514, *SIHMP*, 1:496-497.

Conclusion

goals of establishing a flourishing slave trade in sub-Saharan Africa. Without access to Moroccan textiles and horses, the Portuguese could not have purchased as many Africans as they did. For the Moroccans, especially those near the coastal cities, Portuguese *feitorias* provided market opportunities to sell their various goods. Powerful Moroccan merchants, like *qā'id* Al-`Attar, were able to profit handsomely from this trade, while other Moroccans were able to buy and sell smaller quantities of goods and secure needed silver currency. Jews, serving in their roles both as merchants and middlemen, were able to earn vast sums of money. These trading relationships were not, by any means, created by the Portuguese military conquests in Morocco; they pre-existed it. Nevertheless, the conquests did create a situation where the most favorable terms accrued to the Portuguese.

But the promotion of trade was, for many Portuguese nobles, a secondary activity. The majority of Portuguese nobles served their king in Morocco, and elsewhere in the Portuguese empire, for *honra e proveito* (honor and gain).[3] These words do not connote the virtues of a mercantile life of honest trading and manufacturing, but rather the martial virtues of battle and plunder. Historian Malyn Newitt, using the example of Portuguese India, has argued that it was these values that redirected the Portuguese empire in the early sixteenth century from one based on careful commercial administration, as envisioned by King D. Manuel and his advisors, to one based heavily on predation and plunder.[4]

Because Portugal, unlike Castile, had only one university before 1537, it had a limited number of educated bureaucrats that it could assign to imperial offices. The only choice for Portuguese kings was to call on members of aristocratic (*fidalgo*) families to fill these positions. The family connections and prior military service of most *capitães* and many other top officials in the Moroccan fortresses shows this clearly. In other words, "when a *fidalgo* . . . was appointed to an office, . . . the

---

[3] Joaquim Romero Magalhães, "A sociedade," in *História de Portugal*, ed. José Mattoso (Lisbon: Editorial Estampa, 1994), 3:41-5 and Sussanah Humble Ferreira, "Prestige, Ideology, and Social Politics: The Place of the Portuguese Overseas Expansion in the Politics of Dom Manuel (1495-1521)," *Itinerario* 40 (2000): 21-45.

[4] Malwyn Newitt, "Plunder and the Rewards of Office in the Portuguese Empire," in *The Military Revolution and the State, 1500-1800*, ed. Michael Duffy (Exeter: University of Exeter, 1980), 10-28.

crown was not appointing a salaried bureaucrat but was alienating its authority to a member of a clan with strongly articulated aristocratic and military values and interests." Moreover, although the common soldiers were paid directly by the crown, their commander often increased this pay, creating a personal loyalty stronger than crown loyalty.[5] Additionally, the soldiers' desire for quick wealth might lead them to follow a local commander who could deliver this rather than a commander intent on following royal orders. For instance, Rui Barreto, the *capitão da cidade* of Azamor, wrote to the king in 1514, explaining that it was extremely difficult to command soldiers who were "someone else's men."[6]

Newitt argues, in fact, that the Portuguese system created a "plunder frontier." He furthermore asserts, too cynically it seems, that "plunder was the prime motive force of 'discovery'" and expansion in Portuguese Asia and the rest of the Portuguese empire.[7] Indeed, the Portuguese experience in Morocco follows the logic of the plunder frontier to an extent. Although Portuguese kings repeatedly voiced their commitment to stability within Morocco and alliance with Moroccans, many of the Portuguese *fronteiros* were unable to restrain their greed. They were torn between serving their king and helping themselves. After all, Portuguese royal practice gave twenty percent of all captured booty, whether human or material, to the local *capitão* and another twenty percent to any *alcaide dos mouros* who participated in its seizure. This financial *dis*incentive, as it were, to maintain regional stability caused extensive problems. Moroccans were seen by many Portuguese as a natural resource to be exploited. This mindset led to illegal and unwise abuses, including the exploitation of Moroccan merchants who sold goods in Portuguese cities and the enslavement of allied Moroccans.

There are two corollaries to Newitt's "plunder frontier" hypothesis that are applicable here. First, plunder, despite the problems it may have caused for royal policy makers, was in effect a

---

[5] Malwyn Newitt, "Plunder and the Rewards of Office in the Portuguese Empire," in *The Military Revolution and the State, 1500-1800*, ed. Michael Duffy (Exeter: University of Exeter, 1980), 14-15.

[6] "Letter from Rui Barreto to D. Manuel," Azamor, 21 February 1514, *SIHMP*, 1:492.

[7] Newitt, "Plunder," 16.

deliberate policy. That is, so long as the Portuguese plundered persons or groups not allied with Portugal, Portuguese kings supported it. Plundering sent a clear message that those who were the friends of Portugal would avoid the devastation faced by those who were not.[8] As can be seen from numerous examples offered in this book, this tactic was a typical and royally-approved process operative in Morocco.

Second, the plunder frontier was not a static location; it moved constantly. For instance, if a local leader refused to ally with the Portuguese, then he and his people were fair game for plunder. But, if after a few months or years of this he changed his mind and allied with the Portuguese, they no longer had the right to plunder his wealth. Consequently, those wishing to enrich themselves through plunder had to move on to another unallied region. Because a percentage of plunder was claimed by the king as income and used by his agents to fund imperial expenses, the continual expansion of the plunder frontier became an economic necessity. Afonso de Albuquerque, the governor of India (1509-1515), worried that if all the local Indian leaders concluded peaceful relations with the Portuguese, then he would be unable to pay wages and meet imperial expenses. Peace was bad for empire.[9]

A similar situation befell the Portuguese in Morocco. In one case, Yahya-u-Ta'fuft, the *alcaide dos mouros* of Dukkala from 1511 to 1518, complained that the Portuguese in Safi hated him because he had restored peace to Dukkala in 1517; consequently, they no longer had an easy source of income from the plunder of rebellious Moroccans. Two decades later, in 1536, a large group of Portuguese soldiers in Azamor requested that they be allowed to return to Portugal, the recently-concluded peace with the Sa`adids having precluded any raiding activity and was thus prejudicial to their wealth (*fazenda*).[10] Furthermore, note that it was in the late 1520s, after the Sa`adids had stopped all Portuguese expansionist activities in Morocco, had cut into Portuguese raiding profits, and had begun to slowly tighten their noose around the

---

[8] Newitt, "Plunder," 19-20.

[9] Newitt, "Plunder," 22-23.

[10] For the Yahya-u-Ta'fuft episode, see chapter eight. The 1536 Azamor episode is recounted in chapter two.

Portuguese zones of influence, that King D. João III first seriously considered abandoning the southern Moroccan fortresses (see below).

Unlike Newitt's unidirectional plunder frontier in Portuguese India, the plunder frontier in Morocco was also exploited by non-Portuguese. Small groups of Moroccans, usually called "thieves" in Portuguese sources, raided near Portuguese cities, seizing livestock and taking Portuguese captives. Allied Moroccans were kidnapped by their fellow Moroccans who falsely claimed that they were *mouros de guerra*, meaning that they could legally be enslaved, and then sold at Portuguese slave auctions. Meanwhile, taking advantage of the periodic instability away from the Portuguese fortresses, various tribal groups conducted raids against each other, typically to seize grain and livestock.

Although the notion of the plunder frontier can help us understand Portuguese behavior in Morocco, the Portuguese urge to plunder Morocco for quick gain was tempered by the fact that they needed Moroccan allies and their goodwill in order to maintain their trading and tribute relationships and expand their zone of influence. They sought these things by two key means: treating allies with honor and supporting allies materially. As I have argued elsewhere, the Portuguese viewed honor as a right to respect, both from one's social equals and from one's social inferiors.[11]

Honor mattered deeply to Moroccans as well, not just to the Portuguese. Yahya-u-Ta`fuft, for example, addressed the issue of honor by imposing a fine under the legal code (*qanūn*) he established for Moroccans he governed by his *alcaidaria*: "Whosoever publicly recalls the past dishonor [*`ār*] of anyone owes two *waqiyyas* or twenty *dinars* or a bull." While there were some among the Portuguese leadership in Morocco who treated allied Moroccan elites with respect, many were not treated the way they should have been.[12] Mistreatment ran counter to goodwill.

Material support for allies was extremely important. As discussed in chapter six, allies were given gifts, largely of cloth and

---

[11] Matthew T. Racine, "Service and Honor in Sixteenth-Century Portuguese North Africa: Yahya-u-Ta`fuft and Portuguese Noble Culture," *Sixteenth Century Journal* 32 (2001): 67-90, esp. 68-71.

[12] "*Qanūn* of Yahya-u-Ta`fuft," n.l., 16-25 June 1512, *SIHMP*, 1:318.

clothing (though also including money and spices), when they first allied with the Portuguese. As long as they remained loyal, top *alcaides dos mouros* were paid an annual salary and allowed to keep a twenty percent of booty seized during military operations on behalf of the Portuguese. Meanwhile, the Portuguese provided them with iron for horseshoes, materials to repair town and village defenses, and assistance in ransoming their men who had been captured.

Abandonment

Ultimately, the Portuguese failed in the objective originally articulated by D. João II and D. Manuel to conquer Fez and Marrakech and subject all of Morocco to their suzerainty. There are many reasons for this failure. The two most obvious and perhaps most important of these reasons are the inability of the Portuguese to field a sufficiently large military force to accomplish these goals – both because of the expense and the sheer number of soldiers needed – and the increasingly dispersed nature of the Portuguese empire by the 1520s, which did not allow a concentration of effort in any one area of the globe. Unlike the Spanish, who rallied a substantial number of Indian allies to help them destroy the Aztec capital of Tenochtitlán in 1521, the Portuguese could never assemble an army large enough to challenge seriously Fez or Marrakech.

Despite its ability to enrich many individual Portuguese, Jewish, and Moroccan plunderers and merchants, the Moroccan frontier was never very hospitable to the Portuguese royal treasury. The fortresses were expensive to maintain, both in terms of money and men. As discussed in chapter four, the yearly expenditure on the four Portuguese fortresses in southern Morocco probably averaged approximately 21 million *reis* per year, while income from these same fortresses often fell several million *reis* short of this figure. The southern Moroccan fortresses were operating at a deep loss during the early sixteenth century when the average yearly income for the Portuguese crown was only 80 million *reis*.[13] Thoughts of abandoning

---

[13] Newitt, "Plunder," 18. Writing in the first half of the seventeenth century, Frei Luís de Sousa agreed that abandonment of Safi and Azamor was the only sensible option: "*Anos havia que el-rei tinha entendido com seu grande juízo e bom discurso que cumpria muito a seu Estado e fazenda descarregar-se das duas cidades de Safim e Azamor; porque, quanto ao Estado, era certo não lhe serem de utilidade nenhuma, visto Safim não ter porto, e o rio de Azamor não ser capaz*

the fortresses came as early as the late 1520s. Following the 1524/5 Sa`adid conquest of Marrakech, Portuguese influence in the region slowly deteriorated and their zone of control and alliance began to shrink.

In 1529, King D. João III requested that his councilors and the important nobles of the realm respond to the question of whether or not most of the Moroccan fortresses should be abandoned. The responses, known as *pareceres*, were divided, though most favored maintaining the fortresses. One of the respondents, Gonçalo Mendes Sacoto, the former *capitão* of Safi (1522-1526), saw Morocco as the lynchpin of the Portuguese empire: "Morocco had been taken for the service of God and constituted a light that should it ever cease to shine would being disasters to the rest of the empire." For the moment, D. João III maintained the fortresses.

The next few years were ambivalent ones for the king. In 1531, he concluded a secret negotiation with several influential Jews in Marrakech, promising them that if he or his *capitães* conquered the city, the Jews and their families would be protected. During the following year, the king instructed his Roman ambassador to make a preemptive request of Pope Clement VII for permission to demolish all of his Moroccan fortresses except Ceuta, Tangiers, and Arzila, thus concentrating Portuguese power in the north of Morocco. Then, in 1534, the king asked for another series of *pareceres*. This time the responses were more evenly divided, though those who wished to maintain the fortresses were the most persuasive.

The events of 1540 began to convince even the Portuguese hawks that it was time to think twice about maintaining a large presence in Morocco. During the final months of 1540, Safi had faced almost daily raids from the Shyadma, Gharbiyya, and Shawiyya tribes, now loyal to the Sa`adids. While these raids resulted in the deaths of many more Moroccans than Portuguese, they created a virtual siege around Safi and led to a lack of supplies that, according to *capitão* D. Rodrigo de Castro, had resulted in the starvation deaths of nearly every horse in the city as their grain supplies were redirected to people. While the Portuguese at Safi eventually killed enough Moroccans and negotiated

---

de navios de importância; e quanto à fazenda, era demasiado o custo que lhe faziam, sem resultar dele nenhum fruito de consideração" (*AJ*, 2:208).

with the Sharif in Marrakech to stop the attacks by January 1541, it was clear that the situation was worsening.[14]

It was, as noted previously, the siege, beginning in September 1540, and eventual capture of Santa Cruz by Sa'adid forces in March 1541 that finally swayed the opinion of the realm. In April 1541, D. João III requested a third set of *pareceres*. This time, the responses were favorable to abandonment of all fortresses in the path of the Sa'adids. As a result, the king abandoned Safi and Azamor beginning in October 1541 (the evacuation was completed sometime in early 1542) and resolved to strengthen Mazagão.[15]

The abandonment was a relatively orderly process, with the women and children evacuated first. All of the important financial documents appear to have been returned to Portugal, though few of them have survived into the present. In one instance, the receipts for the *feitoria* of Azamor were transported by ship from Azamor to Vila Nova de Portimão in the Algarve. There the man in charge of these books, Pedro Álvares de Faria, rented a mule at a cost of 740 *reis* so that he could transport himself and the books to Lisbon, "not wanting to risk such important documents to the sea."[16] Other documents undoubtedly were left behind or destroyed, leading to one of the reasons that the documentary record for these fortresses is so patchy. Soldiers were the last to evacuate Safi and Azamor. They were ordered to demolish important defensive structures and then remove or destroy all artillery, ammunition, and powder from the city.[17]

---

[14] *AJ*, 2:146-149.

[15] José Alberto Rodrigues da Silva Tavim, *Os judeus na expansão portuguesa em Marrocos durante o século XVI: origens e actividades duma comunidade* (Braga: Edições APPACDM Distrital de Braga, 1997), 336; Joaquim Veríssimo Serrão, *História de Portugal* (Lisbon: Verbo, 1978), 3:39-41; Maria Augusta Lima Cruz Fagundes, "Documentos inéditos para a história dos portugueses em Azamor," *Arquivos do Centro Cultural Portugues* 2 (1970): 123-124; "L'Évacuation des places portugaises du Maroc sous Jean III," in *SIHMP*, 4:335-349. Texts of the 1529, 1534, and 1541 *pareceres* can be found in *SIHMP*, 2:443-452, 490-494, 521-525, 551-553, 637-639, 649-699, 702-703; 3:1-14, 18-21, 337-383.

[16] Fagundes, "Documentos," 168. This quote also speaks to the nature of maritime journeysduring this period, even brief ones in friendly waters.

[17] "L'Évacuation des places portugaises," *SIHMP*, 4:335-336 and *AJ*, 2:208-211. Several months after Azamor had been completely abandoned, Luís de Loureiro, the *capitão* of Mazagão, recommended to the king that he send some ships upriver to shell Azamor so as to make it inhospitable should the Sa'adids decide to use it as a base

The interest in the abandoned cities did not end immediately. During the early 1550s, the Sa`adids faced attacks from the Turks who were seeking to expand into Morocco. To prevent this, the Sa`adids had to commit the majority of their military might to the eastern part of their kingdom. In 1553, the Portuguese in Mazagão, using information from former Portuguese captives and friendly Moroccans, concluded that it would be easy to retake Azamor "with very few men."[18] King D. João III was not interested.

The headaches did not stop for D. João III once Safi and Azamor had been vacated. The people who had lived in these cities wanted to be reimbursed for the losses of the property they had abandoned. Others, especially high-ranking officials and military personnel, wanted to be reassigned to posts as lucrative or as prestigious as those they had held in Morocco. Over the three years from 1542 to 1544, the king disbursed 6,730,000 *reis* in damages to former residents of Safi and Azamor. Moreover, he granted offices in the Azores and in India to those who had lost their incomes. For example, Lançarote de Freitas, formerly the *feitor* and *almoxarife* of Azamor, became the *feitor* of Cananor in India.[19]

Perhaps it is best to end this book by contemplating Lançarote de Freitas, a Portuguese Finnegan whose Moroccan ending, like that of Joyce's title character, was simultaneously a continuation and new beginning. It is better, perhaps, to contemplate his success, loyalty, and optimism, than to contemplate the broken bodies, minds, and souls of

---

("Letter from Luís de Loureiro to D. João III," Mazagão, 15 December 1542, *SIHMP*, 4:117-118).

[18] "Letter from Vicente Riscado to D. João III," Mazagão, 28 April 1553, *SIHMP*, 5:11-12. Turkish agents actually succeeded in assassinating Sharif Muhammad al-Sheikh in 1557, but were unable to exploit this act to conquer Morocco. Still, the fear of Turkish expansion remained a key factor in Sa`adid policy for the remainder of the sixteenth century. Jamil M. Abun-Nasr, *A History of the Maghrib in the Islamic Period* (New York: Cambridge University Press, 1987), 155-158, 212-214 and Weston Cook, Jr., *The Hundred Years War for Morocco: Gunpowder and the Military Revolution in the Early Modern Muslim World* (San Francisco: Westview Press, 1994), 217-272

[19] Fagundes, "Documentos," 169-171. Chronicler frei Luís de Sousa discovered a note in the papers of the Count of Castanheira that claims the king had to disburse 300,000 *cruzados* (or 120,000,000 *reis*) in 1542 alone in order to pay for the evacuation, to fund construction on Mazagão, and to reimburse people for their income and property losses when Safi and Azamor were abandoned (*AJ*, 2:212). This amount seems excessive, but given the lack of financial records for these cities, it is difficult to assess.

Conclusion

Portuguese men and women held in captivity for years or those many Moroccans, victims of bloodthirsty raids who were either killed or enslaved and dispersed throughout Europe, with no hope of ever again seeing their homes and families.

The story told within these pages is not a happy one, if it can be so judged, but it is a human one. A tale of people put in difficult circumstances making do as best they could. Many died. Many were miserable. Many profited handsomely. The story of the Moroccan frontier is simply the story of human interaction. It may seem more Romantic, more Technicolor, but people acted the way they have always acted and, if current events are any indication, will continue to act for the foreseeable future.

There will be many more *Iliads* to write.

Appendix 1: Maps

Maps

Map 1: Regional Overview

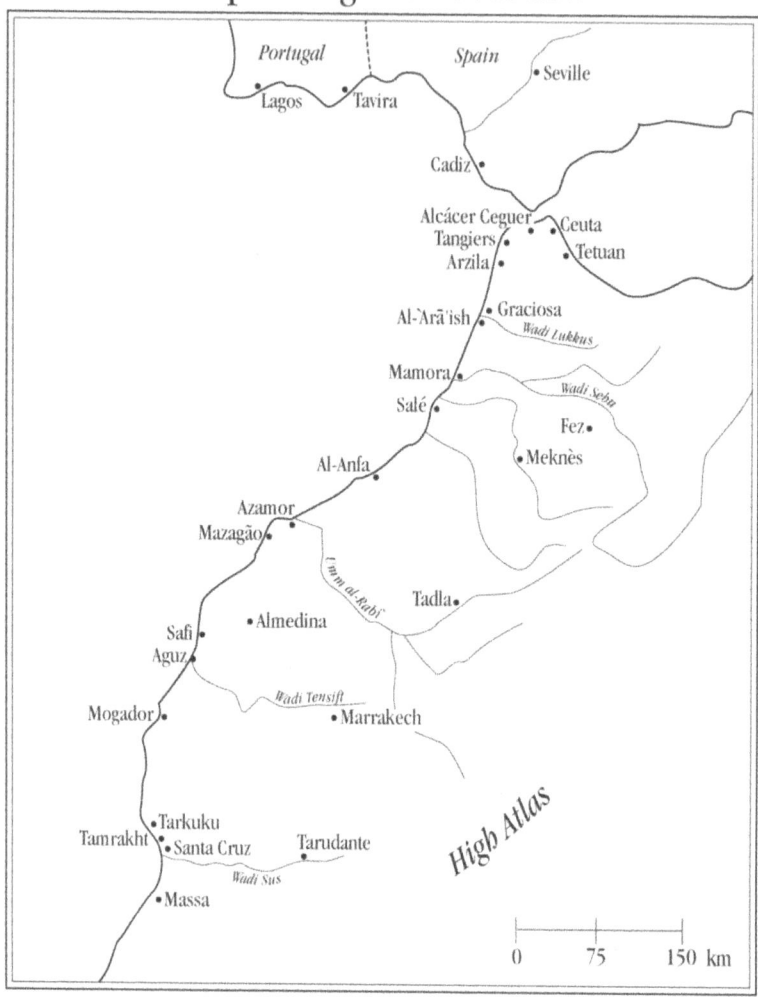

Map 2: Dukkala – Settlements mentioned in the text.

Maps

Map 3: Major Tribes of the Dukkala Region

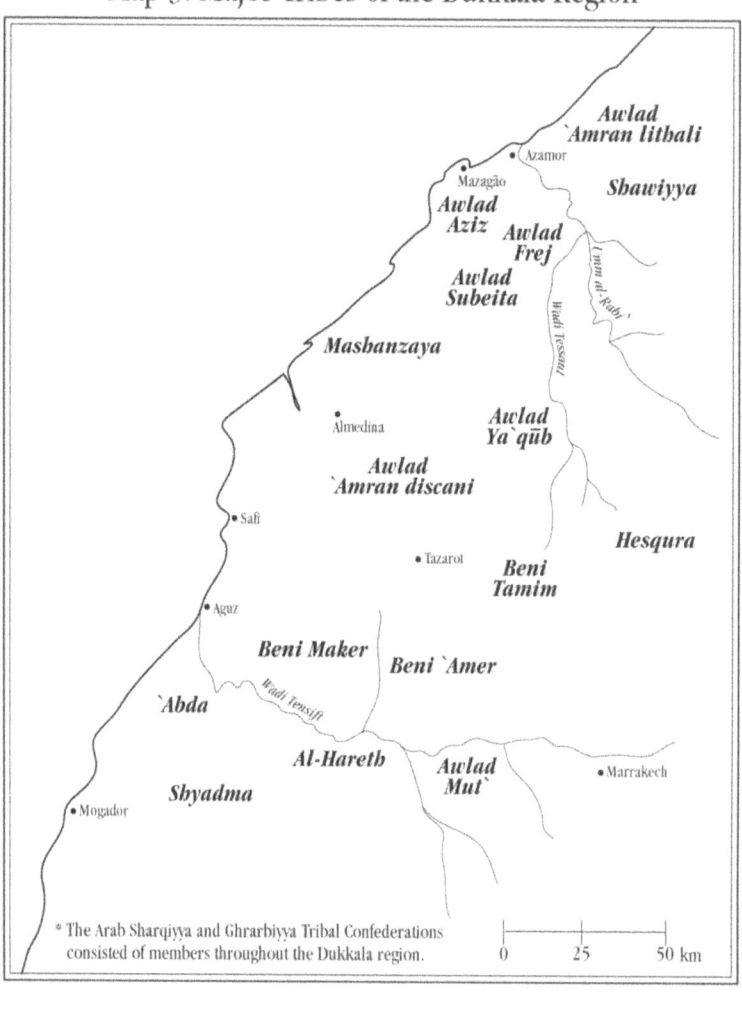

Appendix 2: Important Leaders in Portugal and Morocco

Portuguese Kings

D. Afonso V   (1438-1481)
D. João II   (1481-1495)
D. Manuel   (1495-1521)
D. João III   (1521-1557)
D. Sebastião   (1557-1578)

Moroccan Leaders

Wattasids (Fez)
Muhammad al-Sheikh (1472-1501)
Muhammad al-Burtughali (1501-1526)
Bu Hasun (1526)
Muhammad al-Qaseri (1526-1545)
Ahmed (1547-1549) – Fez conquered by Sa`dids on 31 January 1549

Hintati (Marrakech)
Al-Naser bin Yūsuf al-Hintati (?-1520)
Muhammad Bu Shantuf al Hintati (1520-1524/5)
Muhammad al-Hintati (Lord of the Mountains; ?-1524/5)
(Marrakech conquered by Sa`dids in late 1524 or early 1525)

Sa`dids (Sus and later all Morocco)
Muhammed al-Qa'im (1509-1518)
Ahmed al-A`raj (1518-1544)[1]
Muhammad al-Sheikh (1518-1557)[2]
Note: Ahmed and Muhammad were co-rulers until Muhammad arrested his brother, Ahmed, in 1544

---

[1] Ruler of Marrakech from 1524-1544.

[2] Sultan of Morocco from 1549 until his death.

Appendix 3: List of *Capitães* in Southern Morocco from 1505-1542

Sources for Appendix 3: A. H. de Oliveira Marques, *História de Portugal* 13th ed. (Lisbon: Editorial Presença, 1997), 1:359-361; Joaquim Figanier, *História de Santa Cruz do Cabo de Gué (Agadir) 1505-1541* (Lisboa: Agência Geral das Colónias, 1945), 365; *SIHMP*, 2:602n1, 3:24, 4:425, 5:174, 206; ANTT, CC I, 55, 38; CC II, 92, 90; CC II, 93, 81.

I. Azamor

Rui Barreto and D. João de Meneses	1513-1514
D. Pedro de Sousa	1514-1516
Simão Correia	1516-1518
D. Álvaro de Noronha	1518-1525
Jorge Viegas	1525-1529
António Leite	1529-1530
D. Pedro de Mascarenhas	1530-1534
Lançarote de Freitas (interim)	1534-1535
João Carvalho (interim)	1535
D. Álvaro de Abranches	1535-1537
António Leite	1537-1541
D. Fernando de Noronha	1541-1542

II. Mogador

Diogo de Azambuja	1507-1509
Francisco de Miranda	1509
D. Pedro de Azevedo	1509-1510
Nicolau de Sousa	1510

III. Mazagão

Martim Afonso de Melo	1514-1517
António Leite	1517-1529
António das Neves (substitute)	1520-1521
(Unknown)	1529-1536
Manuel de Sande	1536-1537

João Gomes	1537-1541
António Leite (substitute)	1539
Luís de Loureiro	1541-1548

IV. Safi

Diogo de Azambuja	1508-1509
Pedro de Azevedo	1509-1510
Nuno Fernandes de Ataíde	1510-1516
Nuno Gato (interim)	1516
Dom Nuno de Mascarenhas	1516-1522
Gonçalo Mendes Sacoto	1522-1525
Garcia de Melo	1525-1529
Francisco Lopes Girão	1529-1530
Jerónimo de Melo	1531-1533 [?]
D. João de Faro	1533 [?]-1534
Rui Freire (interim)	1534
Luís de Loureiro (interim)	1534
D. Garcia de Noronha (interim)	1534
D. Jorge de Noronha (interim)	1535
D. Rodrigo de Castro	1535-1541
Luís de Loureiro	1541-1542

V. Santa Cruz

João Lopes de Sequeira	1505-1513
D. Francisco de Castro	1513-1517
Pero Leitão (interim)	1517
D. Francisco de Castro	1517-1521
Simão Gonçalves da Costa (interim)	1521-1523
António Leitão de Gamboa	1523-1525
Luís Sacoto	1525-1528
António Leitão de Gamboa	1528-1529
António Rodrigues de Parada (interim)	1529
Simão Gonçalves da Costa	1530-1533
Rui Dias de Aguiar (interim)	1533
Simão Gonçalves da Câmara (interim)	1533-1534
D. Guterres de Monroi	1534

Capitães

Luís de Loureiro	1534-1538
D. Guterres de Monroi	1538-1541

Appendix 4: Top Portuguese Office Holders Other Than *Capitães*

Note: The dates listed below are those known with certainty. Many times, a person is listed as holding an office during a single year. Nevertheless, this individual may have held the office for several years before or after the date, but there is no proof of the individual's exact term in office.

I. Azamor

[**Note:** Unless otherwise indicated, the information for office holders in Azamor comes from the table between pages 124 and 125 in Maria Augusta Lima Cruz Fagundes, "Documentos Ineditos para a Historia dos Portugueses em Azamor," *Arquivos do Centro Cultural Portugues* 2 (1970).]

Contador

    Nuno Gato, 1513-March/April 1514
    António Leite, March/April 1514-Spring 1520
        Martim Vaz, substitute during parts of 1516 and 1519[1]
        Bastião Leite, substitute during parts of 1518 and 1519[2]
    João Mendes, Spring 1520-1541
        Vasco da Silveira, substituted at end of 1522
        Fernão Pinto, substitute during summer 1523
        Pedro Alvares, substitute during July 1524[3]
        Diogo Machado, substitute from late 1525 to February 1526
        Lançarote de Freitas, interim from February 1526 to early 1528
        Diogo Machado, substitute in 1527[4]
        Manuel Mendes, interim during 1537
        Diogo de Neiva, substitute from late 1537 to early 1538

---

[1] ANTT, CC I, 24, 31, published in Fagundes, 151-152.

[2] ANTT, CC II, 73, 2.

[3] ANTT, CC II, 117, 8.

[4] ANTT, CC I, 35, 89.

Escrivão dos Contos
        Martim Vaz, 1515-1519[5]
        António da Mina, 1520[6]

Feitor
        Martim Reinal, 1486-1501
        João Lopes de Meca, 22 December 1509-
           12 November 1510[7]
        Miguel Moniz, 1513-March 1514
        Lançarote de Freitas, March 1514-April 1519[8]
           Álvaro Nunes, substitute in 1517[9]
           Álvaro do Cadaval, substitute from May 1519-
              August 1520
        Benito Maça, August 1520- December 1524
        Lançarote de Freitas, December 1524-mid-1530[10]
           Benito Maça, substitute during mid-1526[11]
        Alexandre de Freitas, mid-1530-Spring [?] 1535
           Benito Maça, substitute in 1533[12]
        António Barbudo, Spring [?] 1535-Autumn [?] 1537
        João Rodrigues, Autumn [?] 1537-August 1539
        Francisco Gil, August 1539-1541
        Pedro Álvares de Faria, 1541[13]

Almoxarife
        Álvaro do Cadaval, 1513-1519

---

[5] ANTT, CC I, 24, 31, published in Fagundes, 151-152 and ANTT, CC II, 59, 83.

[6] ANTT, CC II, 93, 23.

[7] *SIHMP*, 1:231n1.

[8] ANTT, CC I, 24, 53.

[9] ANTT, CC II, 72, 108.

[10] ANTT, CC II, 121, 180.

[11] ANTT, CC II, 134, 147.

[12] ANTT, CC I, 50, 89.

[13] ANTT, NA 628.

Benito Maça, 1519- December 1524[14]
Lançarote de Freitas, December 1524-mid-1530
    Benito Maça, substitute during mid-1526
Alexandre de Freitas, mid-1530-Spring [?] 1535
António Barbudo, Spring [?] 1535-Autumn [?] 1537[15]
João Rodrigues, Autumn [?] 1537-August 1539
Francisco Gil, August 1539-1541

Porteiro dos Contos da Alfândega
António Sobrinho, 1514[16]
Francisco da Costa Colaço, 1514[17]
António Fernandes, 1514-1515[18]
Afonso Pires, 1517-1523[19]
João Gaioso, 1520[20]

Recebedor da Alfândega
Francisco Gomes, 1523-1529[21]

Escrivão da Alfândega
Pedro Lopes, 1526[22]

Adail
Francisco de Almeida, 1513-December 1516
António Fernandes de Quadros, December 1516-1517
Unknown, 1518
Vasco Fernandes César, 1519-1520
Unknown, 1521

---

[14] ANTT, CC II, 80, 88.

[15] He may have served during or until 1539. See ANTT, CC I, 65, 26.

[16] ANTT, CC II, 46, 94; CC II, 47, 112.

[17] ANTT, CC II, 53, 96.

[18] ANTT, CC II, 53, 34; CC II, 55, 99; CC II, 60, 169.

[19] ANTT, CC II, 68, 113; CC II, 109, 6.

[20] ANTT, CC II, 91, 60.

[21] *GTT*, 10:421.

[22] ANTT, CC II, 134, 147.

António Gonçalves, Spring 1522-1530
    António Fernandes de Quadros, substituted in 1523 and 1525[23]
Unknown, 1530-1536
Vicente Álvares, end 1537-early 1538
Unkown, 1538-1541

Almocadém

Andre Mendes, 1523[24]

Apontador

Francisco da Costa Colaço, 1514 [?][25]
António Fernandes, 1515-1516[26]
Martinho Fernandes, 1516[27]
Afonso Pires, 1521[28]

Ouvidor

Martinho de Aguiar, 1514[29]
Diogo Fragoso, 1517[30]
Fernão Gonçalves, 1523[31]

Juíz dos Órfãos

Diogo Fragoso, 1517[32]
Vicente Rodrigues Evangelho, 1530[33]
Francisco Farzão, 1536 [?]-1541[34]

---

[23] ANTT, CC II, 112, 24 and CC II, 129, 173.

[24] ANTT, CC I, 30, 16.

[25] ANTT, CC II, 53, 96.

[26] ANTT, CC II, 59, 61; CC II, 65, 15.

[27] ANTT, CC II, 64, 19.

[28] ANTT, CC II, 97, 64.

[29] ANTT, CC II, 51, 129.

[30] ANTT, CC I, 21, 100.

[31] *SIHMP*, 2:330n1.

[32] ANTT, CC I, 21, 100.

[33] *SIHMP*, 2:515.

Tabelião
>> Mateus Fernandes, 1513-1516[35]
>> Artur Golayo, 1513-?[36]
>> João Godinho, 1517-1523[37]
>> Gonçalo Coelho, 1523[38]
>> Francisco Pires, 1536[39]

Miscellaneous
> *Piloto da Barra*[40]
>> João da Rua, 1514-1517
>> Ignacio Afonso, 1517-1537
>>> Manuel da Rua, 1517-1525
>>> João Fernandes, 1519-1523[41]
>>> João Dias, 1525-1537

> *Mestre das Obras*
>> Afonso Gonçalves, 1520[42]

> *Mestre da Obra da Ponte*
>> Martim Teixiera, 28 March 1520-1522[43]

> *Vedor das Obras*
>> Nuno Gato, 1513-February 1514[44]
>> Vasco da Pina, March 1514-July 1514[45]

---

[34] *SIHMP*, 5:120.

[35] ANTT, NA 883.

[36] *SIHMP*, 1:401n3.

[37] *SIHMP*, 2:315 and *GTT*, 10:421-424.

[38] *GTT*, 10:421-424.

[39] ANTT, CC I, 57, 6.

[40] Unless otherwise noted, all information on *pilotos da barra* comes from *SIHMP*, 2:266n3.

[41] ANTT, CC II, 108, 87.

[42] *SIHMP*, 2:271.

[43] *SIHMP*, 2:253n4.

[44] ANTT, CC II, 44, 168.

Manuel Lopes, 1516-1517[46]
António Fernandes, 1517-1518[47]

Recebedor dos Mantimentos
Pedro Álvares de Faria, 1513-1516 & ?-1541[48]

Escrivão de Recebedor dos Mantimentos
Bartolomeu de Final, ?-1542[49]

Alcaide do Mar
Lopo Vaz, 1513-1517[50]
Pedro Homem, 1517-?[51]

Escrivão do Campo de El Rey
Gonçalo Lopes, 1523[52]

Alfaqueque mor
João Fernandes, 1516-?[53]

II. Mazagão

Contador
António Leite, 1515-[1517?][54]

---

[45] *SIHMP*, 1:522.

[46] ANTT, CC II, 64, 105 and CC II, 72, 44.

[47] ANTT, NA 751.

[48] ANTT, CC I, 71, 60; ANTT, NA 918; NA 628; Fagundes, 168. He served in the same capacity in Ceuta during at least 1532 to 1537 (ANTT, NA 621, 625, 741, 753).

[49] ANTT, CC I, 71, 60.

[50] *SIHMP*, 1:581n3.

[51] *SIHMP*, 1:581n3.

[52] ANTT, CC II, 108, 22.

[53] ANTT, CC I, 22, 58, published in Fagundes, 145-147.

[54] ANTT, CC II, 62, 19.

Portuguese Office Holders

Escrivão dos Contos
    Duarte Rodrigues, 1516[55]
    Miguel Leite, 1536-1537[56]

Feitor
    João de Oliva, 1540[57]

Escrivão da Feitoria
    Duarte Rodrigues, 1516[58]

Almoxarife
    Álvaro de Cadaval, 1517[59]
    Rui Coteno, 1521-1522[60]
    João Gomes, 1522-1523[61]
    Lopo Lobato, 1533-1536[62]
    Jerónimo do Couto, 1536-1537[63]
    João de Oliva, 1540[64]

Recebedor da Alfândega
    Afonso Feio, 1521[65]

Adail
    Francisco Marreiros, 1537[66]

---

[55] ANTT, CC II, 64, 83.

[56] *SIHMP*, 3:56, 86.

[57] ANTT, CC II, 234, 40, published in José Alberto Rodrigues da Silva Tavim, *Os judeus na expansão portuguesa em Marrocos durante o século XVI: origens e actividades duma comunidade* (Braga: Edições APPACDM Distrital de Braga, 1997), 559.

[58] ANTT, CC II, 64, 83.

[59] ANTT, CC II, 71, 32.

[60] ANTT, CC II, 98, 133 and CC II, 101, 55.

[61] ANTT, NA 581.

[62] ANTT, NA 740.

[63] *SIHMP*, 3:56, 85, 88.

[64] ANTT, CC II, 234, 40, published in Tavim, *Os judeus*, 559.

[65] ANTT, CC II, 95, 154.

[66] *SIHMP*, 3:92 and n.1.

Miscellaneous
    Vedor das Obras
        Vasco da Pina, July 1514-1517 [longer?][67]

    Escrivão das Obras
        Duarte Rodrigues, 1514-1516[68]

    Recebedor dos Manitmentos
        Vasco da Pina, 1513[69]

III. Safi

Contador
        João de Reboreda, 1508[70]
        Nuno Gato 1510-1519 [1522?][71]
        Vasco Martins de Fonseca, 1523[72]
        D. Henrique de Meneses, 1525[73]
        D. Henrique de Noronha, 1527-1541[74]

Escrivão dos Contos
        Bras da Pina, 1512[75]

Feitor
        Rui Fernandes de Almada, July 1491-June 1495[76]
        Lopo de Azevedo, July 1495-February 1498[77]

---

[67] *SIHMP*, 2:176n1.

[68] ANTT, CC II, 64, 83 and *SIHMP*, 1:584.

[69] ANTT, CC II, 43, 19.

[70] ANTT, CC II, 15, 75.

[71] *SIHMP*, 2:377n2.

[72] ANTT, CC II, 107, 81.

[73] ANTT, CC II, 124, 102.

[74] *SIHMP*, 2:411, 569.

[75] *SIHMP*, 1:311.

[76] *SIHMP*, 1:152.

> Nuno de Freitas, February 1498-September 1500[78]
> Nuno Fernandes, October 1500 [?]-April 1501[79]
> Pero Mendes, April 1501-December 1507[80]
> João Lopes de Alvim, December 1507-July 1508[81]
> Heitor Gonçalves, August 1508-September 1510[82]
> Estêvão de Aguiar, September 1510-Spring 1512[83]
> Heitor Gonçalves, Spring 1512-1514[84]
> Estêvão da Gama, 1515[85]
> Álvaro do Tojal, 1515-1516[86]
> João Lopes de Meca, 1517-1518[87]
> Luís Gonçalves, 1519-1522[88]
> João Pires, January 1524-1527 [or more?][89]
> Mendo de Brito, 1534[90]
> Gião Fialho, 1534-1535[91]
> Álvaro de Morais, 1535 [?]-1541[92]

Escrivão da Feitoria
> Cristóvão de Almeida, 1508-1512[93]

---

[77] *SIHMP*, 1:152n1.

[78] *SIHMP*, 1:152n1.

[79] *SIHMP*, 1:152n1.

[80] *SIHMP*, 1:152n1.

[81] *SIHMP*, 1:152n1.

[82] *DCC*, 34; *SIHMP*, 1:152n1; ANTT, CC II, 23, 143.

[83] *DCC*, 34 and ANTT, NA 137.

[84] ANTT, NA 138 and NA 604.

[85] ANTT, CC II, 99, 27.

[86] ANTT, CC II, 58, 122 and CC II, 63, 21.

[87] *SIHMP*, 1:231n1.

[88] *SIHMP*, 2:244n2.

[89] ANTT, CC II, 159, 131 and *SIHMP*, 2:411.

[90] ANTT, CC I, 52, 118.

[91] *SIHMP*, 3:15.

[92] *SIHMP*, 3:259, 503.

[93] ANTT, CC I, 12, 27; CC II, 15, 75.

Almoxarife
    Heitor Gonçalves, 1508
    Sebastião Lopes, 15 August 1508-15 July 1512[94]
    Lourenço Mendes, 1512-1513[95]
    Sebastiao Lopes, 1514-1520[96]
    Luís Gonçalves, 1520[97]
    João Pires, 1522-1527 [or more?][98]
    Gião Fialho, 1534-1535[99]
    Álvaro de Morais, 1535 [?]-1541[100]

Recebedor da Alfândega
    Salvador Gramacho, 1509-1510[101]

Porteiro dos Contos da Alfândega
    João Rodrigues, 1511-1516[102]
    Fernão Vaz, 1537[103]

Adail
    Lopo Barriga, 1508-1516
    Luís Gonçalves, 1519-1522[104]
    Baltasar Rodrigues, 1527-1537[105]
    Lopo Barriga (son of previous Lopo Barriga), ?-1541[106]

---

[94] *DCC*, 93.

[95] ANTT, NA 768.

[96] ANTT, CC II, 44, 98 and CC II, 92, 48.

[97] ANTT, CC II, 93, 32.

[98] ANTT, CC II, 104, 6; CC II, 107, 81; CC II, 124, 102; *SIHMP*, 2:411.

[99] ANTT, CC I, 55, 64 and *SIHMP*, 3:15.

[100] *SIHMP*, 3:259, 503.

[101] ANTT, CC II, 22, 19.

[102] ANTT, CdGA, 334 and ANTT, NA 597, f. 98v and 120v.

[103] *SIHMP*, 3:101.

[104] ANTT, CC II, 93, 32.

[105] *SIHMP*, 2:411, 3:99.

[106] "Letter from Lopo Barriga to D. João III," Safi, 29 June 1541, *SIHMP*, 3:450-451.

Portuguese Office Holders

Almocadém
  Diogo Lopes, 1511 [?]-1528[107]
  João Lopes, 1540 [?]-1541[108]
   Manuel Marques, 1541[109]

Ouvidor
  João de Abreu, 1511-?[110]
  Clement Gil, 1525[111]
  Luis Gonçalves Bocarro, 1537[112]

Tabelião
  Francisco Lopes, 1518[113]
  Francisco Ribeiro, 1523-1542[114]
  Gonçalo Pires, 1537[115]

Miscellaneous
 Recebedor dos Mantimentos
  Lopo Martines, 1508[116]
  António Tinoco, 1510[117]
  Álvaro do Tojal, 1515[118]

 Mestre das Obras
  João Luís, 1513-1524[119]

---

[107] *SIHMP*, 3:264n3 and ANTT, CC I, 39, 37.

[108] *SIHMP*, 3:263.

[109] *SIHMP*, 3:462.

[110] ANTT, NA. 597, f. 22v.

[111] ANTT, CC II, 123, 112.

[112] *SIHMP*, 3:99.

[113] Tavim, *Os judeus*, 536.

[114] ANTT, NA 884.

[115] *SIHMP*, 3:101.

[116] ANTT, CC II, 16, 36.

[117] ANTT, CC II, 24, 77.

[118] ANTT, CC I, 19, 18.

[119] *SIHMP*, 2:48n2.

>   Luís Dias, 1524-1526[120]
>   García da Bologna, 1526-?[121]
>   Lourenço Argueiro, 1540[122]

Vedor das Obras
>   Henrique de Parada, ?-1515[123]
>   Pedro Álvares de Faria, 1515-1517[124]
>   Jorge Machado, 1517-1520 [or longer?][125]
>   Simão Dias, 1540[126]

Recebedor das Obras
>   Pedro Álvares de Faria, 1516[127]

Alfaqueque mor
>   Nuno Gato, 1510-1519 [1522?][128]

IV. Santa Cruz

[**Note:** Unless otherwise indicated, the information for office holders in Santa Cruz comes from Joaquim Figanier, *História de Santa Cruz do Cabo de Gué (Agadir) 1505-1541* (Lisboa: Agência Geral das Colónias, 1945), 366-368.]

Contador
>   Luís Sacoto, 1518-1528[129]
>   Nuno Martins, substitute during 1521

---

[120] *SIHMP*, 2:48n2.

[121] *SIHMP*, 2:48n2.

[122] *SIHMP*, 3:250.

[123] ANTT, CC II, 60, 19.

[124] *SIHMP*, 2:48n3 and ANTT, CC I, 19, 6.

[125] *SIHMP*, 2:48n3 and ANTT, CC II, 92, 48.

[126] *SIHMP*, 3:250.

[127] ANTT, CC I, 20, 105.

[128] *SIHMP*, 1:309-310.

[129] *CSC*, 46n3.

Domingos Lopes Barreto, 1531-1536[130]
Francisco Machado, 20 September 1537-
11 March 1541

Escrivão dos Contos

Baltasar Barreto, late 1520s[131]
Afonso Rodrigues, 1533[132]
Francisco de Camões, 1534[133]

Feitor

João de Ferreira, ?-1513
Afonso Rodrigues, 1513-1517[134]
Pedro Lopes, 1517-September 1518[135]
Sebastião Gonçalves, September 1518-1519
João Gonçalves, 1518-1519 (feitor only)
Vicêncio Ambrum, 15 September 1519-15 June 1520
Francisco Rodrigues, 11 November 1520-12 May 1522
Vicêncio Ambrum, late 1522[136]
Miguel Pacheco, 1523[137]
Vicêncio Ambrum, 1525-1528(?)
António Rodrigues de Parada, 1528-1533
    Manuel Nunes Espargo, substitute in 1531[138]
Manuel Nunes Espargo, 1533-1534

---

[130] ANTT, CC I, 48, 4.

[131] "Letter from Simão Gonçalves da Costa to D. João III," Santa Cruz, 15 September 1529, *SIHMP*, 2:486 and *CSC*, 76n3.

[132] *SIHMP*, 1:470n1.

[133] *SIHMP*, 605-607.

[134] Between May and 30 July 1517 he was in Portugal to defend himself – successfully – against various accusations.

[135] ANTT, CC II, 73, 28.

[136] ANTT, CC II, 104, 83.

[137] ANTT, CC II, 109, 111.

[138] ANTT, CC I, 48, 14.

Vicêncio Ambrum, 1534-1540[139]
    Nuno Martins, substitute in 1538
António da Costa Sacoto, 1540-1541

Escrivão da Feitoria
Francisco Fernandes, 1513-1517 [?][140]
Manuel Rodrigues, 1534-1541[141]

Almoxarife
João de Ferreira, ?-1513
Afonso Rodrigues, 1513-1516
João Gonçalves, 1516-1518[142]
Sebastião Gonçalves, September 1518-1519
Vicêncio Ambrum, 15 September 1519-15 June 1520
Francisco Rodrigues, September 1520-12 May 1522[143]
Vicêncio Ambrum, late 1522[144]
Miguel Pacheco, 1523
Bento da Costa, 1524-1525[145]
Vicêncio Ambrum, 1525-1528(?)
António Rodrigues de Parada, 1528-1533
Manuel Nunes Espargo, 1531-1534[146]
Vicêncio Ambrum, 1534-1540
    Nuno Martins, substitute in 1538
António da Costa Sacoto, 1540-1541

Escrivão do Almoxarifado
Afonso Rodrigues, 1533[147]

---

[139] ANTT, CC I, 43, 42; CC I, 68, 4; Figanier, 324-325 and 333-335.

[140] *SIHMP*, 1:470n1.

[141] *SIHMP*, 2:701, 3:35, 122 and *CSC*, 120-124.

[142] ANTT, CC II, 67, 13; CC II, 69, 1; CC II, 74, 145.

[143] ANTT, CC II, 91, 107.

[144] ANTT, CC II, 104, 83.

[145] ANTT, CC II, 119, 106; CC II, 128, 106.

[146] ANTT, CC I, 48, 4.

[147] *SIHMP*, 1:470n1.

Francisco de Camões, 1534[148]

Porteiro dos Contos da Alfândega
    Estêvão Ramos, 1524-1525[149]
    Tristão da Mota, 1534[150]
    Manuel Rodrigues, late 1534[151]

Adail
    João da Costa, 21 April 1516-15 May 1518
    Fernão Taveira, 3 July 1518-?
    António Rodrigues de Parada, 1529-1537[152]
        Alonso de Sorita, substitute during 1533(?)-1534
    João Dias Casado, 20 August 1538-12 September 1540
    Simão Jorge, 12 September 1540-12 March 1541

Ouvidor
    Francisco da Costa, 1537-1541[153]

Juíz dos Órfãos
    Francisco Machado, 1536[?]-1541[154]

Tabelião
    Bartolomeu de Final, 1524[155]
    João Álvares, 1531[156]

---

[148] *SIHMP*, 1:605-607.

[149] ANTT, CC II, 119, 106; CC II, 127, 54.

[150] ANTT, CC I, 52, 93.

[151] *SIHMP*, 2:701.

[152] ANTT, CC I, 43, 49.

[153] *CSC*, 98

[154] *SIHMP*, 3:53, 341.

[155] *SIHMP*, 2:331.

[156] Tavim, *Os judeus*, 547.

Appendix 5: Weights and Measures

Weights and Measures

Currency

    one ceitil = 1/6 real[1]
    one cruzado = 390 reis (1496-1514); 400 reis (1514-1537)[2]
    one dobra (aka: dinar) = 8 tomins[3] or 4 reis
    one mitical = 420 reis[4]
    one onça of silver = 320 reis[5]
    one tomin = 1/2 real[6]
    one vinten (aka: real de prata) = 20 reis[7]
    one wakuiyya = 10 dinars (dobras)[8]

Weights

    one alcola = 22 to 24 pounds (oddly, this measure was used mainly for oil)[9]
    one arratel = 12 or 16 ounces, depending one the region, and was equal to a Portuguese pound[10]
    one arroba = 25 to 32 arrateis[11]
    one marco = 8 ounces or half an arratel[12]
    one quintal = 4 arrobas (c. 60 kg)[13]

---

[1] *SIHMP*, 2:308n1.

[2] John Vogt, *Portuguese Rule on the Gold Coast, 1469-1682* (Athens, Georgia: University of Georgia Press, 1979), 221. During the first part of the sixteenth century, the *cruzado* was valued for a time in the mid-380 *reis* range (*SIHMP*, 1:224n3).

[3] *SIHMP*, 1:43n1.

[4] *SIHMP*, 1:225.

[5] *SIHMP*, 2:6n1.

[6] *SIHMP*, 1:312n2. On *SIHMP*, 2:316, a Portuguese writes that in 1523 "um tomi, que são quarto reis."

[7] *SIHMP*, 1:263n3.

[8] *SIHMP*, 1:323n2.

[9] *SIHMP*, 1:314n2.

[10] *SIHMP*, 1:43n3.

[11] *SIHMP*, 1:43n2.

[12] *SIHMP*, 1:44n14.

[13] *SIHMP*, 1:43n2.

Measures

    one alqueire = just under 14 liters[14]
    one braça = approximately 2.2 meters[15]
    one cafiz = one moio
    one camel load = 25 alqueires
    one canada = 2.622 liters
    one covado = slightly under 3 palms (approx. 60 cm.)[16]
    one fanega = 4 alqueires[17]
    one farroba = approximately 100 liters[18]
    one légua = five kilometers[19]
    one moio = 828 liters[20]
    one resma = ream of paper (20 quires or 500 sheets)
    one sa` (starts with Arabic letter *sod*) = a Moroccan measure of between 40 and 50 liters[21]
    one vara = 5 palms (approx. one meter)[22]

---

[14] *SIHMP*, 1:44n12.

[15] *SIHMP*, 1:273n2.

[16] *SIHMP*, 1:44n13.

[17] *SIHMP*, 1:301n1.

[18] *SIHMP*, 1:312n1.

[19] *SIHMP*, 1:481n1.

[20] *SIHMP*, 1:90n1.

[21] *SIHMP*, 1:302n1.

[22] *SIHMP*, 1:44n13.

Bibliography of Sources

I. Published Primary Sources

Africanus, Johannes Leonnes (Hassan ibn Muhammad al-Wazzan). *The History and Description of Africa*. Translated by John Pory. 3 vols. London: Hakluyt Society, 1896.

Africanus, Johannes Leonnes (Hassan ibn Muhammad al-Wazzan). *Description de l'Afrique*. Translated by A. Epaulard. 2 vols. Paris: Adrien-Maisonneuve, 1956.

Andrade, Francisco de. *Chronica de D. Joao III*. Coimbra, 1796.

Cenival, Pierre de, David Lopes, Robert Ricard, and Chantal de La ' Véronne. *Les sources inédites de l'histoire du Maroc. Première série – dynastie sa`dienne, archives et bibliothèques de Portugal*. 5 vols. Paris: P. Geuthner, 1934-53.

Coelho, José Ramos Coelho. *Alguns documentos do Archivo Nacional da Torre do Tombo ácerca das navegações e conquistas portuguezas publicados por ordem do governo de sua majestade fidelissima ao celebrar-se a commemoração quadricentenaria do descobrimento da America*. Lisboa: Imprensa Nacional, 1892.

Coelho, P. M. Laranjo and David Lopes. *Documentos inéditos de Marrocos: chancelaria de D. João II*. Lisboa: Imprensa Nacional, 1943.

Ford, J. D. M. and L. G. Moffatt, ed. *Letters of the Court of John III, King of Portugal*. Cambridge, Mass.: Harvard University Press, 1933.

Góis, Damião de. *Crónica do felicíssimo rei D. Manuel*. 4 vols. Coimbra: University of Coimbra, 1949-1955.

Lopes, David. *Textos em aljamía portuguesa; documentos para a historia do dominio português em Safim, extrahidos dos originaes da Torre do Tombo*.
Lisboa: Imprensa nacional, 1897.

--------. *Textos em aljamia portuguesa*. 2nd. ed. Lisbon: Imprensa Nacional, 1940.

Mendonça, Agostinho de Gavy de. *História do cerco de Mazagão*. Lisbon, 1890.

Ordenações Manuelinas. 5 vols. facs. of 1786 ed. ed. Lisbon: Calouste Gulbenkian Foundation, 1984.

Resende, Garcia de. *Cancioneiro Geral*. Lisbon, 1516.

Rodrigues, Bernardo, *Anais de Arzila*, 2 vols. (Lisbon: Academia das Ciências, 1915).

Sousa, Fr. Luís de. *Anais de D. João III*. 2 vols. Lisbon: Livraria Sá da Costa, 1954.

Zurara, Gomes Eanes de. *Crónica da Tomada de Ceuta*. Mem Martins: Publicações Europa-América, 1992.

--------. *Crónica do Conde D. Pedro de Meneses*. Lisbon: Fundação Calouste Gulbenkian, 1997.

Bibliography

II. Secondary Sources

Abulafia, David. "The End of Muslim Sicily." In *Muslims Under Latin Rule, 1100-1300*, ed. James M. Powell, 103-33. Princeton: Princeton University Press, 1990.

-------- and Nora Berend, eds. *Medieval Frontiers: Concepts and Practices*. Burlington, Vermont: Ashgate, 2002.

Abun-Nasr, Jamil M. *A History of the Maghrib in the Islamic Period*. New York: Cambridge University Press, 1987.

Aizenberg, E. "*Una judía muy fermosa*: The Jewess as Sex Object in Medieval Spanish Literature and Lore." *La Corónica* 12 (1984): 187-194.

Albuquerque, Luís de and Francisco Contente Domingues. *Dicionário de história dos descobrimentos portugueses*. 2 vols. Lisbon: Caminho, 1994.

Arnade, Peter. "City, State, and Public Ritual in the Late-Medieval Burgundian Netherlands." *Comparative Studies in Society and History* 39, no. 2 (1997): 300-318.

Assis, Y. T. "Sexual Behaviour in Mediaeval Hispano-Jewish Society." In *Jewish History: Essays in Honour of Chimen Abramsky*, ed. A. Rapaport-Albert and S. Zipperstein, 25-59. London, 1988.

Aubin, Jean and Alfredo Pinheiro Marques. *La Découverte, le Portugal et l'Europe: actes du colloque, Paris, les 26, 27 et 28 mai 1988*. Paris: Fondation Calouste Gulbenkian centre culturel portugais, 1990.

Azevedo, Pedro de. "A inquisição em Mazagão em 1607 e 1609." *Revista de História* 18, 19, and 20 (1916): 182-186, 282-284, 327-337.

Bagby, A. "The Jew in the *Cantigas* of Alfonso X el Sabio." *Speculum* 46 (1971): 670-688.

--------. "The Moslem in the *Cantigas* of Alfonso X el Sabio." *Kentucky Romance Quarterly* 20 (1973): 173-207.

Baião, António, Hernâni Cidade, and Manuel Múrias. *História da expansão portuguesa no mundo*. 3 vols. Lisbon: Editorial Atica, 1937.

Baretta, Silvio R. D. and John Markoff. "Civilization and Barbarism: Cattle Frontiers in Latin America." *Comparative Studies in Society and History* 20, no. 4 (1978): 587-620.

Baroja, Julio Caro. *Los judios en la España moderna y contemporanea*. Vol. 1. 3 vols. Madrid: Ediciones Arion, 1961.

Barros, Maria Filomena Lopes de. *A comuna muçulmana de Lisboa: séculos XIV e XV*. Lisbon: Hugin, 1998.

Barrow, Geoffrey. "Frontier and Settlement: Which Influenced Which? England and Scotland, 1100-1300." In *Medieval Frontier Societies*, ed. Robert Bartlett and Angus MacKay. New York: Oxford University Press, 1989.

Bartlett, Robert. "Colonial Aristocracies of the High Middle Ages." In *Medieval Frontier Societies*, ed. Robert Bartlett and Angus MacKay. New York: Oxford University Press, 1989.

-------- and Angus MacKay, ed. *Medieval Frontier Societies*. New York: Oxford University Press, 1989.

Bataillon, Marcel. "La rêve de la conquête de Fès et le sentiment imperial portugais au XVIe siècle." In *Études sur le Portugal au temps de l'humanisme*, 101-107. Coimbra: University of Coimbra Press, 1952.

Beirante, Maria Ângela. "O resgate de cativos nos reinos de Portugal e Algarve (séc. XII-XV)." In *Actas das III jornadas de história medieval do Algarve e Andaluzia*, 273-282. Loulé: Câmara Municipal de Loulé, 1989.

Bellini, Lígia. "Notes on Medical Scholarship and the Broad Intellectual Milieu in Sixteenth-Century Portugal." *Portuguese Studies* 15 (1999): 11-41.

Bishko, Charles J. "The Castilian as Plainsman: The Medieval Ranching Frontier in La Mancha and Extremadura." In *The New World Looks at its History: Proceedings of the Second International Congress of Historians of the United States and Mexico*, ed. Archibald R. and Thomas F. McGann Lewis, 47-69. Austin: University of Texas Press, 1963.

--------. "The Spanish and Portuguese Reconquest, 1095-1492." In *A History of the Crusades*, ed. Harry W. Hazard, 3, 396-456. Madison: University of Wisconsin Press, 1975.

--------. *Studies in Medieval Spanish Frontier History*. London: Variorum, 1980.

Boswell, John. *The Royal Treasure: Muslim Communities under the Crown of Aragon in the Fourteenth Century*. New Haven: Yale University Press, 1977.

Boucharb, Ahmed. *Dukkāla wa'l-isti`mār al-Burtughālī ila sanat ikhlā' Âsafi wa Azammūr [Dukkala and Portuguese colonization until the year of the evacuation of Safi and Azemor]*. Casablanca: Dar al-thaqafa, 1404/1984.

--------. "Les conséquences socio-culturelles de la conquête ibérique du littoral marocain." In *Relaciones de la peninsula ibérica con el magreb (siglos xiii-xvi): actas del coloquio*, ed. Mercedes García-Arenal and María J. Viguera, 487-521. Madrid: Instituto Hispano-Árabe de Cultura, 1988.

Bibliography

Bourdieu, Pierre. *Outline of a Theory of Practice*. Translated by Richard Nice. New York: Cambridge University Press, 1997.
Bousquet, G. H. *L'Islâm maghebrin, introduction à l'étude générale de l'Islâm*. 4th ed. Algiers: La Maison des livres, 1954.
Boxer, C. R. *The Portuguese Seaborne Empire, 1415-1825*. New York: Alfred A. Knopf, 1969.
--------. *Race Relations in the Portuguese Colonial Empire, 1415-1825*. Oxford: Clarendon Press, 1963.
--------. *Women in Iberian Expansion Overseas, 1415-1815: Some Facts, Fancies and Personalities*. New York: Oxford University Press, 1975.
--------. "'Three Sights to be Seen': Bombay, Tangier, and a Barren Queen, 1661-1684." *Portuguese Studies* 3 (1987): 77-83.
Braga, Isabel M. R. Mendes Drumond. "Contribuição monetária das comarcas portuguesas para a obra da redenção de cativos (1523-1539)." *Brigantia* 14 (1994): 23-34.
-------- and Paulo Drumond Braga. *Ceuta portuguesa (1415-1656)*. Ceuta: Instituto de Estudios Ceutíes, 1998.
--------. *Entre a Cristandade e o Islão: cativos e renegados nas franjas de duas sociedades em confronto*. Ceuta: Instituto de Estudios Ceutíes, 1998.
--------. *Mouriscos e cristãos no Portugal quinhentista: duas culturas e duas concepções religiosas em choque*. Lisbon: Hugin, 1999.
Braga, Paulo Drumond. "D. Maria de Eça, capitoa de Ceuta nos meados do século XVI." In *O rosto feminino da expansão portuguesa*, 2 vols. 1:433-437. Lisbon: Comissão para a Igualdade e para os Direitos das Mulheres, 1994.
--------. "A expansão no norte de África." In *A expansão Quatrocentista*, ed. A. H. de Oliveira Marques. Lisbon: Editorial Estampa, 1998.
Brett, Michael. *Ibn Khaldun and the Medieval Maghrib*. Brookfield, USA: Variorum, 1999.
-------- and Elizabeth Fentress. *The Berbers*. Cambridge, Mass: Blackwell, 1996.
Brodman, James. *Ransoming Captives in Crusader Spain: The Order of Merced on the Christian-Islamic Frontier*. Philadelphia: University of Pennsylvania Press, 1986.
Burns, R. I. "Social Riots on the Christian-Moslem Frontier: Thirteenth-Century Valencia." *American Historical Review* 66 (1961): 378-400.
--------. "Renegades, Adventurers, and Sharp Businessmen: The Thirteenth-Century Spaniard in the Cause of Islam." *Catholic Historical Review* 58 (1972): 341-366.

---------. *Islam Under the Crusaders: Colonial Survival in the Thirteenth-Century Kingdom of Valencia.* Princeton: Princeton University Press, 1973.

---------. "The Language Barrier: The Problem of Bilingualism and Muslim-Christian Interchange in the Medieval Kingdom of Valencia." In *Contributions to Mediterranean Studies*, ed. M. Vassallo. Malta, 1977.

---------. *Moors and Crusaders in Mediterranean Spain.* London: Variorum, 1978.

---------. "Piracy as an Islamic-Christian Interface." *Viator* 11 (1980): 165-178.

---------. *Muslims, Christians, and Jews in the Crusader Kingdom of Valencia.* New York: Cambridge University Press, 1984.

---------. "The Significance of the Frontier in the Middle Ages." In *Medieval Frontier Societies*, ed. Robert Bartlett and Angus MacKay. New York: Oxford University Press, 1989.

---------. "Muslims in the Thirteenth-Century Realms of Aragon: Interaction and Reaction." In *Muslims Under Latin Rule, 1100-1300*, ed. James M. Powell, 57-102. Princeton: Princeton University Press, 1990.

Camamis, G. *Estudio sobre el cautiverio en el siglo de oro.* Madrid, 1977.

Campbell, J. K. *Honour, Family and Patronage: A Study of Insitutions and Moral Values in a Greek Mountain Community.* Oxford: Clarendon Press, 1964.

Caro Baroja, Julio. *Una vision de Marruecos a mediados del siglo xvi: la del primer historiador de los "xarifes," Diego de Torres.* Madrid: Instituto de Estudios Africanos, 1956.

Carpenter, D. "Minorities in Medieval Spain: The Legal Status of Jews and Muslims in the *Siete Partidas*." *Romance Quarterly* 33 (1986): 275-287.

Castañer, José Enrique López de Coca. "Esclavos, alfaqueques y mercaderes en la frontera del mar de alborán, 1490-1516." *Hispania* 38 (1978): 275-300.

---------. "Institutions on the Castilian-Granadan Frontier, 1369-1482." In *Medieval Frontier Societies*, ed. Robert Bartlett and Angus MacKay. New York: Oxford University Press, 1989.

Catz, Rebecca. "Consequences and Repercussions of the Portuguese Expansion on Literature." *Portuguese Studies* 8 (1992): 115-23.

Cenival, Pierre de. "La cathedrale portugaise de Safi." *Hespéris*, 9 (1929): 1-29.

---------. "Les emirs de Hintâta, 'rois' de Marrakech." *Hespéris* 24 (1937): 245-254.

---------. *Chronique de Santa-Cruz du Cap de Gué (Agadir) : texte portugais du XVIe siècle.* Paris: P. Geuthner, 1934.

Bibliography

Chejne, A. *Islam and the West: the moriscos*. Albany: State University of New York Press 1983.

Clark, Peter and Bernard Lepetit, eds. *Capital Cities and their Hinterlands in Early Modern Europe*. Brookfield, Vermont: Scolar Press, 1996.

Coates, Timothy J. *Convicts and Orphans: Forced and State-Sponsored Colonizers in the Portuguese Empire, 1550-1755*. Stanford: Stanford University Press, 2001.

Cohen, Elizabeth S. "Honor and Gender in the Streets of Early Modern Rome." *Journal of Interdisciplinary History* XXII, no. 4 (1992): 597-625.

Cohen, M. "Islam and the Jews: Myth, Counter-Myth, History." *Jerusalem Quarterly* 38 (1986): 125-137.

--------. *Under Crescent and Cross: Jews in the Middle Ages*. Princeton, 1994.

Cohn, Bernard S. "History and Anthropology: The State of Play." *Comparative Studies in Society and History* 22, no. 2 (1980): 198-221.

Contamine, Philippe. *La vie quotidienne pendant la guerre de cent ans: France et Angleterre (XIVème siècle)*. Paris: Hachette, 1976.

Cook Jr., Weston. *The Hundred Years War for Morocco: Gunpowder and the Military Revolution in the Early Modern Muslim World*. San Francisco: Westview Press, 1994.

Cornell, Vincent J. "The Logic of Analogy and Role of the Sufi Shaykh in Post-Marinid Morocco." *International Journal of Middle East Studies* 15 (1983): 67-93.

--------. "Socioeconomic Dimensions of Reconquista and Jihad in Morocco: Portuguese Dukkala and the Sa`did Sus, 1450-1557." *International Journal of Middle East Studies* 22 (1990): 379-418.

Correia, Vergilio. *Lugares d'Além: Azemôr, Mazagão, Çafim*. Lisbon, 1923.

Costa Lobo, António de Sousa Silva. *História da sociedade em Portugal no século XV*. Lisboa: Edições Rolim, 1984.

Cour, Auguste. *L'Établessement des dynasties des chérifs au Maroc et leur rivalité avec les Turcs de la régence d'Alger (1509-1830)*. Paris, 1904.

--------. *Le dynastie marocaine les Beni Wattas, 1420-1554*. Constantine, 1924.

Cronon, William. "Revisiting the Vanishing Frontier: The Legacy of Frederick Jackson Turner." *Western Historical Quarterly* 18 (1987): 157-176.

Cruz, Maria Leonor García da. "As controvérsias ao tempo de D. João III sobre a política portuguesa no Norte de África: compilção de documentos." *Mare Liberum* 14, no. Dec (1997): 117-198.

Cutler, A. "Innocent III and the Distinctive Clothing of Jews and Muslims." *Studies in Medieval Culture* 3 (1970): 92-116.
-------- and H. Cutler. *The Jew as Ally of the Muslim: Medieval Roots of Anti-Semitism*. Notre Dame, 1986.
Davies, Rees. "Frontier Arrangements in Fragmented Societies: Ireland and Wales." In *Medieval Frontier Societies*, ed. Robert Bartlett and Angus MacKay. New York: Oxford University Press, 1989.
Devessa, Juan. "Los orígenes de la Orden de Nuestra Señora de la Merced." In *Las dos ordenes redentoras en la iglesia*, ed. Juan Manuel and Luis Vázquez Ruiz, 37-52. Madrid, 1989.
Dias, João José Alves, ed. *Portugal do renascimento à crise dinástica*. Lisbon: Editorial Presença, 1998.
Dias, Pedro. "As fortificações portuguesas da cidade magrebina de Safi." *Oceanos* 28 (1996): 12-14.
Diffie, Bailey W. and George D. Winius. *Foundations of the Portuguese empire, 1415-1580*. Minneapolis: University of Minnesota Press, 1977.
Duarte, Luís Miguel. "Garcia de Melo em Castro Marim (a actuação de um alcaide-mor no início do século XVI)." In *Actas das III jornadas de história medieval do Algarve e Andaluzia*, 217-236. Loulé: Câmara Municipal de Loulé, 1989.
Dufourcq, Charles E. "Berbérie-Iberie Médiévale." *Revue Historique* 240 (1968): 293-324.
Dutra, Francis A. "The Practice of Medicine in Early Modern Portugal: The Role and Social Status of the *Físico-mor* and the *Surgião-mor*." In *Libraries, History, Diplomacy, and the Performing Arts. Essays in Honor of Carleton Sprague Smith*, ed. Israel J. Katz, 135-169. Stuyvesant, NY: Pendragon Press, 1991.
--------. "The Discovery of Brazil and Its Immediate Aftermath." In *Portugal, The Pathfinder: Journeys from the Medieval toward the Modern World, 1300- ca. 1600*, ed. George D. Winius, 145-168. Madison, Wisconsin: The Hispanic Seminary of Medieval Studies, 1995.
--------. "As ordens militares." In *O tempo de Vasco da Gama*, ed. Diogo Ramada Curto, 229-241. Lisbon: CNCDP, 1998.
Dziubinski, Andrej. "Les chorfa saadiens dans les Sous et à Marrakech jusqu'en 1525." *Africana Bulletin* 10 (1969): 31-51.
Elbl, Martin M. "Portuguese Fortifications in Morocco: A Concise Overview." *Portuguese Studies Review* (2000): 88-108.
--------. "Portuguese Urban Fortifications in Morocco: Borrowing, Adaptation, and Innovation along a Military Frontier." In *City Walls: The Urban Enceinte in Global Perspective*, ed. James D. Tracy, 349-385. New York: Cambridge University Press, 2000.
Erdmann, Carl. *A ideia de cruzada em Portugal*. Coimbra, 1940.

Bibliography

Fagundes, Maria Augusta Lima Cruz. "Documentos ineditos para a história dos portugueses em Azamor." *Arquivos do Centro Cultural Portugues* 2 (1970): 104-179.

Farinha, António Dias. *História de Mazagão durante o período filipino*. Lisboa: Centro de Estudos Históricos Ultramarinos, 1970.

--------. *Os estudos árabes na historiografia posterior a Herculano*. Lisboa: Academia Portuguesa da História, 1978.

--------. "O Islão e os descobrimentos." In *A universidade e os descobrimentos*, 121-126. Lisbon: Imprensa Nacional-Casa da Moeda, 1993.

--------. *Os portugueses em Marrocos*. Lisbon: Instituto Camões, 1999.

Figanier, Joaquim. *História de Santa Cruz do Cabo de Gué (Agadir) 1505-1541*. Lisboa: Agência Geral das Colónias, 1945.

Figueras, G. "Documentos espagnols sur le siege d'Arzila en 1508." *Hespéris* 23 (1936): 3-8.

Fisher, G. *Barbary Legend: War, Trade, and Piracy in North Africa, 1415-1830*. Oxford, 1957.

Fonseca, Luís Adão da. *The Discoveries and the Formation of the Atlantic Ocean: 14th century - 16th century*. Translated by The British Council, Lisbon. Lisbon: CNCDP, 1999.

Frame, Robin. "Military Service in the Lordship of Ireland, 1290-1360: Institutions and Society on the Anglo-Gaelic Frontier." In *Medieval Frontier Societies*, ed. Robert Bartlett and Angus MacKay. New York: Oxford University Press, 1989.

Galbraith, J. S. "The Turbulent Frontier as a Factor in British Expansion." *Comparative Studies in Society and History* 2 (1960): 150-168.

García y García, A. "Jews and Muslims in the Canon Law of the Iberian Peninsula in the Late Medieval and Early Modern Period." *Jewish History* 3 (1988): 41-50.

Gellner, Ernest. *Muslim Society*. New York: Cambridge University Press, 1981.

-------- and Charles Micaud, eds. *Arabs and Berbers: From Tribe to Nation in North Africa*. Lexington, Mass.: Lexington Books, 1972.

Gerber, Jane S. *Jewish Society in Fez, 1450-1700*. Leiden: E. J. Brill, 1980.

Gímenez-Solar, A. "Caballeros españoles en Africa y africanos en España." *Revue Hispanique* 12 (1905): 249-372.

Glick, T. "The Ethnic Systems of Premodern Spain." *Comparative Studies in Sociology* 1 (1978): 157-171.

--------. *Islamic and Christian Spain in the Early Middle Ages: Comparative Perspectives on Social and Cultural Formation*. Princeton: Princeton University Press, 1979.

Goode, William J. *The Celebration of Heroes: Prestige as a Social Control System*. Los Angeles: University of California Press, 1978.

Goodich, Michael, Sophia Menache, and Sylvia Schein, ed. *Cross Cultural Convergences in the Crusader Period: Essays Presented to Aryeh Grabois on his Sixty-Fifth Birthday*. San Francisco: Peter Lang, 1995.

Goodman, Anthony. "Religion and Warfare in the Anglo-Scottish Marches." In *Medieval Frontier Societies*, ed. Robert Bartlett and Angus MacKay. New York: Oxford University Press, 1989.

Goulven, J. *La place de Mazagan sous la domination portugaise*. Paris, 1917.

--------. *Safi au vieux temps des portugais*. Lisbon, 1938.

Gravioto, Carlos Gozalbes. "Andalucía y el contrabando de armas con Marruecos en el siglo XVI." *Archivo Hispalense* 192 (1980): 177-189.

Gros, P. "Deux kanouns marocains du début du XVIe siècle." *Hespéris* 18 (1934): 64-75.

Guy, Donna J. and Thomas E. Sheridan, eds. *Contested Ground: Comparative Frontiers on the Northern and Southern Edges of the Spanish Empire*. Tucson: University of Arizona Press, 1998.

Halperin, Charles J. "The Ideology of Silence: Prejudice and Pragmatism on the Medieval Religious Frontier." *Comparative Studies in Society and History* 26, no. 3 (1984): 442-466.

Harvey, L. P. "Aljamia Portuguesa Revisited." *Portuguese Studies* 2 (1986): 1-14.

--------. *Islamic Spain, 1250 to 1500*. Chicago: University of Chicago Press, 1990.

--------. "When Portugal Expelled its Remaining Muslims (1497)." *Portuguese Studies* 11 (1995): 1-14.

Hennessy, Alistair. *The Frontier in Latin American History*. London: Edward Arnold, 1978.

Hess, Andrew. "The Moriscos: An Ottoman Fifth Column in Sixteenth Century Spain." *American Historical Review* 74 (1974): 1-25.

--------. *The Forgotten Frontier: A History of the Sixteenth-Century Ibero-African Frontier*. Chicago: University of Chicago Press, 1978.

Hirschberg, J. N. *A History of the Jews in North Africa*. 2 vols. 2nd revised ed. Leiden: E. J. Brill, 1981.

Hoffman, Bernard G. *The Structure of Traditional Moroccan Rural Society*. The Hague: Mouton & Co., 1967.

Hollister, C. Warren. *Medieval Europe: A Short History*. 8th ed. San Francisco: McGraw Hill, 1998.

Hower, Alfred, and Richard A. Preto-Rodas. *Empire in Transition: The Portuguese World in the Time of Camões*. Gainesville: University Presses of Florida : University of Florida Press/Center for Latin American Studies, 1985.

Bibliography

Humble, Sussanah. "Prestige, Ideology, and Social Politics: The Place of the Portuguese Overseas Expansion in the Policies of Dom Manuel (1495-1521)." *Itinerario* 40 (2000): 21-45.

Ibarra, Miguel Ángel de Bunes. *Los moriscos en el pensamiento histórico: Historiografía de un grupo marginado.* Madrid: Ediciones Cátedra, 1983.

--------. "La vida en los presidios del norte de África." In *Actas del coloquio las relaciones de la península ibérica con el magreb, siglos XIII al XVI*, 561-590. Madrid, 1988.

--------. *La imagen de los musulmanes y del norte de Africa en la España de los siglos XVI y XVII: los caracteres de una hostilidad.* Madrid, 1989.

--------. "Reflexiones sobre la conversión al Islam de los renegados en los siglos XVI y XVII." *Hispania Sacra* 42 (1990): 181-198.

Iria, Alberto. *Da fundação e governo do castelo ou fortaleza de São Jorge da Mina pelos portugueses e da sua acção missionária após o descobrimento desta costa, notícia histórica e biblio-iconográfica.* Lisboa: Agência Geral do Ultramar, 1958.

Issawi, Charles. "The Christian-Muslim Frontier in the Mediterranean: A History of Two Peninsulas." *Political Science Quarterly* 76 (1961): 544-554.

Jamous, Raymond. *Honneur et baraka: Les structures sociales traditionnelles dans le Rif.* New York: Cambridge University Press, 1981.

Jiménez, Manuel González. "Frontier and Settlement in the Kingdom of Castile (1085-1350)." In *Medieval Frontier Societies*, ed. Robert Bartlett and Angus MacKay. New York: Oxford University Press, 1989.

Johnson, Harold and Maria Beatriz Nizza da Silva. *O império luso-brasileiro, 1500-1620.* Lisbon: Editorial Estampa, 1992.

Johnson, Lyman L. and Sonya Lipsett-Rivera, eds. *The Faces of Honor: Sex, Shame, and Violence in Colonial Latin America.* Albuquerque: University of New Mexico Press, 1998.

Kedar, Benjamin Z. "The Subjected Muslims of the Frankish Levant." In *Muslims Under Latin Rule, 1100-1300*, ed. James M. Powell, 135-74. Princeton: Princeton University Press, 1990.

Kelly, James. *'That Damn'd thing Called Honour': Duelling in Ireland, 1570-1860.* Cork: Cork University Press, 1995.

Khaddari, Majid. *War and Peace in the Law of Islam.* Baltimore, 1955.

Lacoste, Y. "General Characteristics and Fundamental Structures of Mediaeval North African Society." *Economy and Society* 3 (1974): 1-18.

Lamar, Howard Roberts, and Leonard Monteath Thompson. *The Frontier in History: North America and Southern Africa Compared.* New Haven: Yale University Press, 1981.

Lapidus, Ira M. *Muslim Cities in the Later Middle Ages.* Cambridge, MA., 1967.
Laroui, Abdallah. *The History of the Maghrib: An Interpretive Essay.* Translated by Ralph Manheim. Princeton: Princeton University Press, 1977.
Lewis, Bernard. *Cultures in Conflict: Christians, Muslims, and Jews in the Age of Discovery.* New York: Oxford University Press, 1995.
Lockhart, James. *Spanish Peru, 1532-1560: A Social History.* 2nd ed. Madison, Wisconsin: University of Wisconsin Press, 1994.
Lopes, David. *Os arabes nas obras de Alexandre Herculano: notas marginaes de lingua e história portuguesa.* Lisbon: Imprensa nacional, 1911.
--------. *Textos em aljamia portuguesa; estudo filológico e histórico.* 2nd ed. Lisbon: Imprensa nacional, 1940.
--------. *A expansão em Marrocos.* Lisbon: Teorema, 1989.
--------. "Cousas luso-marroquinas: Notas filológicas sôbre particularidades vocabulares do português das praças de África." *Boletim de Filologia* 7 (1941): 1-15.
--------, ed. *História de Arzila durante o domínio português (1471-1550 e 1577-1589).* Coimbra: Imprensa da Universidade, 1924.
Lourie, Elena. "A Society Organized for War: Medieval Spain." *Past and Present* (1966): 55-76.
--------. *Crusade and Colonisation: Muslims, Christians, and Jews in Medieval Aragon.* Aldershot: Variorum, 1990.
Macedo, Helder. "Recognizing the Unknown: Perceptions in the Age of European Expansion." *Portuguese Studies* 8 (1992): 130-6.
MacKay, Angus. "The Ballad and the Frontier in Late Medieval Spain." *Bulletin Of Hispanic Studies* 53 (1976): 15-33.
--------. *Spain in the Middle Ages: From Frontier to Empire, 1000-1500.* London, 1977.
--------. "Religion, Culture, and Ideology on the Late Medieval Castilian-Granadan Frontier." In *Medieval Frontier Societies*, ed. Robert Bartlett and Angus MacKay. New York: Oxford University Press, 1989.
Magalhães Godinho, Vitorino de. "Ceuta e Marrocos." In Idem, *A economia dos descobrimentos henriquinos*, 109-127. Lisbon: Livraria Sá da Costa, 1962.
--------. *L'Économie de l'empire portugais aux XV et XVI siècles.* Paris, 1969.
--------. *Os descobrimentos e a economia mundial.* 4 vols. Lisbon: Editorial Presença, 1982-1985.
Marmon, S. "Concubinage, Islamic." In *Dictionary of the Middle Ages*, 3:527-529. New York: Charles Scribner's Sons, 1983.
--------. *Slavery in the Islamic Middle East.* Princeton, NJ: M. Wiener, 1999.
Martyn, John R. C. *The Siege of Mazagão : A Perilous Moment in the Defence of Christendom against Islam.* New York: Peter Lang, 1994.

Bibliography

Matar, Nabil. *Islam in Britain, 1558-1685*. New York: Cambridge University Press, 1998.

--------. "Muslims in Seventeenth-Century England." *Journal of Islamic Studies* 8, no. 1 (1997): 63-82.

Mattoso, José. *Identificação de um país: ensaio sobre as origens de Portugal, 1096-1325*. 2 vols. Lisbon: Editorial Estampa, 1988.

--------. *História de Portugal*. 8 vols. Lisbon: Editorial Estampa, 1997.

Maxwell, Kenneth. "Portugal, Europe, and the Origins of the Atlantic Commerical System, 1415-1520." *Portuguese Studies* 8 (1992): 3-16.

McCrank, Lawrence J. "Cistercians as Frontiersmen." In *Estudios en homenaje a Don Claudio Sánchez Albornoz en sus 90 años*, 2:313-360. 2 vols. Buenos Aires: Cuadernos de História de España, Anexos, 1983.

Meyerson, Mark. "Prostitution of Muslim Women in the Kingdom of Valencia: Religious and Sexual Discrimination in a Medieval Plural Society." In *The Medieval Mediterranean: Cross-Cultural Contacts*, ed. M. J. Chiat and K. L. Reyerson, 87-95. St. Cloud, MI, 1988.

--------. *The Muslims of Valencia in the Age of Fernando and Isabel: Between Coexistence and Crusade*. Berkeley: University of California, 1991.

Miller, David Harry and Jerome O. Steffen, eds. *The Frontier: Comparative Studies*. Norman: University of Oklahoma Press, 1977.

Mirrer, Louise. *Women, Jews, and Muslims in the Texts of Reconquest Castile*. Ann Arbor, Michigan: University of Michigan Press, 1996.

Montagne, Robert. *The Berbers: Their Social and Political Organization*. Translated by David Seddon. London: Frank Cass, 1973.

Morsy, Magali. "Arbitration as a Political Institution: An Interpretation of the Status of Monarchy in Morocco." In *Islam in Tribal Societies*, ed. Akbar S. Ahmad and David M. Hart, 39-65. Boston: Routledge and Kegan Paul, 1984.

Mottahedeh, Roy P. *Loyalty and Leadership in an Early Islamic Society*. Princeton: Princeton University Press, 1980.

Muldoon, James. *Popes, Lawyers, and Infidels: The Church and the Non-Christian World, 1250-1550*. Philadelphia, 1979.

Newitt, Malwyn. "Plunder and the Rewards of Office in the Portuguese Empire." In *The Military Revolution and the State, 1500-1800*, ed. Michael Duffy, 10-28. Exeter: University of Exeter, 1980.

Nirenberg, David. *Communities of Violence: Persecution of Minorities in the Middle Ages*. Princeton: Princeton University Press, 1996.

O'Callaghan, Joseph F. *A History of Medieval Spain*. Ithaca: Cornell University Press, 1983.

--------. "The Mudejars of Castile and Portugal in the Twelfth and Thirteenth Centuries." In *Muslims Under Latin Rule, 1100-1300*, ed. James M. Powell, 11-56. Princeton: Princeton University Press, 1990.

Oliveira Marques, A. H. de. *Daily Life in Portugal in the Late Middle Ages*. Translated by S. S. Wyatt. Madison: University of Wisconsin Press, 1971.

--------. *Portugal na crise dos séculos XIV e XV*. Lisbon: Editorial Presença, 1987.

--------. *História de Portugal*. 3 vols. 13th ed. Lisbon: Editorial Presença, 1997.

-------- ed. *A Expansão Quatrocentista*. Lisbon: Editorial Estampa, 1998.

Palmer, William. "That 'Insolent Liberty': Honor, Rites of Power, and Persuasion in Sixteenth-Century Ireland." *Renaissance Quarterly* 46 (1993): 308-327.

--------. "Scenes from Provincial Life: History, Honor, and Meaning in the Tudor North." *Renaissance Quarterly* 53 (2000): 425-448.

Pearson, Michael N. *Port Cities and Intruders: The Swahili Coast, India, and Portugal in the Early Modern Era*. Baltimore: The Johns Hopkins University Press, 1998.

Peristiany, J. G., ed. *Honour and Shame: The Values of Mediterranean Society*. Chicago: University of Chicago Press, 1966.

--------, ed. *Mediterranean Family Structures*. New York: Cambridge University Press, 1976.

-------- and Julian Pitt-Rivers, eds. *Honor and Grace in Anthropology*. New York: Cambridge University Press, 1992.

Pires de Lima, Durval R. *História da dominação portuguêsa em Çafim (1506-1542)*. Lisbon, 1930.

Pitt-Rivers, Julian. *The Fate of Shechem or The Politics of Sex: Essays in the Anthropology of the Mediterranean*. New York: Cambridge University Press, 1977.

Powell, James M., ed. *Muslims Under Latin Rule, 1100-1300*. Princeton, New Jersey: Princeton University Press, 1990.

--------. "The Papacy and the Muslim Frontier." In *Muslims Under Latin Rule, 1100-1300*, ed. James M. Powell, 175-203. Princeton: Princeton University Press, 1990.

--------. *A Society Organized for War: The Iberian Municipal Militias in the Central Middle Ages, 1000-1284*. Los Angeles: University of California Press, 1988.

Racine, Matthew T. "Service and Honor in Sixteenth-Century Portuguese North Africa: Yahya-u-Ta`fuft and Portuguese Noble Culture." *Sixteenth Century Journal* 32 (2001): 67-90.

Bibliography

Rau, Virgínia. "Feitores e feitorias: "instrumentos" do comércio internacional português no século XVI." In *Estudos sobre história económica e social do antigo regime*, 141-99. Lisbon: Editorial Presença, 1984.

--------. *Estudos de história medieval*. Lisboa: Editorial Presença, 1986.

Renaud, H. P. J. "Recherches historiques sur les épidémies du Maroc." In *Mélanges d'études luso-marocaines*, 376-381. Lisbon, 1945.

Ricard, Robert. "La côte atlantique du Maroc au début du XVI siècle d'apres Les instructions nautiques." *Hespéris* 7 (1927): 229-258.

--------. "A propos de *rebato*: Note sur la tactique militaire dans les places portugaises du Maroc." *Bulletin hispanique* 35, no. 4 (1933): 448-53.

--------. "Le problème de l'occupation restreinte dans l'Afrique du Nord (xv-xviii siècles)." *Annales d'Histoire Économique et Sociale* 8, no. 41 (1936): 426-437.

--------. "Sur le chronologie des fortifications portugaises d'Azemmour, Mazagan, et Safi." In *III congresso do mundo português*, 1, 107-117. Coimbra, 1940.

--------. "Bastião de Vargas, agent de Jean III de Portugal au Maroc, et le projet d'alliance entre le Portugal et le royaume de Fès (1539-1541)." In *SIHMP*, 3:176-192.

--------. "Documentos sobre las relaciónes de Andalucia con las plazas portuguesas de Marruecos (1541)." *Al-Andalus* 13 (1948): 275-292.

--------. "Les places luso-marocaines et les iles portugaises de l'atlantique." In *SIHMP*, 3:323-329.

--------. "L'Évêché de Safi (1487?-1542)." In *SIHMP*, 3:75-82.

--------. "L'Occupation portugaise d'Agadir (1505-1541)." In *SIHMP*, 3:ix-xx.

--------. "Les travaux de Mazagan en 1541." In *SIHMP*, 4:9-12.

--------. "Contribution à l'étude du commerce genóis au Maroc durant la Periode portugaise (1415-1550)." In *Études sur l'histoire des portugais au Maroc*, 115-142. Coimbra: University of Coimbra, 1955.

--------. "Le commerce de Berbérie et l'organisation économique de l'empire portugais aux XV et XVI siècles." In *Études sur l'histoire des portugais au Maroc*, 81-114. Coimbra: University of Coimbra, 1955.

--------. "L'Evacuation des places portugaises du Maroc sous Jean III." In *SIHMP*, 4:335-349.

Riches, D. "The Phenomenon of Violence." In *The Anthropology of Violence*, ed. D. Riches, 1-27. Oxford, 1986.

Roche, Daniel. *The Culture of Clothing: Dress and Fashion in the Ancien Regime*. New York: Cambridge University Press, 1997.

Rodrigues, Ana Maria S. A. and Maria de Fátima Moura Ferreira. "Mulheres portuguesas em Marrocos: imagens do quotidiano feminino nos séculos XV e XVI." In *O rosto feminino da expansão portuguesa*. 2 vols. 1:417-431. Lisbon: Comissão para a Igualdade e para os Direitos das Mulheres, 1995.

Roque, Ana. "Considerações sobre a mulher no contexto da expansão portuguesa no norte de África (as praças do sul de Marrocos)." In *O rosto feminino da expansão portuguesa*. 2 vols. 1:449-466. Lisbon: Comissão para a Igualdade e para os Direitos das Mulheres, 1995.

Rosenberger, Bernard. "Note sur Kouz: un ancien port à l'embrouchure de l'Oued Tensift." *Hespéris-Tamuda* 8 (1967): 23-66.

-------- and Hamid Triki. "Faimes et épidémies au Maroc aux XVI et XVII siècles." *Hespéris-Tamuda* 14 (1973): 109-176.

-------- and Hamid Triki. "Faimes et épidémies au Maroc aux XVI et XVII siècles." *Hespéris-Tamuda* 15 (1974): 5-103.

Ruff, Julius R. *Violence in Early Modern Europe, 1500-1800*. New York: Cambridge University Press, 2001.

Russell, Peter. *Prince Henry "the Navigator": A Life*. New Haven: Yale University Press, 2001.

--------. *Portugal, Spain, and the African Atlantic, 1343-1490 : Chivalry and Crusade from John of Gaunt to Henry the Navigator*. Brookfield, Vt., USA: Variorum, 1995.

Sá, Isabel dos Guimarães. *Quando o rico se faz pobre: misericórdias, caridade e poder no império português, 1500-1800*. Lisbon: CNCDP, 1997.

--------. "Shaping Social Space in the Centre and Periphery of Portuguese Empire: The Example of the Misericórdias from the Sixteenth to the Eighteenth Century." *Portuguese Studies* 13 (1997): 210-221.

Saldanha, António Vasconcelos de. *As capitanias do Brasil: antecedentes, desenvolvimento e extinção de um fenómeno atlântico*. Lisbon: CNCDP, 2001.

Sanceau, Elaine. *Castelos em África*. Translated by Dr. José Francisco dos Santos. Oporto: Livraria Civilização Editora, 1961.

Santos, João Marinho dos and José Manuel Azuelo e Silva, eds. *Vasco da Gama: a honra, o proveito, a fama e a gloria*. Oporto: Editora Ausência, 1999.

Savage, Jr., William W. and Stephen I. Thompson, eds. *The Frontier: Comparative Studies*. Norman: University of Oklahoma Press, 1979.

Schneider, Jane. "Of Vigilance and Virgins: Honor, Shame, and Access to Resources in Mediterranean Societies." *Ethnology* 10, no. 1 (1971): 1-24.

Schneider, Peter. "Honor and Conflict in a Sicilian Town." *Anthropological Quarterly* 42, no. 3 (1969): 130-54.

Serra Ruiz, R. *Honra e injuria en el derecho medieval español*. Murcia, 1969.

Serrão, Joel. *Dicionário de história de Portugal*. 4 vols. Oporto: Livraria Figueirinhas, 1975.

Serrão, Joaquim Veríssimo. *Cronistas do século XV posteriores a Fernão Lopes*. Amadora: M.E.I.C. Secretaria de Estado da Investigação Científica, 1977.

--------. *História de Portugal*. 14 vols. Lisbon: Verbo, 1977-2000.

--------. *Portugal e o mundo nos séculos XII a XVI: um percurso de dimensão universal*. Lisbon: Verbo, 1994.

Silva, Manuela Santos. "Para o estudo da produção frutícola do concelho de Loulé (Os 'Livros de repartição da fruta' do século XV)." In *Actas das III jornadas de história medieval do Algarve e Andaluzia*, 255-264. Loulé: Câmara Municipal de Loulé, 1989.

Souto, A. Moeyrelles do. "O abandono das praças de norte de África." *Studia* 33 (1971): 251-339.

Spufford, Peter. *Handbook of Medieval Exchange*. London: Office of the Royal Historical Society, 1986.

Stewart, Frank Henderson. *Honor*. Chicago: University of Chicago Press, 1994.

Strocchia, Sharon. "Gender and the Rites of Honor in Italian Renaissance Cities." In *Gender and Society in Renaissance Italy*, ed. Judith Brown and Robert Davis. New York: Longman, 1998.

Subrahmanyam, Sanjay. *The Portuguese Empire in Asia, 1500-1700: A Political and Economic History*. New York: Longman, 1993.

Tavim, José Alberto Rodrigues da Silva. *Os judeus na expansão portuguesa em Marrocos durante o século XVI: origens e actividades duma comunidade*. Braga: Edições APPACDM Distrital de Braga, 1997.

Thomaz, Luís Filipe F. R. "Factions, Interests, and Messianism: The Politics of Portuguese Expansion in the East, 1500-1521." *The Indian Economic and Social History Review* 28 (1991): 97-109.

Thornton, John. *Africa and Africans in the Making of the Atlantic World, 1400-1800*. 2nd. ed. New York: Cambridge University Press, 1998.

Torres, Diego de. *Relación del origen y suceso de los xarifes y del estado de los reinos de Marruecos, Fez, y Tarudante*. Madrid: Siglo Veintiuno de España, 1980.

Tucker, Treva J. "Eminence over Efficacy: Social Status and Cavalry Service in Sixteenth-Century France." *Sixteenth Century Journal* 32 (2001): 1057-1095.

Turner, Frederick Jackson. *The Frontier in American History*. New York: Henry Holt, 1962.

Ventura, Margarida Garcez. "O Algarve nos primóridos da expansão: um sermão milenarista em Lagos (12 de julho de 1415)." In *Actas das III jornadas de história medieval do Algarve e Andaluzia*, 265-272. Loulé: Câmara Municipal de Loulé, 1989.
Vizcargüenaga, Ignacio. "Los orígenes de la Orden Trinitaria." In *Las dos ordenes redentoras en la iglesia*, ed. Juan Manuel and Luis Vázquez Ruiz, 9-35. Madrid, 1989.
Vogt, John. "Crusading and Commercial Elements in the Portuguese Capture of Ceuta." *Muslim World* 59 (1969): 287-299.
--------. "Notes on the Portuguese Cloth Trade in West Africa, 1480-1540." *International Journal of African Historical Studies* 8 (1975): 623-639.
--------. "Santa Barbara's Legion: Portuguese Artillery in the Struggle for Morocco." *Military Affairs* 41 (1977): 176-182.
--------. *Portuguese Rule on the Gold Coast, 1469-1682*. Athens, GA: University of Georgia, 1979.
Von Ehingen, Jurge. *The Diary of Jurge Von Ehingen*. Translated by Malcolm Letts. London, 1929.
Webb, Walter Prescott. *The Great Frontier*. Boston: Houghton Mifflin, 1952.
Weber, David J. "Turner, the Boltonians, and the Borderlands." *American Historical Review* 91 (1986): 66-81.
Wieczynski, Joseph L. *The Russian Frontier: The Impact of Borderlands upon The Course of Early Russian History*. Charlottesville: University Press of Virginia, 1976.
Wilentz, Sean, ed. *Rites of Power: Symbolism, Ritual, and Politics Since the Middle Ages*. Philadelphia: University of Pennsylvania Press, 1985.
Winius, George D. *Portugal, the Pathfinder: Journeys from the Medieval toward the Modern World, 1300-ca. 1600*. Madison: Hispanic Seminary of Medieval Studies, 1995.
Wolfskill, George and Stanley Palmer, ed. *Essays on Frontiers in World History*. College Station: Texas A&M University Press, 1983.
Wolfthal, Diane, ed. *Peace and Negotiation: Strategies for Coexistence in the Middle Ages and the Renaissance*. Turnhout: Brepols, 2000.
Yahya, Dahiru. *Morocco in the Sixteenth Century: Problems and Patterns in African Foreign Policy*. London: Longman, 1981.
Yarrison, James A. "Force as an Instrument of Policy: European Military Incursions and Trade in the Maghreb, 1000-1355." Ph.D. diss., Princeton University, 1982.
Yerushalemi, Y. H. "Professing Jews in Post-Expulsion Spain and Portugal." In *Salo Wittmayer Baron Jubilee Volume*, 2, 1023-1055. Jerusalem, 1974.

Bibliography

--------. *Lisbon Massacre of 1506 and the Royal Image in the Shebet Yehudah*. Cincinnati, Ohio: Hebrew Union College, 1976.

Zafrani, Haim. *Les juifs au Maroc: vie sociale, économique, et religieuse*. Paris: LaRoux, 1972.

INDEX

A

a`yān (i.e., elite secular rulers), 204
Abelhos, Muhammad, 250
Abraham Rute, *rabi mor* of Safi, 21, 50, 64, 69, 71, 72, 73, 116, 141, 191, 195, 201, 267
Abranches, Álvaro de, 41, 54, 76, 253, 300
Abreu, Francisco de, 30
Abreu, João de, 110, 314
adail, 30, 32, 33, 45, 64, 101, 117, 139, 142, 206, 218, 223, 251, 266, 268, 276
adail mor, 32
Adibe, family of Jews, 69
Adibe, José, 69
Adibe, Ya`qūb, 70, 141, 148
Adibe, Yahya, 70, 72
Adibe, Yūsuf, 180
adultery, 56
Afonso V, King D., 12, 13, 14, 15, 16, 40, 123, 152, 229, 247
Afonso, João, 130
agreements, with Jews, 70
agriculture, 48
Aguiar, Inez de, 45
Aguiar, Martinho de, 110, 307
Aguiar, Rui Dias de, 141, 301
Aguz, 22, 158, 266
Al-`Attar, *qā'id*, 50, 133, 134, 139, 141, 284
al-`Aziz, `Abd, 153
Al-A`rā'ish. See, Larache, See, Larache
al-A`raj, Ahmed, 24, 25, 72, 116, 117, 206, 254, 269, 298
Al-Anfa. See, Casablanca, See, Casablanca, See, Casablanca, See, Casablanca
al-Burtughālī, Muhammad, 21
Alcácer Ceguer, 13, 25, 40, 272
Alcácer Kebir, 25
Alcáçovas, Treaty of, 15, 16

alcaide, 16, 56, 64, 118, 160, 161, 162, 170, 175, 180, 194, 198, 202, 205, 249, 271
alcaide do çoquo, 127
alcaide dos mouro, 178
alcaide dos mouros, 39, 78, 82, 83, 84, 113, 161, 162, 175, 179, 182, 185, 198, 201, 202, 256, 264, 275, 285, 286
alcaide mor, 32, 231
Alcoforado, Duarte, 118
alfândega, 34, 125, 126
alfaqueque, 30, 33, 43, 64, 67, 190, 246, 248, 249, 250, 251, 252, 253, 254, 267
alfaqueque mor, 33, 101, 251
alformas, see "guides", 19, 79
Algarve, 13, 56, 101, 124, 155, 245, 247, 257, 290
al-Gharbiyya, Ya`qūb, 127
al-Harran, Muhammad, 228, 232, 259
al-Jadīda. *See,* Mazagão
aljaravias, 131
al-Khemis, 81, 82, 97, 175, 176, 205
Al-Khemis, 193
al-Kurimat, 193, 194
alliance, 9, 25, 81, 87, 145, 151, 152, 157, 159, 161, 162, 167, 168, 169, 171, 173, 176, 179, 182, 184, 191, 193, 194, 195, 196, 197, 200, 254, 267, 285, 289
alliance, a case study, 188
alliance, benefits of, 179
alliances, creation of, 159
Almedina, 20, 79, 81, 91, 98, 113, 134, 163, 168, 180, 182, 191, 193, 194, 199, 221, 261, 277, 279
Almeida, Cristóvão de, 118, 312
Almeida, Francisco de, 30, 101, 142, 306
Almeida, Gonçalo de, 74
Almeida, Gonçalo Ribeiro de, 100

Index

almocadém, 45, 64, 229, 236, 238, 266, 268
*almogaveria*s, 236, 237
Almohads, 188
almonds, 97
almotacé, 33, 127
almoxarife, 34, 52, 55, 102, 117, 118, 126, 144, 231, 263, 265, 291
alms, see also "*esmolas*", 36, 44, 45, 248, 249
al-Mumin, Mawlay `Abd, 273
Al-Naser bin Yūsuf, 198, 220, 298
al-Naser, Mawlay, 50, 178, 180, 192, 193, 194, 200
al-Qā'im, Muhammad, 23
alquices (see also "*haiks*", 132, 133, 147
al-Rahman, `Abd, 83, 173, 176, 180, 185, 186, 228
al-Sheikh, Muhammad, 14, 15, 16, 17, 21, 70, 157, 164, 195, 226, 227, 250, 291, 298
al-Sheikh, Muhammad, Sharif, 259, 262, 269
al-Sheikh, Sheikh Muhammad, 219
Álvares, Bastião, 273
Álvarez, Francisco, 46
Alvelos, Pero Fernandes de, 241
Alvim, João Lopes des, 118, 135
Amada, Inês, 46
Amaral, Afonso do, 92
Ambrum, Vicêncio, 52, 118
Amejjot, Lahsen, 191
amtonas, 134
anadel, 35, 218
Andalusia, 55, 91
Andaluzia, 56, 96, 120, 124, 126, 155, 245
announcements, publication of, 98
apontador, 38, 64
apothecary, see "*boticário*", 51
Arabs, 3, 72, 78, 79, 81, 130, 157, 170, 172, 176, 185, 186, 188, 195, 198, 200, 212, 220, 237, 277
Aranha, Gomes, 111
architects, 104, 209, 215

Arguim, 132, 133, 136, 142
Arruda brothers, architects, 80, 104, 187, 210, 211, 212, 238
artillerymen, 38, 54, 224
artisans, 28, 52, 53, 79, 126, 229, 281
Arzila, iv, 14, 15, 25, 40, 48, 51, 56, 58, 71, 89, 150, 164, 197, 261, 263, 272, 289
assassination, 171
Ataíde, Nuno Fernandes de, 19, 31, 35, 39, 40, 44, 47, 64, 67, 79, 83, 84, 91, 92, 98, 112, 115, 142, 159, 168, 170, 172, 173, 174, 177, 183, 184, 187, 189, 190, 191, 192, 193, 195, 196, 197, 208, 209, 212, 215, 218, 220, 221, 222, 223, 224, 225, 237, 238, 244, 256, 262, 274
atalaias, 39, 214, 218, 222, 260
atalaias da torre, 39
audiencia, 104
Awlad `Amran discani, 47, 188, 189, 190, 193, 198, 200, 221
Awlad `Amran lithali, 84, 188, 189, 191, 198, 199, 200, 221
Awlad `Amran tribe, 47, 84, 113, 183, 187, 188, 189, 190, 191, 192, 193, 194, 195, 196, 197, 198, 199, 200, 201, 202, 203, 221, 264
Awlad Bu `Aziz, 188
Awlad Dūib tribe, 187
Awlad Frej, 188, 192, 193
Awlad Mut`, 196, 200
Awlad Subeita tribe, 138, 177, 184, 188, 191, 200, 203, 221
Awlad Ya`qub, 188, 193, 198, 200, 203
Awlad Ya'qub tribe, 184, 221
Awlad Zid, 192
Azambuja, Diogo de, 18, 20, 29, 30, 49, 50, 54, 71, 112, 118, 131, 157, 179, 180, 209, 211, 267, 300, 301
Azamor, *passim*
Azamor, prior of, 74

Azevedo, Lopo de, 35, 49, 108, 311
Azores, 120, 156, 257, 270, 271, 291

B

bailiffs, 34, 110
bakeries, 97
bakers, 48, 54
banners, 53, 98, 173
Banu Hilal, 188
barbeiros, see also "barbers", 49
barbers, 49, 52
barbers, see also "*barbeiros*", 49
Barbudo, Pedro, 258
barley, 92, 95, 97, 99, 115, 124, 127, 138, 148, 149, 163, 189, 210, 237, 253
Barque Malik, 235
Barreto, Rui, 31, 36, 37, 74, 75, 104, 165, 186, 193, 210, 217, 237, 244, 283, 285, 300
Barriga, Lopo, 64, 80, 223, 266, 267, 268, 279, 313
Barriga, Lopo, captivity of, 267
baskets, 211
beeswax, 80, 116, 124, 133, 141, 147
Belleames, Meymam, 75
Belsbā`, Yahya bin, 173, 180
Benacafiz, 170, 186, 192, 237, 255, 261, 278
Benetto da Ravenna, 215
Beni Maker tribe, 112, 163
Beni Tamer tribe, 255
Benzamiro family, 69, 72, 136, 145
Benzamiro, Abraham, 69, 133
Benzamiro, Ibrahim, 116, 117, 190, 268
Benzamiro, Isaac, 54, 64, 69, 148, 223
Benzamiro, Ismail, 223, 267
Berbers, 3, 23, 78, 81, 157, 163, 167, 172, 176, 188, 220, 221, 224, 236, 255, 326, 330, 334
Berrio, Estêvão Rodrigues, 22, 92, 176, 193, 194, 195

besteiros, see also "crossbowmen", 38
bin `Umar, Selim, 21
bin al-`Ilj, Mūmin bin Yahya, 228
bin Barka, Hammu, 153
bin Daud, Sheikh Melik, 129, 130, 137, 143, 166
bin Mira, `Omar, 189, 190, 197, 264
bin Shahmut, Rahho, 195, 196, 201
Bin Yehuda, 84
bin Zaur, Lahsen, 190, 191
Bishko, Charles J., 6, 7, 11, 251, 325
blacksmiths, 52, 53, 54, 58
boats, 42, 63, 105, 106, 216
Bocarro, Luis Gonçalves, 110, 314
Bogozmão, Sheikh Sa`īd, 184
Bojador, Cape, 18
bordates, 132, 135, 140, 145
boticário, see "apothecary", 51, 52
Boucharb, Ahmed, iv, 3, 4, 95, 96, 163, 242, 325
Bras, Pero, 58
Brazil, 8, 17, 40, 110, 156, 236, 245, 272, 329
bread, 48, 90, 97, 99, 138, 180, 195
bridge, construction of, 73
bridges, 73, 102, 106, 181
Bruges, 13
Bu Dbira, 206
Budara, Yehuda, 145
burial, 36
burnous, 131
Burns, Robert, 2
Burns, Robert I., 3, 4, 7, 77, 169
butchers, 52, 93
butter, 147, 189, 192

C

Cabral, Álvaro, 102
Cadaval, Álvaro do, 102, 161, 202, 257, 265, 266, 283, 305
Cadiz, 129, 130, 225
cal, 79, 104, 143, 169, 210, 211, 212, 213, 220, 234

Index

cal, forneira de, 48
Câmara, Manuel da, 229, 231, 248, 257, 270, 271
Câmara, Simão Gonçalves da, 222, 301
camels, 142, 143, 191
Canary Islands, 17, 240
cannons, 217, 219, 227, 230, 235
capitão, 15, 19, passim
capitão da cidade, 31
capitão do campo, 31, 49, 261
capitoas, 46
captives, 9, 14, 15, 19, 25, 30, 33, 54, 86, 99, 115, 116, 150, 164, 168, 190, 194, 196, 198, 199, 201, 205, 206, 225, 236, 237, 240, 245, 246, 247, 248, 250, 251, 252, 253, 255, 256, 257, 258, 259, 260, 261, 262, 263, 264, 265, 269, 272, 273, 274, 275, 277, 278, 282, 287, 291
captives, sexual exploitation of, 261
captives, treatment of, 254
captivity, 9, 12, 15, 17, 24, 26, 32, 42, 43, 48, 51, 69, 78, 80, 83, 95, 106, 115, 116, 117, 118, 119, 123, 129, 144, 153, 164, 178, 180, 183, 184, 192, 194, 198, 201, 202, 217, 230, 232, 234, 235, 237, 239, 241, 245, 246, 247, 248, 249, 250, 253, 254, 255, 256, 258, 259, 260, 261, 262, 263, 264, 265, 266, 268, 269, 270, 271, 272, 274, 275, 276, 277, 278, 279, 281, 283, 285, 288
captivity, freedom from, 262
caravans, 116, 136, 141, 142, 183, 184
Cardeal Henrique, D. Infante, 45
Cardenal, João, 102
Carneiro, Gonçalo, 53
carpenters, 52, 53
Carvajal, Rodrigo de, 55, 231
Carvalho, Álvaro, 101
Casa dos Contos, 104, 212
Casablanca, iv, 14, 325
Castañer, José Enrique López de Coca, 3, 117, 164, 175, 205, 251, 256, 327
Castelo Real, 18, 157, 211
Castile, 15, 32, 55, 56, 59, 82, 88, 90, 96, 117, 125, 155, 159, 161, 167, 284
Castilians, 6, 16, 17, 18, 55, 118, 125, 128, 157, 240
Castro Marim, 32, 56, 329
Castro, D. Francisco de, 29, 167, 301
Castro, D. Rodrigo de, 25, 30, 37, 39, 41, 45, 47, 60, 91, 117, 119, 206, 217, 234, 240, 241, 254, 259, 269, 289
cathedral, 36, 98, 105, 107, 108, 115
cathedrals, 107
Catherine of Bragança, 26
cativos de conta, 265
cativos de conta (i.e., elite captives), 259, 266, 267, 268, 269, 278
cattle, 81, 92, 116, 123, 177, 199
cavaleiro, 31, 241
cavalry, 20, 38, 39, 43, 82, 92, 97, 106, 178, 184, 185, 193, 199, 202, 208, 218, 230, 236, 237, 279
cavouqueiros, 211
Cerveira, Álvaro Mendes, 58
Ceuta, 1, 2, 10, 11, 12, 13, 15, 25, 26, 33, 40, 43, 44, 46, 47, 48, 57, 58, 87, 89, 91, 93, 95, 124, 125, 133, 155, 164, 209, 222, 228, 245, 247, 249, 256, 258, 260, 272, 289
Chaberim, Muhammad Benelim, 187
Charles II of England, 26
chickens, 93, 97, 237
children, 37, 40, 42, 44, 47, 48, 59, 67, 83, 84, 85, 119, 129, 165, 166, 167, 178, 184, 194, 197, 198, 200, 203, 209, 220, 227, 230, 234, 237, 241, 246, 250, 254, 255, 258, 261, 262, 263,

264, 266, 271, 272, 273, 278, 290
China, 126
Christianity, 8, 36, 43, 47, 49, 65, 66, 74, 76, 84, 85, 86, 87, 88, 107, 115, 118, 164, 174, 175, 236, 249, 257, 259, 262, 282
Chronicle of Santa Cruz do Cabo de Gué, 226
church, 13, 23, 76, 77, 105, 182, 233, 262, 272, 283
churches, 16, 35, 152, 270
cinnamon, 133, 140
cirurgiões, see also "surgeons", 49
cisterns, 106
clergy, 29, 35, 36, 37
cloth, 6, 16, 35, 73, 97, 123, 124, 131, 134, 135, 152, 180, 181, 253, 287
clothing, 37, 72, 73, 87, 124, 131, 133, 143, 161, 173, 179, 180, 195, 198, 201, 205, 259, 288
cloves, 133, 139, 180
cobblers, 52, 58, 234, 255, 278
commodities (trade), 130
Compromisso da Misericórdia de Lisboa, 272
comuna, 69, 77, 85, 160, 161, 182, 249, 250, 281, 324
conflict resolution, 116
construction, 16, 17, 18, 21, 22, 35, 36, 38, 46, 52, 53, 73, 78, 79, 101, 102, 103, 104, 105, 107, 108, 109, 115, 120, 131, 137, 143, 144, 152, 153, 156, 157, 209, 210, 211, 212, 213, 214, 216, 217, 227, 241, 260, 273, 291
construction, religious, 107
construction, royal, 103
contador, 19, 33, 35, 40, 62, 64, 87, 94, 95, 96, 97, 104, 108, 117, 144, 145, 150, 162, 166, 167, 190, 211, 213, 221, 223, 251, 261, 275
contraband, 128, 129
contracts, 51, 69, 126, 132, 133, 135

Cook, Jr, Weston, 8, 128, 151, 204, 291
Cook, Jr., Weston, 128
copper, 124, 136, 137
Cornell, Vincent, 96, 151, 188, 204, 328, 334
Correia, Brites, 46
Correia, Simão, 39, 68, 70, 71, 88, 92, 101, 105, 110, 118, 162, 197, 198, 199, 218, 220, 244, 265, 300
cortes, 11, 155
Costa, Bento da, 271, 272, 278, 317
Costa, Francisco da, 229, 306, 307, 318
Costa, João da, 45, 251, 318
Costa, Simão Gonçalves da, 42, 44, 86, 174, 301, 316
Cotrim, João, 167
couraças, 216
courts, 29, 51
coutos, 56
cows, 92, 143, 165, 195, 208
crime, generally, 109
crimes, forgery, 111
crimes, non-violent, 110
crimes, punishment, 113
crimes, violent, 111
criminals, 12, 56, 57, 78, 113, 114, 116, 199, 275
cristãos novos, see "New Christians", 74
crops, 81, 91, 92, 123, 138, 177, 178, 192, 199, 203
crossbowman, 31, 39, 62
crossbowmen, 39, 41, 55, 156, 224, 230
crossbowmen, see also, 38
cross-cultural justice, 116
crusade, 11, 13, 17, 22, 282
crusades, 164, 180, 208, 249, 333, 334, 337
cucumbers, 97, 139

Index

D

D. Beatriz, wife of João Lopes de Sequeira, 18
D. Fernando, 11, 12, 14, 71, 164, 258, 300
D. Henrique, 10, 11, 12, 13, 69, 87, 277, 311
D. Jaime, Duke of Bragança, 19, 20, 241
D. Manuel, King, *passim*
Dardeiro, Moses, 64, 72, 113, 190
Daroque, Ya`qūb, 73, 253
dates, 97, 139, 268, 304
Daūd, Malik bin, 183
daughters, 26, 28, 30, 40, 45, 55, 190, 195, 228, 231, 234, 261, 266, 269, 270, 271
Davies, Rees, 3, 150, 204, 205, 329
dawwārs, 16, 78, 80, 153, 163, 173, 192
death, ii, 12, 30, 33, 36, 44, 45, 46, 48, 69, 70, 76, 83, 86, 87, 101, 102, 112, 114, 164, 170, 171, 194, 197, 212, 233, 239, 249, 251, 261
degredados, 58, 166
degredados, see also "exiles", 36, 55, 59
devotional objects, 108
Dia, 189, 191, 192, 201
Diálogo de vária história, 268
Dias, António, 1, 6, 10, 53, 153, 215, 330
Dias, Fernão, 41
Dias, Jorge, 53
Dias, Luís, 54, 55, 315
Diogo, *mourisco* traitor, 86
distrust, 176
docks, 32, 53, 105
drugs, 139
Drumond Braga, Isabel, 259
drums, 173, 221, 225
Duarte, King D., 11, 12, 123
Dukkala, iv, 23, 24, 39, 71, 72, 82, 84, 86, 92, 95, 96, 98, 113, 118, 124, 129, 130, 132, 135, 141, 151, 158, 162, 170, 172, 173, 175, 178, 181, 183, 186, 188, 190, 192, 194, 196, 197, 198, 199, 200, 201, 202, 203, 254, 275, 276, 286
duties, import and export, 126

E

Eanes, Afonso, 91
Eça, D. Garcia de, 45
Eça, D. Maria de, 46, 47, 222, 326
Egypt, 135
elche, 262
eleche, 228
embezzlement, 118
engineers, 211
English, ii, v, 14, 25, 26, 124, 128, 135, 204, 215, 245
epidemics, 51
escrivão da ribeira, 35, 94
escrivão das obras, 144
escrivão do anadel-mor dos besteiros, 35
escrivão do campo de El Rey, 35
escrivão dos mantimentos, 34
escrivão, see "scribes", 34, 35, 64, 94, 100, 103, 118, 145, 217, 219, 234, 271
Esmeraldo de Situ Orbis, 80, 123, 124, 157
esmolas, see also "alms", 44
espingardeiros, see also "matchlockmen", 38, 193, 230
estancias, 67, 217, 219, 222, 223
execution, 57, 72, 82, 109, 113, 115, 116, 246
exiles, 36, 40, 42, 55, 56, 58, 59, 63

F

Fagundes, Maria Augusta Lima Cruz (historian), 29, 33, 34, 36, 38, 42, 51, 52, 55, 60, 61, 62, 78, 88, 92, 94, 97, 98, 100, 101, 102, 107, 108, 118, 120, 122, 127, 167, 216, 244, 252, 290, 291
Faiscas, Isabel, 46
falcons, 163, 197
famine, 37
faqīrs, 198, 283

Faria, D. Joana de, 40, 47
Faria, Pedro Álvares de, 103, 290
farmers, 5, 96
fazenda, 41, 286, 288
feitor, 16, 34, 35, 45, 49, 50, 52, 55, 83, 94, 96, 105, 117, 118, 121, 125, 129, 132, 133, 135, 136, 137, 138, 139, 143, 153, 166, 168, 176, 192, 217, 263, 266, 269, 275, 291
feitoria, 16, 19, 28, 34, 35, 45, 49, 70, 71, 104, 105, 108, 118, 120, 125, 126, 132, 135, 136, 138, 139, 141, 148, 152, 153, 165, 180, 210, 217, 219, 220, 271, 284, 290
Fernandes, Bento, 53
Fernandes, João, 45, 58, 101, 102, 252, 308, 309
Fernandes, Jorge, 42
Fernandes, Lourenço, 53
Fernandes, Luís, 46
Fernandes, Manuel, 234, 255, 278
Fernandes, Margarida, 48
Fernandes, Maria, 258
Fernandes, Pero, 241, 273
Fernandes, Valentim, 124, 133
Fernandez, Álvaro, 55
Fernandez, Diego, 55
ferry boats, 53, 105, 106
Fez, 3, 9, 10, 12, 14, 15, 16, 20, 25, 51, 70, 76, 80, 93, 214, 228, 254, 261, 263, 270, 288
figs, 91, 97, 124, 139, 180, 223
fines, 114
firewood, 81, 97, 123, 143, 144, 177, 211
fish, 35, 90, 94, 95, 121, 123, 147
fishermen, 79, 94, 169, 279
fishing, 93
físicos, see also "physicians", 49
flour, 105
Folgado, João, 127
Fonseca, Beatriz da, 43
food, 90, 93, 137
food, shortages of, 98
foral, 160, 161
foreigners, 54, 55, 59, 129

fortresses, abandonment of, 288
fountains, 106, 213
Fragoso, Diogo, 102, 110, 307
Franciscans, 35, 36, 108, 109, 273
Francisco de Holanda, 215
Frazão, João Álvares, 102
Frei António, 273
Frei Fernando, 35
Frei Vicente, 35, 36
Freire, Cristóvão, 266, 269, 270
Freitas, Lançarote de, 34, 250, 263, 264, 291
French, 1, 38, 54, 111, 114, 128, 156, 217, 245
fronteiro, 6
fronteiros, 28, 37, 140, 214, 244, 257, 275, 285
frontier, 2, 3, 4, 5, 6, 7, 8, 9, 17, 31, 36, 56, 59, 65, 69, 72, 88, 89, 90, 98, 100, 109, 115, 117, 119, 121, 150, 152, 155, 158, 159, 164, 169, 203, 204, 205, 207, 236, 239, 241, 242, 250, 274, 279, 282, 283, 285, 286, 288
Frontier. *See, Introduction*
fruit, 47, 124, 125, 195
fruits, 95, 160, 254
fugitives, 56, 58, 59

G

gado de El Rey, 92
Gago, Pedro, 45
Galway, 135
gambling, 57
Gamboa, António Leitão de, 23, 32, 41, 111, 113, 171, 172, 208, 228, 259, 301
gardens, 48, 91, 92, 260
Gato, Nuno, 19, 21, 30, 31, 33, 35, 36, 40, 41, 64, 67, 81, 91, 96, 97, 98, 104, 108, 133, 139, 147, 162, 163, 169, 179, 189, 190, 207, 208, 210, 211, 213, 218, 221, 222, 223, 224, 225, 251, 252, 261, 275
gazelles, 93
Genoa, 54, 55, 129

Index

gente de ordenança, see also "soldiers", 38
gente de pé, see also "infantrymen", 38
Germans, 38, 54
Ghana, 136
Gharbiyya, 84, 97, 170, 176, 178, 183, 185, 188, 191, 195, 196, 197, 198, 200, 221, 238
Gharbiyya tribe, 84, 167, 289
Gibraltar, Straits of, 11, 33, 56
Gil, Inês, 46
glass, 103
goats, 83, 143, 166
Godinho, Vitorino Magalhães, 1, 52, 124, 125, 133, 136, 140, 148
Góis, Damião de, iv, 95, 155, 196, 222, 225, 237, 323
Golaio, Artur, 110
Golayo, Artur, 51, 308
gold, 6, 121, 123, 124, 125, 131, 136, 137, 142, 148, 224, 233
Gold Coast, 121, 131, 152, 320, 339
goldsmiths, 52, 137
Gomes, Francisco, 111, 306
Gomez, Fernando, 271
Gonçalves, Catarina, 45
Gonçalves, Fernão, 101, 111, 307
Gonçalves, Heitor, 69, 132, 133, 135, 166, 167, 176, 191, 192, 275, 312, 313
Gonçalves, Isabel, 46
Gonçalves, João, 46, 52, 53, 55, 316
Gonçalves, Luis, 110, 266, 268, 269, 314
Gonçalves, Simão, 42, 44, 86, 174, 222, 260, 301, 316
Gouveia, Diogo de, 15
Graciosa, 17, 157, 158
grain, 10, 14, 16, 21, 44, 73, 80, 81, 90, 95, 96, 97, 98, 99, 107, 115, 118, 120, 123, 125, 130, 138, 140, 142, 152, 156, 161, 163, 177, 187, 188, 200, 201, 202, 253, 287, 289
grain cellar, 104, 105

Granada, 6, 10, 12, 13, 125, 150, 155, 251
grapes, 48
greed, 47, 190, 236, 242, 270, 274, 277, 279, 285
guias, see "military guides", 79
guides, see "*alformas*", 19, 79, 218, 236

H

haiks, 132, 133, 134
hardtack, 42
Harvey, L. P., 39, 84, 150, 173
hay, 210
Henriques, Luís, 154, 234
Henriques, Vasco, 103
Hesqima tribe, 167
Hesqura tribe, 194
hides, 80, 93, 124, 143
Hintati, 3, 8, 9, 23, 52, 151, 167, 169, 170, 191, 198, 199, 200, 202, 205, 220, 238, 264, 266, 282, 283, 298
holidays, 47
homiziados, 56, 57
honey, 123, 147, 163
honor, 272, 287
honra e proveito, 284
horses, 6, 16, 32, 37, 47, 62, 80, 97, 105, 123, 142, 153, 163, 175, 183, 189, 194, 209, 210, 229, 237, 241, 253, 262, 270, 284, 289
hortelões, see "market gardeners", 91
hostages, 12, 82, 83, 84, 159, 163, 164, 165, 166, 167, 194, 198, 200, 201, 264, 266
hostages, treatment of, 165
houses, 32, 46, 50, 71, 75, 99, 100, 101, 102, 103, 107, 109, 126, 221
houses, demolition, 101
housing, 8, 32, 66, 100, 101
hunting, 90, 93, 99

348

I

Idrisid revolution, 14
incest, 57, 114
India, 17, 126, 131, 133, 139, 156, 284, 286, 287, 291, 335
indigo, 124, 140, 147
Infante Santo, 12, 15, 164, 258
infantry, 20, 38, 166, 230, 237
infantrymen, 37, 82, 218
infrastructure, 125, 128
ink, 144
Inquisition, 76, 86, 257, 258, 259
interpreters, 69, 70, 72, 113, 190, 194
Islam, symbols, 161
Italians, 54, 128, 338
Izzara, 183

J

jailers, 34, 110
jails, 68
Jalofs, 230
Japan, 126
Jerusalem, 154, 155, 328, 339
Jews, 8, 9, 29, 34, 37, 38, 49, 50, 54, 64, 65, 66, 67, 68, 69, 70, 71, 72, 73, 74, 75, 76, 77, 78, 79, 80, 85, 88, 89, 93, 97, 98, 99, 100, 106, 113, 117, 124, 125, 126, 127, 128, 130, 132, 133, 134, 135, 136, 137, 138, 139, 140, 141, 142, 143, 144, 145, 146, 148, 154, 160, 178, 189, 190, 201, 211, 213, 218, 223, 226, 252, 253, 255, 256, 257, 260, 265, 276, 282, 283, 288, 289
Jews, expelled from fortresses, 89
Jews, population, 67
Jews, property ownership, 71
jihād, 169
João de Castilho, 215
João I, King D., 10, 11, 155
João II, King D., 15, 16, 17, 131, 152, 153, 157, 288, 298, 323
João III, King D., iv, 23, 24, 25, 30, 33, 37, 39, 41, 44, 45, 48, 50, 51, 54, 57, 60, 62, 68, 69, 71, 72, 73, 76, 81, 83, 85, 86, 87, 88, 90, 91, 93, 94, 97, 99, 109, 110, 116, 117, 118, 119, 121, 127, 128, 134, 137, 140, 158, 164, 172, 203, 208, 212, 213, 214, 215, 217, 226, 227, 228, 229, 230, 231, 232, 233, 235, 240, 241, 242, 244, 250, 254, 259, 262, 263, 264, 265, 266, 267, 268, 269, 271, 272, 273, 277, 278, 279, 281, 287, 289, 290, 291
João IV, King D., 26
João Ribeiro, 215
Jorge, João, 45
Judaism, 67, 74, 75
judiaria, 66, 68, 70, 93
judicial officials, 34
juíz dos orfãos, 34
juíz dos órfãos, 109

K

keys, 53, 98, 174, 216, 242
kidnapping, 115, 191, 275, 276

L

lacar, 124, 132, 133, 140, 147
Lacoste, Yves, 187
lakes, 81, 196
lambens, 131, 132, 133
Larache, 15, 17, 272
law, Moroccan, 114
Lazaraque, 12
leather, 133, 143
Leitão, Pero, 32, 154, 275, 301
Leite, António, 33, 54, 71, 73, 85, 86, 87, 88, 95, 96, 105, 107, 111, 127, 128, 138, 150, 151, 159, 177, 178, 187, 211, 239, 253, 277, 278, 279
Leme, Martin, 13, 14
Levi, family of Jews, 69
Levi, Meyer, 69, 132, 133
Levi, Yusef, 69
lime, see also "*cal*", 48, 79, 80, 81, 104, 108, 143, 169, 210

Index

Lisbon, vi, i, ii, iv, v, 1, 2, 6, 10, 11, 13, 16, 19, 22, 25, 26, 28, 29, 31, 32, 35, 40, 47, 49, 50, 51, 54, 56, 57, 60, 67, 68, 69, 70, 71, 72, 73, 74, 76, 80, 87, 99, 100, 108, 109, 110, 113, 119, 123, 124, 125, 126, 127, 133, 134, 135, 136, 141, 153, 154, 156, 157, 160, 165, 170, 171, 173, 179, 181, 182, 183, 185, 189, 191, 215, 216, 219, 220, 222, 229, 234, 235, 236, 242, 244, 247, 248, 249, 256, 257, 259, 261, 262, 272, 273, 281, 284, 290
livestock, 81, 90, 92, 97, 99, 130, 138, 160, 178, 209, 239, 287
loans, 13
locks, 53
locksmiths, 52
Lopes, Afonso, 53
Lopes, David, 1, 2, 10, 156, 173, 179, 185, 215, 276
Lopes, Duarte, 99, 127
Lopes, Francisco, 81, 258
Lopes, Sebastião, 263, 313
loquat, 97
Lord of the Mountains, see Mawlay Muhammad, 24, 52, 198
Loureiro, Luís de, 48, 60, 86, 119, 180, 212, 213, 214, 215, 227, 242, 244, 254, 290, 291
Lud, 79, 169
Luís, Rodrigo, 46

M

Maça, Benito, 54, 166
Machado, Pero, 116
MacKay, Angus, v, 117, 155, 239, 251
Madeira, 87, 96, 144, 156, 162, 211, 222, 225, 229, 233, 257
Magro, Rui Gil, 188
Mali, 136
Mamora, 21, 22, 32, 112, 123, 157, 158, 170, 172, 192, 195, 196
mamposteiros, 249, 250

Manuel, D. Bernardo, 238
Marim, Isabel, 48
Marinids, 10, 12, 13, 14, 328
Mariz, Pedro de, 268
market garden, 50, 71
market gardeners, 91
market-gardeners, 52, 54
marlota (i.e., cloak), 171, 180, 201
Marrakech, 3, 9, 11, 12, 20, 23, 39, 41, 52, 72, 81, 130, 132, 134, 170, 184, 185, 191, 195, 196, 199, 200, 201, 202, 206, 214, 238, 266, 269, 288, 289, 290
marriage, 26, 30, 41, 42, 43, 45, 48, 55, 73, 76, 87, 228, 262
marriage, cross-cultural, 43
Martins, Domingos, 43
Maryam, wife of `Abd al-Rahman, 83
Mascarenhas, D. Nuno, 22, 23, 32, 41, 44, 51, 71, 78, 81, 82, 84, 92, 97, 98, 99, 107, 115, 136, 140, 161, 162, 164, 167, 175, 176, 178, 179, 182, 184, 186, 197, 199, 200, 202, 203, 205, 256, 258, 266, 268, 269, 275, 276, 277, 278
Mashanzaya Berbers, 224
masons, 52, 53, 102
Massa, 17, 124, 152, 153, 154, 156, 165, 169, 183, 255, 256
Massa, treaty with Portugal, 153
massacre, 119, 240, 241
matchlockmen, see also "*espingardeiros*", 38, 41, 55, 62, 193, 218, 224, 229, 230
Mawlay `Abd al-Rahman bin Haddu, 83
Mawlay Fares, 83
Mawlay Idris, 72
Mawlay Muhammad, 14, 195, 198
Mawlay Zayyan, 19, 21
Mazagão, vi, 1, 2, 21, 25, 26, 27, 33, 35, 40, 48, 54, 60, 62, 68, 69, 71, 78, 79, 86, 87, 88, 89, 96, 100, 101, 104, 105, 107, 109, 120, 121, 122, 127, 128, 138, 142, 144, 156, 159, 178,

186, 188, 189, 192, 210, 211,
212, 213, 214, 215, 216, 227,
235, 238, 239, 242, 244, 254,
263, 270, 273, 277, 278, 279,
290, 291
Mazagão, abandonment of, 26
Mazagão, Siege of (1562), 25, 215, 258
meat, 47, 92, 93, 95, 123, 138, 147, 177, 229
Medina, Diego de, 22
Medina, Ya`qūb de, 134, 141
Meknès, 192, 200
Melo, Garcia de, 24, 32, 56, 110, 116, 117, 136, 137, 268
Melo, Jorge de, 21, 142, 156
Melo, Lopo de, 266, 267, 269
Melo, Pedro Lourenço de, 209
Menagullo, Cymbealla, 75
Mendes de Vasconcellos, Rui, 15
Meneses, D. João de, 31, 37, 49, 75, 80, 100, 170, 186, 192, 193, 194, 212, 215, 216, 237, 238, 256, 261, 263
Mercedarian Order, 247
merchants, 12, 13, 14, 20, 25, 28, 34, 51, 52, 54, 55, 67, 69, 73, 75, 76, 79, 80, 95, 96, 97, 99, 117, 123, 125, 126, 127, 128, 129, 130, 134, 135, 136, 138, 142, 143, 144, 145, 146, 152, 154, 190, 222, 228, 251, 252, 253, 256, 271, 275, 277, 284, 285, 288
Mers al-Sultan, 192
Mestre Boytac, 22
mestre das obras, 54, 55, 102
Mestre Marcos, 49
Mestre Rodrigo, 33, 50, 71, 72, 75, 76, 90, 93, 94, 99, 128, 213, 277
metalworker, see "*serralheiro*", 53
Mexico City, 141
midwives, 40
military guides, see "*guias*", 79
millenarianism, 155
Mimūn, Sheikh, 39, 167, 168, 180, 194, 199, 278
misericórdias, 272, 274

mistresses, 40, 42
mistrust, 174
Mogador, 18, 22, 157, 158, 211, 300
monasteries, 22, 36, 46, 109, 212, 247, 249
Monroi, D. Guterres de, 30, 55, 80, 227, 228, 230, 231, 232, 233, 264
Monroi, D. Mécia de, 231, 269
moradia, 34, 97, 120
moradores, 28, 250
mosque, 13, 15, 101
mosques, 77, 107, 109
mouraria, 159, 182, 249
mouraria, taxes, 160
mouriscos, 8, 43, 66, 76, 84, 85, 86, 87, 88, 115, 277
mouros de cavalo ("Moroccan cavalrymen"), 39
mouros de guerra (i.e., non-allied Moroccans), 129, 162, 202, 256, 260, 275, 287
mouros de pazes (i.e., allied Muslims), 78, 81, 138, 139, 162, 171, 194, 195, 275
mudéjar, 159, 161, 249
Muhammed al-Sheikh, sharif, 24, 25
mulberry, 97
murder, 64, 72, 112, 113, 114, 172, 175, 199, 255
murder, political motive, 113
Muslim, women, 82
Muslims, 4, 8, 9, 11, 14, 21, 29, 37, 55, 65, 66, 68, 76, 77, 78, 79, 80, 82, 84, 85, 86, 87, 88, 93, 98, 108, 114, 115, 116, 117, 124, 127, 128, 129, 133, 135, 138, 139, 140, 141, 143, 150, 152, 153, 155, 156, 159, 160, 161, 162, 164, 169, 171, 173, 174, 176, 177, 179, 180, 181, 182, 186, 187, 188, 219, 221, 226, 228, 234, 236, 240, 241, 246, 247, 249, 250, 252, 255, 256, 257, 258, 261, 263, 268,

Index

270, 271, 274, 275, 276, 277, 282
Muslims, execution of, 78
Muslims, laborers, 80
Muslims, royal protection of allies, 82
Myra, wife of Mawlay Fares, 83

N

nails, 53, 103, 104, 183
needlework, 48
negotiations, 19
New Christians, 8, 49, 50, 65, 66, 67, 71, 74, 75, 76, 85, 128, 130, 136, 213, 252, 277
New Christians, occupations of, 74
New Christians, property ownership, 75
New Christians, see, generally, Chapter 3, 65
Newitt, Malyn, 284
Noronha, D. Afonso de, 47
Noronha, D. Álvaro de, 22, 32, 49, 73, 81, 106, 114, 133, 134, 138, 167, 177, 180, 181, 183, 184, 186, 200, 202, 203, 211, 239, 276, 277
Noronha, D. Isabel de, 222
Noronha, D. Rodrigo de, 174, 199, 222, 268
Noronha, Henrique de, 43, 87
notaries, 34, 51, 52, 102, 110
notaries, see "*tabelião*", 51, 52
Nun, Cape, 18

O

oaths, 12, 172, 173
oaths, Muslim allies, 173
Odivelas, 30
Oeres, 163
olive oil, 86, 91, 180, 229, 249
olives, 91
onions, 97, 139
orchards, 91, 92, 97
Ordenações Manuelinas, 56, 111, 113, 114, 172

orphans, 44, 109, 160
Orthodoxae fidei, 17
Osório, Jerónimo, ii
ouvidores, 34, 110, 173
ouvidores (i.e., chief magistrates), 109, 110, 111, 229
oxen, 83, 103, 166

P

Pacheco Pereira, Duarte, 80, 123, 124, 157
Padre João Nunes, 259
padreira, 48
painters, 53
paper, 144
Paris, iv, v, 1, 15, 245
payroll, 38, 39, 58, 61
pensions, 44, 213
pepper, 133, 139
Pereira, Rui, 103
Perez, João, 206
pharmacist, see "apothecary", 51, 52
physicians, 28, 49, 50, 52, 71, 75, 76, 94, 213, 277
physicians, see also "*físicos*", 49
piers, 105
pigs, 93
Pina, Vasco de, 144, 211, 213
Pires, Gonçalo, 52, 314
Pires, Mateus, 31
Pius II, Pope, 249
Pombal, Marquês de, 26
Ponce de León, Rodrigo, 239
population of fortresses, 28
porteiro dos contos, 39, 58, 64
Portugal, v, 1, 10, 11, 13, 14, 15, 16, 17, 18, 19, 21, 26, 30, 32, 33, 36, 41, 42, 43, 44, 45, 46, 47, 48, 50, 56, 57, 58, 59, 64, 65, 66, 67, 68, 69, 71, 72, 75, 76, 77, 85, 87, 88, 91, 93, 100, 101, 103, 105, 108, 109, 111, 113, 116, 118, 120, 123, 124, 125, 127, 128, 135, 139, 141, 142, 143, 144, 145, 152, 153, 154, 155, 158, 160, 161, 165, 167, 168, 169, 170, 172, 173,

175, 181, 183, 184, 185, 191,
192, 194, 196, 197, 204, 210,
214, 216, 222, 229, 240, 245,
247, 248, 249, 250, 251, 252,
253, 256, 257, 258, 263, 268,
271, 272, 274, 282, 284, 286,
290
priests, 35, 108, 259
proselytizing, 65, 160
prostitutes, 40, 42, 43, 48, 114

Q

qā'id (generally), 14, 15, 21, 23,
130, 141, 176, 180, 183, 184,
228, 254
qanūn (i.e., legal code), 287
Qassim, 206, 254
Qsima tribe, 17
Quemadmodum magnis (papal bull),
249
quittance, 35, 49, 269

R

rabi mor, 21, 50, 68, 69, 180, 201
raiding, 16, 23, 30, 39, 42, 53, 80,
82, 92, 95, 99, 111, 129, 142,
146, 162, 178, 192, 207, 214,
218, 236, 238, 241, 256, 261,
265, 266, 286
raids, 11, 25, 30, 31, 34, 37, 38, 54,
80, 91, 105, 112, 117, 130, 138,
142, 170, 183, 185, 186, 204,
212, 213, 223, 236, 237, 238,
240, 241, 245, 247, 249, 255,
256, 276, 283, 287, 289
raisins, 124, 139
ransom, 43, 54, 67, 171, 233, 245,
247, 248, 249, 250, 251, 252,
254, 259, 260, 262, 263, 265,
266, 267, 269, 270, 272, 273,
278, 280, 283
rape, 111, 112, 114, 172, 198, 260,
269, 270
real estate transactions, 75
rebate (i.e., attack alert), 214, 215
recebedor de alfandega, 111
recebedor dos mantimentos, 35

regateira, 48
Rego, Antão do, 263
religious animosity, 175
religious conversion, 118
rent, 72, 102, 143, 267
Riscado, João, 45
ritual, Christian, 37
robbery, 78, 115, 275
Rodrigues, Afonso, 50, 94, 103,
105, 129, 130, 135, 143, 144,
168, 211, 217
Rodrigues, Bernardo, iv, 261
Rodrigues, Catarina, 102
Rodrigues, Cristóvão, 53
Rodrigues, João, 22, 39, 43, 58, 64,
93, 102
rope, 52, 105, 258
royal fifth, 94, 264, 276, 278
Royal officials, generally, 29
Ruff, Julius R., 116, 208
Ruis, Diogo, 100
Rute, family of Jews, 69

S

Sa`adids, 3, 8, 9, 23, 24, 25, 42, 69,
70, 82, 84, 85, 86, 88, 121, 128,
129, 130, 137, 144, 151, 169,
184, 185, 204, 205, 206, 207,
208, 215, 219, 220, 227, 232,
233, 234, 244, 253, 254, 255,
259, 266, 272, 274, 276, 282,
283, 286, 289, 290, 291
Sa`īd-u-Mubarek, 171
Sacoto, Gonçalo Mendes, 23, 62,
115, 117, 140, 158, 240, 244,
264, 265, 277, 289
Sacoto, Luís, 240
Sacouto, Luís de, 43
Safi, 2, 16, 17, 18, 19, 20, 21, 22,
23, 24, 25, 29, 30, 31, 32, 33,
35, 36, 37, 38, 39, 40, 41, 42,
44, 45, 46, 47, 49, 50, 51, 52,
54, 58, 60, 61, 62, 64, 65, 67,
69, 70, 71, 72, 73, 75, 77, 78,
79, 80, 81, 82, 83, 84, 86, 87,
88, 90, 91, 92, 93, 95, 96, 97,
98, 99, 101, 102, 103, 104, 105,

Index

106, 107, 108, 109, 110, 112, 115, 116, 117, 118, 119, 120, 121, 122, 123, 124, 126, 127, 130, 131, 132, 133, 134, 135, 136, 137, 138, 139, 140, 141, 142, 143, 147, 148, 149, 152, 153, 159, 161, 162, 163, 164, 166, 167, 168, 169, 170, 171, 172, 173, 174, 175, 176, 177, 178, 179, 180, 181, 182, 183, 184, 185, 187, 188, 189, 190, 191, 192, 193, 194, 195, 196, 197, 198, 199, 200, 201, 202, 203, 205, 206, 208, 209, 210, 211, 212, 213, 214, 215, 216, 217, 218, 220, 221, 222, 223, 224, 225, 226, 227, 229, 237, 238, 241, 244, 251, 254, 256, 257, 258, 261, 262, 263, 266, 267, 268, 269, 273, 274, 275, 276, 277, 279, 286, 288, 289, 290, 291
Salé, 123, 192, 254
Sanchez, Diego, 55
Santa Cruz, 2, 18, 21, 23, 24, 25, 29, 30, 31, 32, 35, 40, 41, 42, 43, 44, 45, 46, 50, 51, 52, 55, 60, 62, 68, 69, 72, 73, 78, 80, 86, 87, 94, 98, 101, 103, 104, 105, 108, 109, 111, 118, 119, 120, 122, 124, 129, 130, 133, 135, 137, 138, 139, 141, 143, 144, 145, 152, 154, 156, 166, 167, 168, 171, 172, 174, 175, 180, 183, 184, 208, 211, 215, 216, 217, 219, 220, 222, 226, 227, 228, 229, 230, 231, 232, 233, 234, 235, 239, 240, 241, 242, 244, 251, 255, 257, 258, 259, 262, 263, 269, 270, 271, 272, 273, 274, 276, 278, 281, 290
Santarém, 19, 21, 156, 247
Santiago, Order of, 32
São Jorge da Mina, 18, 118, 121, 131, 132, 136, 142, 332
sawyers, 52
scribes, 34, 69, 100, 110

Sebastião, King D., 26, 56, 155, 298
Seita, 170
Seja tribe, 170, 197, 221
Senabria, Goterres de, 231
Sequeira, D. Beatriz de, 46
Sequeira, João Lopes de, 17, 18, 31, 46, 154, 156, 167, 255
serralheiro, see "metalworkers", 52, 53, 75
Seville, 55, 155
shackles, 54, 198, 259
shad, 16, 124, 153
Sharquiyya, region of Morocco, 83, 184, 185, 186, 188, 189, 192, 193, 195, 196, 200, 201, 202, 203, 220
Shawiyya region, 93, 97, 99, 105, 106, 150, 161, 173, 180, 183, 264, 265
Shawiyya tribe, 95, 106, 127, 169, 180, 181, 257, 264, 265, 279, 289
Shawiyya, region of, 20
sheep, 93, 143, 147, 165, 189, 192, 195
ships, 16, 18, 20, 32, 63, 80, 94, 98, 105, 152, 153, 154, 216, 217, 226, 228, 232, 233, 235, 244, 247, 290
Shyadma tribe, 163, 200, 220, 221, 289
Sidi Yahya, 153
Sidi Ya'qūb, 180
siege warfare, generally, 214
sieges, 9, 10, 13, 15, 18, 25, 30, 31, 55, 67, 91, 162, 166, 170, 174, 175, 189, 193, 194, 207, 208, 214, 215, 216, 217, 218, 219, 220, 221, 222, 223, 225, 226, 227, 228, 229, 230, 231, 234, 235, 236, 239, 244, 257, 289, 290
Silva, D. Beatriz da, 41
Silva, Manuel da, 41
Silveira, Manuel da, 266, 267, 269

silver, 64, 83, 114, 123, 131, 132, 136, 137, 167, 180, 201, 223, 265, 269, 272, 281, 284, 320
Sintra, 158, 173
Sintra, Treaty of, 18
slaughterhouses, 102
slavery, 30, 48, 80, 111, 112, 114, 129, 130, 131, 140, 166, 167, 199, 201, 202, 236, 245, 246, 257, 261, 262, 263, 274, 275, 276, 277, 279, 284, 287
slaves, 6, 16, 47, 48, 49, 78, 79, 80, 99, 115, 116, 123, 125, 129, 130, 131, 133, 136, 139, 142, 152, 168, 190, 192, 194, 236, 242, 245, 257, 260, 261, 262, 264, 267, 269, 270, 274, 276, 279, 280
sodomy, 114, 260
soldiers, 28, 31, 33, 37, 38, 39, 42, 43, 49, 51, 54, 58, 62, 63, 67, 79, 80, 81, 105, 120, 129, 152, 157, 178, 186, 192, 193, 197, 216, 218, 219, 223, 228, 229, 230, 231, 233, 236, 240, 244, 271, 285, 286, 288
Sousa, D. Pedro de, 31, 32, 238
Southampton, 134
Souto, Bento do, 260
Spanish, ii, 4, 6, 8, 11, 16, 26, 66, 67, 74, 77, 78, 155, 186, 207, 251, 288
spices, 6, 131, 134, 139, 145, 288
stipends, 30, 39, 45, 50, 64, 70, 94, 97, 179
straw, 97
Subida, Alonso de, 46, 51, 55
Sufis, 151
sūq (i.e., market), 96, 98, 126
surgeons, 49, 52, 281
surgeons, see also "*cirurgiões*", 49, 50
Sus region, 3, 23, 96, 137, 140, 143, 151, 157, 226, 276
Sutil, D. João, bishop of Safi, 93, 181
suzerainty, 152, 185, 204, 236, 256, 288

symbols, 47, 168, 171, 172, 173, 181, 198, 205, 240, 248, 258

T

Ta`fuft, Yahya-u-, 2, 23, 39, 47, 64, 72, 82, 84, 98, 113, 114, 118, 161, 170, 171, 174, 175, 176, 177, 179, 181, 184, 185, 186, 194, 195, 197, 198, 199, 202, 214, 242, 264, 267, 275, 276, 286, 287
tabelião, see "notaries", 51, 52
Tadla, 50, 133, 253
Tafuf, 170, 186, 192, 237, 278
tailors, 74, 281
Tamrakht, 130, 180
Tangiers, 1, 11, 12, 13, 14, 15, 25, 26, 32, 57, 58, 71, 89, 107, 150, 164, 272, 289
Tarkuku, 55, 129
Tarudante, 54, 70, 157, 228, 230, 231, 232, 233, 240, 258, 270, 271, 272, 273
Taveira, Fernão, 130, 139, 276
taverns, 54
Tavim, José A. R. da Silva, 73
taxes, 16, 34, 35, 70, 73, 94, 153, 154, 156, 160, 181
Tazarote, 163
Tednest, 172
Teixeira, Martim, 102, 106
Tejeste, 170
tença, see also "stipends", 39, 50, 179, 251
Tenochtitlán, 288
Tensift, 158, 195
Tetuan, 13
textiles, 69, 80, 124, 131, 132, 134, 140, 141, 152
tiles, 52, 101, 103, 104
Tit, 20
Toledo, Treaty of, 16
treason, 56, 174, 200
treasury, 104, 212
treaties, 15, 16, 17, 18, 19, 20, 25, 41, 47, 82, 152, 153, 154, 158,

Index

161, 162, 163, 166, 167, 168, 173, 178, 189, 190, 264
Tribunal dos Cativos, 247, 248, 250, 272, 273
tribute, 4, 7, 16, 20, 47, 70, 81, 90, 95, 96, 97, 98, 109, 115, 137, 138, 142, 151, 152, 153, 156, 160, 161, 162, 163, 176, 182, 187, 189, 191, 192, 205, 287
Trinitarian Order, 247, 248, 249
trust, 76, 84, 159, 164, 165, 168, 174, 176, 186, 197, 200, 235, 252
Turks, 13, 230, 291
Turner, Frederick Jackson, 4, 5, 6, 7, 328, 338, 339
turnips, 97, 139
Tuson, Ya`qūb, 133, 138

U

Uarar, lake, 196
Umm al-Rabi`, 21, 35, 53, 63, 73, 93, 102, 105, 123, 127, 134, 150, 153, 156, 237, 279
United States, 5, 7, 325
Urban II, Pope, 208

V

Vaz, Afonso, 44, 86, 208, 242
Vaz, Estêvão, 134, 135
Vaz, Martim, 167
vedor das obras (i.e., construction overseer), 103, 144, 210
vegetables, 80, 95, 126, 229
Vicente, Álvaro, 43
Viegas, Jorge, 75, 87, 99, 127, 213, 244, 277
Vieira, Henrique, 233, 272
vigário capelão da casa, 35
Vila Nova de Mazagão, 26
vineyards, 92, 260
violence, 9, 17, 77, 78, 80, 111, 115, 204, 205, 206, 207, 208, 223, 233, 234, 236, 239, 240, 241, 242, 245, 279, 282
viúvas de vivos, see also "women, widows", 43

W

Wadi Lukkus, 17, 157
Wadi Massa, 124
Wadi Sebu, 22, 123, 157, 170
walls, defensive, 216
Washman, `Ali bin, 112, 176, 267
Wattasids, 3, 8, 9, 14, 16, 17, 21, 22, 23, 24, 25, 50, 53, 72, 76, 83, 85, 92, 151, 157, 158, 164, 169, 170, 178, 180, 181, 183, 186, 192, 193, 194, 195, 196, 200, 201, 205, 207, 218, 237, 250, 252, 253, 254, 264, 274, 282, 283
Webb, Walter Prescott, 6
Webb, Wlter Prescott, 6, 339
wheat, 37, 45, 83, 92, 95, 96, 97, 98, 99, 120, 122, 123, 124, 139, 148, 149, 152, 163, 166, 189, 191, 200, 229, 237, 242, 260
wills, 36, 46, 55
wine, 47, 90, 92, 223, 229, 249
witchcraft, 57, 219
wives, see also "marriage", ii, 15, 17, 18, 20, 28, 40, 41, 42, 43, 44, 45, 46, 47, 67, 75, 82, 83, 84, 85, 87, 101, 111, 127, 165, 167, 190, 194, 196, 200, 208, 219, 222, 227, 231, 234, 241, 250, 254, 261, 264, 270, 272, 279
women, 8, 28, 37, 40, 41, 42, 43, 44, 45, 46, 47, 48, 57, 59, 73, 76, 80, 82, 83, 84, 111, 112, 119, 166, 194, 198, 218, 219, 220, 230, 234, 237, 241, 250, 254, 255, 260, 261, 262, 263, 264, 271, 273, 279, 281, 290
Women, 40, 42, 43, 46, 47, 82, 119, 241
women, and combat, 219
women, Muslim, 82
women, poor, 44
women, property owners, 46
women, property ownership, 102
women, unmarried, 42, 43
women, widows, 43, 45

wood, 81, 103, 104, 105, 143, 144, 183, 211

Y

Yūsuf al-Hintati, Al-Nasr bin, 185

Z

zamujeiros, 91
zāwiyas, 151, 169, 204

www.ingramcontent.com/pod-product-compliance
Lightning Source LLC
Chambersburg PA
CBHW072002150426
43194CB00008B/970